TEILHARD DE CHARDIN:
THEOLOGY, HUMANITY AND COSMOS

STUDIES IN PHILOSOPHICAL THEOLOGY, 29

Editorial Profile:
Philosophical theology is the study of philosophical problems which arise in
reflection upon religious beliefs and theological doctrines.

1 H. de Vries, *Theologie im Pianissimo & zwischen Rationalität und Dekonstruktion*,
   Kampen, 1989
2 S. Breton, *La pensée du rien*, Kampen, 1992
3 Ch. Schwöbel, *God: Action and Revelation*, Kampen, 1992
4 V. Brümmer (ed.), *Interpreting the Universe as Creation*, Kampen, 1991
5 L.J. van den Brom, *Divine Presence in the World*, Kampen, 1993
6 M. Sarot, *God, Passibility and Corporeality*, Kampen, 1992
7 G. van den Brink, *Almighty God*, Kampen, 1993
8 P.-C. Lai, *Towards a Trinitarian Theology of Religions: A Study of Paul
   Tillich's Thought*, Kampen, 1994
9 L. Velecky, *Aquinas' Five Arguments in the* Summa Theologiae *Ia 2, 3*, Kampen, 1994
10 W. Dupré, *Patterns in Meaning: Reflections on Meaning and Truth in Cultural
   Reality, Religious Traditions, and Dialogical Encounters*, Kampen, 1994
11 P.T. Erne, *Lebenskunst. Aneignung ästhetischer Erfahrung*, Kampen, 1994
12 U. Perone, *Trotz/dem Subjekt*, Leuven, 1998
13 H.J. Adriaanse, *Vom Christentum aus: Aufsätze und Vorträge zur Religionsphilosophie*, Kampen, 1995
14 D.A. Pailin, *Probing the Foundations: A Study in Theistic Reconstruction*,
   Kampen, 1994
15 M. Potepa, *Schleiermachers hermeneutische Dialektik*, Kampen, 1996
16 E. Herrmann, *Scientific Theory and Religious Belief: An Essay on the
   Rationality of Views of Life*, Kampen, 1995
17 V. Brümmer & M. Sarot, *Happiness, Well-Being and the Meaning of Life: A
   Dialogue of Social Science and Religion*, Kampen, 1996
18 T.L. Hettema, *Reading for Good. Narrative Theology and Ethics in the Joseph
   Story from the Perspective of Ricoeur's Hermeneutics*, Kampen, 1996
19 H. Düringer, *Universale Vernunft und partikularer Glaube. Eine theologische
   Auswertung des Werkes von Jürgen Habermas*, Leuven, 1999
20 E. Dekker, *Middle Knowledge*, Leuven, 2000
21 T. Ekstrand, *Max Weber in a Theological Perspective*, Leuven, 2000
22 C. Helmer & K. de Troyer (eds), *Truth: Interdisciplinary Dialogues in a Pluralistic Age*, Leuven, 2003
23 L. Boeve & L.P. Hemming (eds), *Divinising Experience. Essays in the History
   of Religious Experience from Origen to Ricœur*, Leuven, 2004
24 P.D. Murray, *Reason, Truth and Theology in Pragmatist Perspective*, Leuven, 2004
25 S. van Erp, *The Art of Theology. Hans Urs von Balthasar's Theological
   Aesthetics and the Foundations of Faith*, Leuven, 2004
26 T.A. Smedes, *Chaos, Complexity, and God. Divine Action and Scientism*,
   Leuven, 2004
27 R. Re Manning, *Paul Tillich's Theology of Culture and Art*, Leuven, 2005
28 P. Jonkers & R. Welten *God in France: Eight Contemporary French Thinkers
   on God*, Leuven, 2005

TEILHARD DE CHARDIN

THEOLOGY, HUMANITY AND COSMOS

by

DAVID GRUMETT

PEETERS
LEUVEN – PARIS – DUDLEY, MA
2005

Library of Congress Cataloging-in-Publication Data

Grumett, David.
   Teilhard de Chardin: theology, humanity and cosmos / by David Grumett.
   p. cm. -- (Studies in philosophical theology; 29)
   Includes bibliographical references and index.
   ISBN 90-429-1650-8 (alk. paper)
   1. Teilhard de Chardin, Pierre. 2. Theology. I. Title. II. Series.

B2430.T374G76 2005
230'.2'092--dc22

                                                                    2005047441

© 2005 - Peeters, Bondgenotenlaan 153, 3000 Leuven, Belgium.

ISBN 90-429-1650-8
D. 2005/0602/85

In order to understand certain orientations and emphases of his thought, in order to do justice to what was both most daring and most timely in it, a work of historical reconstruction has become necessary. We must bring to mind again the situation of the religious and conservative world in France around 1900, the interior exile of Catholic society, the theology current at that time, as well as the positivist, determinist and antireligious mentality then dominant. Neither the denigrators nor the admirers of Teilhard ordinarily perceived the historical importance of his effort to establish, in the face of obstacles coming from two antagonistic poles, a spiritual interpretation of universal evolution that included the transcendence of humankind, the value of personal being, freedom, openness to God, consummation in Christ.

(Henri Cardinal de Lubac,
At the Service of the Church:
Henri de Lubac Reflects on the Circumstances that Occasioned his Writings,
San Francisco: Communio, 1993, p. 110.)

For my parents

TABLE OF CONTENTS

ACKNOWLEDGEMENTS

My interest in Teilhard was born in the old Divinity Faculty building in St John's Street, Cambridge, when I was seeking a topic for my doctoral thesis. I finally chose to focus on Teilhard's classic theological manifesto *The Divine Milieu*. Douglas Hedley agreed to supervise the project, advocating a clear focus, close textual reading and thorough research. The work was made possible by a research award by the Arts and Humanities Research Council, formerly part of the British Academy. Brian Hebblethwaite and George Pattison provided further encouragement to pursue what was by Cambridge standards an unorthodox topic. Membership of the community of graduate students at King's was a tremendous privilege, and I gained much from its intellectual energy and diversity. Martin Shaw prompted me to gain immediate experience of the Ignatian spiritual tradition. Ursula King and Ben Quash offered invaluable comments on a hot summer's afternoon at Peterhouse.

Since then, several people have supported the development of this work. At Exeter, I have derived great benefit from discussions with Christopher Southgate and Mark Wynn, and from participation in the theological community there. Paul Avis has motivated me to think more about the significance of Teilhard's work for ecclesiology, and Mike Higton and John McDowell have helped me to clarify some theological concepts. Fraser Watts has guided me to some issues in science and religion. Robert Bonfils SJ has generously made available material in the Archives Françaises de la Compagnie de Jésus. I have been privileged to use the transcriptions of the later portions of Teilhard's *Journal* painstakingly made by Nicole Schmitz-Moormann, without which this resource would have been almost impossible to read. Petà Dunstan, Kester Gillard, Ro Hopper and Michael Howarth have given invaluable practical assistance, and Carolina Armenteros and Maggi Dawn offered warm hospitality during research visits to Paris and Cambridge.

ABBREVIATIONS

Works and Correspondence of Teilhard de Chardin

AE   *Activation of Energy*, San Diego: Harvest, 1978.
AM   *The Appearance of Man*, London: Collins, 1965.
CE   *Christianity and Evolution*, San Diego: Harvest, 1974.
DM   *The Divine Milieu*, Brighton: Sussex Academic Press, 2004.
FM   *The Future of Man*, London: Collins, 1964.
HE   *Human Energy*, London: Collins, 1969.
HM   *The Heart of Matter*, San Diego: Harvest, 1974.
HP   *The Human Phenomenon*, Brighton: Sussex Academic Press, 2003.
HU   *Hymn of the Universe*, London: Collins, 1965.
J   *Journal, 1914–1919*, eds. Nicole and Karl Schmitz-Moormann, Paris: Fayard, 1975; and unpublished journal.
LE   *Letters from Egypt, 1905–1908*, New York: Herder & Herder, 1965.
LH   *Letters from Hastings, 1908–1912*, New York: Herder & Herder, 1968.
LI   *Lettres intimes à Auguste Valensin, Bruno de Solages, Henri de Lubac, André Ravier, 1919–1955*, Paris: Aubier Montaigne, 1972.
LLS   *Letters to Lucile Swan*, Washington, DC: Georgetown University Press, 1993.
LLZ   *Letters to Léontine Zanta*, New York: Harper & Row, 1969.
LP   *Letters from Paris, 1912–1914*, New York: Herder & Herder, 1967.
LT   *Letters from a Traveller, 1923–1955*, London: Collins, 1962.
LTF   *Letters to Two Friends, 1926–1952*, London: Rapp & Whiting, 1970.
MM   *The Making of a Mind: Letters from a Soldier-Priest, 1914–1919*, London: Collins, 1965.
MPN   *Man's Place in Nature*, London: Collins, 1966.
NR   *Notes de retraites, 1919–1954*, Paris: Seuil, 2003.
SC   *Science and Christ*, London: Collins, 1968.
TBC   *Pierre Teilhard de Chardin – Maurice Blondel: Correspondence*, New York: Herder & Herder, 1976.
TF   *Toward the Future*, San Diego: Harvest, 1975.
VP   *The Vision of the Past*, London: Collins, 1966.
WW   *Writings in Time of War*, London: Collins, 1968.

Reference Works and Journals

ANF   *Ante-Nicene Fathers of the Christian Church*, 10 vols.; Grand Rapids, Mich.: Eerdmans, 1993.
AP   *Archives de philosophie*

DEC   *Decrees of the Ecumenical Councils*, 2 vols.; London: Sheed &
        Ward, 1990.
MT   *Modern Theology*
NPNF   *Nicene and Post-Nicene Fathers of the Christian Church*, 28 vols.;
        Grand Rapids, Mich.: Eerdmans, 1961.
NRT   *Nouvelle revue théologique*
PE   *The Papal Encyclicals*, 5 vols.; Pierian: Ann Arbor, 1990.
RMM   *Revue de métaphysique et de morale*
RSR   *Recherches de science religieuse*
RTAM   *Recherches de théologie ancienne et médiévale*
SP   *Studia patristica*
ST   Thomas Aquinas, *Summa theologiae*, 60 vols.; London: Blackfriars,
        1962–76.
TI   Karl Rahner, *Theological Investigations*, 23 vols.; New York: Cross-
        road, 1974–92.
TS   *Theological Studies*

PROLOGUE

The retrieval of a theology

Pierre Teilhard de Chardin died on Easter Sunday 1955. During the two following decades, his oeuvre attracted tremendous interest from theologians and many other people who would not otherwise have been engaged in theological reflection, however broadly that activity is conceived. Many of these were members of traditional religious institutions, and many were not. Most critical, expository and comparative studies of Teilhard's oeuvre produced since then have concentrated on his scientific concepts and theories, such as evolution, convergence and the noosphere. Teilhard indeed devoted a considerable portion of his life's work to exploration of the natural sciences, and to palaeontology in particular, as well as to the speculative questions which these presented, and in so doing developed new theories and concepts about human development, life and consciousness. The resulting theories were bold, inspiring, and widely disseminated and discussed, to the extent that Émile Poulat identifies Teilhard's impact on postwar French religion as greater than that made by any other theologian.[1] In Britain, only John Robinson achieved similar renown, and in Germany, Paul Tillich. The 'phenomenon of Teilhard' has been regarded by some as a remarkable example of religious enquiry and reflection in an increasingly secular age, and by others as an instance and even a cause of the decline of religious institutions and their displacement by vacuous new age spirituality.[2]

The posthumous fame which Teilhard acquired was, unfortunately, gained at the expense of any proper appraisal of him as a French theologian of the first half of the twentieth century. His identity, whether as theologian, scientist, mystic, or philosopher, has been passionately contested, often on the basis of questionable assumptions and broad generalizations about his oeuvre. The phenomenon of 'Teilhardianism', as the body of 'orthodoxy' that was created by many of his most ardent disci-

---

[1] Émile Poulat, *Les Prêtres-ouvriers: naissance et fin* (Paris: Cerf, 2nd edn, 1999), p. 545.

[2] Instances of these divergent responses are, respectively, Ursula King, *The Spirit of One Earth: Reflections on Teilhard de Chardin and Global Spirituality* (New York: Paragon, 1989); David H. Lane, *The Phenomenon of Teilhard: Prophet for a New Age* (Macon, Ga.: Mercer University Press, 1996).

ples has been termed, needs to be distinguished from the theology of Teilhard itself so that the latter can be subject to proper scrutiny. Even Jacques Maritain draws a clear distinction between the faith and religious experience of Teilhard himself, and the ideas propagated by the 'literature of propaganda and its enraptured ecclesiastical retinue'. Unfortunately, Maritain proceeds to make extensive criticisms of the latter and leaves little space for discussion of the former.[3]

One of the aims of this study will be to clarify the mutual relation of the multiple facets of Teilhard's persona and to argue for the integrity of his theology and for its guiding influence over all other elements of his work. From Teilhard's own testimony, it is clear that scientific endeavour occupied a secondary place in his life in comparison with his faith and theology. The year after learning that the Curia was investigating the orthodoxy of his views on original sin, he writes to Auguste Valensin and places in perspective the relative significance of his scientific and religious activities:

> There is no need for me to tell you that geology has a minor role, basically, in the begetting of this Gospel to me. I need a contact with the Real to animate me and to nourish me — work with the Real, too, so that I may participate in the 'human effort' and practise what I preach, the alliance between Human and Christian. Geology has been this to me. But I believe that any other experience would have had the same results for me.[4]

Teilhard's scientific endeavours were, in other words, of functional rather than absolute importance to his theology: they made possible this 'contact with the real'. Étienne Gilson states of Teilhard that 'under the continual flow of scientific or other alluvions he kept intact and miraculously preserved the nugget of pure gold which was the piety and faith of his childhood'.[5] Further evidence that this pearl of great price was not lost is found in works produced shortly before Teilhard's death. Mathias Trennert-Helwig comments: 'When Teilhard titled his autobiography in 1950 *The Heart of Matter* it is clear that he never did away with the religious heritage of his family, even though he transformed its content through the crises of his life.'[6] The title of this essay of Teilhard's

---

[3] Jacques Maritain, 'Teilhard de Chardin and Teilhardianism', in *The Peasant of the Garonne: An Old Layman Questions Himself about the Present Time* (London: Chapman, 1968), p. 116.

[4] Letter to Auguste Valensin, 26 May 1925, *LI*, p. 120; trans. in Claude Cuénot, *Teilhard de Chardin: A Biographical Study* (London: Burns & Oates, 1965), p. 33, n. 27.

[5] Étienne Gilson, «Trois leçons sur le thomisme et sa situation présente», *Seminarium* 17 (1965), p. 727; trans. in Robert Speaight, *Teilhard de Chardin: A Biography* (London: Collins, 1967), p. 326.

alludes, of course, to the Sacred Heart of Christ, which fired his theological imagination throughout his life. Teilhard's preservation of these core religious beliefs becomes even more apparent in his final essay, 'The Christic', in which he declares: 'Today, after forty years of continuous thought, it is still exactly the same fundamental vision that I feel I must present.'[7] Indeed, this essay can be seen as his 'East Coker' moment, a homecoming following a remarkable *exitus* and *reditus* in which he finds in his beginning his end, and in his end, his beginning.[8] Teilhard's theology could reasonably be described as 'radical' and 'orthodox'. Because it is both of these things, however, he never himself uses either term to designate it.

Jacques Maritain states that Teilhard's 'ardent metaphysical and theological concern played a central role in his thought'.[9] Indeed, in *The Human Phenomenon* Teilhard states of the Omega Point (which was the name he gave to the final synthesizing goal of the evolution of the created order): 'I probably would never have dared to consider or form the rational hypothesis of it, if I had not already found in my consciousness as a believer not only the speculative model for it, but its living reality.'[10] Teilhard has been neglected as a theologian motivated by concrete and mystical religious experience partly because he was prevented, during his lifetime, from publishing any of the works which later captured public imagination. The only essays on explicitly theological topics published before his death were very early ones produced during his time as a theology student in the Jesuit scholasticate at Ore Place, Hastings: a journal article and an encyclopaedia entry.[11] These received little attention at the time, as might be expected, and have not since been republished.[12] The posthumous appearance of Teilhard's oeuvre, by contrast, excited a wide variety of public reactions, both popular and scholarly, to

---

[6] Mathias Trennert-Helwig, 'The Church as Axis of Convergence in Teilhard's Theology and Life', *Zygon* 30 (1995), p. 77.

[7] 'The Christic' (1955), *HM*, p. 83.

[8] See T.S. Eliot, *Four Quartets* (London: Faber & Faber, 1959), pp. 19–27.

[9] Maritain, 'On two studies dealing with the theology of Père Teilhard', in *The Peasant of the Garonne*, p. 269.

[10] *HP*, p. 211.

[11] «Les Miracles de Lourdes et les enquêtes canoniques», *Études* 118 (1909), pp. 161–83; «Homme: IV: l'homme devant les enseignements de l'Église et devant la philosophie spiritualiste», *Dictionnaire apologétique de la foi catholique*, II (4 vols.; Paris: Beauchesne, 4th edn, 1924–28), §§501–514.

[12] Although see Thomas Becker, *Geist und Materie in den ersten Schriften Pierre Teilhard de Chardins*, Freiburger theologische Studien 134 (Freiburg: Herder, 1987), which provides a detailed discussion of these and some early scientific writings.

which he had no opportunity to respond. Although many of his theological manuscripts had received wide private circulation prior to his death, long periods of exile in China, New York and elsewhere prevented him engaging effectively in the debates which surrounded even those. Nevertheless, Teilhard remained hopeful that, if he laid out his theories clearly, they would eventually be corrected and amplified by criticism.[13] I hope that this study, published in Louvain, the city in which *The Divine Milieu* almost went to press in 1929, will make a small contribution to that task.[14]

An additional complicating factor in the interpretation of Teilhard has been the order of publication of his oeuvre, most of which consists of essays collated into volumes by his former secretary Jeanne Mortier, aided by other executors, and published in the years following his death in 1955. These appeared with especial rapidity in France, beginning with *Le Phénomène humain* and *L'Apparition de l'homme* before the end of the same year, and followed by *La Vision du passé* in 1957. *The Phenomenon of Man* was the first work to be translated into English, appearing under that title in 1959. Aidan Nichols provides a perspective on how Teilhard's theology was at this time occluded by the zeitgeist into which it was received:

> Unfortunately the Catholic *pietas* of Teilhard towards the mystery of the Word incarnate, the Church, the Blessed Virgin and the Eucharist — essential, on his view, to our personal contribution to divine world-making — proved less easily communicable in the period (the 1960s) when his writings, long ecclesiastically inhibited, became generally available, than a secularising reading of his thought which confirmed the 'horizontalism' of the times.[15]

It is ironic that had Teilhard been permitted to publish his theology during his lifetime and in accordance with his own theological priorities, it would probably have received more orthodox interpretation and constituted less of a threat to magisterial teaching.[16] In fact, a hermeneutic

---

[13] 'The New Spirit, 1942' (1942), *FM*, p. 82.

[14] For the circumstances surrounding this event, see letter to Auguste Valensin of 29 September 1929 and «Les Révisions du *Milieu divin*», *LI*, pp. 201, 471–82.

[15] Aidan Nichols, *Catholic Thought Since the Enlightenment: A Survey* (Leominster: Gracewing, 1998), p. 141.

[16] The events surrounding Teilhard's life and theology, and the posthumous life of both, provide important lessons about the futility of using authority to define valid topics for theological discussion and research and to prevent the consideration of other topics. For details of recent Curial statements on Teilhard, see Jean Lacouture, 'Obedience and Teilhard', in *Jesuits: A Multibiography* (London: Harvill, 1996), pp. 431–41; Antonio Russo, «Rome et Teilhard», *RSR* 69 (1981), pp. 485–507.

became established which, to the extent that it engaged with Teilhard's theology, tended to interpret it in light of his scientific theories. Many advocates of Teilhard's thought have undermined it in the eyes of mainstream, orthodox theologians by perpetuating this methodology and failing to grasp its underlying christological emphasis.[17] Richard Kropf, towards the end of his exhaustive study of Teilhard's use of scripture, places his scientific work in his proper context, stating: 'Teilhard was a Christian mystic who from the very beginning of his career was attempting to reinterpret scientific theory in the light of Christian doctrine'.[18] The argument of this study will be exactly this: that Teilhard's theology provides the hermeneutic for the whole of his thought.

Many of Teilhard's interpreters, both detractors and advocates, have subsumed his theology within an intellectual synthesis originating in the early period of the reception of his work. This Procrustean treatment is particularly unfortunate because Teilhard left explicit warnings throughout his oeuvre against conflating different modes of analysis. In the first sentence of the preface to *The Human Phenomenon,* he states that the work is *not* written from a theological perspective: 'To be properly understood, the book I present here must not be read as a metaphysical work, still less as some kind of theological essay, but solely and exclusively as a scientific study.'[19] In many other places, Teilhard indicates to his readers that he is adopting scientific, palaeontological, biological, experiential, or neutral perspectives.[20] Elsewhere he affirms: 'I am writing for my fellow philosophers and theologians.'[21] Preoccupied with the difficulties posed by multiple readerships, he suggests that certain of his essays might have caused confusion because their argument, being intended for 'non-believers', did not progress beyond its first phenomenal phase.[22]

This is not to say, however, that the papers which were primarily scientific in nature were produced with no missionary intention. Teilhard

---

[17] Richard W. Kropf, *Teilhard, Scripture and Revelation: A Study of Teilhard de Chardin's Reinterpretation of Pauline Themes* (Rutherford, NJ: Fairleigh Dickinson, 1980), p. 295.

[18] Kropf, *Teilhard, Scripture and Revelation,* pp. 252–53. When the occasion required, Teilhard read the New Testament in Greek. (See *NR*, p. 166, n. 48.)

[19] *HP*, p. 1.

[20] Respectively 'The Reflection of Energy' (1952), *AE*, p. 322; 'The Transformist Question' (1921), *VP*, p. 8; 'On the Probable Coming of an "Ultra-humanity"' (1950), *FM*, p. 270; 'Universalization and Union' (1942), *AE*, p. 94, n. 1; 'The Zest for Living' (1950), *AE*, p. 241.

[21] 'Christ the Evolver' (1942), *CE*, p. 138.

[22] 'Outline of a Dialectic of Spirit' (1946), *AE*, p. 150.

approaches Christian apologetics by challenging and extending the metaphysical horizons of his readers, rather than by assailing them with explicit revealed truth. This missionary intent is one reason why he maintains an appropriate separation between scientific and theological levels of analysis: he wishes to preclude the possibility that theology and science can reach opposing and irreconcilable conclusions about the world, which forms their common subject matter.[23] To reflect on the boundaries of these two disciplines and their mutual relation as part of a contribution to addressing conflicts about creation and evolution is, indeed, one of Teilhard's principal concerns. Theologically, he inhabits the Anselmnian tradition of placing reason at the service of faith in its quest for understanding.[24] As Prior of Bec, Anselm affirms: 'I do not seek to understand so that I may believe; but I believe so that I may understand. For I believe this also, that "unless I believe, I shall not understand".'[25] Teilhard does not aim to present a systematic theology, but to contribute to this work of theological reflection motivated by *'fides quaerens intellectum'*.[26] The search of faith for understanding is not an enterprise in which only the individual Christian should be engaged, however. It is properly an activity of the Church as a whole, of whom Teilhard states: 'She will never keep the faith luminous for her children and for those outside her except by seeking.'[27] The whole Church needs to envision itself as an 'Ecclesia *quaerens*'. This Anselmian character of Teilhard's theology is especially apparent in the essays with a profoundly mystical content, which conserve a genre of theological reflection in which poetry, philosophy, mystical reflection and praise are inalienably conjoined.[28] In such essays, Teilhard does not wish to deny historic views of Christian perfection but to amplify them, believing that the 'traditional attitude towards God of spiritually minded Christians is retained whole and entire in views that appear to be so novel'.[29] Teilhard wishes to understand creation via God, as does Aquinas in the first part of the *Summa theologiae*, and not God via creation. In common

---

[23] 'Basis and Foundations of the Idea of Evolution' (1926), *VP*, pp. 135–36.

[24] See Wilhelm Dupré, 'Anselm and Teilhard de Chardin: Remarks on the Modification of the Ontological Argument in the Thought of Teilhard de Chardin', *Analecta Anselmiana* 4 (1975), pp. 323–31.

[25] Anselm, *Proslogion*, §I (Notre Dame, Ind.: University of Notre Dame Press, 1979), p. 115; cf. Is 7.9.

[26] 'Christianity and Evolution' (1945), *CE*, p. 173.

[27] Letter to Victor Fontoynant, 26 July 1917, quoted in *SC*, p. 10.

[28] 'Pantheism and Christianity' (1923), *CE*, p. 60.

[29] 'Historical Representations of Original Sin' (1922), *CE*, p. 53; cf. 'The Concept of Christian Perfection' (1942), *TF*, p. 102.

with Aquinas, and also Aristotle, he sees no difference between natural science (*scientia naturalis*) and the philosophy of nature (*philosophia naturalis*): to develop metaphysical theories about the constitution of the world and to investigate the world experimentally form one single enterprise guided by theological principles.

This study will offer a systematic account of Teilhard as a philosophical theologian, and will identify his intellectual origins in the philosophical and theological currents of late nineteenth and early twentieth century France. Prominent figures of this era include the Catholic lay philosopher Maurice Blondel, the Jesuit theologians Pierre Charles, Ferdinand Prat and Pierre Rousselot, and the philosophers Henri Bergson and Victor Delbos. These people mediate crucial intellectual currents to Teilhard: Spinozist immanentism from Delbos, the later Leibniz from Blondel, new perspectives on Aquinas from Rousselot, the Pauline tradition from Prat, and elements of Plotinus and Aristotle from Bergson. Contemporary theologians like Charles, Prat and Rousselot are not usually cited explicitly because their work was considered controversial: Teilhard shared his essays with colleagues, and it was standard practice for letters to be read by superiors. He criticizes Bergsonian cosmology explicitly, in contrast, because in so doing he finds common cause with the magisterium, which had placed works of Bergson's on the Index. The correspondence between Teilhard and Blondel about drafts of Teilhard's early work is especially pertinent, yet has received limited attention from interpreters.[30] Owing to the time interval of three decades or more between the writing and publication of his early essays, Teilhard mediates fin de siècle theological and philosophical debates into the 1960s and 1970s: in other words, from one period of intense intellectual and social ferment into another. In order to demonstrate this, I will devote considerable attention to the antecedents of his theology, focusing on points at which these are most clearly identifiable. Teilhard is imbued with the Thomist and Ignatian traditions and perceives the need to interpret this heritage in terms relevant to the concerns of modern science, philosophy, politics and society.

---

[30] *TBC.* See Franco Polato, *Blondel e Teilhard de Chardin (convergenze e divergenze)*, Studi e Ricerche 18 (Bologna: Zanichelli, 1966); Marie-Jeanne Coutagne, «Le Christ et l'énigme du monde: la christologie blondélienne, 1916–1925», in *Le Christ de Maurice Blondel*, ed. René Virgoulay (Paris: Desclée, 2003), pp. 85–114; Christopher Mooney, 'Blondel and Teilhard de Chardin: An Exchange of Letters', *Thought* 37 (1962), pp. 543–62; Christian d'Armagnac, «De Blondel à Teilhard de Chardin: nature et intériorité», *AP* 21 (1958), pp. 298–312.

One way of approaching the study of Teilhard's theology is to regard
it as combining the different theories of human religious personality
characteristic of Rousselot and Blondel. Rousselot identifies two tendencies in theories of Christian love.[31] The first regards the union between
human and God as consisting in the completion of the human person, of
which the instance par excellence is Aquinas's conception of the vision
of God as the telos of humanity. The second theory represents union as
achievable only following the dissolution of the person in, for instance,
religious ecstasy or extreme self-denial. Rousselot prefers the first
approach. Blondel argues, however, that whilst the essence of the completion of the human person is action, this leads to passion and ultimately to death. This means that the divine will eventually comes to
replace human will, requiring the *death* of the human in both 'partial'
deaths, and ultimately in final and complete bodily death.[32] Teilhard preserves Rousselot's preference for the completion of the human person in
his theology of action, whilst appropriating Blondel's insights into the
unique communicative value of death in his theology of passion. Among
Teilhard's achievements is to translate Blondel's voluntarist philosophy
of action and passion as healing a rupture in the divided human *will* into
the intellectualist cosmology of the Thomism which Rousselot espouses,
which is grounded in *illumination* and the capacity of humanity for the
vision of God.

The structure of this study is primarily intended to facilitate an account
of the main components of Teilhard's philosophical theology. It will
also provide a sense of the progression of his theological interests
through his life. Chapter 1 will examine the concepts of matter and spirit
and their mutual relation. Initially, Teilhard argues that matter is indestructible and self-sufficient, but later identifies matter as a deficiency in
spirit, as plurality and multiplicity, which can only be unified by the
soul. This chapter will show the extent to which Teilhard's theology is,
from its origins, metaphysically grounded. His appropriation of patristic
and Neoplatonic themes will also become evident here.

Chapters 2 and 3 will examine the theories of action and passion,
which in *The Mystical Milieu* and *The Divine Milieu* form the two halves

---

[31] Pierre Rousselot, *Pour l'histoire du problème de l'amour au Moyen-Âge*, Extrait
des Beiträge zur Geschichte der Philosophie des Mittelalters 6 (Münster: Aschendorff,
1908); trans. *The Problem of Love in the Middle Ages: A Historical Contribution* (Milwaukee, Wis.: Marquette University Press, 2001).

[32] Maurice Blondel, papers of 5 and 19 December 1919, *TBC*, pp. 24–26, 44–45.

of a dialectic of spiritual ascent. Humanity attempts to understand itself and the meaning of its existence, Teilhard believes, by reflecting on the place of its action and passion in the universe and their relation to the action of God. Teilhard gives prominence to his theology of action in order to counter an exaggerated theological concern with suffering and passivity. Although passion, conceived as 'undergoing', ultimately comprises the greater half of the dialectic with action, he argues, it can only truly be experienced by the person of action. The importance which Teilhard attaches to passion is in consequence frequently overlooked, but I will be giving it full attention. Both action and passion possess creative and transformative power, and provide the possibility of communion with God. Each ultimately draws the person out of the material context in which he or she is situated into a greater and truer reality.

Chapter 4 will conclude, in some respects, the first half of the study, describing how, in Teilhard's cosmology, matter and soul are formed into the stuff of an enduring, habitable world by Christ, who is present in both action and passion, as well as being their transcendent source. This theology of Christ as the bond of substance makes possible a combined theory of eucharistic and general substance that provides suggestive openings for current ecumenical and interfaith theological work. Teilhard shows how Christ, uniting human and divine natures in the Incarnation, binds together the matter and spirit of the cosmos, and is in this sense 'cosmic'.

Chapter 5 will address a much-neglected area of Teilhard's theology, that of seeing. The gift of vision transforms the way in which believers in Christ see the world, translating the theology of Christ's presence in substance developed in the previous chapter into a lived reality. This new vision is given in and by the divine 'milieu', which is literally a middle space of perception existing between the universe and God. Because the divine milieu is a theory about how the world is experienced in action and passion, this chapter will therefore also pursue the argument of chapters 2 and 3. Chapter 6 will consider the ethics of virtue and the specific 'operative' virtues of purity, faith and fidelity. The context of spiritual ascent distinguishes this ethics of virtue from current prevailing theories of 'virtue ethics' based on practice and character, suggesting instead that virtue is infused and brings with it a striving for excellence. Divinization is the final product of virtuous living, and it is ultimately not individual persons, but humanity collectively, who will be transfigured.

Chapters 7 and 8 will present the practical consequences of this theology for evolution and society respectively. They will situate these topics in the context of the debates and commitments of Teilhard's own lifetime — Darwinian and Lamarckian theories of evolution, and Action Française and Christian social democratic movements — rather than in the period of publication of his oeuvre following his death. Chapter 7 will show how the fundamental convictions that human evolution requires an active and providential principle of life, rather than random selection, and is completed by a final consummation, constitute developments of the metaphysics of chapters 1 to 4. The relation of theology to the natural sciences will also be considered. Chapter 8 will examine Teilhard's responses to fascism and Marxism and identify two key principles for political theology: that Christian faith holds believers to account for their own society and its politics, and that there are good reasons for hope in the future. The light in which the 'other' is seen, originating in the discussion of vision in chapter 5, becomes a distinctively religious political principle, and global social democracy offers, it will be argued, the only feasible political future for world government.

The relative importance of different types of analysis will modulate through different points of the study. Sometimes, Teilhard's theology will best be understood by simple exposition of what he himself has said. In other places, gaps in his exposition will need to be filled, or context provided. Elsewhere, antecedents in patristic theology, the cosmology of Thomas Aquinas, or French theology will assume primary significance. The unifying aim of the study is to present Teilhard's theology as a coherent whole in a way which is both attentive to textual and historical detail and which seeks to understand Teilhard and the problems and questions he addresses in context and with appropriate imagination. I will make clear during the course of this exercise whether ideas presented are Teilhard's own, those on which evidence shows that he drew, or others that illuminate, complement or raise pertinent questions about his analysis. His explicit references to other theologians are sparse and sometimes vague, often owing to the circumstances in which much of his work is composed, such as in battlefields or during pauses in expeditions. It is hard to imagine theological libraries being close to hand. The references to other theologians which do appear are especially valuable, therefore, and I have made greater efforts than previous interpreters of Teilhard to identify exact primary sources for these and to give them a suitably prominent place in exposition and analysis. A related objective of this study is the modest but crucial one of presenting the raw material of Teilhard's theology. Since my interpretation of him as a theologian rooted in historic catholic Christianity will appear quixotic to many of his enthusiasts and detractors, I have devoted more space in the text to presentation and quotation than would probably be needed for a less contested figure.

So much of Teilhard's work is contained in essays, with several of the volumes of essays comprising material produced over a wide time period. In references, I have therefore cited the title of each essay as it appears at the head of the page in the collected works, which is sometimes abbreviated, and the year of writing. Some works were published one or two years after writing, but because many remained unpublished during Teilhard's lifetime, the year of writing, rather than any publication date, has been the only consistently available one to use. Use of this date also facilitates clear focus on the progression of Teilhard's thought, particularly in periods when several essays are produced in rapid succession. The year of writing is included, along with the abbreviated title of the collection in which the essay occurs, in all references, unless the essay has recently been cited. English translations of Teilhard's works are cited exactly as given, except that in cases where masculine English nouns or pronouns in the text or titles of essays have been derived from French ones, these are rendered inclusively, in line with the policy applied to the revision of the translations of Teilhard's collected works in course of publication by Sussex Academic Press. The bibliography includes the full titles of all essays cited, and marks with asterisks a selection from various volumes that provides an engaging and representative sample of Teilhard's theology. It also provides a comprehensive bibliography of the most useful secondary literature.

1. COSMOS

During his early life in Sarcenat, near Clermont-Ferrand in the Auvergne in the shadow of the Puy-de-Dôme, Teilhard acquired a powerful sense of the materiality of the world and of the embodied character of human existence in the world. This is described in some of his early letters from Egypt, where he spent three years teaching in the School of the Holy Family in Cairo, run by the Lyons province of the Jesuit order. This correspondence is filled with vivid descriptions of the geology, flora and fauna of the country in which he was living.[1] The abiding attraction that matter continued to exert on Teilhard's imagination is expressed in many of his wartime writings. The remarkable 'Hymn to Matter' praises matter as perilous, mighty, universal, impenetrable and mortal, as inexhaustible potentiality, universal power and melodious fountain of water. Teilhard addresses matter thus:

> Without you, without your onslaughts, without your uprootings of us, we should remain all our lives inert, stagnant, puerile, ignorant both of ourselves and of God. You who batter us and then dress our wounds, you who resist us and yield to us, you who wreck and build, you who shackle and liberate, the sap of our souls, the hand of God, the flesh of Christ: it is you, matter, that I bless.[2]

Teilhard defines matter as

> the assemblage of things, energies and creatures which surround us to the extent that these are palpable, sensible and 'natural' (in the theological sense of the word). Matter is the common milieu, universal and tangible, infinitely shifting and varied, in which we live.[3]

Matter is beyond human objectification and is the cause of the limitations intrinsic to the human condition, which culminate ultimately in death. It also constitutes the shared world in which human life is set. When matter acts on the human body, the soul experiences the fragility and commonality of the material, embodied existence in which it partakes with other beings.

---

[1] e.g. letter of 1 October 1905, *LE*, pp. 34–39.
[2] 'The Spiritual Power of Matter' (1919), *HU*, p. 69.
[3] *DM*, p. 66.

Teilhard gradually develops an account of matter that recognizes matter's dependence for its consistency on other elements of the cosmic order. Reflecting on the early development of his cosmology, Teilhard refers to 'an instinctive predilection for matter (regarded as more absolute than the rest) that I corrected only much later'.[4] His reaction against this preference is strong, and he later argues that matter, far from being the ultimate principle of the cosmos, is in fact dependent on, and implies, a hierarchy of principles above it. The consistency of matter that enables it to act so decisively on the human body requires the existence of a universal principle that sustains materiality, and is as such non-material. The body, moreover, is not only formed passively in its encounters with matter, but transforms matter through its own activity. Teilhard's early reflections, dominated by a vision of the *Sturm und Drang* to which matter subjects the apparently passive body, are superseded by a dialectic of action and passion in which matter is *object* as well as subject. Humanity participates moreover, through action and passion, in the absolute principle beyond the material to a degree proportionate to its place on the scale of universal perfection. The soul experiences this participation as freedom when active, and as suffering, or undergoing, when passive.

Paul Tillich refers to the time when, long after describing life and its ambiguities in the third volume of his *Systematic Theology*, he read *The Human Phenomenon*. Tillich recounts his subsequent realization that he and Teilhard shared a common concern that theology 'must relate its understanding of man to an understanding of universal nature, for man is a part of nature and statements about nature underlie every statement about him'.[5] The two theologians address this shared concern in different ways, however. Tillich pursues his project by identifying voids existing within human culture, and by correlating Christian symbols with them interprets the sacred possibilities they offer. Teilhard, by contrast, considers the universal nature of the cosmos as comprising material and spiritual principles, and posits an absolute, unifying metaphysical principle, who is God. His theology originates as an attempt to understand how God creates, sustains and animates the cosmos of which humanity forms a part.

---

[4] 'My Universe' (1918), *HM*, p. 198.
[5] Paul Tillich, *Systematic Theology*, III (3 vols.; University of Chicago Press, 1951–63), p. 5.

Creation: the fall into matter

By the time of his war writings and later, Teilhard argues that matter is not itself an active or indestructible cosmic principle, but implies the existence of such a principle on which it is dependent for its consistency. This inference of an immaterial sustaining principle can be seen as a conscious move away from an Aristotelian conception of matter as self-sufficient and itself constituting substance towards a Plotinian view of matter as unlimited (ἄπειρος), indefinite (ἀόριστος), and dependent for its consistency on an external forming principle.[6] Teilhard identifies matter with privation: 'An initial and extremely dispersed Multiple, which is the lowest aspect of the world, the form in which it comes closest to Non-being.'[7] Matter is the principle of the cosmos contrary to order, being a 'dead-weight, a husk to be discarded' and 'dim, heavy, passive, loaded with suffering, evil', and the flesh is a 'prison in which the soul suffocates'.[8] Plotinus describes this dispersal and multiplicity using the image of the 'mud of darkness' (βόρβορος σκοτεινός) derived from the Orphic imagery in the *Phaedo* of 'lying in the mire' (ἐν βορβόρῳ κείσεται)[9]. He identifies matter (ὕλη), in similar terms to Teilhard, as 'utterly vile' and 'utterly evil' (πάντον αἰσχρόν, πάντον κακόν).[10] In characteristically Leibnizian mode, Teilhard portrays matter as a principle of disunity:

> With every monad folding back jealously upon itself and claiming the right to bring all the others into subjection, the whole throng of monads is dissociated and scattered.[11]

In this deprived state, in which matter lacks unity and possesses no real or permanent value, its nature cannot be comprehended by the human

---

[6] Plotinus, *Enneads*, II.4 (33) 15; 11 (7 vols.; Harvard University Press, 1966–88), pp. 142–47, 130–35. An excellent survey of the similarities and contrasts between Teilhard and Plotinus is given in Mary T. Clark, 'The Divine Milieu in Philosophical Perspective', *The Downside Review* 80 (1962), pp. 12–25.

[7] 'The Names of Matter' (1919), *HM*, p. 226; cf. «Homme: IV» (1912), §508. A useful overview is given in D. Dixon Sutherland, 'A Theological Anthropology of Evil: A Comparison in the Thought of Paul Ricoeur and Teilhard de Chardin', *Neue Zeitschrift für systematische Theologie und Religionsphilosophie* 34 (1992), pp. 85–100.

[8] 'Cosmic Life' (1916), *WW*, p. 38; 'The Great Monad' (1918), p. 190; cf. Plotinus, *Enneads*, IV.8 (6) 3; 1, pp. 404–405, 398–99.

[9] Plotinus, *Enneads*, I.8 (51) 17–18, p. 310; Plato, *Phaedo*, 69c6, *Works* I, (12 vols.; Harvard University Press, 1914–30), p. 240.

[10] Plotinus, *Enneads*, II.4 (33) 16, pp. 148–49.

[11] 'The Struggle Against the Multitude' (1917), *WW*, p. 103.

mind.[12] Its principal deficiency, expressed in Neoplatonic terms, is its lack of any forming principle.

Teilhard discusses several original fall narratives that have inspired theological accounts of this cosmic multiplicity. The locus classicus in Judeao-Christian scripture has been the Genesis 3 myth: Adam and Eve, created free and adult by God, misuse the free will with which they were created by eating from the tree of the knowledge of good and evil. The consequences of their sinful act, which according to Augustine include guilt for it, have since been transmitted through the whole of humanity.[13] Teilhard signals his familiarity with the images of the fall as an initial accident, or a culpable act which 'broke the primal unity of things',[14] employed by the first Tridentine canon on original sin:

> If any one does not confess that the first man, Adam, when he had trans-gressed the commandment of God in Paradise, immediately lost the holi-ness and justice wherein he had been constituted; and that he incurred, through the offence of that prevarication, the wrath and indignation of God, and consequently death, with which God had previously threatened him, and, together with death, captivity under his power who thenceforth had the empire of death, that is to say, the devil, and that the entire Adam, through that offence of prevarication, was changed, in body and soul, for the worse; let him be anathema.[15]

Teilhard rejects this depiction of the fall decisively, complaining that it 'has already ceased to be for us anything but a strait-jacket and a verbal imposition, the *letter* of which can no longer satisfy us either intellectu-ally or emotionally'.[16] Many of the well-known intellectual difficulties with the literal reading of the account of the sin of Adam and Eve arise in the course of attempts to reconcile the concept of a 'first man' with theories of biological evolution. For instance, identifying the first male being in whom all the relevant generic characteristics were sufficiently evolved to qualify him for inclusion in the category 'man' would be impossible. More serious in practice are the emotional consequences of the literal reading, implicit in much of Teilhard's criticism of it. The peculiarly Augustinian concept of *reactus* (guilt) inherited by humanity for the sin of Adam has often occluded consideration of the fundamental fact of sin itself (*vitium*), its actual genesis, and the practical responses to it that are urgently needed to preserve the world from further sinful

---

[12] 'Pantheism and Christianity' (1923), *CE*, pp. 57–58.
[13] 'My Universe' (1924), *SC*, p. 80; 'Christology and Evolution' (1933), *CE*, p. 86.
[14] 'The Phenomenon of Spirituality' (1937), *HE*, p. 101.
[15] 'Ut fides nostra', *DEC* II, p. 666.
[16] 'Christology and Evolution', p. 86.

degeneration. The excessive focus by theologians on *reactus* helps to explain, Teilhard suggests, why they have so often regarded humanity as actually sinful rather than potentially good.

An alternative account of the fall is provided by the Watcher legend. This account also supplies cosmology appropriate to a different interpretation of the Eden narrative. Popular in pre-Augustinian theology, the myth has more recently inspired John Hick's philosophical theodicy. Recounted in the opening verses of Genesis 6, it narrates the fall of angels as a result of their sinful union with earthly women, from whom warrior-giants were in consequence born:

> When people began to multiply on the face of the ground, and daughters were born to them, the sons of God (בְּנֵי־הָאֱלֹהִים) saw that they were fair; and they took wives for themselves of all that they chose. Then the LORD said, 'My spirit shall not abide in mortals for ever, for they are flesh; their days shall be one hundred and twenty years.' The Nephilim were on the earth in those days — and also afterwards — when the sons of God went in to the daughters of humans, who bore children. These were the heroes that were of old, warriors of renown.[17]

This account of the fall suggests that human sinfulness possesses a cosmic origin rather than a specifically moral one, even if that sinfulness is interpreted literally. This revised hamartiology inspires Teilhard to consider the possibility that humanity was created perfect but then descended to a lower level of being characterised by plurality and a deficiency of goodness. He speculates:

> As a consequence of an infidelity similar to that of the angels, this pre-humankind would have become less spiritual, and more material; and it is in fact this materialization which would have produced the woeful multiplicity.[18]

Teilhard considers this account of a cosmic fall of spirit to be more credible than the standard Eden narrative because it 'satisfactorily explains our complete inability to distinguish in the past the least trace of an earthly paradise'. In resisting anachronistic literal readings of Genesis 3, he advances an interpretation that is undoubtedly closer to the allegorical intent that motivated its composition and transmission. He states:

---

[17] Gen 6.1–4. John Hick, *Evil and the God of Love* (Basingstoke: Macmillan, 2nd edn, 1977), pp. 201–218; Norman Powell Williams, *The Ideas of the Fall and of Original Sin* (London: Longmans, Green & Co., 1927), pp. 21–31. I Enoch 6–8 gives the most detailed version of the legend. Jude 14, cf. 6, attests to the prophetic status of Enoch's writing. See *The Ethiopian Book of Enoch*, I (2 vols.; Oxford: Clarendon, 1978), pp. 67–84.

[18] 'Historical Representations of Original Sin' (1922), *CE*, p. 50.

> Adam and Eve began their existence in a sphere of the world different from
> ours. Through their fall they sank into a lower sphere (now our own); in
> other words they were embodied as matter in, incarnated in, fitted into, the
> strictly animal sphere into which we are now born: they were *reborn* at a
> lower level than that of their first state.[19]

This allegorical portrayal of the Adam and Eve suggests that the narrative of the fall of the angels inspires Teilhard's allegorical reading of the
Eden one. He argues that both accounts give, according to the 'most
recent advances in exegesis ... not "visual" information about humanity's *history* but teaching about its *nature*'.[20] The fall of the individual is
a repetition of the cosmic fall.[21] Sin does not originate in an event occurring within time, but in the act of the creation of time and space itself.
Sin is the 'essential reaction of the finite to the creative act' and the
'*reverse side* of all creation':

> Il n'est pas un acte qui s'est posé 'intra' *universem*; — Il est un évènement
> qui a accompagné la formation de l'Univers, de façon à se mélanger com-
> plètement à la création, avant tout temps et tout espace. La faute originelle
> est mêlée à l'essai même du Monde. — Aussi loin que nous regardions, en
> arrière et autour de nous, tout et *sub peccato*, — comme aussi *sub Christo*.
> — Il correspond à une certaine involution des choses, à une matérialisation
> universelle dont l'influence du Christ fait ressortir l'esprit.[22]

Two years later, Teilhard states:

> Original sin expresses, translates, personifies, in an instantaneous and
> localized act, the perennial and universal law of imperfection which oper-
> ates in humankind *in virtue* of its being *in fieri* [in process of becoming].
> One might even, perhaps, go so far as to say that since the creative act (by
> definition) causes being to rise up to God from the confines of nothingness
> (that is, from the depth of the multiple, which means from some other mat-
> ter), all creation begins with it, as its accompanying risk and shadow, some
> fault; in other words, it has its counterpart in some redemption. Seen in this
> way, the drama of Eden would be the very drama of the whole of human
> history concentrated in a symbol profoundly expressive of reality.[23]

---

[19] 'Historical Representations of Original Sin', pp. 48–49.

[20] 'Reflections on Original Sin' (1947), *CE*, p. 191.

[21] 17 March 1919, *NR*, p. 52.

[22] *J*, 29 May 1920, cahier VIII: 'It isn't an act committed *within* the universe; — It is
an event which accompanied the formation of the universe, so as to mix itself completely
with creation, before all time and all space. Original sin is implicated in the initial creation of the world. — As far as we can see, behind and around us, everything is *under sin*
— but also *under Christ*. — It corresponds to a fall into being, to a universal material-
ization which Christ's influence causes to emerge into spirit.'

[23] 'Historical Representations of Original Sin', pp. 51–52.

The role for Adam implicit in the figurative reading of the Eden narrative espoused by Teilhard converges with that of Enkidu in the Gilgamesh creation myth. This hirsute noble savage, in many respects Adam's Babylonian twin, is presented more as a mediator between animal and human life than as a first human being created fully formed.[24] Created half-man and half-beast, Enkidu lives among the animals to begin with, but is enticed by the sacred prostitute Shamhat, sent by Gilgamesh, and by their union the human kingdom is founded. Some of the features of this story are equally apparent in the Hebrew account of creation, not least Adam's rejection of kinship with the animal kingdom, despite naming its members.[25] What is most significant, however, is that the Gilgamesh narrative suggests in the ambiguous figure of Enkidu an evolutionary interpretation of creation. He is a being enshrouded in hair who consumes vegetation and drinks water with gazelles and cattle prior to his seduction. There is no evidence that Teilhard was aware of the Gilgamesh myth. Nevertheless, it suggests that an evolutionary reading of early creation myths is by no means inconsistent with their original intention.

Teilhard offers one allegorical reading of the Eden narrative particularly apposite to this reformed cosmology. He refers to the homily of Gregory of Nazianzus 'On the Theophany, or Birthday of Christ', which 'explains the expulsion from Eden as the fall in a "denser" form of life'. Of Adam's ejection from paradise, the Bishop of Sasima states:

> For his sin he was banished, at once from the Tree of Life, and from Paradise, and from God; and put on the coats of skins ... that is, perhaps, the thicker [sic] flesh, both mortal and contradictory.[26]

This translation represents the coats of skins as an analogy for the 'coarser flesh', thus imputing to them a penitential status, and in so doing imposes on the passage a sense that Gregory does not wish to convey. Donald Winslow gives the more literal rendering of Gregory's παχ-υτέραν as 'thicker skins',[27] and this is closer to what Teilhard believes

---

[24] *Gilgamesh*, I.ii–iv, in *Myths from Mesopotamia*, ed. Stephanie Dalley (Oxford University Press, 1991), pp. 53–56.

[25] Gn 2.20.

[26] Gregory of Nazianzus, 'Homily 38: On the Theophany, or Birthday of Christ', §12, in *NPNF*, series II, VII, p. 348; cf. Gn 3.21; 'Reflections on Original Sin', p. 191, n. 7. The Vulgate renders the כָּתְנוֹת עוֹר 'tunicas pellicias'. Teilhard notes this term in passing in *J*, 24 March 1921, cahier VIII, where he relates it to the universality of sin destroying all life in the Flood, though not specifically to materiality.

[27] Donald F. Winslow, *The Dynamics of Salvation: A Study in Gregory of Nazianzus* (Cambridge, Mass.: Philadelphia Patristic Foundation, 1979), pp. 68–69.

the essential meaning of the expulsion from paradise to be: not a fall
from a sanctified spiritual state into sinful embodiment, but a change in
the nature of embodiment and an increase in the *weight* of the flesh.[28]
The body ceases to share in the contemplation of the soul, becoming a
hindrance to the soul and requiring its direction.[29] This theme of the
heaviness of the soul becomes dominant in emerging Christian orthodoxy. Augustine quotes the Wisdom of Solomon: 'The body, which is
corruptible, weighs down the soul, and our earthly habitation drags
down the mind to think many things.'[30] He later employs the Plotinian
analogy of the body finding its proper position in the cosmos according
to its weight.[31] The cosmology invoked here is based, therefore, on an
inverse relation of weight to spirit: the more that matter dominates soul
in the combined substance of the body, the lower the position it occupies
in the hierarchy of created being.

Teilhard compares these allegorical readings of Genesis with the doctrine of an 'original sin "pan-cosmic" in nature' of the Alexandrian tradition, and in a reference to Pierre Charles, recalls: 'I have some idea
that the same views were re-adopted and taught at Louvain some few
years ago'.[32] Teilhard associates with Charles more specifically the
hypothesis that the first man was a spiritual creation and subsequently
fell into materiality.[33] The Belgian Jesuit was instrumental in efforts
made during the 1920s, which almost succeeded, to publish *The Divine
Milieu* in the *Museum Lessianum* series founded at Louvain.[34] The

[28] Cf. retreat note of 25 July 1922, *NR*, p. 101; and extensive notes in *J*, 9–18 May
1921, cahier VIII.

[29] Gary A. Anderson, 'The Garments of Skin in Apocryphal Narrative and Biblical
Commentary', in *Studies in Ancient Midrash*, ed. James Kugel (Harvard University Center for Jewish Studies, 2001), pp. 101–143, identifies the tensions between the Eden
account of the clothing in skin representing the *ontological* state of sinful embodiment
and images of Adam and Eve covering their nudity for fear of committing a *moral* sin.

[30] Wisd 9.15; Augustine, *Confessions*, VII.xvii (23) (2 vols.; London: Heinemann,
1912), I, pp. 384–85.

[31] Augustine, *Confessions*, XIII.ix (10), vol. II, pp. 390–91; cf. Plotinus, *Enneads*, 2.1
(40) 3, pp. 14–17.

[32] 'Reflections on Original Sin', p. 191, n. 7. In a letter of 3 October 1923, *LLZ*, p. 57,
Teilhard commends Pierre Charles's new collection *La Prière de toutes les heures* (2
vols.; Bruges: Beyaert, 1923); trans. *Prayer for all Times* (1 vol.; London: Fount, 1983),
written in a strikingly similar genre to the sections of *The Divine Milieu* in which Christ
is directly addressed.

[33] See Bruno de Solages, *Teilhard de Chardin: témoignage et étude sur le développement de sa pensée* (Toulouse: Privat, 1966), pp. 326–27, which discusses a note written
by Teilhard to the author; René d'Ouince, *Un prophète en procès: Teilhard de Chardin
dans l'Église de son temps* (Paris: Aubier Montaigne, 1970), p. 56.

[34] Haiyan Wang, *Le Phénomène Teilhard: l'aventure du livre 'Le Milieu divin'*
(Saint-Étienne: Aubin, 1999).

'Alexandrian' theology with which Charles is associated existed, of course, over a period of at least four centuries, from its origins in Philo to its conclusion in the writings of the Cappadocian Fathers. Although this means that there is no uniform Alexandrian theory of the fall,[35] the teachings of Philo and the pre-Caesarean Origen provide two good examples of the characteristics which Teilhard is identifying when using the term 'Alexandrian' generically. Philo interprets the tunics of skin in terms similar to those of Gregory of Nazianzus, suggesting that the tunics represent, quite simply, the natural skin of the human body, and therefore human embodiment.[36] In so far as the body is material, it contains an evil tendency, and insofar as it is spiritual it possesses the potential for goodness. Philo describes the creation of good and evil inclinations by God, then depicts the divine contemplation of the deeds of humanity:

> Having set up these standards in the soul, He watched, as a judge might, to see to which it would tend. And when He saw it inclining to wickedness, and making light of holiness and godly fear, out of which comes the winning of immortal life, He drove it from the paradise.

Philo defends his creation allegory in the following robust terms:

> These are no mythical fictions, such as poets and sophists delight in, but modes of making ideas visible, bidding us resort to allegorical interpretation guided in our renderings by what lies beneath the surface.[37]

An allegorical reading of the expulsion from Eden, far from diminishing its significance, in fact reveals the episode's true meaning by 'making ideas visible'. Philo focuses on the *Phaedrus* movement of ascent and descent, stating that souls 'descending into the body as though into a stream have sometimes been caught up in the swirl of its rushing torrent and swallowed up thereby'.[38] Notably, this is a descent of individual souls, like the one that Gregory describes, rather than the collective fall of every soul. Sin is represented by the weight of embodiment: Philo conceives of humanity not as a *massa peccati* in the sense of 'one mass

---

[35] F.R. Tennant, *The Sources of the Doctrines of the Fall and Original Sin* (Cambridge University Press, 1903), pp. 273–345, provides a useful overview of the theologies of sin developed by many of these pre-Augustinian theologians.

[36] Philo, *Questions and Answers on Genesis*, I.liii, *Works* suppl. I (12 vols.; London: Heinemann, 1929-54), pp. 30–31. The translation is based on an Aramaic copy.

[37] Philo, *On the Account of the World's Creation Given by Moses*, lv–lvi, *Works* I, pp. 122–25; see Émile Bréhier, *Les Idées philosophiques et religieuses de Philon d'Alexandrie* (Paris: Vrin, 1908; 3rd edn, 1950).

[38] Philo, *On the Giants*, iii, *Works* II, pp. 450–51; cf. *On Dreams*, i.22, *Works* V, pp. 370–71; Plato, *Phaedrus*, 246a–254e, *Works* I, pp. 470–99.

coming from inherited sin and the penalty of mortality', as does Augustine,[39] but in the very literal sense of the differentiated weight of individual bodies.

This cosmology is also adopted by Origen, who recounts a prenatal fall from the transcendental sphere in the course of which the soul becomes enmeshed in matter. Fire and heat represent the divine principle, and he therefore describes the fall of individual souls not as the gaining of weight but as a *cooling* in their temperature.[40] Plotinus employs a similar cosmology: fire is splendid beyond all material bodies and gives form to water, air and earth, which are the other three elements, by providing them with colour and heat.[41] Fire is given equal primacy among the simple bodies by Aristotle, who reasons, like his Pythagorean predecessors, that fire is the only simple body which is fed by the form.[42] Origen even speculates on the derivation of ψῡχή (soul) from ψῡχρός (cool) in order to establish the heat connection. The world, on its creation by God was varied and diverse, and therefore some souls have cooled and others have not. Origen nonetheless insists on the creation of all souls equal and alike, in order to remove from God any culpability for individual descents.[43] This use of fire and heat imagery to represent features of the cosmos is particularly suggestive because Teilhard identifies the divine principle of the universe by similar means. He refers to the search of the mystic for the 'devouring fire which they could identify with the Divine that summons them from all sides', and to the moment when God takes possession of the soul as 'the fire coming down'.[44] The fire metaphors in Teilhard's work describe the spiritual

---

[39] Cf. Augustine, *De diversis quaestionibus VII ad Simplicianum*, I, q. 2, 20, in *Earlier Writings*, ed. John Burleigh (London: SCM, 1953), pp. 403–404.

[40] Origen, *On First Principles*, II, 8.3 (New York: Harper, 1966), pp. 122–27; cf. Aristotle, *On the Soul*, I.2, *Works* VIII (23 vols.; Harvard University Press, 1926–91), pp. 30–31, notes both this and an opposing etymology that derives ζῆν (to live) from ζεῖν (to boil).

[41] Plotinus, *Enneads*, I.6 (1) 3, pp. 240–43; see A.H. Armstrong, *The Architecture of the Intelligible Universe in the Philosophy of Plotinus: An Analytical and Historical Study* (Cambridge University Press, 1940), pp. 54–55.

[42] Aristotle, *On Coming-To-Be and Passing-Away*, 335a16–19, *Works* III, p. 307.

[43] Origen, *On First Principles*, II, 9.2–3, 6, pp. 354–59, 364–67; *Traité des principes*, I (5 vols.; Paris: Cerf, 1978–84), pp. 342–49. See also Origen, *Homélies sur la Genèse*, eds. Henri de Lubac and Louis Doutreleau, Sources Chrétiennes 7b (Paris: Cerf, 1944; rev. 2nd edn, 2003); Henri de Lubac, *Histoire et l'esprit: l'intelligence de l'Écriture d'après Origène* (Paris: Aubier, 1950); Ferdinand Prat, *Origène: le théologien et l'exégète* (Paris: Bloud, 1907).

[44] 'The Mystical Milieu' (1917), *WW*, p. 129.

illumination of the cosmos in Christ, and will be considered in greater detail in the context of vision.

Later Christian typology, based typically on scriptural notions of purity rather than philosophical ones, inverts this representational scheme. Heat and fire come to be associated with the *lowest* level of being (Gehenna, or Hell) and not the highest. The result of this inversion seems to be ambivalence about what exactly takes place at the moment of conflagration: destruction or consummation? In modern accounts, emphasis is frequently placed on the fire of judgement punishing and destroying sinful humanity.[45] The linking of the fire with the flood of Genesis 7 in the principal scriptural source II Peter 3.3–10 reinforces this interpretation. Although the inundation occurs as punishment for the sinful union of angels with women, the comparison of the deluge of water with the deluge of fire forces recognition of the *baptismal* tradition of the flood. The water represents, according to the Easter Anthems of Romans 6.9–11, dying to sin and being alive to God in Christ Jesus. Teilhard accentuates this second affirmative aspect of conflagration, writing of God:

> When he enters into us to destroy, as it seems, the virtues and the forces that we have distilled with so much loving care out of the sap of the earth, it will be as a loving fire to consummate our completion in union.[46]

Fire suggests, therefore, not only judgement, but renewal and *consummation*.[47] This resonates with the Stoic understanding of the ἐκπυροσις, or dissolution of the universe into fire, as a cyclical and repeatable event that brings purification or κάθαρσις.[48] Teilhard's opinion that the final parousia is 'more akin to a maturing than to a destruction' corresponds well with the evolutionary historical cosmology which he develops.[49]

The Alexandrians, Teilhard states with approval, are exceptional in eschewing the tendency of theologians to 'borrow' the representation of original sin 'almost literally from the first chapters of Genesis'.[50] He notes that when the Alexandrians admit the

---

[45] For instance, E. Lussier, 'Universal Conflagration at the Parousia', *Catholic Biblical Quarterly* 12 (1950), pp. 243–47.

[46] *DM*, p. 59.

[47] Francis X. Murphy, 'Conflagration: The Eschatological Perspective from Origen to John Chrysostom', *SP* 18, 1 (Kalamazoo, Mich.: Cistercian, 1985), pp. 179–85.

[48] Michael Lapidge, 'Stoic Cosmology', in *The Stoics*, ed. John M. Rist (Berkeley: University of California Press, 1978), pp. 180–84.

[49] 'The Stuff of the Universe' (1953), *AE*, p. 382.

[50] 'Historical Representations of Original Sin', p. 45.

idea of a genesis or a fulfilment of the one from the elements of the world, these elements still remain … the source of all sin and all suffering — because of their temporary condition of disorder, itself the inevitable consequence of the still continuing process of attaining their union — but they no longer need a prior evil to explain their appearance and their initial distribution. They are no longer the shattered fragments of the amphora, but the dust of the elemental clay.[51]

A figure of crucial importance for Teilhard's developing awareness of Alexandrian cosmology is Henri Rondet. Teilhard cites the Lyons theologian in support of his position in the essay 'Reflections on Original Sin', in which Teilhard considers contemporary church theology in the light of modern scientific theories about creation and evolution. Rondet had just published a collection of studies *Problèmes pour la réflexion chrétienne*.[52] Referring to this work, Teilhard argues that the power of sin was established prior to the creation of the temporal order, rather than within the temporal order:

> In its allegedly traditional form, original sin is generally presented as a 'serial' event, linking up (with an earlier and a later) *inside* history. Yet, for conclusive physical and theological reasons, surely we should treat it, on the contrary, as a reality which belongs to the trans-historic order, affecting (like a colour or a dimension) the whole of our experiential vision of the world.[53]

In consequence, 'original sin ceases to be an isolated *act* and becomes a *state*'. In opposition to the Augustinian inversion of the relation between sin and temporality, this conception of original sin as affecting humanity collectively does not require the derivation of the 'whole human race from one single couple'. Sin is no longer regarded as the result of the misuse of human free will within temporality, and becomes a *condition for* temporality. If history is itself contingent on sin, then the redemption of the world by Christ is necessary absolutely, rather than necessary in order to remedy the adverse consequences of a historically contingent event that might not have occurred. This reversal, Teilhard contends,

> far from weakening the dogmatic characteristics of the Fall, intensifies them… Redemption is indeed universal, since it corrects a state of affairs (the universal presence of disorder) which is tied up with [lié à] the most basic structure of the universe in process of creation.[54]

---

[51] 'The Road of the West' (1932), *TF*, p. 57.

[52] 'Reflections on Original Sin', p. 197; Henri Rondet, *Problèmes pour la réflexion chrétienne: Le Péché originel, L'Enfer et autres études* (Paris: Spes, 1946), cf. *Le Mystère du péché originel* (Le Puy: X. Mappus, 1943).

[53] 'Reflections on Original Sin', pp. 188–89.

[54] 'Reflections on Original Sin', pp. 196–97.

As if to repay Teilhard's compliment to him, Rondet cites Teilhard in his later study *Le Péché originel*, observing that Teilhard is 'less concerned with the individual fault, the revolt of one person against God, than he is with the moral shortcomings of collective mankind.'[55] Rondet goes on to consider where this theology of sin as collective ontological fallenness places the crucial point of moral decision: Teilhard 'puts back to the end of time the moral choice which the scholastics located in the earthly paradise'. Adam's partaking in the fruit of the tree of the knowledge of good and evil does not, once conceived as a condition for temporality, inhibit future free choice. The alternatives are not sin or freedom, but sin *and* freedom on the one hand, and non-existence on the other. The transgression of Adam continually presents humanity with the option of accepting its liberty to assent to the absolute spiritual principle which will redeem and consummate the world, and which makes possible the action and passion of human existence.[56]

Historically, the literal reading of Genesis 3 to account for the power of sin in the world develops under the substantial authority of Paul of Tarsus. The apostle to the Gentiles certainly demonstrates his familiarity with the alternative account in the myth of the fall of the angels, alluding to it when explaining why women should cover their heads.[57] Nevertheless, Paul's theological attention is dedicated wholly to the sin of Adam and Eve construed as an event which took place in time and consisted in their misuse of God-given free will, and in expounding the consequences of that sin for humanity. This is in spite of his concern in many places with the consequences of lust, which are described not in the Eden account but in the Watcher legend. In Romans, Paul portrays Adam as the one man through whom sin entered the world. Death was the result of Adam's sin, and has since spread through all humankind.[58]

---

[55] Henri Rondet, *Le Péché originel dans la tradition patristique et théologique* (Paris: Fayard, 1967), trans. *Original Sin: The Patristic and Theological Background* (Shannon: Ecclesia, 1972), pp. 252–54.

[56] See 'The Grand Option' (1939), pp. 37–60. For comparison of Teilhard's notion of the cosmic fall with that of Schelling, see Marietta Grindler, „Der Rückgang von Raum und Zeit zu Unendlichkeit und Ewigkeit", in *Das holistische Evolutionsmodell Pierre Teilhard de Chardins: ein Vergleich mit den Entwicklungsgedanken bei Plotin, Schelling und Bergson* (Aachen: Shaker, 2000), pp. 352–53. Donald Gray, 'Involution and the problem of evil', in *The One and the Many: Teilhard de Chardin's Vision of Unity* (London: Burns & Oates, 1969), pp. 52–74, identifies a third 'Neoplatonic' position in Teilhard's final years, following the 'biblical' and 'Alexandrian' ones. I have chosen not to develop this distinction owing to the close association of Alexandrian theology with Neoplatonism.

[57] I Cor 15.22.

[58] Rom 5.12–19.

The obedient sacrifice of Christ cancels out the sin of Adam: indeed, Christ is the Second Adam.

It is significant that Augustine is the first major theologian to refute the identification of the Sons of God as angels.[59] Until then, the passage formed part of the wider cosmic hamartiology which Teilhard embraces. Augustine regards the Watcher legend as of less importance than had previously been considered on the grounds that the Sons of God referred to in Genesis 6 were purely human messengers. He remains in principle agnostic over the question of whether or not 'spirits with bodies of air' could experience lust or procreate with women, but is unable to believe that the angels would have committed so grave a fault at any time later than the creation of the world. He also presents a semantic argument for his inversion of the traditional hierarchy of stories, stating that an ordinary human messenger in scripture is frequently designated an ἄγγελος, and that this is true of the supposedly heavenly beings of Genesis 3. Denial that the fall possesses cosmic origins naturally suits Augustine's own theological agenda of placing full responsibility for this catastrophe on humankind, which misused its free will.[60] His aim of accounting for a universal sinful state might have been achieved more convincingly, however, by accepting an allegorical interpretation of the expulsion from Eden such as the one that Teilhard espouses, rather than by defending its historicity and then having to develop an account of the subsequent transmission of sin through humanity from its particular originating act.

The unification of matter

Matter, being a principle of disunity and multiplicity, is dependent on a spiritual principle to provide it with form. Following Teilhard's early 'predilection for matter', his metaphysics becomes more Cartesian: extension persists, but is in practice little more than a mental construct. Matter remains in theory indestructible, but because it is infinitely divisible is equally 'boundless plurality, mere dust'.[61] This is why

---

[59] F.B. Huey and John H. Walton, 'Are the "Sons of God" in Genesis 6 Angels?', in *The Genesis Debate* (Nashville: Thomas Nelson, 1986), pp. 184–209. Huey shows (p. 190) that the interpretation of the Sons of God as angels was considered orthodox by the Greek Fathers and that its first major refutation was by Augustine in *De civitate Dei*, XV.23 (7 vols.; Harvard University Press, 1957–72), IV, pp. 546–61.

[60] Augustine, *De civitate Dei*, XIII.15; XIV.13, vol. IV, pp. 182–85, 334–45.

[61] 'Science and Christ' (1921), *SC*, p. 29.

Descartes states that even a stone, apparently the most solid of material substances, would no longer possess the property of hardness if liquefied or reduced to powder.[62] Extension is no more than one of the 'garments under which corporeal substance appears', and is not an objective primary quality of an external body in the Lockean sense.[63] The point on which Teilhard diverges with Descartes, however, regards the concept of substance: this is not simply matter as revealed by the sum of its attributes, as Descartes believed, because this would imply that objects in the world can exist in a self-sufficient unity, which Teilhard always argues is impossible. Teilhard states that matter in isolation is 'incapable by its very nature of giving rise to the world that surrounds us and gives us substance.'[64] In fact, substance possesses its own distinct existence in an object, sustaining the object in which it dwells within a hierarchy of being and enabling that object to exist and be perceived as a unity.

In his early works, Teilhard employs Leibnizian terminology to describe the relation between the unifying principle of the cosmos and the entities dependent on it. This is significant because Leibniz's metaphysics was itself developed under the same Neoplatonizing influence that was decisive in Alexandria.[65] Leibniz provides Teilhard with a means of describing the relation of the many to the transcendent One. Teilhard later calls this 'Omega', yet evident even in his early works, before he develops this concept, is an insistence on the cosmic setting of the single entity, or monad. The concept of individuation can ultimately only make sense, he believes, if situated within an ontology of the transcendent One present within it to preserve its unity. In each person, as well as each substance, is present

---

[62] René Descartes, *Principles of Philosophy*, II.11 (Dordrecht: Reidel, 1983), p. 44.

[63] René Descartes, 'Third Meditation', §45, in *Meditations on First Philosophy*, *The Philosophical Works of Descartes*, II (3 vols.; Cambridge University Press, 1984), p. 31; John Locke, *Essay Concerning Human Understanding*, II.23, §§9–29 (Oxford: Clarendon, 1975), pp. 300–312.

[64] 'The Spirit of the Earth' (1931), *HE*, p. 23.

[65] An excellent discussion of the Plotinian motifs which Leibniz employs, both consciously and unconsciously, is Georges Rodier, «Sur une des origines de la philosophie de Leibniz», *RMM* 10 (1902), pp. 552–64. For the mystical orientation of Leibniz, see Allison Coudert, Richard Popkin and Gordon Weiner (eds.), *Leibniz, Mysticism and Religion* (London: Kluwer, 1998); Emily Grosholz, 'Plato and Leibniz against the Materialists', *Journal of the History of Ideas* 57 (1996), pp. 255–76. Anne Becco, «Leibniz et François Mercure van Helmont: bagatelle pour des monades», in *Magia naturalis und die Entstehung der modernen Naturwissenschaften* (Wiesbaden: Steiner, 1978), pp. 119–42, discusses his links with Henry More and Cambridge Platonism.

besides a body and a soul, a certain physical entity that relates them in their entirety to the universe (the final universe) in which they reach their fulfilment. This is because, strictly speaking, there is in the universe only one single individuality (one single monad), that of the whole (conceived in its organized plurality).[66]

The presence of the One in the many therefore needs to be seen as a necessary consequence of the ontological priority of the One over the many, rather than an indication of latent monism or immanentism. It is not the case that the identity of each particular monad is annihilated in that of the whole, nor that the One is coextensive with the many. On the contrary, every monad is dependent on a superior monad for its individuality. In some in his wartime writings, Teilhard describes the One in ways susceptible of a pantheist interpretation, distinguishing it from the cosmos no more clearly than by affirming the difficulty of its perception and the fact that it is greater than the elements it unifies.[67] Nevertheless, during the 1920s he begins to refer more conspicuously to the transcendent character of the unifying principle in terms that exclude the possibility of it originating *within* the created order:

> The entire cosmos, as one complete whole, is held up, 'informed', by the powerful energy of a higher, and unique Monad which gives to everything below itself its definitive intelligibility and its definitive power of action and reaction.[68]

The single monad, which forms and informs every inferior monad, thus provides a power of attraction which gives to the cosmos a 'higher principle of unity'.[69]

Teilhard identifies the *Phaedrus* as a source for this dynamic relationship between individuation and unification.[70] He presumably has in mind the contrast between the two main themes of the dialogue. These are the separation characteristic of the method of composition and division which speech and deductive reason employ, versus the ascent of the soul in the higher stages of the dialectic to contemplate the good. The contemplative ascent is motivated by the love of beauty and truth and described in the opening portion of the dialogue.[71] What remains unclear, however, is the means by which the unification of individual

---

[66] 'The Universal Element' (1919), *WW*, pp. 296–97.
[67] 'The Great Monad' (1918), *HM*, p. 191.
[68] 'My Universe' (1924), *SC*, p. 57.
[69] *DM*, p. 23.
[70] 'Pantheism and Christianity' (1923), *CE*, pp. 57–58.
[71] Plato, *Phaedrus*, 265e–272c, 245c–256d, *Works* I, pp. 534–55, 468–503.

monads will be effected. In other words, how will the unifying principle act on and within the cosmos? Teilhard believes that the cosmos is still undergoing its unification, and does not therefore employ his theory of a unifying monad to account for a static cosmic consistency already fully realized. Instead, he develops an account of a dynamic and progressive unification effected through time. The unity of each monad is partly real but partly anticipated: 'If the consciousness of each monad is to be explicable, that monad must be conceived not as an atom juxtaposed with other atoms, but as a partial centre of the Whole, a particular actualizing of the Whole.'[72] Teilhard is already formulating this view in his early encyclopaedia essay:

> Les individus ne sont pas tellement isolé que leur noyau ne se frange d'une zone de liaisons et d'interdépendence. Par son insertion dans le monde, chaque monade devient un centre d'action mystérieuse, et peut-être indéfinie; en tant qu'a sujetti à constituer un même Cosmos, il est vraisemblable que «tout tient à tout».[73]

The unification principle is, in other words, imperfectly actualized in every individual monad. In *The Divine Milieu*, Teilhard describes how, from the perspective of the individual soul, matter appears to fall into two distinct zones defined by this movement from individuation towards unification:

> The zone already left behind or arrived at, to which we should not return, or at which we should not pause, lest we fall back — this is the zone of matter in the material and carnal sense; and the zone offered to our renewed efforts towards progress, search, conquest and 'divinization', the zone of matter taken in the spiritual sense.[74]

Teilhard continues by describing how the division between the two senses of matter perceived during the spiritual ascent of the soul is determined by individual perspective: 'The frontier between these two zones is essentially relative and shifting.'[75] Although each monad possesses its own 'Jacob's ladder', a general upward movement of the meeting point

---

[72] 'Pantheism and Christianity' (1923), *CE*, p. 61.

[73] «Homme» (1912), §504: 'Individuals are not so isolated that their core isn't surrounded by a zone of connections and interdependence. By its insertion in the world, each monad becomes a centre of mysterious and perhaps indeterminate action; because each monad constitutes an identical Cosmos, it is likely that "all is due to all".'

[74] *DM*, p. 68. The use of 'carnal' gives a pejorative association that is not intended by the original *charnelle*, whose principal connotations are *la chair* (the flesh) and *charnu* (fleshy).

[75] *DM*, pp. 68–69.

of fleshy matter and spiritual matter may nevertheless be identified. Teilhard describes this as the '"drift" of matter towards spirit'. He therefore transforms Leibnizian monadology in a similar way to Heidegger, whose description is redolent of Teilhard's:

> Because each monad, in a way of its own, is the world insofar as it presents the world, every drive is in consensus with the universe. Because of the consonance [*Einstimmigkeit*] every prehensive drive has with the universe, the monads themselves are also interconnected with one another. The idea of the monad as prehensive drive tending toward transition implies that the world belongs in each case to the monad in a perspectival refraction, that all monads as units of drive are thus oriented in advance toward a predisposed harmony of the totality of beings: *harmonia praestabilita*.[76]

The leitmotif of pre-established harmony assigned to Leibniz does not exclude dynamic striving towards unity, but motivates it. Heidegger argues that the essence of the μονάς is not the individuation which Leibniz had emphasized, but *unification*. It is in this sense that the whole universe is potentially present in every single monad. Teilhard also conceives of a 'potency of unity scattered throughout the universal multiple', which is '*by nature convergent*'.[77] He states that each individual carries within itself a part of the final end of the cosmos.[78] What Carol Vale describes as a 'movement away from the metaphysics of *esse* to one of *unire*'[79] is therefore implicit in Teilhard's earliest work.

Wayne Hankey argues that one reason why much twentieth century interpretation of Aquinas has, in contrast, privileged *esse* over *unire*, is that the concern with materiality and process implicit in *unire* has been considered to sit uneasily with the doctrine of creation ex nihilo developed to contradict the pagan preoccupation with matter as eternal.[80] Teil-

---

[76] Martin Heidegger, 'From the Last Marburg Lecture Course', in *Pathmarks* (Cambridge University Press, 1998), p. 79.

[77] 'How I Believe' (1934), *CE*, p. 108; 'The Road of the West', p. 46.

[78] 19 March 1919, *NR*, p. 58.

[79] Carol Jean Vale, 'Teilhard de Chardin: Ontogenesis vs. Ontology', *TS* 53 (1992), p. 317. This article is notable for its attempt to relate Teilhard's metaphysics to recent debates in the interpretation of Thomas Aquinas. Vale argues that the doctrine of participation needs to be understood using an analogy of intrinsic attribution as well as the analogy of proper proportionality, and that this dual conception provides the basis for a metaphysics of *unire* such as Teilhard's. James Lyons, *The Cosmic Christ in Origen and Teilhard de Chardin: A Comparative Study* (Oxford University Press, 1982), p. 178, likewise argues that being must be understood as *unire* rather than *esse* in order to 'take into account the condition upon which the possibility of participated being rests'.

[80] Wayne Hankey, 'Aquinas's First Principle: Being or Unity?', *Dionysius* 4 (1980), pp. 133–72.

hard indeed does not accept the doctrine of creation from nothing.[81] A determination to defend the doctrine of creation ex nihilo certainly seems, in contrast, to be one of the factors motivating Jacques Maritain's assessment that Teilhard's concept of creation as unification 'is a view of Hegelian theogony rather than of Christian theology'.[82] Proper appreciation of the Neoplatonic dimension of Thomas Aquinas's thought allows, however, ontology, the metaphysics of being, to be combined with a *hen*ology, or metaphysics of unification.[83] Unity is not a purely intellectual need, but an essential requirement of created being. To combine the perspectives of *esse* and *unire* is, indeed, the fundamental challenge facing any theology which takes embodiment and change seriously.

Karl Rahner compares his own theory of the unity of matter and spirit with that contained in Teilhard's collection *Man's Place in Nature*, and identifies clear similarities:

> All creaturely spirituality has an essential connection with matter, because ultimately speaking, although in very varied ways, creaturely spirituality is a receptive and intercommunicative spirituality (even in the case of the 'angels'), and matter in the metaphysical sense is the necessary condition for finite spiritual beings to exercise an intercommunicative influence upon one another. We must assume here the concept of an essential self-transcendence on the part of an existing creature sustained by God as its ultimate cause, and on the basis of this assumption we can freely assert that the development of biologically organized materiality is orientated in terms of an ever-increasing complexity and interiority towards spirit, until finally, under the dynamic impulse of God's creative power, and through a process of self-transcendence of this kind, it becomes spirit.[84]

Teilhard employs philosophical analysis, like Rahner, as necessary preparation for a theory of revelation. The 'essential self-transcendence' of the creature, which Rahner attributes to the fact that its telos subsists in God, impels the creature from philosophical analysis into specifically theological reflection. In the case of matter, although it is in some way being born in human minds, it is equally the deep from which substance emerges.[85] Spirit therefore exists in a condition of mutual dependence with matter. From this, it follows that both philosophical and theological

---

[81] *J*, 1 January 1946, cahier XIV.

[82] Jacques Maritain, 'On two studies dealing with the theology of Père Teilhard', in *The Peasant of the Garonne: An Old Layman Questions Himself about the Present Time* (London: Chapman, 1968), p. 264.

[83] See e.g. Proclus, *The Elements of Theology*, §§113–65 (Oxford: Clarendon, 2000), pp. 100–145.

[84] Karl Rahner, 'Christology', *TI* II, p. 218.

[85] 'The Names of Matter' (1919), *HM*, p. 225.

analysis are required to provide a complete account of the created order and its telos, or purpose.

The supremacy of spirit

Teilhard affirms that 'what binds the monads together is not, properly speaking, the body, but the soul', and that the *'only consistence* beings possess comes to them from their *synthetic element,* in other words from what, at a more perfect or less perfect degree, is *their soul, their spirit'.*[86] These statements are similar to those made by Thomas Aquinas describing the relation of body to soul in less explicitly metaphysical terms as one of dependence,[87] and are characteristic of Teilhard's tendency to appropriate the cosmology of Aquinas and the Thomist tradition, and in doing so, to give its principles a more materialistic interpretation than its authors intended. Teilhard's description of the body-soul relation is, moreover, a key element of continuity between his cosmology and that of Thomism: only spirit can provide matter with its unifying principle. In *The Divine Milieu,* Teilhard asserts that 'all that is sensible exists for the spirit', and this includes matter. A more precise formulation is: 'All reality, even material reality, around every one of us, exists for our souls.'[88] In *The Human Phenomenon,* matter is portrayed in the first chapter as that which *precedes* energy, life and thought, which provide its successively higher organizing principles. Plotinian cosmology is once again evident here. Matter is dependent on soul, which 'immediately imposes the form of the things on it because matter's indefiniteness distresses it, as if it were in fear of being outside the realm of being and could not endure to stay for long in non-being'.[89] Matter is also needed by soul, however, to provide soul with a receptacle on which to act and in which to dwell: Teilhard would certainly disagree with Plato's suggestion that space itself can act as a receptacle that 'provides room for all things that have birth'.[90]

---

[86] 'Creative Union' (1917), *WW*, p. 168; 'Science and Christ' (1921), *SC*, pp. 29–30.
[87] e.g. *ST*, Ia, q. 91, a. 4, ad 3; cf. First Decree, Council of Vienne, *DEC* I, p. 361.
[88] *DM*, pp. 16, 14.
[89] Plotinus, *Enneads*, II.4 (33) 10, pp. 126–29.
[90] Plato, *Timaeus*, 52b, *Works* IX, pp. 122–23. For Teilhard's knowledge of this text, see his letter to Claude Rivière of 22 January 1943, discussing the musical analogy for the harmony of the cosmos, quoted in Robert Speaight, *Teilhard de Chardin: A Biography* (London: Collins, 1967), p. 261.

The spiritual principle, notwithstanding its superiority to matter in the order of being, remains bound to it and dependent on it in the order of generation. Spirit is inalienably embodied:

> Even if it is Spirit that constantly carries matter along and supports it in the ascent towards consciousness, it is matter, in return, that enables Spirit to subsist by constantly providing it with a point upon which to act, and supplying it with nourishment.[91]

In defining the second part of this dependency relation, Teilhard refers to Justin Martyr's description of the conversion, or restoration, of the matter of the cosmos. Teilhard here indicates yet again his indebtedness to the *ressourcement* of contemporary theology from patristic texts. Justin states: 'The body is the house of the soul; and the soul the house of the spirit. These three, in all those who cherish a sincere hope and unquestioning faith in God, will be saved.'[92] Teilhard attributes to the Greek Fathers in general the view that 'Christ cannot sanctify the Spirit without ... uplifting and saving the totality of matter'.[93] An important point which distinguishes some of these theologians from others, however, is their opinion about whether the instaurated matter is created or uncreated. Justin himself appears ambivalent about this, in contrast with Irenaeus's clearly-stated view that matter is the creation of God.[94] If matter is indeed a divine creation, then its restoration may be accomplished without the transgression of the distinction between created and uncreated. Salvation, according to this cosmology, comprises a reordering of the *created* order. It would, of course, be possible to defend a theology of purely spiritual salvation occurring within a cosmos in which matter was uncreated, without undermining the distinction between the created and uncreated orders: materiality would then simply be left unredeemed. Such a theory would, however, sit uneasily with the express Pauline teaching that in the resurrection of the dead it is essentially the *material* body which is changed.[95]

In Teilhard's praise of Justin Martyr can be seen lingering elements of his early fascination with matter. Justin's view that matter can be 'con-

---

[91] 'My Universe' (1924), *SC*, p. 50.

[92] Justin Martyr, 'Fragments of the Lost Work on the Resurrection', §10, *ANF* I, pp. 298–99.

[93] 'The Road of the West', p. 51; 'The New Spirit, 1942' (1942), *FM*, p. 94.

[94] Irenaeus, *Against Heresies*, II, 10.4, *ANF* I, p. 370; D.S. Wallace-Hadrill, *The Greek Patristic View of Nature* (Manchester University Press, 1968), pp. 66; Konstantin Ruzhitaky, 'The Teaching of the Holy Fathers and other Church Writers on Matter', *Journal of the Moscow Patriarchate*, 1989, 1, pp. 17–18.

[95] I Cor 15.34–58.

verted' is indeed based on the assumption that matter is indestructible. Teilhard, however, develops the belief that matter is a 'deposit that is slowly formed in the tissues of our soul', and a 'tendency, a direction ... the side of Spirit that we meet as we fall back',[96] and thinks that matter will ultimately be transformed into spirit. Teilhard's view is closer to Origen's than to Justin's: matter is a *manifestation* of the turn away from God and not an uncreated element of the cosmos.[97] Nevertheless, Teilhard continues to insist on the positive potential of matter, which in the words of Kevin Corrigan 'emerges in relation to the life-bearing activity of the productive form or creative Author'.[98] Spirit, as previously discussed, has 'more consistence than matter in the universe', being the 'primal substance of things',[99] whereas matter is 'transparent and malleable in relation to spirit'.[100] The spiritual potential of matter can therefore be actuated only within a spiritual order. Outside this order, matter is a 'mirage', because the created order 'does not hold together "from below" but "from above"'.[101] Spirit does not always recognize its superior position in relation to matter, however. A Faustian tendency to 'self-worship' and 'autonomy and solitude' is present in spirit, which mistakenly identifies the telos of the cosmos to be material rather than spiritual.[102] Teilhard portrays this error by referring to the Faust legend, which suggests that humanity has, quite literally, surrendered its spirit to material power, and has thus disrupted the natural ordering of material principles by spiritual ones. Teilhard's interpretation of Faust is close to that of Goethe, who portrays the legend as a social and historical allegory rather than a story about the fall and eventual redemption of a single man.[103]

Paul Haffner has argued that Teilhard 'held a panpsychistic notion of reality, in which all matter has a spiritual dimension', and that in Teil-

---

[96] 'Cosmic Life' (1916), 'The Eternal Feminine' (1918), *WW*, pp. 40, 195.

[97] Wallace-Hadrill, *Greek Patristic View of Nature*, p. 147; P.M. O'Cleirigh, 'Prime Matter in Origen's World Picture', *SP* 16 (Berlin: Akademie, 1985), pp. 260–63.

[98] Kevin Corrigan, 'Plotinus and St Gregory of Nyssa: Can Matter really have a Positive Function?', *SP* 27 (Leuven: Peeters, 1993), p. 20.

[99] 'The Spirit of the Earth' (1931), 'Human Energy' (1937), *HE*, pp. 38–39, 119.

[100] 'Human Energy', p. 130.

[101] 'How I Believe' (1934), *CE*, p. 113. See further the comments in Henri de Lubac, 'Tradition and innovation in the position of the problem of God in Father Teilhard de Chardin', in *Theology in History* (San Francisco: Ignatius, 1996), p. 512.

[102] 'Faith in Humanity' (1947), 'The Spiritual Repercussions of the Atom Bomb' (1946), *FM*, pp. 188–89, 147; 'Catholicism and Science' (1946), *SC*, pp. 190–91.

[103] Johann Wolfgang von Goethe, *Faust: A Tragedy* (New York: Norton, 2nd edn, 2001).

hard's cosmology, the 'soul is not sufficiently distinct from matter'.[104] A few of Teilhard's statements could be interpreted in this way: he refers, for instance, to the 'coalescence between life and matter', and to matter and consciousness as bound together.[105] Perhaps most provocatively, he states: 'There is neither spirit nor matter in the world; the "stuff of the universe" is *spirit-matter*.'[106] Such assertions are exceptional, however. The burden of evidence suggests that the 'spirit-matter' thesis should be regarded either as hyperbole or an exploration of an idea undertaken during the 1930s that was later discarded. The view that Teilhard mostly defends is summarized in Chalcedonian terms as a 'dynamic contact ... established, without producing confusion, between the forces of matter and spirit'.[107] It is in this sense that the relation between matter and spirit should be understood: *fusion* rather than *con*fusion. The consistency of the cosmos remains always dependent on the action of spirit. Refusal to accept some type of relationality such as this would, Teilhard argues, amount to a Manichean or Catharistic denigration of the materiality of the created order.[108] This type of radical separation of spirit from matter has been deemed incompatible with the axioms of Christian theology, and he opposes it emphatically:

> In the light of pure reason, nothing in the universe is intelligible, living, and consistent except through an element of synthesis, in other words a spirit, or from on high. Within the cosmos all the elements are dependent upon one another ontologically, in the ascending order of their true being (which means of their consciousness); and the entire cosmos, as one complete whole, is held up, 'informed', by the powerful energy of a higher, and unique, Monad which gives to everything below itself its definitive intelligibility and its definitive power of action and reaction.[109]

This unifying principle is at once both metaphysical, bestowing consistency, and epistemological, providing intelligibility:

> The explanation of the world and its consistence are to be found in a higher soul of progressive attraction and solidification, without which the radical plurality of the universe would never have emerged from its dust. To the informed observer, analysis of matter reveals the priority and primacy of Spirit.[110]

[104] Paul Haffner, *Mystery of Creation* (Leominster: Gracewing, 1995), pp. 75–76.
[105] 'Basis and Foundations of the Idea of Evolution' (1926), 'Humanity's Place in Nature' (1942), *VP*, pp. 118, 227.
[106] 'Sketch of a Personalistic Universe' (1936), *HE*, pp. 57–58.
[107] 'Reality and Significance of Human Orthogenesis' (1951), *VP*, p. 255.
[108] 'Two Converse Forms of Spirit' (1950), *AE*, p. 221, n.
[109] 'My Universe' (1924), *SC*, p. 57.
[110] 'Science and Christ' (1921), *SC*, p. 31.

In philosophical terms Teilhard demonstrates, in the words of Brian
Hebblethwaite, the 'greater reasonableness of interpreting the universe
from the standpoint of its highest product ... the world of mind, than that
of reducing the more complicated to the less complicated and trying to
interpret mind in terms of the combination of material particles alone'.[111]
The higher soul to which Teilhard refers is an identifiable feature of the
tradition of natural theology, but he conceives the redemption and sanctification that it effects in strikingly dynamic terms: 'God is seen to be
the supreme centre in which the multiplicity of lower forms of being
becomes an organic whole — the focus at which matter is consummated
in spirit.'[112] The matter of the cosmos is thus given consistency by a
spiritual principle: the action of God on the cosmos and within it.

---

[111] Brian Hebblethwaite, *The Ocean of Truth* (Cambridge University Press, 1988),
p. 58.
  [112] 'The Evolution of Chastity' (1934), *TF*, p. 83.

2. ACTION

Teilhard's metaphysics is governed by the principle that the soul is dependent on matter in its spiritual ascent. Equally, and as part of this, soul provides matter with its organizing principle. In human action, soul and matter, and spiritual and material principles, are fused, and matter is subdued, formed and reformed. This encounter of soul and matter possesses momentous spiritual consequences for both. Soul gives form to matter and implicates matter in a telos. Teilhard affirms: 'The human soul is the first fully formed purchase point that the Multiple can fasten onto as it is drawn up by the Creation towards unity.'[1] Perhaps less obviously, but even more importantly from the human point of view, matter provides a 'ladder' which the soul ascends as it imposes order on matter. As John of Damascus affirms, matter is the medium through which salvation is accomplished, and is for this reason worthy of honour.[2]

Teilhard's own life of action, and particularly his service as a stretcher bearer during the First World War, is crucial in shaping his concept of action.[3] Participation in war liberated him from daily social conventions and implicated his action in large-scale collective projects.[4] This experience was shared by a whole generation of French clergy and members of religious orders, who were not exempted from their nation's military draft. Few performed the official role of chaplain owing to the large numbers consequently serving in the forces.[5] Had they enjoyed the associated officer status, some might have been afforded a little protection

---

[1] 'My Universe' (1924), *SC*, p. 47.

[2] 'I do not worship matter; I worship the Creator of matter who became matter for my sake, who willed to take His abode in matter; who worked out my salvation through matter. Never will I cease honouring the matter which wrought my salvation!... God has filled it with His grace and power. Through it my salvation has come to me.' (John of Damascus, *On the Divine Images: The Apologies Against those who Attack the Divine Images*, I, 16 (New York: St Vladimir's, 1980), p. 23.)

[3] See *MM*.

[4] Jean Maalouf, *Le Mystère du mal dans l'oeuvre de Teilhard de Chardin* (Paris: Cerf, 1986), p. 29.

[5] Annette Becker, *War and Faith: The Religious Imagination in France, 1914–1930* (Oxford: Berg, 1998), p. 33, records that of the 32,699 priests, monks and seminarians mobilized, just 1500 worked as military chaplains. Vincent Lapomarda, 'France', in *The Jesuits and the Third Reich* (Lewiston, Ma.: Mellen, 1989), p. 266, states that 841 out of about 3,000 French Jesuits served in the armed forces during the Great War in various capacities.

from the most acute battlefield dangers. Most clergy and religious, by contrast, served as ordinary soldiers, or like Teilhard, as medical orderlies. Teilhard was awarded the Croix de Guerre and Médaille Militaire, and following the war was created a Chevalier de la Légion d'honneur following nomination by his regiment.[6] Working as a stretcher-bearer, collecting the injured and dying from the battlefield, he was very fortunate to receive no injuries. Annette Becker states: 'Statistics prove that to have escaped death or serious wounding between 1914 and 1918 was such an extraordinary display of chance that it inevitably caused questioning amazement.'[7]

The other great enterprise to which Teilhard committed his life was palaeontology (the study of fossils). A decisive moment in his research arrived in April 1923, when he embarked on his first expedition to China. He was then entering a crucible of great religious, political and scientific exploits. Jean Lacouture notes: 'From the Jesuit standpoint, China was, and had been for three centuries, the ultimate arena of grand ventures.'[8] Francis Xavier, Alessandro Valignano, Matthew Ricci, Benedict de Goes, Johann Adam Schall von Bell and Fleming Fernand Verbiest are among the best known of hundreds of Jesuits associated with the region in the later seventeenth and eighteenth centuries, and were themselves preceded by the Franciscan emissaries to the Mongol emperors, John of Piancarpino and John of Montecorvino.[9] During Teilhard's residence in China, the country was becoming an increasingly hostile war zone. By the time of his second stay, in the period from 1926 to 1927, forces loyal to the fledgling Chinese Communist Party were fighting the nationalist Kuomintang government, and the country had been partitioned. Although Teilhard was never exposed to serious physical danger in China, his movements were hindered by both fighting and the predations of bandits.[10] It is significant that he produced *The Divine*

---

[6] Claude Cuénot, *Teilhard de Chardin: A Biographical Study* (London: Burns & Oates, 1965), p. 25.

[7] Becker, *War and Faith*, p. 68. Teilhard's own acts of bravery and citations are recorded in 'Teilhard de Chardin's War Service', *MM*, p. 41.

[8] Jean Lacouture, 'Obedience and Teilhard', in *Jesuits: A Multibiography* (London: Harvill, 1996), p. 418.

[9] See George H. Dunne, *Generation of Giants: The First Jesuits in China* (London: Burns & Oates, 1962); Christopher Dawson, *The Mongol Mission: Narratives and Letters of the Franciscan Missionaries in Mongolia and China in the Thirteenth and Fourteenth Centuries* (London: Sheed & Ward, 1955).

[10] See letters to Henri Breuil, 16 July 1923, *LT*, p. 80; Auguste Valensin, 27 June 1926, *LI*, p. 135; Claude Aragonnès, 8 July, 13 December 1926, *LT*, pp. 129, 137; Léontine Zanta, 7 May 1927, *LLZ*, p. 78.

Milieu, the work which most clearly describes his theology of action, at a time when he was himself living the *vita activa*.

The integration of faith and action is a foundational theological principle of Teilhard's. He states: 'The general influence and practice of the Church has always been to dignify, exalt and transfigure in God the duties inherent in our lives, the search for natural truth, and the development of human action.' By contrast, he protests, the 'great objection brought against Christianity in our time, and the real source of the distrust which renders entire blocks of humanity immune to the influence of the Church' is the 'suspicion that our religion makes its followers inhuman'.[11] Action forms, Teilhard believes, the essence of humanity, and needs therefore to be placed at the centre of its theology. He challenges misconceptions about the demands of Christian faith, widespread both within and beyond the Church of his day, and argues that faith in Christ affirms the natural, active aspirations of humankind 'written in their hearts by nature'.[12] The presentation of a theology that testifies to the intrinsic goodness of human action, notwithstanding its imperfection, prior to any specifically religious redemption, is an abiding concern of Teilhard's. In an early essay, he states that the Christian faith 'jettisons neither the rational method of conquering the world, nor humankind's confidence in itself: on the contrary, it stimulates and inspires them'.[13]

Intention and freedom

The scriptural origins of Teilhard's theology of action are to be found in his opposition to an excessively legalistic interpretation of the Pauline tradition, especially as laid out in the Letter to the Romans. Teilhard emphasizes the importance in Paul's theology not of sin, guilt and judgment, but of the individual human action being part of a general theory of the role of works in the life of faith. The definition of 'works' that Teilhard employs is not restricted to specifically 'religious' practices such as prayer and fasting. His theology of action is, above all, one that

---

[11] *DM*, pp. 8, 26.

[12] *DM*, p. 9. Thomas Merton, 'The universe as epiphany', in *Love and Living*, eds. Naomi Burton Stone and Patrick Hart (London: Sheldon, 1979), pp. 171–84, which is essentially a review of *The Divine Milieu*, portrays Teilhard convincingly as a Christian humanist. It is surprising, given that Teilhard and Merton are the two most widely-known catholic spiritual writers of the twentieth century, that Merton's review of *The Divine Milieu* has received no comment in Teilhard scholarship.

[13] 'Operative Faith' (1918), *WW*, p. 244.

locates the value of action in the actual performance of the act itself, rather than in the intention motivating it, or in the action's wider consequences. Teilhard is especially critical of a theology of action based on what he terms its 'purity of intention'. He describes this concept in his first wartime essay:

> The pure heart, the right intention, are the organs of the higher life towards which, it would appear, all the soul's hopes are directed: the fundamental principle in the building up of the Body of Christ is *making use of the subjective moral value* of human acts.[14]

Teilhard defines purity of intention as the doctrine that action which conforms to the will of God is the only mark of Christian faithfulness. This doctrine would suggest, he argues, that the fruits of the earth and our stewardship of them possess no intrinsic value. They are simply means through which humanity may develop ever greater obedience to God, and love of God. Teilhard commences *The Divine Milieu* with a critique of this moral theology.[15] In another essay, he complains that many theologians suggest that the only reason humanity has to work is in order to give proof of its good will.[16] To illustrate what he means, Teilhard critically quotes an imagined spiritual director counselling his tutee with the following words: 'What will always endure, is this: that you have acted in all things conformably to the will of God.'[17] Henri de Lubac describes the doctrine of purity of intention as a 'subjectivist doctrine, that would imply, if its internal logic were fully appreciated, a scepticism or a contempt directed at the action itself, considered in its proper finality and its objective result.'[18]

Notwithstanding its fundamental flaw, the doctrine of purity of intention contains an 'enormous amount of truth'. It 'expresses vigorously the primary worth of the divine will' and 'reveals a sort of unique milieu, unchanging ... in which we can place ourselves without ever having to withdraw'. It also provides the 'golden key which unlocks our inward personal world to God's presence'. Nevertheless, the hope that accompanies a pure intention fails to bring spiritual peace or joy.[19] Although the value of intention 'infuses a priceless soul into all our actions ... it

---

[14] 'Cosmic Life' (1916), *WW*, p. 53.

[15] *DM*, pp. 11–13.

[16] 'My Universe', p. 67.

[17] *DM*, p. 11.

[18] Henri de Lubac, 'Père Teilhard and the morality of intention', in *The Religion of Teilhard de Chardin* (London: Collins, 1970), p. 260.

[19] *DM*, p. 12.

does not confer the hope of resurrection upon their bodies. Yet that hope is what we need if our joy is to be complete.'[20] Teilhard's critique of privatized Christian piety is similar to the one given by Immanuel Kant in the *Critique of Practical Reason*. Kant praises the moral teaching of the Gospel for providing a moral principle which, despite its purity, is well-suited to the limitations of finite humanity.[21] He understands Christian morality in pietist Lutheran terms close to those which form the object of Teilhard's critique. Kant critically defines the conception of virtue that this tradition proposes as '*holiness* in the supposed *possession* of a complete *purity* of dispositions of the will'.[22] He proceeds, of course, to propose his own definition of virtue founded on his doctrine of universal reason. At one level, Teilhard pursues this Kantian project of freeing the human soul from a conception of the moral law as opposing human freedom. Teilhard suggests however, in opposition to Kant's position in the second critique, that respect for the moral law and reverence for duty[23] cannot alone provide a full account of human moral action. The subject of action is embodied humanity, and action's object is the material world. Only action possessing an objective aim beyond itself that transcends human subjectivity can, Teilhard argues, justify the human hope for joy. His position is clearly anti-Kantian in that it opposes intention and good will as the touchstones of moral goodness. Teilhard might also have Friedrich Nietzsche in sight as an opponent. In *The Anti-Christ*, the most French of the German *philosophes* inveighs against what he regards as the depressive and enervating morality of pity intrinsic to Christian practice, and its devaluing of nature and natural values.[24] Teilhard also wishes, like Nietzsche, to develop a theory of action that reclaims freedom and materiality as its cardinal values, but wishes to give this theory a specifically Christian identity.

Teilhard's fundamental dissatisfaction with the definition of the goodness of action in terms of the purity of the intention motivating it is that this fails to provide an adequate account of action in a profoundly dynamic and interconnected cosmos. In *The Divine Milieu*, he describes the 'explicit consciousness of being an atom or a citizen of the universe'

---

[20] *DM*, pp. 12–13.

[21] Immanuel Kant, *Critique of Practical Reason*, AK 5:86 (Cambridge University Press, 1997), p. 73.

[22] Kant, *Practical Reason*, AK 5:84, p. 72.

[23] Kant, *Practical Reason*, AK 5:82, p. 70.

[24] Friedrich Nietzsche, *The Anti-Christ*, §§7, 38, in *Twilight of the Idols/The Anti-Christ* (London: Penguin, 1990), pp. 130–31, 161–62. See e.g. 'The Atomism of Spirit' (1941), *AE*, pp. 52–53.

which has resulted from a 'collective awakening' of humanity. He suggests that a pietistic morality of performing one's duty in accordance with one's station in life has, in the twentieth century, been transposed into the privatized pursuit of a self-interest which lacks any ultimate purpose and or acceptance of responsibility to wider society. What both pietistic and egoistic moralities lack is reference to a shared world of relationships and responsibilities. Purity of intention reveals a *unique* milieu,[25] and this is its problem: it cannot reveal a *divine* milieu.

Teilhard opposes the concept of action based on purity of intention with one grounded in freedom, which emerges from his critical engagement with two related traditions: Spinozism and existentialism. Fundamental to Spinozist philosophy is the connaturality of God and nature, which Teilhard defends in a letter to Auguste Valensin: «Vous opposez la morale chrétienne à la morale spinozienne en disant que la première nous dit seulement de devenir 'semblables à Dieu'. Je n'accepte pas l'opposition. — Pour le Chrétien, être συμμορφος χριστῳ, c'est participer, sous la similitude de conduite, à un être commun; — c'est réellement, 'devenir le Christ', 'devenir Dieu'.»[26] Nevertheless, by the following year Teilhard is employing the term 'Spinozism' pejoratively, and arguing that Spinoza's monism is incompatible with Christian theology.[27] Whereas Spinoza characterizes union as consisting of absorption and fusion, Teilhard believes that union can only be established by differentiation, even stating that Spinoza's monist metaphysics has failed to be anything more than ideology.[28] Teilhard objects that its totalizing quality denies to humanity any meaningful initiative of action and response in the world, and that it posits action and passion as two perspectives of a single immanent reality, rather than as implying a transcendent principle. Teilhard also elucidates the negative consequences of Spinozism for christology: its pantheism suggests the 'concept of a hypostatic union extended to the whole universe'.[29] This makes Christ a 'being so unique that his subsistence, his person, his "I", takes the place

---

[25] *DM*, p. 12.

[26] Letter to Auguste Valensin, 17 December 1922, *LI*, p. 89. 'You oppose Christian morality to Spinozist morality by claiming that the first calls us only to become "similar to God". I fail to accept this opposition. — For the Christian, to be formed in Christ is to participate, by means of an identical impulsion, in a common being — it is really "to become Christ", "to become God".'

[27] 'Pantheism and Christianity' (1923), *CE*, p. 56; 'Action and Activation' (1945), *SC*, p. 185.

[28] *HP*, p. 212.

[29] 'Pantheism and Christianity', p. 69.

of the subsistence, the personality, of all the elements incorporated in his mystical body'. Teilhard is determined, in contrast, to establish concepts of freedom and the Incarnation that preserve individuated substances rather than annihilating them in a generic substance.

The critique of pantheism which Teilhard presents needs to be regarded in the wider context provided by the seminal study of Spinoza's moral system made by Victor Delbos.[30] This was a constructive examination of Spinoza's theory of the self, in which an essential identity is established in the human will between *le volontaire* (the voluntary) and *le voulu* (the willed). In other words, there exists no essential distinction between the abstract object of the will, and the object actually pursued in practical action. In his final chapter, Delbos attacks this assumed identity and the doctrine of immanence which, he contends, is associated with it. He argues that there must occur a rupture of the will into its two constituent parts, separated by a 'potential infinite which cannot be contented with anything finite'.[31] This cleavage is of great concern to Teilhard: it creates a divided self, or a 'double life' of loyalty to both God (spirit), who is the abstract object of will, and the world (matter), which is the concrete object of will.[32]

This discussion of infinity within finitude is distinctly Pascalian,[33] and needs to be related to Teilhard's Blondelian critique of atheist existentialism, which formed at that time the principal variety of existentialism in France. Teilhard complains of the 'ever more solitary introspection of the individual by the individual' associated with its philosophy, and impugns its theory of 'closed being' according to which every individual is tragically shut up 'each on his own, each inside himself'.[34] Links between Delbos and Blondel were close: they shared a supervisor at the Sorbonne, the prolific Émile Boutroux, and Delbos's manuscript was on Blondel's desk whilst he was composing *L'Action*.[35] Blondel transforms

---

[30] Victor Delbos, *Le Problème moral dans la philosophie de Spinoza et dans l'histoire du spinozisme* (Paris: Alcan, 1893).

[31] Delbos, *Le Problème moral*, p. 549.

[32] *DM*, p. 10.

[33] See especially Pascal's Pensée 199 (Sellier, 72) on the Disproportion of Man, *Pensées* (London: Penguin, rev. edn, 1995), pp. 59–65.

[34] 'On Looking at a Cyclotron' (1953), 'A Phenomenon of Counter-Evolution' (1949), *AE*, pp. 356–57, 190.

[35] John J. McNeill, *The Blondelian Synthesis: A Study of the Influence of German Philosophical Sources on the Formation of Blondel's Method and Thought* (Leiden: Brill, 1966), pp. 7–9. For their reviews of each other's books, see Victor Delbos, «Maurice Blondel, *L'Action*», *Revue philosophique de la France et de l'étranger* 38 (1894), pp. 634–41; Maurice Blondel (writing as Bernard Aimant), «Une des sources de la pen-

the Pascalian *espace infini* with which Delbos opposes Spinoza's 'tendency to persist in being' into the 'radical will to be', and in so doing lays foundations for a specifically Christian form of existentialism in which *le voluntaire* and *le voulu* are separated, but reunited in an Absolute which is not immanent but transcendent.[36] Teilhard embraces this Blondelian metaphysics of action. Émile Rideau places Teilhard within the Christian existentialist tradition on the grounds that, in his theology, each portion of multiple and finite individual humanity is confronted with the problem of its destiny in relation to an absolute.[37] Teilhard did not, however, regard himself as an existentialist, which in France so frequently connoted atheism. By internalizing the absolute within the self, in contrast with the Kierkegaardian model of the self existing in relation with the absolute, emerging French existentialism was to deny the possibility of the kind of material and transcendent orientation within the world that, in Teilhard's opinion, is fundamental to moral life.

Acts of faith

In an allusion to Blondel's *L'Action*, Teilhard affirms that the philosophy of action permits a more convincing analysis of the real that a philosophy concerned solely with intelligible forms.[38] Blondel's problem is the same as that of Aquinas's *Summa contra gentiles*: why do beings act? Aquinas identifies both the origin and the end of human action as residing in God,[39] although denies that the ultimate origin of human activity exists within the created order. In fact, in his cosmology created

sée moderne: l'évolution du spinozisme», *Annales de philosophie chrétienne* 64 (1894), p. 261. See also Maurice Blondel, «Un interprète de Spinoza: Victor Delbos, 1862–1916», *Chronicum spinozanum* 1 (1921), pp. 290–300.

[36] See especially Maurice Blondel, «L'Évolution du spinozisme et l'accès qu'elle ouvre à la transcendance», *L'Archivio di Filosofia* 11, 4 (1932), pp. 3–12, and in *Dialogues avec les philosophes: Descartes, Spinoza, Malebranche, Pascal, Saint Augustin* (Paris: Aubier Montaigne, 1966), pp. 11–40.

[37] Émile Rideau, *Teilhard de Chardin: A Guide to his Thought* (London: Collins, 1967), pp. 110–45.

[38] 'The Mysticism of Science' (1939), *HE*, p. 167; 'Action and Activation', p. 176. Cf. Maurice Blondel, *L'Action: essai d'une critique de la vie et d'une science de la pratique* (Paris: Alcan, 1893); trans. *Action: Essay on a Critique of Life and a Science of Practice* (Notre Dame, Ind.: University of Notre Dame Press, 2003).

[39] Thomas Aquinas, *Summa contra gentiles*, II–III (5 vols.; Notre Dame, Ind.: University of Notre Dame Press, 1975).

beings possess only the potential for activity, which is actualized by divine power: 'God, who is pure and primary act, must of all things be the most active spreading his likeness abroad, and so must of all things be the most powerful or actively potential source of activity.'[40] Blondel transforms this metaphysics, arguing that human action is not the actualization of potential being by an external source. Rather, in human action, the 'deliberate and willed act naturalizes the absolute in the relative itself'. In truly voluntary action, a 'secret nuptial takes place between the human will and the divine will' which amounts to a 'synthesis of man and God'.[41]

Teilhard appropriates this collaborative concept of action in preference to the classic Thomist one. It implies, he argues, an open world 'from which we can at every moment expect something completely new to emerge', and makes possible irreversible gains in the total value of the world. Action possesses an absolute value that is 'unique and indispensable to the plenitude of the real'.[42] This transformation of Thomist *actus essendi* ontology enables Teilhard to refute the various negative philosophies of action that were common contemporary currency, such as the positivist ironism of Rénan and Taine, the poetic decadence of Baudelaire, and the pessimism of Schopenhauer. Teilhard suggests that such theories are the indirect products of cosmologies such as Aquinas's, according to which human action possesses no real, concrete value. The theories of the 'sceptic and the dilettante, the scribe and the pharisee'[43] contradict, however, the fundamental requirements which human flourishing places on philosophy to account for the relation of humanity to an absolute. Teilhard's aim is to eliminate the 'various forms of agnosticism, explicit or implicit, that have tried to base morality on a pure social empiricism or again on a pure individual aestheticism'.[44]

Teilhard's conception of the act of faith can be illuminated by a brief examination of his reading of Karl Barth's *God in Action*. Teilhard notes with approval Barth's statement that revelation is an essentially human matter, in the sense that it is given by God through Christ to humanity

---

[40] Thomas Aquinas, *On the Power of God*, q. 1, a. 1 (2 vols.; London: Burns, Oates & Washbourne, 1932–34), I, p. 4, trans. *Selected Philosophical Writings*, ed. Timothy McDermott (Oxford University Press, 1998), p. 66.

[41] Blondel, *Action*, §§367, 371, pp. 339, 342–43.

[42] 'Action and Activation', pp. 176–77.

[43] 'The Spirit of the Earth' (1931), *HE*, p. 37.

[44] 'Christianity in the World' (1933), *SC*, p. 104.

and has no meaning outside this relational context.[45] Teilhard nevertheless disagrees with the anthropology used by Barth to justify this context. Barth's reason for defining the created order as existing in a state of complete dependence on Christ is that humanity is lost and the world is profane.[46] Barth regards this attempt to perceive clearly the worldliness of the world to be a positive one which frees the world and humanity from the burden of attempting to be or to become something which they are not. Teilhard nevertheless considers this concern with the profanity of the world to be an inappropriately «antipodial», or oppositional, assessment of the human condition in relation to God.[47] He notes critically Barth's statement that the grace of God in the person of Jesus Christ 'excludes every thought of co-operation, either of man, or of any other creature', with divine grace, labeling this opinion «pessimisme radical».[48] Mary Carrington points out that Barth's refusal of human cooperation with God is explained by Barth's 'total rejection of what to him was the elevation of the converse of such views into the near worship of man'.[49] Although Barth believes that humanity is called to participate in and to further the purposes of God, he resists any suggestion that human action can be regarded as participation in divine grace itself. Hence Barth's response to liberal Protestant historical criticism of the Gospels and Teilhard's rejection of the christology of Loisy and other modernists are motivated by similar concerns. Liberal protestant and modernist biblical critics both perform useful functions in undermining pre-critical readings of scripture. What must be resisted, however, is any temptation to turn human reason into the judge of God, because this would deny to divine revelation its power of confronting and subverting every human epistemology. Critical readings of scripture in fact prepare the way for the revelation of more fundamental truths about Christ. Teilhard, despite his affinity with Barth on this point, nevertheless regards humanity as naturally imperfect rather than completely estranged from God, and as called to become more fully conscious of itself and the created order. In Teilhard's theology, human dependence on Christ makes co-operation between God and humanity possible, in the course of

---

[45] Note on Karl Barth, *God in Action* (Edinburgh: T&T Clark, 1936), p. 57, in carnet de lecture.

[46] Barth, *God in Action*, pp. 26–27.

[47] Note on Barth, *God in Action*, p. 34, in carnet de lecture.

[48] Note on Barth, *God in Action*, p. 20, in carnet de lecture.

[49] Mary C. Carrington, 'Teilhard de Chardin and Karl Barth', *The Teilhard Review* 17, 2 (1982), p. 20.

which humanity, under divine grace, works out its salvation and participates in Christ's salvation of the larger created order.

It would be easy to overstate the opposition between Barth and Teilhard over the relation between action and salvation, not least as a result
of their two sharply contrasting styles of theological presentation. Barth
is not saying that human action has no place in the scheme of salvation,
any more than Teilhard is suggesting that humanity is able to secure salvation purely by its own initiative. The key point at issue between them
seems to be the status of the relation of humanity to God. In Barth's theology, this is established by election in Christ and can only exist within
election, whereas Teilhard understands a primordial relation between
God and humanity, which he does not develop in specifically christological terms, always to have existed. In Teilhard's theology, the work
of Christ consists, therefore, in realizing this primordial relation in all its
fullness. Teilhard is always careful to avoid diminishing the world in
order to magnify the work of God, which is a tendency he detects in
Barth's theology.[50]

Fundamental to this reappraisal of the role of divine activity in human
action is Pierre Rousselot's doctrine of the 'act of faith'. Rousselot and
Teilhard studied together at Ore Place, Hastings during the academic
year 1908–1909, and worked together in Paris during the year
1913–1914.[51] Teilhard, in his exposition of Rousselot's doctrine, states:
'The essential note of the psychological act of faith is to perceive as possible, and accept as more probable, a conclusion which ... cannot be
contained in any analytical premises. *To believe is to effect an intellectual synthesis.*'[52] This synthesis consists not only of one act of faith but
of successive acts in which the human and the divine 'attain a vital
recognition of one another'. The act of faith is, in this sense, supernatural.[53] Affirmations such as these of the need for personal assent to
ecclesial dogma now seem uncontroversial to most Christians. Nevertheless, any suggestion that Church teaching should not receive immediate
assent from believers purely by virtue of being Church teaching, but that
it needed to be accompanied by a separate 'psychological' assent, was

[50] *J*, 1 October 1944, cahier XIII.
[51] For biography of Rousselot, see Léonce de Grandmaison, foreword to Pierre Rousselot, *L'Intellectualisme de saint Thomas* (Paris: Beauchesne, 2nd edn, 1924), pp. v–xl;
Élie Marty, *Le Témoignage de Pierre Rousselot SJ, d'après ses écrits et sa correspondance* (Paris: Beauchesne, 1941).
[52] 'How I Believe' (1934), *CE*, pp. 98–99.
[53] 'My Fundamental Vision' (1948), *TF*, p. 190, n. 23; 'The Directions and Conditions of the Future' (1948), *FM*, p. 237; retreat note of 20 July 1922, *NR*, p. 95.

regarded by Church authorities as subversive and dangerous. In an article with far-reaching consequences, Rousselot considers the doctrine of the act of faith to be necessary to account for the connaturality of supernatural, divine grace with the objective, symbolic faith of the Church, or what Hegel describes as 'positive religion'.[54] A 'perception of credibility' is needed because only that allows assent from within the order of nature to truths revealed in the order of grace. Rousselot argues that faith is not dependent simply on the will to believe. Also required for the act of faith to be confirmed is a predisposition in human intelligence for revelation, which is due to grace. It is necessary, in other words, to renounce the concept of purely 'scientific' or 'natural' faith associated with scholastic theology. These propositions might not appear unreasonable, especially in light of Aquinas's opinion that faith is 'perceived by the subject wherein it resides, by the interior act of the heart'.[55] Even so, the doctrine of the act of faith had been censured by Wlodimir Ledochowski, the Jesuit Superior General, five years after Rousselot's death in combat at Éparges, and no Jesuit was permitted to defend its truth or probability in writing or orally, whether in public or in private.[56]

Just as threatening to the magisterium as the 'act of faith' doctrine itself was the underlying metaphysic of continuity between the natural and supernatural realms on which it was founded. Teilhard perceives, however, that far from undermining Christian religion, this continuity provides a clearer spiritual orientation for it:

> By their faith, of course, disciples of Christ are led to place the goal of their hopes higher and farther off than other people. The vision of this higher goal does not tend to destroy but on the contrary is destined to recast and elevate the aspirations and progress of what Tertullian has called the 'naturally Christian soul'. Christians — and here is one of the most certain and precious portions of their creed — do not become so by simply negating but by transcending the world to which they belong.[57]

As the first Latin Father states: 'O noble testimony of the soul by nature Christian! ... It looks not to the Capitol, but to the heavens. It knows

---

[54] Pierre Rousselot, «Les Yeux de la foi», *RSR* 1 (1910), pp. 241–59, 444–75; trans. in *The Eyes of Faith. Answer to Two Attacks* (New York: Fordham University Press, 1990).

[55] *ST*, Ia, q. 87, a. 2, ad 1.

[56] Wlodimir Ledochowski, Letter to Provincials of 15 July 1920, 'Doctrina de actu fidei a P. Petro Rousselot p.m. proposita prohibetinur', *Acta Romana Societatis Iesu* 3 (1919–23), pp. 229–33; discussed in Avery Dulles, 'Principal Theses of the Position of Pierre Rousselot', in Rousselot, *Eyes of Faith*, p. 113.

[57] 'The Mysticism of Science', p. 178.

that there is the throne of the living God, as from Him and from thence itself came down.'[58] This praise of the soul is echoed in Henri de Lubac's Blondelian identification of an 'original assent springing from being itself, which the entire role of my free will is to ratify, whatever the cost'.[59] Teilhard infers from this conception of the soul the existence of a 'world ripe for conversion' because it consists of naturally Christian souls possessing a potential for faith that needs to be actualized.

In defending this conception of the soul as *naturaliter christiana*, Teilhard challenges two corrupt varieties of Augustinianism. Firstly, he focuses on the 'Baianism' that he perceived to be prevalent in the contemporary Church, which in its judgment of humanity places excessive emphasis on individual human sinfulness and the need for individual salvation, and fails in contrast to give a proper appraisal of sin as being a fact of creation.[60] Michel Baius, a harbinger of the Jansenist movement, had believed the whole of human nature to exist in a state of radical separation from God as a result of its concupiscence, and to contain within itself no trace of God's image unless granted to it by an external power.[61] The implication of such extreme dualism as this was that the soul exists as a purely psychic entity rather than a spiritual one, because if it were a spiritual one, it would possess some kind of intrinsic relation to God. Moreover, the absolute needfulness of divine grace which Baius's theory posited fatally undermined the gratuity of grace, which is the corollary of divine freedom. The second corrupt variety of Augustinianism that Teilhard attacks is Jansenism, which can be regarded as a more highly developed form of Baianism and was certainly more widely diffused. Jansenists, being highly critical of scholastic anthropology, drew on the Augustinian tradition in opposition to Thomist orthodoxy, and especially on its doctrine of grace.[62] The Augustinian tradition in general provided valuable resources to theologians wishing to decon-

---

[58] Tertullian, *The Apology*, §17, *ANF* III, p. 32.

[59] Henri de Lubac, 'A Meditation on the Principle of the Moral Life', *Communio (US)* 26 (1999), p. 423, originally in *Revue apologétique* 65 (1937), pp. 257–66; cf. 'The Heart of the Problem' (1949), *FM*, p. 265.

[60] 'Modern Unbelief' (1933), *SC*, p. 116; *J*, 30 January 1917, p. 188.

[61] This little-known figure was central to the debates surrounding Augustinianism in which Teilhard's thought was formed. See the article of one of Teilhard's tutors at Hastings, Xavier-Marie le Bachelet, «Baius», in *Dictionnaire de théologie catholique*, II (15 vols.; Paris: Letouzey et Ané, 1915–50), cols. 38–111; Henri de Lubac, «Deux Augustiniens fourvoyés: Baius et Jansénius», *RSR* 21 (1931), pp. 422–43, 513–40.

[62] A letter of 29 September 1910, *LH*, p. 113, written by Teilhard on his return from Louvain, indicates his knowledge of the *Augustinus* of Jansenius which was composed there.

struct the theological tradition portrayed in *Aeterni patris*, which described Aquinas as the 'chief and master' of the scholastics and as the figure who performed the great work of 'diligently collecting, and sifting, and storing up, as it were, in one place, for the use and convenience of posterity the rich and fertile harvests of Christian learning scattered abroad in the voluminous works of the holy Fathers'.[63] Teilhard is nevertheless fundamentally opposed to the notion of a division between souls inclined wholly to grace and those disposed wholly to concupiscence characteristic of the Jansenist strand of the Augustinian heritage. Teilhard considers dichotomies such as these to lie at the root of systematic theologies whose principal axioms are fall, expiation, and the corruptibility of the material world. Like Baianist theologies, Jansenism effectively denies any divine initiative in the salvation of souls and exclude the possibility of what De Lubac describes in *Surnaturel* as the 'natural desire' for God inherent in souls due to the goodness of the created order and prior to any special grace specifically granted to them. Owing to the irresistibility of divine grace, souls are subject either to a supernatural determinism if they are under grace, or to a natural determinism if they are not.[64] Teilhard, as part of his criticism of these theologies, subtitles an article in which he challenges Jansenist conceptions of the soul with the Vulgate version of the Matthean affirmation of

[63] *Aeterni patris*, §§17, 14, *PE* II, pp. 22–23. See Jacob Schmutz, 'Escaping the Aristotelian Bond: The Critique of Metaphysics in Twentieth-Century French Philosophy', *Dionysius* 17 (1999), pp. 197–200. Twentieth century *nouvelle théologie* is most commonly associated with the retrieval of patristic texts, but this is a well-established French tradition. For their crucial importance to Gallicanism, especially among the Jesuits, see J.L. Quantin and Antionina Bevan, 'The Fathers in Seventeenth Century Roman Catholic Theology', in *Reception of the Church Fathers in the West*, ed. Irena Backus, II (2 vols.: Leiden: Brill, 1997), pp. 951–86, most of which deals with French theology.

[64] See Henri de Lubac, *Surnaturel: études historiques* (Paris: Aubier Montagne, 1946; Desclée, 2nd edn, 1991). Teilhard describes the work as containing «distinctions capitales» (*J*, 24 November 1946, cahier XIV). De Lubac studied in the same institutions as Teilhard: the Maison Saint-Louis in St Helier, Jersey from 1920 to 1923, and Ore Place, Hastings from 1925 to 1926, before returning to Fourvière in 1926 at the conclusion of the exile. *Surnaturel* emerged from the Sunday seminars held at Hastings during De Lubac's year there under the aegis of Joseph Huby and known as «La Pensée». (Jean-Pierre Wagner, *Henri de Lubac* (Paris: Cerf, 2001), pp. 12–13; Georges Chantraine, «La Théologie du surnaturel selon Henri de Lubac», *NRT* 119 (1997), pp. 218–20; Bernard Sesboüé, «Le Surnaturel chez Henri de Lubac: un conflit autour d'une théologie», *RSR* 80 (1992), p. 374.) The decision to return the scholasticate to Fourvière was made in June 1926 once the former Rector and new Provincial, Jean-Baptiste Costa de Beauregard, had assumed office. (L. Rosette, «Hastings», in *Établissements des Jésuites en France depuis quatre siècles*, ed. Pierre Delattre, II (5 vols.; Enghien: Wetteren, 1939–57), cols. 807–808.)

Christ's, 'I have come not to abolish but to fulfil.'[65] In other words, salvation in Christ completes a movement of the soul rather than initiating one.

Teilhard is equally critical of the Pelagian theology of sanctification. Pelagius's soteriology was diametrically opposed to the Jansenist one, suggesting that human nature possessed absolute autonomy in relation to God. The British monk conceived divine grace as a once-for-all gift that had already been granted to its recipients, and once given, was completely sufficient for incorporating the recipient into the body of the elect. The view that material and spiritual human progress possess absolute religious value has often been designated Pelagian, but Teilhard quite rightly resists this conclusion. 'I stand', he says, 'at the antipodes of Pelagianism.'[66] Teilhard specifically refutes the designation of his theology of action as Pelagian, stating that he uses the concept of activity 'without in any way denying, far from it, all that occurs between grace and will in the infra-experiential spheres of the soul.'[67] Teilhard states of Christian believers:

> Without any tendency to deviate into any naturalism or Pelagianism, they find that they, as much as and even more that the unbeliever, can and must have a passionate concern for a terrestrial progress which is essential to the consummation of the kingdom of God.[68]

What unites the theologies of Baianism and Jansenism with, at the opposite extreme, Pelagianism, in opposition to the true heritage of Augustine, is that all three deny the pre-established relation that Leibniz argues exists between humankind and God, and which Teilhard wishes always to affirm. To posit such a *harmonia praestabilita* is far from denying the polarities of natural and supernatural. It provides, by contrast, the foundations for an understanding of the essential relatedness of humanity to God which forms the basis of faith. Pelgianism, like Jansenism, teaches that living under grace is unproblematic once that grace has been received. Teilhard, however, wishes both to challenge religious believers who count themselves as being 'under grace' without any act of faith, and to provide those believers who do not identify themselves with religious institutions with their own grammar of assent.

---

[65] 'The Sense of Humanity' (1929), *TF*, pp. 13, 28; cf. Matt 5.17.

[66] Letter to Père Lévie, 2 March 1932, quoted in Robert Speaight, *Teilhard de Chardin: A Biography* (London: Collins, 1967), p. 147.

[67] *DM*, p. 7, n. 7.

[68] 'The Concept of Christian Perfection' (1942), *TF*, p. 104.

The bond of action

Teilhard, in his engagement with the Pauline, Augustinian, Spinozist and existentialist traditions, wishes to define human action as being at once both material and spiritual. The ultimate object of human action lies beyond any particular objects which it produces, and yet is only truly spiritual to the extent that it forms and transforms the materiality of the world. Teilhard prays:

> The more I examine myself, the more I discover this psychological truth: that we shall never lift a finger to do the smallest task unless we are moved, however obscurely, by the conviction that we are contributing infinitesimally (at least indirectly) to the building of something definitive — that is, to your work, my God. This may well sound strange or exaggerated to those who act without thoroughly scrutinizing themselves. And yet it is a fundamental law of their action. It requires no less than the pull of what we call the Absolute — no less than you yourself — to set in motion the frail liberty which you have given us. And that being so, everything which diminishes my explicit faith in the heavenly value of the results of my effort, diminishes irremediably my power to act.[69]

Action is not just any activity or habit, but a movement of soul and body that occurs following reflection.[70] Action expresses an absolute, abiding or heavenly value, which is its aim and final cause. A true action requires the 'underlying intention ... of constructing "a work of abiding value"'.[71] The absolute or heavenly value of an action also provides its efficient cause: human liberty is not annihilated by its final cause, but made possible and completed by it. In 1918, Teilhard identifies a tendency in his theology to reduce the different modes of causation to their formal cause.[72] He subsequently defines efficient causality far more carefully, describing its preservation as the defining feature of 'Christian naturalism': action, in other words, despite its supernatural quality, remains a real movement of the body by the soul. Teilhard quotes in his support the definition of 'Christian naturalism' given by the catholic evolutionist Henry de Dorlodot: 'The tendency to attribute to the natural action of secondary causes all that is not excluded therefrom either by reason or the positive data of the natural sciences, and to have recourse

---

[69] *DM*, p. 13.

[70] Beatrice Bruteau, 'Sri Aurobindo and Teilhard de Chardin on the Problem of Action', *International Philosophical Quarterly* 12 (1972), p. 194.

[71] 'How I Believe' (1934), *CE*, pp. 110–11.

[72] *J*, 1 October 1918, p. 351.

to a special Divine intervention distinct from God's general governing activity only if it is absolutely necessary to do so.'[73]

This argument that action possesses a cosmic function which binds together the contingent and the absolute needs to be seen as part of a wider French critique of both Kantian philosophical rationalism and Thomist theological rationalism. Kant was the bête noire of neo-Thomist scholastics because his philosophy posited an autonomous human soul of which the cosmos and the deity were both considered to be products.[74] He had argued in the *Critique of Pure Reason* that the pure cognitive faculty of the soul could in no way prove the existence of God by rational reflection: 'the principles of reason's natural use do not lead at all to any theology'.[75] Aquinas, by contrast, was correctly regarded as arguing the opposite, opposing the *fides quaerens intellectum* tradition which had culminated in Anselm's *Cur Deus Homo* and *Proslogion* with a more precise and systematic separation of faith and reason. This is why Aquinas opposes ontological arguments yet inaugurates the *Summa theologiae* with the cosmological proofs of the Five Ways.[76] This preservation of reason within very closely defined bounds was the chief concern of Réginald Garrigou-Lagrange and other strict observance Thomists of the first quarter of the twentieth century, who in their anxiety to preserve the rational foundation of their metaphysics, perceived Kant to be the initiator of scepticism and relativism.[77] This demarcation of philosophy within theological bounds was essential if philosophy were to fulfil its function of demonstrating that the revealed truth of the Church was not contrary to reason.

Teilhard affirms, with Thomists and against Kant, that a supernatural realm of faith exists apart from the world constructed by human reason.

---

[73] 'The Transformist Question' (1921), *VP*, p. 25, n. 1; cf. Henry de Dorlodot, *Le Darwinisme au point de vue de l'orthodoxie catholique* (Brussels: Vroment, new edn, 1921); trans. *Darwinism and Catholic Thought* (London: Burns, Oates & Washbourne, 1922), p. 94.

[74] Pierre Colin, «Le Kantisme interdit», in *L'Audace et le soupçon: la crise moderniste dans le catholicisme français (1893–1914)* (Malakoff: Desclée, 1997), pp. 199–237, provides an excellent overview of the theological reception of Kant in this period.

[75] Immanuel Kant, *Critique of Pure Reason*, §A636/B664 (Cambridge University Press, 1997), p. 586.

[76] For a lucid and straightforward exposition of Aquinas's position, see Max Charlesworth, *Philosophy and Religion: From Plato to Postmodernism* (Oxford: Oneworld, 2002), pp. 63–74.

[77] Teilhard recalls his meeting with Garrigou-Lagrange in Rome in 1948: 'We smiled and spoke of Auvergne.' (Cuénot, *Teilhard*, p. 269.)

French neo-Kantianism was particularly anti-metaphysical, and Kant was perceived by contemporary catholic theologians as the 'Luther' of German philosophy due to his separation of faith from reason.[78] Nevertheless, Teilhard sides with Kant against the Thomist tradition in employing reason to reflect autonomously on faith and action. He wishes to mediate between Kantians and neo-Thomists by employing reason in a creative, autonomous way that does not undermine the basic tenets of Christian faith, and for this task challenges the Thomist subordination of philosophy to theology. This was significant because Leo XIII had directed theologians to study Thomist philosophy in his 1879 encyclical *Aeterni patris*, and it therefore possessed normative status in Catholic theology. Philosophy was typically regarded as the servant of the Church and of theology, rather than as an independently established realm of reflection on acts of faith able to maintain itself without recourse to revealed truth.

Teilhard believes that a person can be led to faith by reason. He does not wish to establish a new Christian rationalism, however, but to use reason to reflect on the character of faith as expressed in action and passion. Teilhard shares with Blondel a synthetic concept of these two sides of the praxis of human life, positing in experience a unity of the several parts of intuition that transforms a merely possible experience into an actual one. René Virgoulay describes this as *réalisme intégral*, and it is essentially a transcendental unity of apperception grounded not in consciousness, as for Kant, but in action, whose horizon becomes ever wider and finally universal.[79] Teilhard states:

> In order to become explicit... our consciousness, rising above the growing (but still much too limited) circles of family, country and race, shall finally discover that the *only truly natural and real human unity* is the spirit of the earth.[80]

The stages of action transcend the empirical act itself, and action is seen to synthesize willing, knowing and being in a spiritual unity. Action is unavoidably an affirmation of universal value. Blondel similarly states:

---

[78] McNeill, *Blondelian Synthesis*, pp. 43, 45; cf. 'Operative Faith' (1918), *WW*, p. 244.

[79] René Virgoulay, *Blondel et le modernisme: la philosophie de l'action et les sciences religieuses, 1896–1913* (Paris: Cerf, 1980), p. 286. Kant, *Critique of Pure Reason*, §A158/B197, p. 283, gives the supreme principle of all synthetic judgments: 'Every object stands under the necessary conditions of the synthetic unity of the manifold of intuition in a possible experience.'

[80] 'The Spirit of the Earth' (1931), *HE*, p. 32.

In acting, man does not limit his outlook to the family, to the city, to humanity. He projects his intention still further. As the Stoics said quite rightly, he inserts himself into the universe as a whole.[81]

These comments encapsulate the structure of the middle part of Blondel's *L'Action*, which comprises a detailed examination of the phenomenon of action in the progressively expanding stages of sense intuition, consciousness, will, individual action and collective action.[82] Teilhard shares this conception of the dependence of the soul on the wider cosmos of which it forms a part. To bring the soul to full recognition of the extent of its dependence on the cosmos for its action, he proposes a movement of recollection remarkably similar to Blondel's:

> If we wish to live our humanity and our Christianity to the full, we must overcome this insensitivity which tends to conceal things from us to the extent that they are too close to us or too vast. Let us, then, perform the salutary exercise which consists in starting with those elements of our conscious life in which our awareness of ourselves as persons is most fully developed, and moving beyond these to consider the spread of our being in the world. We shall be astonished at the extent and the intimacy of our relations with the universe.[83]

Teilhard therefore considers the phenomenon of action in progressively wider spheres. Its origins are to be found in the individual self and in the sensation, willing and movement of the body. The horizon of action then extends through the family, the country, and collective humanity, leading finally to a universal principle. This is literally an *ecstasis*[84]: a stepping outside of the self. Teilhard's sustained critique of the theory of the autonomous self becomes particularly apparent at this point. He does not accept that a theory of the self can be constructed by psychology, sociology or other social sciences and then become the object of theological reflection. Theology provides, on the contrary, the beginning, the middle and the end of reflection on the self, due to the primordial dependence of that self on God in its faith, action and passion.

Teilhard believes, like Aquinas, that this dependence is manifested in the phenomenon of *power*.[85] The two men nevertheless construe the nature of this power in very different ways. Aquinas envisions power as

---

[81] Blondel, *Action*, §279, p. 263.
[82] Blondel, *Action*, §§43–322, pp. 54–299.
[83] *DM*, pp. 16–17.
[84] 'The Atomism of Spirit' (1941), *AE*, p. 47.
[85] Aquinas, *On the Power of God*, q. 1, a. 1, vol. I, pp. 4–5; see Stephen L. Brock, 'Agent-causality and finality', in *Action and Conduct: Thomas Aquinas and the Theory of Action* (Edinburgh: T&T Clark, 1998), pp. 95–136.

an essentially static bond between the effect and the agent that communicates some feature from the agent to the thing acted on. Teilhard, by contrast, conceives of a bond of cosmic dependence rooted in the materiality of human life, and defines the nature of this dependence in explicitly sacramental terms:

> By Baptism in cosmic matter and the sacramental water we are more Christ than we are ourselves — and it is precisely in virtue of this predominance in us of Christ that we can hope one day to be fully ourselves.[86]

The dependence of the human soul on God in Christ necessarily implies, Teilhard argues, the dependence of the wider created order on God in Christ. To illustrate this, he makes an analogy between human baptism and the Incarnation:

> the movement carried out by the man [i.e. Christ] who plunges into the world, in order first to share in things and then to carry them along with him — this movement, let me emphasize, is an exact replica of the baptismal act.[87]

Teilhard believes that the relation between God and the soul which action implies can only be understood in terms of the interconnecting material bonds which construct the cosmos. In *The Divine Milieu*, he argues that 'At the heart of our universe, each soul exists for God, in Our Lord.' This proposition, he adds, 'does no more than express the fundamental catholic dogma which all other dogmas merely explain or define'.[88] Action requires not just purity of will, nor even the merging of the individual human will with divine will, as in Blondel's philosophy of action, but the 'strengthening and purification of the reality and urgency contained in the most powerful interconnection revealed ... in every order of the physical and human world'.[89] It is here that Teilhard sides with the patristic tradition against Blondel, who in arguing for the infinity of the voluntary act effectively disavows its concrete, material setting.[90] The obedience of the acting person is, Teilhard argues, obedience to a God who manifests himself to the acting person in and through dependence on the material world.

---

[86] 'My Universe' (1924), *SC*, p. 58.
[87] 'The Evolution of Chastity' (1934), *TF*, p. 73.
[88] *DM*, p. 14.
[89] *DM*, p. 16.
[90] On the tension between Blondel and patristic theology, see Jean-Luc Marion, «La Conversion de la volonté selon *L'Action*», *Revue Philosophique de la France et de l'Étranger* 177 (1987), p. 38.

Teilhard warns against too legalistic an understanding of this dependence, for instance by means of narratives based on possession such as the parable of the wicked tenants of the vineyard.[91] Ownership analogies usually fail to provide a sufficiently physical image of the nature of the dependence of humanity on God and of the mediation of the various levels of universality which bind the individuated soul to the absolute. Whilst voicing these hesitations, Teilhard distances himself from pantheistic and purely materialistic interpretations of dependence, which he describes as 'perverse':

> God cannot in any way be intermixed with or lost in the participated being which he sustains and animates and holds together, but he is at the birth, and the growth and the final term of all things.[92]

In his early correspondence with Teilhard, Blondel reminds him of the importance of always preserving the real distinction between the natural and the transcendent to which the previous passage alludes:

> One should be on guard against the dangers of immanentism; the more one represents Christ as an innate presence in souls and in the world itself, the more vital it is to lay sharp stress on the absolute transcendence of the divine gift, on the inescapably supernatural character of the plan towards deification, and thus on the moral transformation and the spiritual expansion which are demanded by and achieved through grace.[93]

Teilhard provides a more natural target than Blondel for imputations of immanentism, owing to his emphasis on the materiality of the cosmos. Nevertheless, he is just as anxious as Blondel to defend the separation of God from universe. God dwells in the universe because God is greater than the universe, not because God exists as part of it. The transcendent absolute makes itself immanent in the cosmos, but acts always as a unitive cause rather than as an efficient one.[94]

Creation and transformation

Humanity is progressively being emancipated from the material forces which formerly dominated it, and is entering a new stage of maturity. It is now ready to become adult, or what amounts to the same thing, is

---

[91] Mt 21.33–41.
[92] 'Cosmic Life' (1916), *WW*, p. 47.
[93] Paper of 5 December 1919, *TBC*, pp. 26–27.
[94] 'Outline of a Dialectic of Spirit' (1946), *AE*, pp. 148, 150.

already 'becoming' or 'emerging' as adult.[95] As these various references to the same sentiment show, it is unclear whether Teilhard considers humanity to be on the threshold of this stage, entering it, or
already in it. Whichever is the case, something new is being born into
the world. In other parts of his work, Teilhard reverses this focus on the
future state of humanity by depicting the movement into adulthood
using images of what is being left behind. Humanity is like a child
come of age, and is advancing beyond its childish form of living.[96]
These phrases sound remarkably similar to Dietrich Bonhoeffer's
descriptions of a 'world that has come of age'.[97] Teilhard implicitly
accepts Bonhoeffer's analysis of the 'attack by Christian apologetic on
the adulthood of the world'[98], although does not of course share his
view that a new religionless faith devoid of traditional Christian symbols is the correct response. Teilhard wishes, in fact, to develop a theology of action as part of an apologia for classical Christianity, showing how faith can be at once both fully religious and fully human. He
therefore refers to coming-of-age in other places as a specifically religious and spiritual progression, looking forward to a time when 'consciousness will be truly adult and of age', and affirming that
'humankind has at last become fully conscious of its powers'.[99] This
depiction of the advent of adulthood as a shift in consciousness is
closely linked with the notion of 'awakening'. Teilhard writes of an
'age suddenly woken into consciousness of its future', and of an 'awakening of consciousness'.[100] Bonhoeffer similarly states: 'The world that
has become conscious of itself and the laws that govern its own existence has grown self-confident in what seems to us to be an uncanny
way.'[101]

[95] *DM*, p. 28; 'The Death-Barrier and Co-Reflection' *AE*, (1955), p. 403; 'The Transformist Question' (1921), *VP*, p. 25; 'The Mysticism of Science' (1939), *HE*, p. 163.

[96] *HP*, p. 161; 'The Spirit of the Earth', p. 32; cf. I Cor 13.11.

[97] Dietrich Bonhoeffer, letter to Eberhard Bethge, 30 June 1944, in *Letters and
Papers from Prison: The Enlarged Edition*, ed. Eberhard Bethge (London: SCM,
1986), p. 341. For the affinity between Teilhard and Bonhoeffer, see the excellent essay
of W.J.P. Boyd, 'Teilhard de Chardin and Modern Protestant Theology', in *Teilhard
Reassessed*, ed. Anthony Hanson (London: Darton, Longman & Todd, 1970), pp. 126–
43. Boyd argues that their similarities are due to the fundamental place that both give
to christology.

[98] 'Mastery of the World and the Kingdom of God' (1916), *WW*, p. 86.

[99] 'My Universe', p. 83; 'Historical Representations of Original Sin' (1922), *CE*,
p. 53.

[100] 'Christology and Evolution' (1933), *CE*, p. 93; 'Super-Humanity, Super-Christ,
Super-Charity' (1943), *SC*, p. 151.

[101] Bonhoeffer, letter to Bethge, 8 June 1944, in *Letters and Papers*, p. 326.

The challenge Teilhard confronts is how to conceive of particular actions in cosmic terms without removing agency from individual souls and vesting it in a higher or ultimate principle. In particular, he is anxious to distance himself from Blondelian voluntarism, which suggests that in action the human and divine wills are merged. In an important early synopsis of his theology of action, Teilhard notes: 'The First Cause is not involved in effects; it acts upon individual natures and on the movement of the whole.'[102] In other words, God does not govern the world by directly determining efficient causes, but by means of an arrangement of causes ordered by final causality to provide the 'texture' of causes within the universe.[103] Although this might seem little more than a return to textbook Thomism, Teilhard wishes to challenge a cardinal tenet of this cosmology by refusing the absolute separation of production (*eductio*) from creation (*creatio*), protesting that this dichotomy 'denies any absolute value to the work of secondary causes'.[104] The severing of production from creation remains an abiding complaint:

> It is sound Scholastic philosophy, as everyone knows, that being, in the form of *Ens a se*, is posited exhaustively and repletively, and instantaneously, at the ontological origin of all things. Following this in a second phase, all the rest (i.e. 'the world') appears in turn only as an entirely gratuitous supplement or addition: the guests at the divine banquet. Strictly deduced from a particular metaphysics of potency and act, this thesis of creation's complete gratuitousness was acceptable in the Thomistic framework of a static universe.[105]

The concept of *Ens a se* (being-in-itself) is unsuited to Teilhard's metaphysics, however. What the modern experience of action and evolution requires, he believes, is not an Aristotelian Prime Mover acting *a retro* (starting from the beginning) as the cause of subsequent events, but a final cause acting *ab ante* (drawing us ahead).[106] This is an implicit criticism of Bergson's philosophy of history, which posits a primordial origin but no final unity. Bergson states: 'Harmony is rather behind us than before. It is due to an identity of impulsion and not to a common aspiration.'[107] In contrast to the Bergsonian unity grounded in memory, Teil-

---

[102] 'The Modes of Divine Action in the Universe' (1920), *CE*, p. 28.

[103] The concept of the four causes as providing the 'texture of the universe' is employed in Olivia Blanchette, *The Perfection of the Universe According to Aquinas: A Teleological Cosmology* (University Park: Pennsylvania State University Press, 1999).

[104] 'On the Notion of Creative Transformation' (1920), *CE*, p. 22.

[105] 'The Contingence of the Universe' (1953), *CE*, pp. 224–25.

[106] 'The God of Evolution' (1953), *CE*, p. 240.

[107] Henri Bergson, *Creative Evolution* (London: Macmillan, 1911), p. 54.

hard posits a unity founded in action as continuous co-operative creation:

> To create, even when we use the word omnipotence, must no longer be understood as an instantaneous act but as a process or controlled movement of synthesis... The creative act takes the form, for those beings which are its object, of transition from a state of initial dispersion to one of ultimate harmony.[108]

The work of creation is therefore 'comprehensible only as a gradual process of arrangement and unification'.[109]

At the core of Teilhard's critique of Thomist cosmology is the simple principle that 'God *does not make*: He *makes things make themselves.*' This Teilhard defines as a theory of creation 'of evolutionary type'.[110] In another discussion, he states: 'When the primal cause operates, it does not insert itself among the elements of this world but acts directly on their natures, so that God, as one might say, does not so much "make" things as "make them make themselves".'[111] Aristotelian ontology fails, in contrast, to grasp this complementarity between God and being in the creative act.[112] Teilhard states:

> There is not one moment when God creates, and one moment when the secondary causes develop. There is always only one creative action (identical with conservation) which continually raises creatures towards fuller-being, by means of their secondary activity and their earlier advances. Understood in this way, creation is not a periodic intrusion of the First Cause: it is an act co-extensive with the whole duration of the universe.'[113]

This theology of creation contains clear implications for the understanding of divine action, which is 'not to be observed either here or there (except to some degree in the mystical relationship of spirit with Spirit) but to be spread throughout the sustained, completed and to some extent super-animated complex of secondary activities.'[114] The corollary of this is, as Thomas Merton states, that God needs humankind, 'since without humankind God's creative plan cannot be fulfilled'.[115]

---

[108] 'Christology and Evolution', pp. 82–83.
[109] 'Reflections on Original Sin' (1947), *CE*, p. 194.
[110] 'The Modes of Divine Action in the Universe', p. 28; 'What Should We Think of Transformism?' (1930), *VP*, p. 154.
[111] 'The Transformist Question', p. 25.
[112] 'The Contingence of the Universe', p. 227.
[113] 'On the Notion of Creative Transformation', p. 23.
[114] 'The Basis and Foundations of the Idea of Evolution' (1926), *VP*, p. 134.
[115] Merton, 'Teilhard's Gamble', in *Love and Living*, p. 186.

Blondel was seeking, in his philosophy of action, to respond to Kantian scepticism not by speculation, as the German idealists had done, but by conceiving of action as a synthesis of willing, knowing and being. Teilhard accepts this critique of Kant, stating for instance that the psychological motivation to act requires belief in the 'absolute value of something in that effort'.[116] In another place, he identifies the compatibility of Blondel's theory with his own view that 'if human activity is to be set in motion, nothing less is required than the attraction of a result that cannot be destroyed'.[117] Teilhard describes an 'absolute, that is to say a divine goal' as being the 'sole possible instigator of reflective life', and as a profound need which humanity seeks beneath all particular religious forms. Humanity needs to 'trust in the infallibility and finally beatifying value of the action' in which it is involved.[118] Although Teilhard and Blondel agree about the importance of this universal dimension of action, their theories about the relative significance of the spiritual and material dimensions of the 'result that cannot be destroyed' diverge. The differences are evident in their correspondence exchanged during 1919, and concern the value which each attaches to the material results of action. Teilhard writes to Blondel:

> I do not attribute a definitive or absolute value to the various constructions which humankind is led to establish through its struggle with the natural order. I believe they will disappear, recast into a totally new, unimaginable plane of existence. But I hold that they play a provisional and essential role — being irreplaceable, unavoidable *phases* we must go through (we or the species) in the course of our metamorphosis.[119]

Teilhard is here challenging, albeit apologetically, Blondel's devaluation of the material results of action. The changes which action effects in nature, Blondel believes, possess no absolute value, and simply form necessary stages in a progression towards a final consummation. Teilhard believes that Blondel's philosophy of action does not go far enough in challenging the acosmism of the received Kantian tradition. Teilhard wishes to provide an account of the materiality of human action, whereas for Kant, the ground of the material world is given by the understanding, which '*contains the ground of the world of sense and so too of its laws*'.[120] Teilhard asserts, in contrast:

---

[116] 'My Universe', p. 42.

[117] 'How I Believe' (1934), *CE*, p. 110.

[118] 'The Spirit of the Earth', 'Human Energy' (1937), *HE*, pp. 44, 124.

[119] Paper of 12 December 1919, *TBC*, p. 34.

[120] Immanuel Kant, *Groundwork of the Metaphysics of Morals*, AK 4:453 (Cambridge University Press, 1997), p. 58.

> Human action can be related to Christ, and can co-operate in the fulfilment
> of Christ, not only by the intention, the fidelity, and the obedience in which
> — as an addition — it is clothed, but also by the actual *material content* of
> the work done.[121]

As John Milbank has stated of Aristotelian cosmology: 'It is hard to
conceive of a procession out of an active subject as a positive gain in
being, still less as a gain in being for the subject. But this is surely
how one wishes to categorize all meaningful human constructs. The
human person, who is the producer of significant objects, regards such
objects as worthy of maintenance, implying that their absence would
mean a loss.'[122] The challenge posed by the similar though more
abstract Thomist principle, derived from Aristotle, that an effect cannot be greater than its cause, is the one which Teilhard is seeking to
address. He argues that action produces effects which are indeed
greater than their causes, in so far as they endure beyond the lifetime
of their producer and possess in some cases far greater powers and
consequences:

> *Free will can be put into motion*, in the smallest matter, *only by the appeal
> of a definitive result*, of a *'Ktema eis aei'* — an everlasting possession —
> promised to its effort.[123]

Teilhard quotes on several occasions this description by Thucydides of
his hope that his *History of the Peloponnesian War* will provide a 'possession for all time'.[124] The κτῆμα εἰς αἰεὶ refers to the belief that eternal didactic truth can be manifested in history. In Thucydides' account
itself, this hope is bound up with a cyclical historiography in which the
narrative remains relevant because the same events of realist power politics will recur in successive generations. Teilhard proposes a linear theory of history, however. In his cosmology, the possession of action is
eternal because action intervenes in the flux of repeatable events and
thus realizes the telos of history. Indeed, Teilhard's cosmology suggests
that it is precisely action that establishes the modern, linear, Christian
view of history.

---

[121] 'Note on the Universal Christ' (1920), *SC*, p. 17.

[122] John Milbank, *The Word Made Strange: Theology, Language, and Culture*
(Oxford: Blackwell, 1997), p. 124.

[123] 'My Universe', p. 43.

[124] 'How I Believe', p. 111; 'Action and Activation' (1945), *SC*, p. 177; 'The Singularities of the Human Species' (1954), *AM*, p. 263; 'The Death-Barrier and Co-Reflection' (1955), *AE*, p. 402; cf. Thucydides, *History of the Peloponnesian War*, I, xxii.4
(4 vols.; London: Heinemann, 1919–23), I, pp. 40–41.

Communion with God in action

Action has, in different traditions of Christian theology, been understood to possess very different effects. A theory of action with no metaphysical grounding might conceive it as the means of preserving a community in the midst of a sinful world, enabling its members to promote the interests of their neighbours by attempting to preserve them in faith and prevent them from falling away from God and into sin. A more satisfactory conception of action, such as that proposed by Karol Wojtyla, is as self-determination through which the acting person is revealed.[125] Both definitions are reasonable so far as they go, but neither fully expresses the communion between God and humanity that occurs in action.

Teilhard describes in *The Divine Milieu* a fourfold movement of action and passion in which the human soul is commanded to 'put on Christ'.[126] This movement consists of the four principal 'actions of life' to which Paul of Tarsus refers as 'labouring with' (*collaborare*), 'suffering with' (*compati*), 'dying with' (*commori*) and 'being raised with' (*con-ressuscitare*).[127] In moving through these phases, which Teilhard argues are fundamental to Pauline theology, the soul experiences both action and passion, as well as a future resurrected unity lying beyond them. No previous study of Teilhard has drawn proper attention to this crucial fourfold movement. The verses of scripture to which he refers are not included in Richard Kopf's excellently thorough study of biblical sources used by Teilhard,[128] and are not referenced or translated in the newly revised translation of *The Divine Milieu*. Teilhard's identification of the four terms as a 'famous series of words' might have misled some interpreters into searching for them in one single place. Their significance lies not, however, in any common textual origin. Labouring with, suffering with, dying with and being raised with form a theological series of moments in the life of the soul: action, passion, death and resurrection. Their source might well have been the monumental study of Paul by Teilhard's teacher at Hastings, Ferdinand Prat, in which the

---

[125] Karol Wojtyla, *The Acting Person*, Analecta Husserliana 10 (Dordrecht: Reidel, 1979).

[126] *DM*, p. 8; cf. Rom 13.14. A footnote added to the newly revised translation offers Gal 3.27 instead, but that is descriptive and not imperative.

[127] *collaborare*: Phil 1.27, 4.3; *compati*: Rom 8.17, I Cor 12.26; *commori*: II Tm 2.11, cf. II Cor 7.3; *con-ressuscitare*: Eph 2.6, Col 2.12, 3.1.

[128] Richard W. Kropf, *Teilhard, Scripture and Revelation: A Study of Teilhard de Chardin's Reinterpretation of Pauline Themes* (Rutherford, NJ: Fairleigh Dickinson University Press, 1980), pp. 303–315.

four terms are discussed together in conjunction with various others.[129]
This succession of *co-* moments expresses the fact that human action is
neither simply participation in the action of a higher being, nor
autonomous action capable of creating its own ends, but that it occurs in
co-operation with the action of Christ:

> It is through the collaboration which he stimulates in us that Christ, start-
> ing from all created things, is consummated and attains his plenitude... We
> may, perhaps, imagine that the creation was finished long ago. But this
> would be quite wrong. It continues still more magnificently, and at the
> highest levels of the world. *Omnis creatura adhuc ingemiscit et parturit.*
> And we serve to complete it, even by the humblest work of our hands. This
> is, ultimately, the meaning and value of our acts.[130]

Teilhard's quotation of the Romans passage, which suggests that a continuing creative process is at work in the world — 'The whole creation
has been groaning in labour pains until now' — points to the fusion of
creation, christology and cosmology in his theology of action.

In regarding the collaboration between humanity and divinity that
occurs in action as grounded in the unification of the soul by God, Teilhard is clearly inspired once again by Blondel. Teilhard states:

> What basically characterizes the Divine Milieu is that it constitutes a
> dynamic reality in which all opposition between Universal and Personal is
> being wiped out.[131]

The concept of milieu enables Teilhard to understand the unification
process in a similar way to Blondel, whose reaction against his German
sources becomes particularly evident at this point.[132] The milieu is neither an expansion of subjectivity in which the ego itself becomes the
universal, as with Fichtean idealism, nor the domination of subjectivity
by an absolute, as in the realism of Spinoza. Rather, the mediation
between subjectivity and the absolute is transformed when the absolute
reveals itself within the milieu, with neither element dominating the relation. This could be conceived, employing a spatial metaphor, as the col-
lapsing of the 'distance' between subjectivity and the absolute made
necessary by Blondel's argument that action cannot be confined within
subjectivity or even within universality. This is because the motivation

---

[129] Ferdinand Prat, *The Theology of Saint Paul*, II (2 vols.; London: Burns, Oates &
Washbourne), pp. 18–19; trans. of *La Théologie de saint Paul* (2 vols.; Paris: Beauchesne, 1908–1912).

[130] *DM*, p. 20; cf. Rom 8.22.

[131] 'The Christic' (1955), *HM*, p. 95.

[132] McNeill, *Blondelian Synthesis*, pp. 43, 45

to action is due ultimately to an absolute spiritual principle. The culmination of this phenomenological part of Blondel's philosophy of action
is a specific form of communion of the soul with both God and humanity: 'the profound unity of wills and the universal extension of action'.[133]

In 'The Universal Element', Teilhard refers to a 'Unique Essential
(*unum necessarium*) in whose activity we are included'.[134] He also
describes the 'one thing needful' or the 'unique necessary being' as one
surrounding the acting person, and therefore one within whom the acting
person is contained.[135] The *unum necessarium*, which provides the
essay's subtitle, is present everywhere whilst remaining a centre. Indeed,
the 'one thing necessary' is present everywhere because it is a centre,
communicated by means of action to the material world. It also sustains
the dialectic of Blondel's *L'Action* between the soul and the absolute.
The inevitability and necessity of dialectical movement, which Teilhard
describes as the 'essential aspiration' of humanity towards God,[136]
springs from the gap between contingent and absolute that Blondel
describes:

> In my action there is something I have not yet been able to understand and
> equal, something which keeps it from falling back into nothingness and
> which is something only in being nothing of what I have willed up to now.
> What I have voluntarily posited, therefore, can neither surpass nor maintain
> itself. It is this conflict that explains the forced presence of a new affirma-
> tion in consciousness; and it is the reality of this necessary presence that
> makes possible in us the consciousness of this very conflict. There is a 'one
> thing necessary'. The entire movement of determinism brings us to this
> term, for it is from this term that the determinism itself begins, the whole
> meaning of which is to bring us back to it.[137]

The idea of the *unum necessarium*, although used by Blondel, far predates him, originating in the Vulgate translation of Christ's words to
Martha in Luke's Gospel: 'porro unum est necessarium / Maria optimam
partem elegit quae non auferetur ab ea'.[138] This passage has been of
tremendous importance in theological reflection on the relation of action
to contemplation, with most of its interpreters considering its message to
be that contemplation, represented by Mary, provides a higher form of

---

[133] Blondel, *Action*, §245, p. 234.
[134] 'The Universal Element' (1919), *WW*, pp. 290–91.
[135] 'The Spiritual Power of Matter' (1919), *HU*, p. 65; *DM*, p. 83.
[136] *DM*, p. 84.
[137] Blondel, *Action*, §339, p. 314.
[138] Lk 10.42. 'For only one thing is necessary. Mary has chosen the better part, which
will not be taken away from her.'

spiritual life than the action associated with Martha. Johannes Eckhart is
one of few preachers to argue for the reversed priority of the action of
Martha being superior to the contemplation of Mary. He observes of
Martha:

> She saw how Mary was possessed with a longing for her soul's satisfac-
> tion. Martha knew Mary better than Mary knew Martha, for she had lived
> long and well, and life gives the finest understanding.[139]

Martha, being the owner of a house and probably a widow or an elder
sister, has already experienced the yearning of Mary, and according to
Eckhart, knows that Mary will be unable to enter fully into the contemplative life until she has lived the active life more intensely. Teilhard
also suggests, like Eckhart, that active contemplation is superior to passive contemplation, and that the *unum necessarium* is Christ, who unifies and sustains all action and contemplation.[140]

The soul and the universe of which it forms a part are, Teilhard
believes, converging in a movement of unification towards Christ and in
Christ. Christ will only become fully present in the world, however, at
the end of history. In the meantime, the human soul enjoys a spiritual
communion with God (as opposed to full physical unity) derived from
God's creative power in which its action shares. Teilhard declares:

> In action, first of all, I adhere to the creative power of God; I coincide with
> it; I become not only its instrument but its living extension. And as there is
> nothing more personal in beings than their will, I merge myself, in a sense,
> through my heart, with the very heart of God. This contact is continuous
> because I am always acting.[141]

In this state of communion, the soul is 'wedded to a *creative* effort'.
Teilhard's descriptions of this communion are reminiscent of the Augustinian notion of God working *in nobis sine nobis*, 'in us without us',
referred to by Aquinas in several places.[142] In human action, natural and

---

[139] Meister Eckhart, *Sermons and Treatises*, ed. Maurice O'C. Walshe, I (3 vols.;
Shaftesbury: Element, 1987), pp. 79–90, at p. 80. The Assumption sermon may also be
found in Meister Eckhart, *Selected Writings*, ed. Oliver Davies (London: Penguin, 1994),
pp. 193–202; *Meister Eckhart: Teacher and Preacher*, eds. Bernard McGinn with Frank
Tobin and Elvira Borgstadt (New York: Paulist, 1986), pp. 338–45.

[140] In a letter of 23 May 1910, *LH*, pp. 96–97, Teilhard refers to Luke 10.41–42,
employing the passage as a counsel of moderation that activity must be rooted in Christ.
See also his discussion of the passage in retreat notes of 19–27 October 1940, 18–26
October 1941, *NR*, pp. 151, 179, 185.

[141] *DM*, p. 21.

[142] *DM*, p. 7, although Teilhard employs the phrase ten years earlier in *J*, 5 March
1916, p. 48; cf. *ST*, IaIIae, q. 55, a. 4; q. 63, a. 2. Odon Lottin, «Les Premières défini-

supernatural acts are fused: 'Any increase that I can bring upon myself or upon things is translated into some increase in my power to love and some progress in Christ's blessed hold upon the universe.' God is therefore 'inexhaustibly attainable in the totality of our action'.[143] The moment of consummation comes not at the end of a particular action, in other words, but at the final time when all actions are completed. Blondel states:

> To think of God is an action; yet we also do not act without co-operating with Him and without having Him collaborate with us by a sort of necessary *theergy* which integrates the part of the divine in the human operation, in order to achieve the equation of voluntary action in consciousness. And it is because action is a synthesis of man with God that it is in perpetual becoming, as if stirred by the inspiration of an infinite growth.[144]

This conception of action as participation in becoming assumes great importance in Teilhard's later works, in which he develops his theory of evolution. The fact that his theology of creative and transformative action posits communion between actor and absolute — though not a merging of divine and human wills, as with Blondel — shows that Teilhard is not promoting an aristocratic ethic attainable by only a few exemplary heroes, in the mode of Machiavelli's Prince or Nietzsche's Superman. Indeed, Teilhard argues that it is precisely because charity is, as Zarathustra complains, conceived as 'static and resigned', rather than as embodying the classical noble virtues, that 'Nietzsche's superman is now eclipsing the loving-kindness of the Gospel'.[145] The necessary mediation of Christ, whilst precluding egoistic conceptions of virtue, gives great dignity to actions, whether they be great public achievements or ordinary material labour. This is because God

> awaits us every instant in our action, in the work of the moment. There is a sense in which he is at the tip of my pen, my spade, my brush, my needle — of my heart and of my mind. By pressing the stroke, the line, or the stitch, on which I am engaged, to its ultimate natural finish, I shall lay hold of that last end towards which my most interior will tends.[146]

---

tions et classifications des vertus au Moyen-Âge», *Revue des sciences philosophiqes et théologiques* 18 (1929), pp. 371–72, provides an excellent descriptive overview of the distinction between infused and acquired virtue, discussing the importance of Peter of Poitiers's modification of the Lombardine definition of virtue as acquired. Peter insists on the divine origin of all virtues (cardinal, theological and spiritual), which Lottin affirms «feront loi dans les écoles théologiques».

[143] *DM*, pp. 21–22.
[144] Blondel, *Action*, §352, p. 325.
[145] 'The Atomism of Spirit' (1941), *AE*, p. 53.
[146] *DM*, pp. 22–23.

This description echoes the petition made in George Herbert's prayer: 'Teach me, my God and King, / In all things thee to see, / And what I do in anything, / To do it as for thee.'[147] Ordinary material labour is not a spiritual encumbrance, but affords the sole possibility of spiritual progression. Bergson avers, in terms similar to Teilhard's: 'We must not suppose that our pen-stroke is self-sufficient, that it can be isolated from the rest of things. We shall see that it carries with it, whether we will or no, all that we tried to abstract from.'[148] Teilhard construes this wider context as specifically teleological. In action

> we complete in ourselves the subject of the divine union; and through it again we somehow make to grow in stature the divine term of the One with whom we are united, our Lord Jesus Christ. Consequently, whatever our human role may be, whether we are artists, workers or scholars, we can, if we are Christians, speed towards the object of our work as though towards an opening on to the supreme fulfilment of our beings.[149]

The most ordinary material work must, if the whole cosmos is to be brought to readiness for final union in Christ, be included in the process of spiritual progression. Poetic genius may be due to a 'flash of the absolute' and inspired by the 'feeling of the Whole',[150] but so are other types of action. It is not selected portions of the cosmos that are sanctified, but the whole cosmos in its entirety.

Teilhard nevertheless believes that action widens personal horizons. Each reality attained and left behind reveals an ideal of 'higher spiritual content'.[151] The religion which awakens action is not an opium, but calls humanity to cosmic responsibility in which it progresses towards heaven *through* earth.[152] Teilhard's metaphysics of action is aimed at binding human actions to God's work in sustaining the cosmos and directing its history. Action therefore possesses an inherently transcendental character. Its final intention is God, who gathers up its particular ends and projects into a wider plan along with subjects themselves. Although action is predicated on the separation of *essentia* (essence) from *esse* (being), and of the supernatural from the natural, it assumes the possibility of their reunification. In action, God makes possible once again the identity of *esse* with *essentia*, of nature with supernature.

---

[147] 'The Elixir', in *George Herbert*, ed. Louis L. Martz (Oxford University Press, 1994), p. 163.

[148] Bergson, *Creative Evolution*, p. 300.

[149] *DM*, pp. 21–22.

[150] 'Pantheism and Christianity' (1923), *CE*, p. 59.

[151] *DM*, p. 30.

[152] 'Christology and Evolution' (1933), *CE*, p. 93.

Detachment: the end of action

Teilhard identifies detachment as the culmination of action. In so doing, he departs from the pattern of some of the spiritual masters who had nourished him during his Jesuit training. Detachment is, for instance, only the second of the thirty steps of John Climacus (following renunciation of the world), who exhorts the Christian to emulate Lot by fleeing from the city being destroyed in punishment for its wickedness.[153] It possesses a quite different role in Teilhard's thought, however, appearing not at the beginning an active spiritual quest but at its conclusion. True detachment is possible only once the believer has gained awareness of the ultimate intention of their action and of its dependence on the world. It does not precede, but follows, communion with God.

The detached soul is no longer determined by the materiality of the cosmos. It is therefore at this final moment of action — the separation from the world that action finally brings — that the peace and the joy of communion with Christ may be discovered. At the beginning of the analysis of action in *The Divine Milieu*, the fact that purity of intention cannot bring peace and joy is identified as being its principal deficiency as the basis for a theology of action. Although purity of intention there entails detachment, this is simply detachment from the world rather than detachment in communion with God in Christ through the world. Teilhard enunciates the paradoxical relation of the person of action to the world: 'Those who devote themselves to human duty according to the Christian formula, though outwardly they may seem to be immersed in the concerns of the earth, are in fact, down to the very depths of their being, people of great detachment.'[154] This detachment is intrinsic to the life of action:

> To create, or organize, material energy, truth or beauty, brings with it an inner torment which prevents those who face its hazards from sinking into the quiet and closed-in life in which grows the vice of egoism and attachment (in the technical sense). Honest workers not only surrender their calm and peace once and for all, but must learn continually to jettison the form which their labour or art or thought first took, and go in search of new forms. To pause, to bask in or possess results, would be a betrayal of action. Again and again they must go beyond themselves, tear themselves

---

[153] John Climacus, *The Ladder of Divine Ascent* (London: Faber & Faber, 1959). For similarities with the Ignatian ascent motif, see Vincenzo Poggi, «Saint Jean Climaque et saint Ignace de Loyola», *Proche Orient Chrétien* 32 (1982), pp. 50–85.

[154] *DM*, p. 29.

away from themselves, leaving behind them their most cherished beginnings.[155]

Action brings the material peace of its subject to an end. The necessary
participation by the absolute in human action nevertheless draws the acting person beyond their own self to find peace and joy in a more profound dynamic unity of matter and spirit. Teilhard therefore describes
his principal wartime duty of venturing out as a stretcher-bearer into the
part of the battlefield between the front lines to help to collect the
injured and dying as a 'release from day-to-day slavery'[156], and not in
spite of the dangers he encountered. He contrasts these experiences at
the front with a surreal incident that took place close to it when a farmer
apprehended him whilst he was trespassing on the farmer's land:

> As I was cutting across the fields on my way back to the trenches ... I was
> suddenly stopped by a peasant who reproached me for walking across his
> ploughland. The fellow was perfectly justified. But as I listened to him, I
> felt an inner shock, a dizziness, as though I were falling from a great
> height... To all appearances we were similar beings, he and I. We used the
> same words; but he was imprisoned in what concerned him as an individ-
> ualistic 'man of the soil' — and I was living with the life of the Front.[157]

This striking encounter with the *Glebae adscriptus*, rebuked by Schleiermacher in his third speech on *Bildung* (self-development) to the cultured
despisers of religion, illustrates the sense possessing the person of action
of the unspiritual character of the rules that humankind institutes to reg-

---

[155] *DM*, p. 29.

[156] 'Nostalgia for the Front' (1917), *HM*, p. 173.

[157] 'Nostalgia for the Front', p. 177. Teilhard inverts, in this arresting description, the
imagery of the 'vertigo' (ἴλιγγος) experienced by the person contemplating the nature of
existence in Gregory of Nyssa, *Homilies on Ecclesiastes*, VII, 413.5–414.8 (Berlin: De
Gruyter, 1993), pp. 125–26: 'It is like a person who finds himself on a mountain — suppose it is a sheer precipitous rock face, which in its lower part stretches up with a verti-
cal smooth surface for a vast distance, and high above rises that peak, which from its
beetling crag plunges down to an immense depth — what he is likely to experience when
with his toe he feels the ridge overhanging the drop and finds neither foothold nor hand-
hold — that, I believe, is the experience of the soul when it goes beyond what is accessi-
ble to time-bound thoughts in search of what is before time and has no extension. Having
nothing to catch hold of, neither place, nor time, nor space, nor anything else of the kind
which offers a foothold to our intellect, but slipping in all directions from what it cannot
grasp, it becomes giddy and perplexed, and turns back again to what is akin to it, content
to know only enough about the transcendent to be sure that it is something other than
what can be known.' Teilhard also refers, in a sense closer to Gregory's, to the vertigo
experienced on contemplating death, in a retreat note of 20 July 1921, *NR*, p. 83; cf. note
of 16–24 October 1942, *NR*, p. 222; *J*, 20 January 1918, p. 264. For a brief discussion
which relates vertigo to an awareness of living in the finite, see Janine Langan, 'Pascal
and Teilhard de Chardin: *frères spirituels*', *Communio (US)* 12 (1985), pp. 425–35.

ulate society.[158] Teilhard sometimes prefers the term 'renunciation' to detachment when talking about action, or employs the two synonymously.[159] 'Detachment' leaves fewer possibilities for confusion than 'renunciation', because the term contains fewer negative connotations. As Teilhard articulates his theology more precisely, 'detachment' therefore becomes his standard concept in discussions of action. It suggests a degree of independence from the rules and customs that prevail in society at any particular time that is derived from the spiritual character of action.

Teilhard's identification of detachment as the final stage in the human experience of action is similar to that of Meister Eckhart, who describes pure detachment as

> the best and highest virtue whereby a man may chiefly and most firmly join himself to God, and whereby a man may become by grace what God is by nature, and whereby a man may come closest to his image when he was in God, wherein there was no difference between him and God, before God made creatures.[160]

Teilhard believes that detachment profoundly alters the state of being of the material world, bringing it closer to readiness for consummation by God in Christ. Detachment from the material world does not sustain a dichotomy between material and spiritual being, however, as Eckhart believes, but makes possible the spiritual ordering of material being so that matter undergoes a progressive spiritual transformation. Christopher Mooney observes: 'Detachment from the world is not necessarily incompatible with a driving and passionate desire to develop that same world.'[161] Teilhard indeed believes that detachment is essential to the human task of developing and completing the world. Yet detachment also provides the means of bringing peace and joy into the world in what Jürgen Moltmann describes as 'sabbath rest': 'the earthly presence of God in the sabbath stillness, which we perceive only when everything in

---

[158] See F.D.E. Schleiermacher, *On Religion: Speeches to its Cultured Despisers* (Cambridge University Press, 2nd edn, 1997), pp. 55–71.

[159] See 'Mastery of the World and the Kingdom of God' (1916), *WW*, p. 89, where both terms are used; 'Note on the Presentation of the Gospel' (1919), *HM*, p. 221, where only 'renunciation' is used. Neither of these terms should be confused with 'resignation', which Teilhard uses in relation to passion rather than action.

[160] Meister Eckhart, 'On Detachment', in *Sermons and Treatises*, ed. Walshe, III, p. 117; Meister Eckhart, *The Essential Sermons, Commentaries, Treatises and Defense*, eds. Edmund Colledge and Bernard McGinn (London: SPCK, 1981), p. 285.

[161] Christopher Mooney, 'Blondel and Teilhard de Chardin: An Exchange of Letters', *Thought* 37 (1962), p. 548.

us has fallen silent'.[162] Rest is implicit in every true action: once an action is complete, the actor is free to contemplate the new creation of God that their action has brought about, and the necessary presence of God in that creation.

---

[162] Jürgen Moltmann, *The Way of Jesus Christ: Christology in Messianic Dimensions* (London: SCM, 1990), p. 302.

3. PASSION

Limitation, suffering and death comprise fundamental aspects of the soul's passive state. In these passivities, the soul experiences God either as other, or as wholly absent. Moments of passivity might well be combined with moments of action, but Teilhard insists that activity and passivity provide quite distinct ways of regarding the soul: although the two might sometimes coexist, they cannot be merged. Passivities possess no part in action because the definition of action implies that the human soul co-operates with the absolute. This fundamental distinction between passivity and activity is axiomatic both to Teilhard's theology and to the metaphysics of Aquinas, from whom he derives it. Aquinas regards the distinction as intrinsic to the definition of cause and effect: a thing is active in relation to events that it causes, and passive in relation to causes that act upon it. So far as the cosmos as a whole is concerned, only God is pure act, or in other words, only in God are action and power identical,[1] and every part of the created order is passive in relation to God.

Teilhard accepts the essence of this distinction between action and passivity founded on power and cause. Nevertheless, he wishes to conceive of action and passion as *experiences* of the human soul rather than as elements of a set of relations of cause and effect, and this becomes especially apparent in his consideration of passion. Teilhard introduces a psychological element into the contrast in a way characteristic of Spinozist cosmology, according to which actions necessarily arise from adequate ideas in the mind, whilst passions, or things undergone, arise from inadequate ideas and the bodily nature associated with them.[2] Ideas are given to the human soul, Teilhard will argue, primarily by its relations with other parts of the created order rather than by it relation with God: the soul's relation to God can only be conceived through the created order, and not as an abstract direct association. The soul will, on some occasions, have the experience of being wholly in act, co-operating with God rather than deriving its action from a more fundamental passive

---

[1] Thomas Aquinas, *Summa contra gentiles*, II, 9 (5 vols.; Notre Dame, Ind.: University of Notre Dame Press, 1975), pp. 40–41; cf. «Homme» (1912), §502, where humanity is described as the «source en quelque façon première d'action, et sujet ultime de 'passion'».

relation to God. On others, the soul will feel that it is entirely passive. Nevertheless, Teilhard argues that the soul's relation to God is not always one of passion, as Aquinas believes, and that passion is, like action, an experience of the soul rather than a purely metaphysical aspect of its continued being.

Teilhard's theology of passion challenges current prevalent conceptions of passion based on emotion and subjectivity in two ways, suggesting that they fail to encompass a sufficient breadth of human experience and that they wrongly equate desire with freedom rather than with suffering. The term 'passion' is frequently used to convey a range of more or less specific meanings which include emotion, enjoyment, love and sensuality. Such terms convey, however, only one part of its more ancient genealogy. 'Passion', derived from the late Latin *passio* encountered chiefly in Christian theology, originates in the verb *pati*, meaning 'to suffer'. This suggests that passion is anything which is not action: or, in Teilhard's words, that which is not done by the soul, but is undergone by it.[3] Modern philosophy and even theology, frequently under the tutelage of introspective psychological theories, often presume the term 'passion' to refer to a strong and uncontrollable emotion originating in the soul that is 'expressed' in the performance of certain outward acts. The corollary of this presumption is that *passio* is, as an experience, essentially private. This metaphysics inverts, however, the subject-object relation which passion imposes on the soul: passion is, in itself, not liberating but enslaving, even if the enslavement it brings contains within itself the seeds of any subsequent liberating consequences. In Hegel's master-slave dialectic, for instance, although the slave receives greater spiritual recognition from the master than the master does from the slave, the slave remains in material bondage until the point of liberation. Passion is not about being in control, but about being subject to the control of another. Vestiges of the earlier concept of passion persist as testimony to this. For instance, the equivalent Greek term πάθος preserves the association of feeling with *undergoing*. Moreover, the language of passion continues to be used in Christian theology to describe the suffering of Christ and its culmination in his crucifixion.

Teilhard does not give much consideration to passion in his early essays. This apparent lack of concern is explained by the simple fact that he is addressing different theological issues in those essays. Reflection

---

[2] Benedict Spinoza, *Ethics*, III, prop. 3; IV, prop. 2 (London: Penguin, 1996), pp. 74, 118.

[3] *DM*, p. 36: «Ce qui n'est pas agi, en nous, est, par définition, subi.»

on passion was sufficiently prominent in contemporary theology for him not to feel the need to promote discussion of the topic further. Indeed, his theology of action develops as a reaction against the popular passion-centred piety which he saw around him. Teilhard does, however, discuss passion in several places, most notably in *The Divine Milieu*, in which he presents his clearest and most comprehensive theology of this experience. Proper consideration of this aspect of his work will provide an overdue antidote to studies which fail to give a proper account of its place in his theology, and then critique that incomplete account as if it were Teilhard's own. This task is especially pressing because he might sometimes seem to adopt a callous attitude to the individual suffering which comprises the essence of passion. Even R.C. Zaehner, inspired by Stanley Kubrick's film *The Clockwork Orange,* ruminates critically that Teilhard believes that the 'weak should be sacrificed at the altar of the strong in their superb convergence on Omega Point which is the Cosmic Christ'.[4] This description perverts Teilhard's actual theology of suffering, which is based on the recognition of the intrinsic imperfection of the human condition resulting from the material, embodied existence of humanity in the cosmos. Teilhard's perspective shares, in a curious way, some features with that of the Jewish post-Holocaust theologian Ignaz Maybaum, who regards suffering on a mass scale as a form of vicarious atonement for the sins of the world.[5] Nevertheless, whilst Maybaum considers sin to be a specific offence or offences, Teilhard believes that what is 'atoned' for is not so much moral sin as the imperfection intrinsic to the human condition.

The quest for a response to the human experience of suffering lies at the heart of Teilhard's theology. Close to the beginning of the second section of *The Divine Milieu*, Teilhard describes the priorities of the active and passive perspectives of the soul as follows:

> From our point of view, the active occupies first place because we prefer it and because it is more easily perceived. But in the reality of things the passive is immeasurably the wider and the deeper part.[6]

Teilhard is not, therefore, opposed to the theology of passion per se, but to a particular popular form of that theology. In fact, he identifies three

---

[4] R.C. Zaehner, *Our Savage God* (London: Collins, 1974), p. 262. Zaehner makes a similar point in his *Evolution in Religion: A Study in Sri Aurobindo and Pierre Teilhard de Chardin* (Oxford: Clarendon, 1971), p. 38.

[5] Ignaz Maybaum, *The Face of God after Auschwitz* (Amsterdam: Polak & Van Gennep, 1965), p. 72.

[6] *DM*, p. 36.

different types of passion: growth, external diminishment and internal diminishment.[7] He thus follows Thomas Aquinas, who distinguishes three uses of the term 'passive': the loss of something natural to inclination or congenial to it (the strictest sense); any alteration or change that includes some kind of loss, whether congenial or not (the less strict sense); any acquisition by a thing of its potential, with no loss included (the broadest sense).[8] The first two definitions encompassing loss correspond to Teilhard's category of passivity of *diminishment*, and the third definition based on the acquisition of potential, to his category of passivity of *growth*. The first and second definitions approximate, moreover, to his distinction between internal and external passivities of diminishment respectively. Similarities may also be identified with the 'two different forms of passiveness' identified by Karol Wojtyla: something happening *with* (or to) a person from the outside (external diminishment), and something happening *in* a person as part of his or her inner dynamism (growth and internal diminishment).[9]

Teilhard's experience of passion, and his sharing in the passion of close family members, is less well-known than his love of the active life. He is sometimes criticized by theologians who insist on the importance of personal experience in the development of theology for himself giving it a low priority in his theology and for having himself little experience of suffering. So far as the content of his theology is concerned, this is a potentially serious charge for many systematic theologians, who under the influence of post-Holocaust theology consider the failure to provide a satisfactory account of suffering based preferably on personal testimony to be among the most serious faults of which a theologian can be guilty. Theologians who espouse this view are, of course, correct that much compelling theological reflection has emerged from the depths of personal suffering during the course of the twentieth century, but Teilhard's oeuvre needs to be seen as part of this tradition rather than as superseded by it. In 1902, Teilhard was exiled from France as part of the expulsion of religious teaching communities by Émile Combes, spending three years at the Maison Saint-Louis philosophy scholasticate of the French Jesuits on Jersey and four years at its theology scholasticate at

[7] *DM*, pp. 36–54.

[8] *ST*, Ia, q. 79, a. 2 (on mind); IaIIae, q. 22, a. 1 (on feelings). In the latter article, probably written later, the first two senses are dealt with as a single sense possessing two forms.

[9] Karol Wojtyla, *The Acting Person*, Analecta Husserliana 10 (Dordrecht: Reidel, 1979), pp. 62–63.

Ore Place, Hastings.[10] Patrick Cabanel has suggested that this little-known expulsion of Christians from twentieth century Western Europe effectively provided a prelude for the expulsions of Jews and other minority groups by the Vichy regime during the 1940s.[11] In 1926, Teilhard was exiled again, this time from Paris to China, following official investigation of his writings on original sin after a conference paper had been mislaid and despatched to Rome for Curial investigation.[12] He nevertheless accepted decisions that none of his mature theological works be published after they failed to be granted the necessary nihil obstat and imprimatur.[13] In 1950, following publication of the encyclical *Humani generis*, Teilhard was exiled a third time, on this occasion from Paris to New York, where he died five years later.[14]

Teilhard's own family was also afflicted by suffering. By 1926, when Teilhard began writing *The Divine Milieu*, six of his ten sisters and brothers had died at young ages, and he often refers to their anniversaries in letters to his parents.[15] The lives of his two adult sisters are par-

[10] René d'Ouince, *Un prophète en procès: Teilhard de Chardin dans l'Église de son temps* (Paris: Aubier Montaigne, 1970), pp. 50–60, gives the best description of these houses. See also Pierre Clavel, «De Newman à Teilhard: une piste de recherche — 1: Ore Place à l'arrivée de Teilhard en 1908», in *Newman et l'histoire*, eds. Claude Lepelley and Paul Veyriras (Presses Universitaires de Lyon, 1992), pp. 245–55.

[11] Patrick Cabanel, «Le Grand exil des congrégations enseignantes au début du xxe siècle», *Revue d'histoire de l'Église de France* 81 (1995), pp. 207–217; Nicholas Atkin, 'The Politics of Legality: The Religious Orders in France, 1901–1945', in *Religion, Society and Politics in France Since 1789*, eds. Frank Tallett and Nicholas Atkin (London: Hambledon, 1991), pp. 149–65.

[12] See D'Ouince, *Un prophète en procès: Teilhard de Chardin dans l'Église de son temps*, pp. 100–137; Henri de Lubac, 'Tradition and obedience', in *The Eternal Feminine: A Study on the Poem by Teilhard de Chardin* (London: Collins, 1971), pp. 190–99.

[13] Malachi Martin, *The Jesuits: The Society of Jesus and the Betrayal of the Roman Catholic Church* (London: Simon & Schuster, 1988), p. 298, refers to 'the publication of *The Divine Milieu* in 1927' as evidence of Teilhard's failure to remain obedient to the Church. In fact, the nihil obstat required as permission to publish the work was not granted and he made no attempt to publish it. The first formal publication was in 1957, two years after his death. For a detailed account, see Haiyan Wang, *Le Phénomène Teilhard: l'aventure du livre 'Le Milieu divin'* (Saint-Étienne: Aubin, 1999). Much of Martin's work comprises a highly speculative and idiosyncratic interpretation of historical facts.

[14] Robert Speaight, *Teilhard de Chardin: A Biography* (London: Collins, 1967), pp. 298–300.

[15] Marielle did not survive childhood. Albéric, a naval officer, died in 1902. Louise was struck by a fatal attack of meningitis in 1904, and died aged 13. Gonzague was killed in 1914, aged 20, during an assault on a German trench, and Olivier in 1918, also in combat. Victor was to die in 1934, and Gabriel, an air force staff officer, in 1943. (Letters of 5 August, 7 and 26 September 1906, *LE*, pp. 107, 118, 119; 22 September 1912, *LP*, p. 30; 2 April 1930, *LI*, p. 216; 25 November 1942, *LT*, pp. 285–86, 307.) Claude

ticularly noteworthy: Teilhard enjoyed close relations with them as a result of the vocation to different forms of religious life that all three shared, and both women have been subjects of biographical work. Françoise was Superior of the Little Sisters of the Poor, an Augustinian order founded to provide hospitality and care for the elderly, and died in 1911, aged 32, from a smallpox infection contracted in China.[16] Teilhard's other sister, Marguerite-Marie, became permanently bedridden in about 1902 following an attack of pleurisy which developed into spinal tuberculosis, yet worked creatively throughout her decades of invalidity to alleviate the suffering of others, founding the Catholic Union of the Sick in 1922 and acting as its president from 1927 until her death in 1936.[17] Among her many enterprises was the production of her sister's biography. In his moving preface to a collection of Marguerite-Marie's writings, Teilhard reflects:

> O Marguerite, my sister, while I, given body and soul to the positive forces of the universe, was wandering over continents and oceans, my whole being passionately taken up in watching the rise and fall of all the earth's tints and shades, you lay motionless, stretched out on your bed of sickness; silently, deep within yourself, you were transforming into light the world's most grievous shadows. In the eyes of the Creator, which of us, tell me, which of us will have had the better part?[18]

Teilhard's rhetorical question to his sister confirms that he considers passion to possess, at the very least, equal spiritual significance to action. Bodies in passion, just like those in action, are 'in a sense driven out of themselves, compelled to depart from the prevailing forms of life'.[19]

Cuénot, *Teilhard de Chardin: A Biographical Study* (London: Burns & Oates, 1965), pp. 135–36, records that by 1936, only three brothers were left of ten children in 1900. René Virgoulay, «La Question du mal dans la pensée et l'expérience spirituelle du P. Teilhard de Chardin», *RSR* 56 (1982), pp. 44–45, records the deaths but omits that of Marielle. The son of Teilhard's last remaining brother Joseph was drowned in 1947, aged 26. (Letter of 28 July 1947, *LLS*, p. 207.)

[16] Marguerite-Marie Teilhard de Chardin, *Françoise Teilhard de Chardin, Petite-Soeur des Pauvres: soeur Marie Albéric du Sacré-Coeur, 1879–1911: lettres et témoignages* (Paris: Beauchesne, 1975; Clermont-Ferrand: Bellet, 1914), or alternative edn, *Soeur Marie-Albéric du Sacré-Coeur, petite soeur des pauvres, 1879–1911* (Rennes: Oberthur, 1935). See letter of 7 June 1911, *LH*, pp. 148–49.

[17] Marguerite-Marie Teilhard de Chardin, *L'Énergie spirituelle de la souffrance*, ed. Monique Givelet (Paris: Seuil, 1951) comprises a collection of her essays. See Cuénot, *Teilhard*, pp. 2, 55; Henri de Lubac, *The Faith of Teilhard de Chardin and Note on the Apologetics of Teilhard de Chardin* (London: Burns & Oates, 1965), p. 5; *LI*, p. 256, n. 1.

[18] Reproduced as 'The Spiritual Energy of Suffering' (1950), *AE*, p. 249.

[19] 'The Significance and Positive Value of Suffering' (1933), *HE*, p. 50.

Growth and recollection

Teilhard distinguishes three types of passion. The first type, passivities of growth, comprises the 'friendly and favourable energies, those which support our effort and point the way to success'.[20] Although Teilhard does not give any examples of this form of passion, it clearly includes the biological growth and functioning of the human body, and chance circumstances and events which promote the body's flourishing but which cannot be counted as actions because they are not instances of conscious co-operation of the soul with God. That growth is a form of passion, rather than of action, follows from Teilhard's radical definition of action. Indeed, bodies 'undergo life as much as [they] undergo death', and in the scheme of *The Human Phenomenon*, growth is therefore classified as a form of evil.[21] Passivities of growth are disclosed not by an outward movement of consciousness, as is the possibility of action, but by inward reflection. Teilhard describes the process of their discovery within himself in the following terms:

> Leaving the zone of everyday occupations and relationships where everything seems clear, I went down into my innermost self, to the deep abyss from which I feel dimly that my power of action emanates. But as I moved further and further away from the conventional certainties by which social life is superficially illuminated, I became aware that I was losing contact with myself. At each step of the descent a new person was disclosed within me of whose name I was no longer sure, and who no longer obeyed me. And when I had to stop my exploration because the path faded from beneath my steps, I found a bottomless abyss at my feet, and out of it came, arising I know not from where, the current I dare to call *my* life.[22]

This introspective reflection performs a function analogous to that of the negative dialectic in the realm of action: the ever-expanding circle of consciousness established by action becomes an ever-deepening locus of inward contemplation.

Two aspects of this movement, both derived from Bergsonian metaphysics, require elucidation. The first is its unconscious element, which reflective consciousness encounters when seeking to discern the source of its growth, and the second is the *élan vital*, which Teilhard describes as the torrent of life which bears humanity along in time.[23] Henri Berg-

---

[20] *DM*, p. 37.
[21] *DM*, p. 76; *HP*, p. 225. This definition is obviously ontological and not moral.
[22] *DM*, pp. 37–38.
[23] *DM*, p. 38.

son's influence on Teilhard is decisive here, and might well originate prior to the publication of *Creative Evolution* in 1907, when Bergson became the centre of national intellectual attention. From 1883 to 1888, Bergson was teaching in Clermont-Ferrand, very close to the Teilhard family home at Sarcenat, holding a chair in philosophy at the Lycée Blaise-Pascal and working through the same period at the Faculté des Lettres in the town.[24] Joseph Desaymard draws attention to the flourishing Gallic intellectualism in the city, with «le public clermontois» following philosophical debates in journals and participating in them at public conferences.[25] Teilhard's father Emmanuel, a landed farmer and noted historian of the Auvergne, was a member of regional intellectual circles and permanent secretary of the Academy of Sciences, Belles-Lettres and Arts of the city,[26] and it is likely that the family would, via him, have been exposed to early Bergsonian ideas. In particular, it was during this period that Bergson was advancing his theories about consciousness and duration contained in his *thèse principale, Time and Free Will.*[27]

The Bergsonian conception of the recovery of the unconscious being made possible by recollection of the *élan vital* pervades the discussion of growth in *The Divine Milieu*. Teilhard asks:

> What science will ever be able to reveal to us the origin, nature and character of this conscious power to will and to love which constitutes our life? It is certainly not our effort, nor the effort of anyone around us, which sets this current in motion. And it is certainly not our anxious care, nor that of any of our friends, which prevents its ebb or controls its turbulence. We can, of course, trace back through generations some of the antecedents of the torrent which bears us along; and we can, by means of certain moral and physical disciplines and stimulants, regularise or enlarge the aperture through which the torrent is released into us. But neither that geography nor those artifices help us in theory or in practice to harness the sources of life. My self is given to me far more than it is formed by me. We cannot, Scripture says, add a single hour to the span of our life. Still less can we add a unit to the potential of our love, or accelerate by another unit the fundamental rhythm which regulates the ripening of our minds and hearts. In the last resort, the profound life, the fontal life, the new-born life, escape our grasp entirely.[28]

---

[24] See Henri Bergson, *Cours* (4 vols.; Paris: Presses universitaires de France, 1990–2000).

[25] Joseph Desaymard, *H. Bergson à Clermont-Ferrand* (Clermont-Ferrand: Bellet, 1910), p. 8.

[26] *LE*, p. 209, n. 1.

[27] Henri Bergson, *Essai sur les données immédiates de la conscience* (Paris: Alcan, 1889); trans. *Time and Free Will: An Essay on the Immediate Data of Consciousness* (London: Macmillan, 1910).

[28] *DM*, p. 38.

The springs of human will and human love, Teilhard maintains, defy human investigation and explanation, and cannot ultimately be individuated in particular persons. This is a distinctively Bergsonian revolt against a description of the world based on mechanical and mathematical laws.[29] The misguided tendency to divide human life into elements and then to order these elements in series has, Bergson argues, been the dominant trend in Western philosophy and science: 'The cardinal error which, from Aristotle onwards, has vitiated most of the philosophies of nature, is to see in vegetative, instinctive and rational life, three successive degrees of the development of one and the same tendency, whereas they are three divergent directions of an activity that has split up as it grew.' Bergson conceives of humanity as comprising both *instinct*, which points towards unconsciousness and knowledge of matter, and *intelligence*, which points towards consciousness and knowledge of form.[30] Intelligence will seek some things but never find them, and instinct is able to find some others but will never itself be motivated to seek them. A third unifying faculty is needed: '*Intuition* is that faculty of the human mind which shares with instinct an immediacy of relation to life and which shares a reflective power with intelligence.'[31] For Teilhard and Bergson, as for Loisy, religion is important to human life because it constitutes an intuition about that life. By means of intuition, which is grounded in consciousness and reflection, the primordial unity of instinct and intelligence can be recovered and the processes of human growth understood.[32]

Bergson appropriates the Platonic doctrine of ἀνάμνησις (recollection), developed in the *Meno* and *Phaedo* and deployed by his master Plotinus, to provide the basis of his explanation of the relation between consciousness and life. In the *Enneads*, introspection makes possible the retrieval of innate knowledge of the forms.[33] This is illustrated in the *Phaedrus*, when the chariot of the soul, on being struck by the beauty of the face, *recollects* the true nature of beauty seen when cir-

---

[29] Robert Grogin, *The Bergsonian Controversy in France, 1900–1914* (University of Calgary Press, 1988), p. 21.

[30] Henri Bergson, *Creative Evolution* (London: Macmillan, 1911), pp. 152, 157. Bergson explores the concept of recollection in *Matière et mémoire* (Paris: Alcan, 1896); trans. *Matter and Memory* (London: Macmillan, 1911).

[31] Grogin, *Bergsonian Controversy*, p. 29.

[32] Ian W. Alexander, *Bergson: Philosopher of Reflection* (London: Bowes & Bowes, 1957), p. 54.

[33] Plotinus, *Enneads*, IV.3 (27) 25 – IV.4 (28) 12 (7 vols.; London: Heinemann, 1966–68), pp. 110–71.

cling the forms prior to its embodiment.[34] Bergson would first have become acquainted with Plotinus via the promotion of Neoplatonism by Victor Cousin during the mid-nineteenth century and the first French translations of the *Enneads* by Marie-Nicolas Bouillet published in the period 1857–61.[35] Bergson lectured on Plotinus at the College de France and himself selected the topics: the psychology of Plotinus, based on *Ennead* IV, and *Ennead* VI.9 (9), which concerns the Good as the One. ἀνάμνησις might appear to be the antithesis of vitalism, being concerned with the recollection of eternal forms rather than with engagement in material life, yet as A.H. Armstrong notes, it is part of Plotinus's introduction of values that are 'inextricably bound up with change and process into his eternal world'.[36] Bergson, like Plotinus, makes human mental operations pivotal to the combination of spirit and matter. Nevertheless, because Bergson regards the Plotinian tradition as too intellectualized, he transforms the concept of ἀνάμνησις from a principle of knowledge into a principle of activity, or as Teilhard defines it, growth. Life is not contained in a series of discrete events, Bergson and Teilhard argue, but is a continuous movement from the past into the future.

The second of Bergson's concepts which Teilhard critically appropriates is that of the *élan vital*, which posits an 'elemental universal force immanent in nature which purposively strives to fulfill itself'.[37] Teilhard describes this stream of consciousness and life in an early essay:

> This personal driving force is prior to and higher than free will; it is written into our character, into the rhythm of our thoughts, and into the crude surge of our passions; and it is life's heritage to us, it is the *constant evidence* in us of the *vast vital current*.[38]

By the time of writing *The Divine Milieu*, Teilhard modifies this interpretation of the *élan vital*, in keeping with his recognition of the limita-

---

[34] Hence Friedrich Nietzsche's assertion that 'there would be no Platonic philosophy at all if Athens had not possessed such beautiful youths'. *Twilight of the Idols*, §23, in *Twilight of the Idols/The Anti-Christ* (London: Penguin, 1990), p. 91.

[35] *Les Ennéades de Plotin*, trans. Marie-Nicolas Bouillet (3 vols.; Paris: Hachette, 1857–61). For contemporary study of Plotinus, see René Arnou, *Le Désir de Dieu dans la philosophie de Plotin* (Paris: Alcan, 1921); Paul Henry, «Bulletin critique des études plotiniennes (1929–31)», *NRT* 8 (1932), pp. 707–735; 9 (1933), pp. 785–803; 10 (1934), pp. 906–925.

[36] A.H. Armstrong, 'Beauty and the discovery of divinity in the thought of Plotinus', in *Plotinian and Christian Studies* (London: Variorum, 1979), XIX, p. 159.

[37] Grogin, *Bergsonian Controversy*, p. 75.

[38] 'Cosmic Life' (1916), *WW*, pp. 26–27.

tions of human intuition. The *élan vital* cannot be defined, he now suggests, in so confident a manner:

> Our mind is disturbed when we try to plumb the depths of the world beneath us. But it reels still more when we try to number the favourable chances which must coincide at every moment if the least of living things is to survive and to succeed in its tasks.[39]

In *The Divine Milieu*, Teilhard identifies the *élan vital* with a temporal locus which combines two qualities: 'interior development, through which our ideas and affections and our human and religious attitudes are gradually formed', and 'exterior success by which we always find ourselves at the exact point where the whole sum of the energies of the universe meet together to bring about in us the effect which God desires'.[40] The *élan vital* is manifested whenever these two factors coincide.

Human diminishment in suffering

Following his discussion of growth, Teilhard turns to consider the second and third categories of passion, which he defines as 'diminishment'. He conducts most of this discussion in the first person, describing the passion of diminishment as resulting from

> the hostile powers which laboriously obstruct our tendencies, hamper or deflect our progress towards greater-being, and thwart our real or apparent capacities for development[41]

External passivities of diminishment are those diminishments whose source lies outside us, and include various forms of chance, coincidence and misfortune. *Internal* passivities of diminishment are those which originate within us and which 'form the darkest element and the most despairingly useless years of our life'.[42] External passivities of diminishment require only brief discussion. In *The Human Phenomenon*, Teilhard describes external diminishments generically as 'evil in the form of disorder and failure'.[43] They deny human aspiration and human hope their objects: whereas action and growth are both positive developments of human life, diminishments quite simply diminish it.

[39] *DM*, p. 39.
[40] *DM*, p. 40.
[41] *DM*, p. 37.
[42] *DM*, p. 42.
[43] *HP*, p. 225.

Teilhard recognizes that providence may in some circumstances convert the negative effects of external diminishments into good. Suffering might divert human activity onto better objects or projects, as in the case of Job, 'whose final happiness was greater than his first', or direct it towards less material fields for its satisfaction. Exterior shocks are, moreover, indispensable in separating individuals from their customary routines.[44] Humanity is able to overcome external diminishments, and can benefit from doing so. Dietrich Bonhoeffer therefore states: 'False developments and failures do not make the world doubt the necessity of the course that it is taking, or of its development; they are accepted with fortitude and detachment as part of the bargain.'[45] As Jesus tells his disciples, occasions for stumbling are bound to arise.[46] Bergson writes in *Creative Evolution*: 'From the bottom to the top of the organized world we do indeed find one great effort; but most often this effort turns short, sometimes paralysed by contrary forces, sometimes diverted from what it should do by what it does, absorbed by the form it is engaged in taking, hypnotized by it as if by a mirror. Even in its most perfect works, though it seems to have triumphed over external resistances and also over its own, it is at the mercy of the materiality which it has had to assume.'[47] Teilhard would agree with Bergson's assessment of human progress, but not with his apparent conclusion that all forms of diminishment may be overcome by human means. Teilhard agrees that external diminishment may be overcome, but then describes another form of diminishment which cannot be transcended by human power.

This second type of diminishment encompasses more serious types of suffering: congenital natural failings, physical defects, and intellectual and moral weakness, as well as the various sources of physical disintegration which appear during the course of human life, including disease, psychological instability and old age.[48] These internal diminishments, in contrast with external ones, can be neither evaded nor overcome. Teilhard is acutely aware of inhabiting a universe 'immersed in accidents and fate, where everything can happen, even the most absurd'.[49] In *The Human Phenomenon*, Teilhard places these diminishments in the twin

[44] *HP*, p. 97.
[45] Dietrich Bonhoeffer, letter to Eberhard Bethge, 8 June 1944, in *Letters and Papers from Prison: The Enlarged Edition*, ed. Eberhard Bethge (London: SCM, 1986), p. 326.
[46] *HP*, p. 225; cf. Mt 18.7.
[47] Bergson, *Creative Evolution*, p. 134.
[48] *DM*, p. 42.
[49] Letter of 28 July 1947, *LLS*, p. 207.

categories of 'evils of decomposition' and 'evils in the form of solitude and anguish'.[50] The close attention that he gives to internal diminishment is in sharp contrast with what is often asserted to be his excessively optimistic view of human power and progress, and is developed with his own experiences already discussed in the background. Teilhard had endured and shared in sufficient suffering to realize that, sometimes, it does *not* bring indirect benefits, neither to society nor to the person it diminishes. Indeed, the long-term effects of suffering can sometimes be just as dreadful as its immediate ones, leaving physical and psychological scars on persons, communities and nations for generations. Teilhard states:

> We see diminishments, both in us and around us, which do not appear to be compensated by any advantage on any perceivable plane: premature deaths, stupid accidents, weaknesses affecting the highest reaches of our being. Under such blows, we do not move upward in any perceptible direction; we disappear or remain grievously diminished.[51]

The absurdity, from a human perspective, of internal diminishment, cannot be resolved by the providentialist theories used to account for growth and external diminishment. Frequently, the losses which internal diminishment brings 'do not seem to be compensated by any appreciable advantage, even spiritual'.[52] These contradictions can, however, be resolved in God. Indeed, the divine role in their resolution is analogous to its function in action: any resolution of the contradictions which internal diminishment poses implies the action of the absolute mediating current reality and future hope. Teilhard affirms: 'Christ gathers up for the life of tomorrow our stifled ambitions, our inadequate understandings, our uncompleted or clumsy but sincere endeavours.'[53]

Cosmologically, Teilhard's account of passion derives much from Aquinas, who at this point is indebted to the Neoplatonic tradition mediated to him via Augustine and Pseudo-Dionysius, which regards evil as a weakness and a deficiency of goodness rather than as a separate power opposing goodness.[54] There exists in this tradition a strong association of suffering with corporeal multiplicity and disunity. As Jacques Maritain states: 'It is in the order of things that man be involved in sorrow, suffering and death, because by his very essence he is involved in nature

---

[50] *HP*, p. 225.
[51] *DM*, p. 48.
[52] 'My Universe' (1924), *SC*, p. 73.
[53] 'The Struggle Against the Multitude' (1917), *WW*, p. 111.
[54] *ST*, IaIIae, q. 55, a. 3, resp.

which is corporeal, subjected to the change of production and destruc-tion.'[55] The negative effects of bad choices and bad actions in the world is unsurprising because they are grounded in a basic ontological defi-ciency in the human person, who occupies the very lowest position in the hierarchy of intelligent beings. The frequent failure of humanity to act morally is due to the weakness, or privation, of being and goodness from which it suffers. As already discussed, Teilhard employs this Neo-platonic ontology within a dynamic cosmological scheme, stating that 'by virtue of his very perfections, God cannot ordain that the elements of a world in process of growth — or at least of a fallen world in process of rising again — should avoid shocks and diminishments, even moral ones'.[56] In a footnote, Teilhard states that this is

> because [God's] perfections cannot run counter to the nature of things, and because a world, assumed to be progressing towards perfection, or 'rising upward', is of its nature precisely still partially disorganized.

Teilhard continues by pointing out that a world in which there was no trace or threat of evil would be a world already consummated, and in so doing removes some of the peculiarly modern burden of proof that is often supposed to rest on theists to provide religious sceptics with an explanation for the existence of evil and suffering in a world created and governed by God. Teilhard correctly perceives that fundamental axioms of faith and creation, above all the imperfection of humanity and the goodness of God, provide sufficiently convincing reasons to account for the effects of diminishment in the cosmos. Indeed, the presence of diminishment poses in many respects less of a theological problem than would its absence.

Teilhard distinguishes three stages of internal diminishment, and approaches them with full awareness of their repelling character:

> At the first approach of the diminishments we cannot hope to find God except by loathing what is coming upon us and doing our best to avoid it. The more we repel suffering at this moment, with our whole heart and our whole strength, the more closely we adhere to the heart and action of God.[57]

Diminishment inspires fear and horror, and cannot be embraced freely. As Stephen Brock notes: 'Passion undergone voluntarily is not passion

---

[55] Jacques Maritain, *Saint Thomas and the Problem of Evil* (Milwaukee, Mich.: Mar-quette University Press, 1942), p. 11.

[56] *DM*, pp. 46–47.

[57] *DM*, p. 45.

to the fullest degree; it retains something of the nature of action.'[58] Humanity is naturally inclined, therefore, to 'fight to the bitter end against every form of diminution and pain'.[59] The moment of *repulsion* must for this reason be the first moment of the human experience of the passion of diminishment. The fear and loathing which the contemplation of diminishment induces constitute as much a part of Christian life as does action. Indeed, only the person who cherishes the *vita activa* is able to recognize the full horror of the most acute diminishments of the *vita passiva*. Teilhard portrays the *vita passiva* as being essentially the diminishment of the *vita activa*. That the initial human response to internal diminishments is to repel them provides, moreover, one of the reasons for describing them as 'passions' rather than 'passivities'. Only the former term captures the element of emotional struggle intrinsic to suffering. The suffering being is not a disembodied object, but a human subject.

Efforts to repel diminishment might succeed for a finite time, but will not do so indefinitely: if the perpetual repulsion of diminishment were possible, then it would make no sense to regard it as diminishment. The second moment of the diminishment therefore occurs when *diminishment is victorious*. Teilhard states: 'At one moment or another, no matter how well we resist, we shall feel the constraining grip of the forces of diminishment, against which we have been fighting, gradually gaining mastery over the forces of life, and dragging us, physically vanquished, to the ground.'[60] The third and final moment of the passion of diminishment is therefore *resignation*, which Teilhard describes as follows:

> I can only unite myself to the will of God (as endured passively) when all my strength is spent, at the point where my activity, fully extended and straining towards better-being [le mieux-être] ... finds itself continually balanced by forces tending to halt or overwhelm me. Unless I do everything I can to advance or resist, I shall not find myself at the required point — I shall not submit to God as much as I might have done or as much as he wishes. If, on the contrary, I persevere courageously, I shall rejoin God across evil, deeper down than evil; I shall draw close to him; and at that moment the optimum of my 'communion in resignation' necessarily coincides (by definition) with the maximum of fidelity to the human task.[61]

[58] Stephen Brock, *Action and Conduct: Thomas Aquinas and the Theory of Action* (Edinburgh: T&T Clark, 1998), p. 158.

[59] 'The Sense of Humanity' (1929), *TF*, pp. 32–33.

[60] *DM*, pp. 45–46.

[61] *DM*, pp. 53–54.

Teilhard describes these moments of submission to God as 'partial deaths'. They are not the voluntary submission of the human will to the will of God, but the breaking of the human will in the experience of desolation. There is a resonance here with the dark night of the soul of John of the Cross, which Blondel discusses in his first paper for Teilhard:

> When St John of the Cross ... bids us cross the dark night, it is not a matter of his scorning physical reality, of his failing to appreciate aesthetic beauty or of his denying the needs of the heart; quite to the contrary, he wants first to eradicate us from all sensualism, all rationalism, all physicism, in short, rid us of the various forms of anthropomorphic egoism. For abnegation alone, he says, enjoys, possesses, and knows everything through a decentration and a transfer of the self over to God, such that one feels himself, in the elevated state of union, in divine contact with everything, but beyond the images and concepts which are, and always will be, too anthropomorphic in character.[62]

John, in presenting his exposition in two sections, distinguishes the unspiritual night of correction from the spiritual night of purification.[63] The unspiritual night of the soul alters human behaviour by affecting human emotion, and many people have experienced it. The spiritual night, on the other hand, lays the soul bare, purifies it, and prepares it for union with God. John believes that very few people experience the spiritual night. Teilhard does not specify how widely his concept of internal diminishment might be applied, but it seems clear that he considers it capable of describing a wider range of human experience than John's spiritual night, even though internal diminishment shares many of its characteristics. The only possible human response to the 'partial deaths' which internal diminishment brings is, despite their repelling nature, obedience and acceptance. Henri de Lubac states: 'Passivities — as the very word indicates — are such only when they become ours: ours, by virtue of an initial acceptance or assumption, a ratification by the will; or at any rate from the moment when, reflected on by us and echoing in us, they cease to exercise their pressure simply as brute force, and present themselves to us as an actual interior state and as an attitude of obedience and love proposed to our freedom. They then become in a true sense our passivities, without ceasing to be other than us; and the operation that God effects in us through them cannot be replaced by any

---

[62] Paper of 5 December 1919, *TBC*, p. 26.

[63] John of the Cross, *The Dark Night of the Soul* (London: Rider, 2002). This work forms strictly the final two books of a composite work *The Ascent of Mount Carmel and the Dark Night*, which locates purgation as the *culmination* of a spiritual movement.

activity that we ourselves could initiate.'[64] Blondel affirms in similar language: 'What we undergo passively, we become and we make be only by making this passion active and voluntary.'[65]

Internal diminishment implies, like action, the dependence of humanity on God. The orientation of humanity to the absolute implicit in action cannot be only for action. Receptivity to the absolute implies acceptance of everything that it gives, including passion. Indeed, both Teilhard and Blondel argue that suffering constitutes a more profound bond with the absolute than action. Blondel states that suffering 'keeps us from wanting the least in order to incline us to want the most', and that the 'heart of a person is measured by the acceptance they show for suffering', even though the 'one who faces it, desires and loves it, cannot at the same time keep from hating it'. Blondel continues: 'In the face of real grief, there are no beautiful theories that do not seem vain or absurd. As soon as we bring something living and suffering close to them, systems sound empty, thoughts remain ineffective. Suffering is what is new, unexplained, unknown, infinite, what cuts through life like a revealing sword.'[66] Teilhard conveys a similar sense of suffering as the experience of infinity in his depiction of it as an 'agonizing flight from the experiential zones'.[67] It is in dying to self that new life is gained. What is lost in the dark night is not so much the self as an illusion of self. The night of the soul disassembles the 'therapeutic self' created by human projections and replaces it with a 'more healthy sense of self'.[68] In sacrifice, the self receives back more than it has given, and in resignation a future hope is born.[69] Teilhard prays:

> At that last moment when I feel I am losing hold of myself and am absolutely passive in the hands of the great unknown energies that have formed me; in all those dark moments, O God, grant that I may understand that it is you (provided only my faith is strong enough) who are painfully parting the fibres of my being to penetrate to the very marrow of my substance and bear me away within yourself.[70]

---

[64] Henri de Lubac, *The Religion of Teilhard de Chardin* (London: Collins, 1970), p. 56.

[65] Maurice Blondel, *Action: Essay on a Critique of Life and a Science of Practice*, §459 (Notre Dame, Ind.: University of Notre Dame Press, 1984), p. 419.

[66] Blondel, *Action*, §§380–81, pp. 350–51.

[67] *DM*, p. 63.

[68] Denys Turner, *The Darkness of God: Negativity in Christian Mysticism* (Cambridge University Press, 1999), pp. 244, 229.

[69] Blondel, *Action*, §468, p. 426.

[70] *DM*, pp. 50–51.

Resignation is suffering *in Christo*. As the moment of death draws near, and the bond between body and soul is loosened, the soul ceases to act as the subject of its own bond and becomes assimilated into a higher, divine source of union. This dying to self in passive diminishment has been compared by Lee Robbins with the reassimilation of the transpersonal shadow into the subject in Jungian psychology, in that it forms a necessary stage in the spiritual growth and integration of both the individual and of its larger community.[71]

Diminishment gives to the human soul a new vision of the world and of its unity which affirms the existence of God, in whose hands the 'forces of diminishment have perceptibly become the tool that cuts, sculpts and polishes within us the stone which is destined to occupy a precise place in the heavenly Jerusalem'.[72] Teilhard says of God: 'As a result of his omnipotence encroaching upon our faith, events which show themselves experientially in our lives as pure loss will become an immediate factor in the union we dream of establishing with him.' This unification of the soul *in Deo* is brought about by a migration and a partial death, in which the soul is reduced to nothing in the other in an 'ecstasy which will save us from ourselves so that we be subordinated to God'. At this moment of the surrender of self, suffering souls 'end by adoring what they were struggling against'.[73] Teilhard portrays this moment using the image of Jacob wrestling with the angel, which is one that greatly inspired him and to which he refers in several essays. Jacob's opponent in the struggle, who is God, is unable to overpower him, and at daybreak Jacob does not allow God to depart without blessing him. Teilhard states: 'I shall only touch God in the world of matter when, like Jacob, I have been vanquished by him.'[74] Although Jacob struggles against the grip of his opponent, he also worships that grip.[75] His struggle is, in one sense, with God, but also in a larger sense with and on behalf of 'the multitude' or 'multiplicity', in other words, with the entire fallen human condition.[76] God transfigures the contradictions experienced by humanity in the struggle and resignation, repulsion and adoration, which form its life in the material world.

---

[71] Lee Robbins, 'Being in Darkness: A Jungian Commentary on Teilhard's "Passivities of Diminishment"', *Anima* 11, 1 (1984), pp. 17–23. This excellent article is written by a practising psychologist.

[72] *DM*, p. 49.

[73] *DM*, p. 35; cf. Gen 32.22–32.

[74] 'The Mass on the World' (1923), *HM*, p. 126.

[75] 'Cosmic Life' (1916), *WW*, p. 65.

[76] 'The Struggle Against the Multitude' (1917), *WW*, p. 112.

It is significant that Teilhard develops his theology of internal diminishment, informed by his own experience of suffering and persecution, in
the period prior to what many theologians have argued is the breakdown
of the 'plausibility structure' of theodicy in the face of the Nazi genocide
of the 1930s and 1940s.[77] He is not alone in this respect: Vladimir
Soloviev also offers extensive reflections on the topic of evil around the
same time in the *Three Conversations* of the final period of his life.[78]
Hans Urs von Balthasar states that Soloviev's work anticipates the apoc-
alypse and the Antichrist, and demurs that Teilhard's includes no equivalent.[79] It is correct that Teilhard does not reflect on the implications of the
Holocaust for future political society, being more concerned with the
implications for theology of the clash between fascism and communism,
as were most other Christian theologians of his generation and the following one. Teilhard nonetheless anticipates as much as Soloviev the
breakdown of the 'plausibility structure' developed to account for the
existence of evil. Balthasar writes as if Teilhard ends his account of passion with external diminishment. In fact, Teilhard offers an analysis of
suffering which includes levels of distinction between different forms
that are frequently omitted, and one which possesses convincing metaphysical foundations as well as emotional ones. As Donald MacKinnon
suggests, Teilhard goes some way towards grounding 'at a more personal
tragic depth our understanding of redemption'.[80] Teilhard provides, moreover, an account of human action that confronts humanity with the possibility that it might by its own actions protect the world from future totalitarian evil. This aspect of his response to suffering is similar to that of
Hannah Arendt. Both figures argue that tremendous responsibility rests
on humankind for the preservation of the shared world it inhabits. Teilhard so often defends the importance of creative action, and this is also
important for Arendt, who describes action as the 'actualization of the
human condition of natality' whose result is 'infinitely improbable'.[81]

Teilhard remained in China for almost the whole of the period
between 1932 and 1946, and was therefore far removed from the Euro-

---

[77] For discussion of this structure, see Brian Hebblethwaite, *Evil, Suffering and Religion* (London: SPCK, rev. edn, 2000), p. 13.

[78] Vladimir Soloviev, *War, Progress, and the End of History: Three Conversations,
including a Short Story of the Anti-Christ* (Herndon, Va.: Lindisfarne, 1990).

[79] Hans Urs von Balthasar, 'Soloviev', in *The Glory of the Lord: A Theological Aesthetics*, III (7 vols.; Edinburgh: T&T Clark, 1982–91), p. 290.

[80] Donald MacKinnon, 'Re-Review: Pierre Teilhard de Chardin's *Le Milieu divin*',
The Modern Churchman 25 (1983), pp. 49–53.

[81] Hannah Arendt, *The Human Condition* (University of Chicago Press, 1989), p. 178.

pean genocides of this dark era. He does, however, discuss the earlier massacres of Christians in Armenia, with which Jesuits had been confronted in the course of their missionary work in the region. There was, in particular, a sizeable Jesuit presence in Adana, a town situated close to Tarsus and the Mediterranean coast, in the vicinity of the modern border of Turkey and Syria, where the Lyons Province of the Society of Jesus possessed a house and their College of St Paul.[82] This was one of the areas of greatest turmoil in a troubled region: about 250,000 Armenians had been massacred in Turkey in the period 1894–96, and further genocides had been committed in the Russian part of Armenia in 1905. Killings took place in Adana itself in April 1909, whilst Teilhard was studying in Hastings, as part of the Iltihadist Young Turk uprising in which about 25,000 Armenians were killed.[83] In a letter to his parents, Teilhard comments: 'You can imagine that the East has caused much talk here ... especially Turkey. I don't think our missionaries have been harmed, not even in Adana. But a young Father whose whole family belongs to the Armenian Committee has had some tense moments of anxiety. His brother in Constantinople was expressly followed to be murdered and only escaped with great difficulty. The rest of his family is in Adana and he hasn't received word from them yet.'[84] As Teilhard's letter indicates, Europeans living in the region were by no means immune from Ottoman persecution. The boarding school, orphanage, clinic and half-constructed hospital of the Sisters of Saint Joseph of Lyons, also situated in Adana, had all been incinerated.[85] Teilhard and his colleagues were therefore already well aware of the inadequacies of the 'plausibility structure' constructed by some theologians to account for evil in the world, and this awareness pervades his own theology of passion.[86]

[82] Each of the four French Jesuit provinces took responsibility for missions in different regions. Lyons was entrusted with Armenia, Syria and Egypt. (*LE*, p. 7)

[83] For details, see Vahakn N. Dadrian, *The History of the Armenian Genocide: Ethnic Conflict from the Balkans to Anatolia to the Caucasus* (New York: Bergham, 6th rev. edn, 2004), pp. 179–84. This massacre preceded the somewhat better-known genocide of about 2.5 million people living in the region during the First World War, of whom about 1.5 million were Armenian and about 500,000 Greek.

[84] Letter of 26 April 1909, *LH*, p. 42. The footnote gives details of the Jesuit presence in Armenia. For a contemporary account of these genocides, see Anonymous, «L'Oeuvre de la 'Jeune Turquie': Notes de Constantinople», *Études* 118 (1909), pp. 199–235. Teilhard states that a subsequent anonymous article about Turkey in *Études* is by Guillaume de Jerphanion. (Letter of 5 Feburary 1913, *LP*, p. 57.) It seems likely that Jerphanion was also responsible for the earlier article.

[85] *LH*, p. 42, n. 1.

[86] An important comparative study of modern European mass murder is Robert Mel-

The Heart of Christ in the heart of the world

Teilhard describes humanity's participation in the passion of Christ as culminating in an 'impassioned unfolding, heavy with sorrow, in the arms of the Cross'. In attaining this point at which the world's suffering is gathered together, the soul becomes able to 'expand more freely' and to 'open itself, generously and tenderly — with and in Christ — to sympathy with all suffering, to "cosmic compassion"'.[87] Teilhard's theology of the cross is not one of quasi-legal expiation in which the sins of humanity are assumed by Christ or cancelled out by him. Christ on the cross shares, by contrast, in the suffering of humanity, which shares in the suffering of Christ through its internal diminishment. Blondel states: 'To live in God, one must allow the egoism of the old, the former, man to perish, and open oneself to the expanding, crucifying entry of a God who does not stoop down to our size, who would have us grow up to His, an increase beyond anything we could imagine had we not had the Revelation.'[88] The cross, being an instrument of suffering, breaks open Christ in order that broken humanity may be drawn into the heart of his substance, in which the true meaning of passion resides, so that it might share in that passion and in so doing be transformed and reformed by it.[89] The cross itself becomes thus anointed with the suffering of Christ and of humanity. Teilhard states:

> The Cross was placed on the crest of the road which leads to the highest peaks of creation. But, in the growing light of Revelation, its arms which at first were bare, show themselves to have put on Christ: 'Crux inuncta'. At first sight the bleeding body may seem funereal to us. Is it not from the night that it shines forth? But if we go nearer we shall recognize the flaming Seraph of Alvernia, whose passion and compassion are incendium mentis. Christians are asked to live, not in the shadow of the Cross, but in the fire of its creative action.[90]

The Seraph of Alvernia is the angel who marked Francis of Assisi with the stigmata, the five wounds of Christ, which killed him two years later.

---

son, *Revolution and Genocide: On the Origins of the Armenian Genocide and the Holocaust* (University of Calgary Press, 1992). De Lubac notes that Adolf Hitler, in his speech to Nazi military leaders of 22 April 1939 concerning Poland, challenged them with the question: 'Who still talks today about the extermination of the Armenians?' (*LH*, p. 42, n. 1.)

[87] 'Cosmic Life', p. 68.
[88] Paper of 19 December 1919, *TBC*, p. 44.
[89] Letter of 23 August 1929, *LLZ*, p. 95.
[90] *DM*, p. 64.

Teilhard says of the saint: 'Francis is so dear and close to me! I believe he assists me in my difficulties and blesses my work.'[91] A footnote to the newly revised translation of *The Divine Milieu* describes this incident on the mountain by stating that Francis 'had a vision of the heavenly figure' of the Seraph.[92] This fails to grasp the full intent of the passage, however, which is to portray the sharing of humanity in the passion of Christ. Teilhard is clearly drawing on Bonaventure's *Life of Saint Francis* here because he describes the 'passion and compassion' which the Seraph inflicts on Francis using Bonaventure's striking phrase 'incendium mentis'. This means not the 'embrace of the spirit' but the 'conflagration of the soul'. The latter rendering seems much closer both to Bonaventure's meaning and to the intent of the fire imagery so often employed by Teilhard in his spiritual oeuvre. In the words of Bonaventure:

> While Francis was praying on the mountainside, he saw a Seraph with six fiery and shining wings descend from the height of heaven. And when in swift flight the Seraph had reached a spot in the air near the man of God, there appeared between the wings the figure of a man crucified, with his hands and feet extended in the form of a cross and fastened to a cross... Eventually he understood by a revelation from the Lord that ... he was to be totally transformed into the likeness of Christ crucified, not by the martyrdom of his flesh, but by the *fire of his love consuming his soul*.
>   As the vision disappeared, it left in his heart a marvellous ardour and imprinted on his body markings that were no less marvellous. Immediately the marks of nails began to appear in his hands and feet just as he had seen a little before in the figure of the man crucified.[93]

Francis had sought martyrdom during the Fifth Crusade, even entering the enemy camp to preach the Gospel and appearing before Sultan Melek-el-Kamel, who refused, to Francis's chagrin, to put him to death. The *incendium mentis*, the 'fire of divine love consuming his soul', therefore becomes an alternative living passion granted to Francis by the vision of God.

The divine love of Christ is embodied and expressed most completely in his Sacred Heart, to which Teilhard was devoted from childhood until

---

[91] Gabriel M. Allegra, *My Conversations with Teilhard de Chardin on the Primacy of Christ, Peking, 1942–1945* (Chicago: Franciscan Herald Press, 1970), p. 55.

[92] *DM*, p. 64, n. 61.

[93] Bonaventure, *The Life of Saint Francis*, 13.3–4, in *The Soul's Journey into God. The Tree of Life. The Life of St Francis,* ed. Ewert Cousins (Mahwah, NJ: Paulist, 1978), pp. 305–306, emphasis added. The crucial phrase reads 'sed per incendium mentis totum in Christi crucifixi similitudinem transformandum', and is discussed in 'Rite expiatis: Encyclical of Pius XI on St Francis of Assisi', 30 April 1926, §28, *PE* III, p. 299, promulgated just a few months before Teilhard commenced work on *The Divine Milieu*.

death: 'A mysterious patch of crimson and gold in the very centre of the Saviour's breast.'[94] Teilhard states:

> It is in the Sacred Heart that the conjunction of the Divine and the cosmic has taken place... There lies the power that, from the beginning, has attracted me and conquered me... All the later development of my interior life has been nothing other than *the evolution of that seed*.[95]

The modern origins of this devotion lie in the visions of the French nun Marguerite-Marie Alacoque at Paray-le-Monial in the 1670s. The Teilhard family possessed close associations with the cult: Teilhard's sister was named Marguerite-Marie, and Paray is situated in the Bourgogne about 70 miles from the family home near Clermont-Ferrand.[96] The national prominence of the Sacred Heart cult increased, moreover, during the first decades of Teilhard's life. Pilgrimage to Paray proliferated in the period following the nation's traumatic defeat in the Franco-Prussian War, and the basilica of the Sacré-Coeur was constructed between 1876 and 1910 on the Butte de Montmartre overlooking Paris to atone for the massacre of the Commune which concluded the war. The Sacred Heart cult possessed close historic associations with the French nation, and so its profile grew once more during the First World War, when the Heart became the symbol of national unity in suffering.[97] During this war, millions of families 'enthroned' the Heart in their homes, army camps were consecrated to the Heart, and medals bearing its emblem were struck and worn by troops at the front. This and other catholic symbols were conspicuously deployed to build a national spiritual identity — the *union sacrée* — in opposition to the perceived corruption of Ger-

---

[94] 'The Heart of Matter' (1950), *HM*, p. 43.

[95] *J*, 17 October 1919, cahier VI, quoted in Robert Faricy, *All Things in Christ: Teilhard de Chardin's Spirituality* (London: Fount, 1981), pp. 13–14.

[96] Faricy, *All Things in Christ*, pp. 14–16, quotes letters written by Teilhard to his mother Berthe in the period 1914–16 that indicate the central place of devotion to the Sacred Heart in their family; cf. letter of 19 May 1908, *LE*, p. 246. See also Faricy's later article 'The Heart of Christ in the Spirituality of Teilhard de Chardin', *Gregorianum* 69 (1988), pp. 261–77.

[97] For discussion of the Sacred Heart cult in the early period of Teilhard's life, see Annette Becker, *War and Faith: The Religious Imagination in France, 1914–1930* (Oxford: Berg, 1998), pp. 85–96; and for its wider political importance, Ivan Strenski, *Contesting Sacrifice: Religion, Nationalism and Social Thought in France* (University of Chicago Press, 2002), pp. 25–27. A comprehensive study, itself indicative of the tremendous importance attached to the devotion, is Auguste Hamon, *Histoire de la dévotion du Sacré-Coeur* (5 vols.; Paris: Beauchesne, 1939). See also Jean-Vincent Bainvel, *Devotion to the Sacred Heart: The Doctrine and its History* (London: Burns, Oates & Washbourne, trans. from 5th edn, 1924).

man Lutheranism.[98] Teilhard expresses reservations about this popular cult however, «célébrée comme si la Patrie primait l'Église»[99], in a letter to his cousin written shortly before she departed on pilgrimage to Paray: 'Our Lord's heart is indeed ineffably beautiful and satisfying; it exhausts all reality and answers all the soul's needs. The very thought of it is almost more than the mind can encompass. Why must this devotion be ruined by so much mawkishness and false sentimentality? ... It pains me to see pictures of it scattered about here, there and everywhere.'[100]

Teilhard responds by affirming, in line with standard catholic teaching, that devotion to the Sacred Heart must always direct attention beyond itself to its proper reference, who is the person of Christ.[101] Heart imagery impels Teilhard towards a more physical and emotive theology of the passion than that suggested by an exclusive focus on the 'wood' of the cross as providing an instrument of suffering. Christopher Mooney states that the Sacred Heart 'enabled Teilhard to "materialize" what was divine, to bring into a single concrete focus both his attraction for matter and his adoration of the person of Christ'.[102] The Heart bore added personal significance for Teilhard because it was the emblem which Ignatius Loyola had left to the Jesuit movement. In his first short story 'The Picture', Teilhard describes a vision of the Heart. The image to which the title refers portrays Christ offering his Heart to humankind, and in the course of the narrative the outline of his figure becomes indistinct, radiant, and vibrant, with the vibrance then filling the entire surrounding space. Teilhard affirms that these properties 'seemed to emanate from Christ, and above all from his heart'.[103] The Heart is «comme l'élément à l'ignifier».[104] This emanating fire later becomes the 'divine milieu', which Teilhard describes specifically as a *breast*: 'It has therefore the properties of a centre, that is, above all, the absolute

---

[98] Literary examples include Joseph Lahitton, *Le Chemin de croix national pour le temps de la guerre* (Mont de Marsan: Legrand, 1914); Henri Massis, *Le Sacrifice* (Paris: Plon, 1917).

[99] *J*, 16 February 1916, p. 36.

[100] Letter to Marguerite Teillard-Chambon, 31 March 1917, *MM*, p. 192.

[101] On this theme, see Karl Rahner, 'Devotion to the Sacred Heart', *TI* III, pp. 321–52. See also Annice Callahan, *Karl Rahner's Spirituality of the Pierced Heart: A Reinterpretation of Devotion to the Sacred Heart* (Lanham, Md.: University Press of America, 1985); Giorgio Buccellati, 'Ascension, Parousia, and the Sacred Heart: Structural Correlations', *Communio (US)* 25 (1998), pp. 69–103.

[102] Christopher Mooney, *Teilhard de Chardin and the Mystery of Christ* (London: Collins, 1966), pp. 27–28.

[103] 'Christ in the World of Matter' (1916), *HU*, pp. 43–44.

[104] Retreat note of 20 July 1922, *NR*, p. 96.

and final power to unite (and consequently to complete) all beings within its breast [au sein de lui-même].'[105]

This intimacy in universality is an ancient quality of Johannine heart spirituality: the Beloved Disciple reclines close to the breast (στῆθος) of Jesus at the Last Supper, and it is in the fourth gospel that one of the soldiers beholding the crucifixion pierces Jesus's side (πλευρόν), out of which flows blood and water.[106] Christ's prophecy that out of his heart or belly (κοιλία) shall flow streams of living water motivates a rich tradition of cosmic christology with a pronounced physical dimension: the water becomes an allegory for the four rivers which emanate out of Eden and water the earth, and Christ is identified with the 'Stricken Rock with streaming side' at Horeb in the wilderness which quenches the desperate thirst of the Israelites.[107] Teilhard probably became acquainted with these traditions via Cistercian mystics like Angela of Foligno, who were instrumental in propagating Sacred Heart devotion.[108] In opposition to the sentimentalism of the popular wartime cult, they preserve a doctrine of the Heart of Jesus 'clearly directed towards worship of Christ — of Christ considered in the ways in which he influences the whole mystical body, and in consequence, the whole human social organism'.[109]

Teilhard accepts a standard theology of the Passion that Christ, through his death, substitutes himself for humanity[110] and takes its sufferings upon himself. He nevertheless objects to a purely expiatory account, amplifying in opposition to this the atonement principle that physical evil can conquer moral evil. He says of Christ:

> On Calvary He is still, and primarily, *the centre* on which all earthly sufferings converge and in which they are *all assuaged*... The only way we can appreciate the immensity of his agony is to see in it an anguish that reflects every anguish ever experienced, a 'cosmic' suffering. During his Passion, Christ felt that he bore upon his soul, alone and battered, the weight of all human sorrows — in a fantastic synthesis no words can express. All these he took to himself, and all these he suffered.[111]

---

[105] *DM*, p. 76. The newly revised English translation loses this suggestive and crucial association by rendering Teilhard's final phrase simply as 'within itself'.

[106] Jn 13.25, 19.34; cf. retreat note of 23 October – 1 November, *NR*, p. 316.

[107] Jn 7.38; cf. Gen 2.10–14, Ex 17.6; cf. George Hugh Bourne, 'Lord, enthroned in heavenly splendour', *New English Hymnal*, 296 (Norwich: Canterbury Press, 1995). See Michel Fédou, «Origène et le langage du coeur», *Christus* 190 (2001), pp. 58–62.

[108] For details, see Michel Rondet, «La Tradition médiévale», *Christus* 190 (2001), pp. 63–66, and the remainder of this issue; cf. *DM*, p. 78.

[109] 'The Awaited Word' (1940), *TF*, p. 98.

[110] 'The Priest' (1918), *WW*, p. 221.

[111] 'Cosmic Life' (1916), *WW*, p. 67.

Christ assumes on the cross all the physical sufferings of the world. Teilhard's language in evoking Christ's participation in humanity's physical suffering is strikingly similar to that of Hans Urs von Balthasar. Nevertheless, Balthasar's description is more anthropological, identifying the Heart as the 'real centre of spiritual and corporeal man' and as the 'very centre of God' by means of an *analogy* with the human heart.[112] Teilhard's approach, by contrast, is not only christological but cosmological: Christ shares the suffering of humanity and the whole cosmos, which is groaning in travail with him in expectation of its redemption.[113] By virtue of this transforming work

> the most obscure and hateful part of the world becomes the most luminous and divine of all. Beneath the countless servitudes and disappointments of the world the formative power of Christ can be discerned, moulding us and substituting himself for us.[114]

This is an active, physical substitution in which Christ becomes really present in the suffering of the world. The notion that the suffering of humanity is subsumed into the suffering of Christ is lucidly expressed by another Jesuit, Gerald Manley Hopkins, in his poem 'The Wreck of the Deutschland'.[115] Its narrative unfolds the drowning in a shipwreck of five Franciscan nuns, and number symbolism conveys, in the words of John Riches, 'the sacrifice of Christ imprinted upon nature': 'Five! The finding and sake / And cipher of suffering Christ.' Hopkins exclaims: 'Joy fall to thee, father Francis, / Drawn to the Life that died; / With the gnarls of the nails in thee, niche of the lance, his / Lovescape crucified.'[116] The imagery of Christ's passion evokes the suffering which

---

[112] Hans Urs von Balthasar, *Heart of the World* (San Francisco: Ignatius, 1979), p. 14.

[113] Rom 8.22. When Teilhard refers to 'the heart of matter', he means to describe the physical presence of the sacrifice of Christ in the world. The second definite article of the French title *Le Coeur de la matière* is sometimes retained in translation, but Teilhard states that he does not intend in any way to promote the eponymous novel of Graham Greene, which he describes as 'a study in despair'. (Letter of 10 October 1948, *LTF*, p. 190.)

[114] 'My Universe' (1924), *SC*, p. 73.

[115] For the affinity of Teilhard with Hopkins, see Günter Schiwy, *Teilhard de Chardin: sein Leben und seine Zeit*, I (2 vols., Munich: Kösel, 1981), p. 157.

[116] 'The Wreck of the Deutschland', lines 169–170, 177–80, in *Gerald Manley Hopkins*, ed. Catherine Phillips (Oxford University Press, 1995), pp. 103–104. See John Riches, 'Balthasar's Sacramental Spirituality and Hopkins' Poetry of Nature: The Sacrifice Imprinted upon Nature', in *Christ: The Sacramental Word*, eds. David Brown and Ann Loades (London: SPCK, 1996), pp. 168–80; David A. Downes, *The Ignatian Personality of Gerard Manley Hopkins* (Lanham, Md.: University Press of America, 1990); J. Robert Barth, *The Sacramental Vision of Gerald Manley Hopkins* (Regina: Campion College, 1989).

diminishment brings to the human person, who literally recollects and puts on that passion. This method of imagining the Passion is classically Ignatian. As Philip Endean reminds the reader: 'The truth of the gospel is there not only to be "reflected on", but also to be "reflected", as in a mirror; in Ignatius's Spanish, the one word may have both significances.'[117]

Reflection provides a means of scriptural meditation on the material world that fully engages human feelings in the drama of practical living and the search to participate in the activity of God in Christ in the world. Meditation does not consist of private inner reflection but emerges from humanity's active and passive engagements with the material world. The perception of the sacrifice of Christ in nature that forms part of Teilhard's theology of passion possesses at least one ancient precedent in the theology of Justin Martyr.[118] Justin perceives the cross of Christ in the material world: in the mast of a ship, in a farmer's plough, in tools of industry, in governmental insignia, and above all, in the human figure and face. He refers to the *Timaeus* doctrine of the Demiurge forming the two parts of the soul of the world, 'one against the other, the middle of one to the middle of the other, like a great cross' and being placed around the extremities of the cosmos to bind it together, and gives this a specifically Christian interpretation.[119] In Justin's view, the cross preserves the consistency of the cosmos in an all-embracing unity. The Sacred Heart of Christ in matter performs a similar function in Teilhard's cosmology. The Universal Christ emerges 'from the Cross' but is 'born from an expansion of the Heart'.[120]

Death: the end of passion

The culmination of life is the passion of sharing in the death of Christ. Teilhard states: 'It is then, most of all, that we must *appear* to be entirely lost, with *nothing* (of the terrestrial order) that our experience could recognize as compensation. When such a death, slow or rapid, takes place in us, we must open our hearts wide to the hope of union:

---

[117] Philip Endean, *Karl Rahner and Ignatian Spirituality* (Oxford University Press, 2001), p. 242. See also Christoph Théobald, «Une manière ignatienne de faire la théologie», *NRT* 119 (1997), pp. 375–96.

[118] Justin Martyr, *First Apology*, ANF I, 55; 60, pp. 181, 183.

[119] Plato, *Timaeus*, 36c–d, *Works* VII, pp. 70–73.

[120] 'The Awaited Word', p. 99.

never, if we so will it, will the animating power of the world have mastered us so fully.'[121] The final and total internal diminishment of life is death, in which 'all our slow or swift diminishments flow out and merge'. Materially, death is the point at which the body is finally dissolved into total multiplicity, but spiritually is the moment of ultimate consummation and unification. Teilhard affirms of death:

> It is the sum and type of all the forces which diminish us, and against which we must fight without being able to hope for a personal, direct and immediate victory. Now the great victory of the Creator and Redeemer, within our Christian perspectives, is to have transformed what is in itself a universal power of diminishment and extinction into an essentially life-giving factor. God must, in some way or other, make room for himself, hollowing us out and emptying us, if he is finally to penetrate into us. And to assimilate us in him, he must break the molecules of our being to recast and remould us. The function of death is to provide the necessary entrance into our inmost selves. It will make us undergo the required dissociation. It will put us into the state organically needed if the divine fire is to descend upon us. And in that way its fatal power to decompose and dissolve will be harnessed to the most sublime operations of life. What was, by nature, empty and void, a return to plurality, can become, in any human existence, fullness and unity in God.[122]

At the ultimate kenotic, self-surrendering moment of death, humanity becomes open to the transforming power of Christ. Only in sharing in the self-emptying passion of Christ can death be followed by resurrection. Teilhard affirms that humankind must 'overcome death by finding God in it'.[123] He states in an early essay: 'Only one effort, and it is one made possible by confidence in Christ, is worth making. It may be expressed thus: "to believe so resolutely in the power (*vertu*) of death that we can cause life to arise from the blackest depths of its shadows".'[124] Although death is, as Henri de Lubac states, the 'perfect passivity', it is equally the 'door that opens onto transfiguration'.[125]

Teilhard reflects on the nature of death during the course of his correspondence with Blondel, who had stated in *L'Action* that death 'transports the one who loves into what he loves and what is loved into what is loving'.[126] In his first paper to Teilhard, however, Blondel critically

---

[121] 'My Universe' p. 73.
[122] *DM*, pp. 43, 49–50.
[123] *DM*, p. 43.
[124] 'Operative Faith' (1918), *WW*, p. 242.
[125] De Lubac, *Religion of Teilhard de Chardin*, p. 56.
[126] Blondel, *Action*, §382, p. 351.

comments of the essays of Teilhard's that he has received: 'We have to give up the whole of creation for the precious Pearl, to die in the world to be nourished by a new life. Hence the dark night which the soul must cross, without a smooth transit from matter to spirit... The test, renunciation and abnegation are not necessary for the sake of penitence alone; they are essential in light of man's (and through man, the universe's) destiny to attain deification.'[127] Teilhard makes clear in his response to Blondel his fundamental agreement with Blondel's position: that the 'completion of the world is only consummated through a death, a "night", a reversal, an ex-centration, and a quasi-depersonalisation of the monads'.[128] Teilhard in fact gives diminishment greater prominence by the time of writing *The Divine Milieu* than Blondel affords it in *L'Action*. Moreover, although Blondel accounts for suffering existentially, he does not normally conceive it in an explicitly christological context. In *The Divine Milieu*, by contrast, Teilhard considers the transfiguration of death, which encompasses both 'partial' deaths and final physical death, as possible only in the passion of Christ, which enables the transition of the soul to new life:

> Death causes us to lose our footing completely in ourselves so as to deliver us over to the powers of heaven and earth. This is its final terror — but it is also, for the mystic, the climax of his bliss: it is our final entry, there to remain for ever, into the milieu that dominates, that carries us off, that consumes.[129]

In death, the human soul enters into Christ and thereby into a principle of spiritual unity greater than itself:

> For a being, to die normally means to sink back into the Multiple, but it can also be for it the reshaping that is indispensable to its entry under the dominion of a higher soul. The bread we eat appears to be decomposed within us, but it nevertheless becomes our flesh. Could there not also be dissociations in the course of which the elements would never cease to be dominated by a unity that breaks them up only to give them a new form? In every union the dominated term becomes one with the dominant only by first ceasing to be itself. In the case of the definitive union with God in Omega, we can see that if the world is to be divinised it must, in each one of us and in its totality, lose its visible form. From the Christian point of view that, in virtue of the death of Christ, is the life-giving function of human death.[130]

---

[127] Paper of 5 December 1919, *TBC*, p. 26.
[128] Paper of 12 December 1919, *TBC*, p. 31.
[129] 'The Mystical Milieu' (1917), *WW*, p. 133.
[130] 'My Universe', p. 63.

The human soul, in dying to the world following its growth, external diminishment and internal diminishment, becomes separated from its own bodily substance, which thus loses its human form and is recast into part of the divine substance of Christ.

4. SUBSTANCE

Teilhard's prime metaphysical concern in his early work is to understand how the material universe, existing in a state of plurality and multiplicity, can possess the consistency and coherence needed to make action and passion possible. He is opposed to the *materialist illusion* of regarding the 'elements of analysis as "more real" that the terms of synthesis'.[1] Matter can only be given consistency by the action on it of an external unifying power, and how this power acts requires theological explanation. The origin of the unifying power cannot, Teilhard argues, be located within the cosmos — such a cosmology would amount to immanentism and pantheism — but must subsist outside it. Opposition to materialist cosmology persists in Teilhard's later thought, in which he envisages matter to be subordinated to intellect as part of a 'tri-zonal structure' of reality comprising elements, substances, and thought.[2] Matter, in other words, occupies the lowest level in a hierarchy of being, beneath substances and spiritual principles. Teilhard employs the image of wax to illustrate how matter persists even though its form is changed by these higher principles. Matter contains infinite potential within itself, being an 'ever plastic wax, that can indefinitely be remodelled or recast by our hands'.[3] This analogy could well be derived from Justin Martyr, who identifies the ultimate forming principle of matter thus:

> God indeed occupies the position of an artificer, to wit, a potter; and matter occupies the place of clay, or wax, or some such thing. That, then, which is formed of matter, be it an image or a statue, is destructible; but the matter itself is indestructible, such as clay or wax, or any other such kind of matter.[4]

Teilhard evokes, in other places, cosmology similar to that of the Cambridge Platonist Ralph Cudworth in referring to the 'real internal plasticity' of molecules.[5] Such descriptions depict the mutability of unformed matter, but equally suggest that matter can be formed and reformed by human

---

[1] 'How I Believe' (1934)', *CE*, p. 105.
[2] 'The Evolution of Responsibility' (1951), *AE*, p. 208.
[3] 'Action and Activation' (1945), *SC*, pp. 176–77.
[4] Justin Martyr, 'Fragments on the Resurrection', §6, *ANF* I, p. 296.
[5] *MPN*, p. 28; cf. Ralph Cudworth, *The True Intellectual System of the Universe*, I, iii.37, §§5, 23 (Stuttgart: Frommann, 1964), pp. 150, 167.

action and passion. Action and passion, being grounded in the absolute, do not themselves, however, provide the actual source of the substantial unity of matter. That power is given to the cosmos ultimately by God.

Any account of the unity of the cosmos therefore needs to be grounded in the effect of divine action on it, both directly and via human agency. The category of substance is too often employed for the purely philosophical purpose of establishing metaphysics as a self-authenticating body of truth independent of the theological realm. In Teilhard's cosmology, however, substance becomes a profoundly theological concept. His approach is quite different from that of theologians hostile to metaphysics. John Milbank, for instance, asserts that any kind of metaphysical theology must be 'evacuated' and 'overcome' on the grounds that metaphysics compromises proper theological goals and method.[6] From this perspective, any concern with questions of substance, nature and spirit is likely to be regarded as undermining theology. In Teilhard's view, however, metaphysics prepares the way for theology by posing questions to which the only convincing response is a theological one. Theology engages with the aporia, or gaps, left in purportedly all-encompassing philosophical discourse not by annihilating the discourse which generates those aporia, but by demonstrating the necessity for their solution of the revelation of God in Christ.

The bond of substance

The intellectual origins of Teilhard's metaphysics of substance are clearly identified in a paper from Maurice Blondel, in which the latter refers to the correspondence between Gottfried Leibniz and the Jesuit teacher Bartolomaeus Des Bosses that had provided the topic for his *thèse secondaire* at the Sorbonne.[7] Blondel's supervisor, Émile Boutroux,

---

[6] John Milbank, *The Word Made Strange: Theology, Language, and Culture* (Oxford: Blackwell, 1997), pp. 49–50, 110–11.

[7] Maurice Blondel, *De vinculo substantiali et de substantia composita apud Leibnitium* (Paris: Alcan, 1893); trans. *Le Lien substantiel et la substance composée d'après Leibniz* (Louvain: Nauwelaerts, 1972). See Christiane Frémont, *L'Être et la relation; avec trente-sept lettres de Leibniz au R.P. Des Bosses* (Paris: Vrin, 2nd edn, 1999). An abridged translation is G.W. Leibniz, 'Correspondence with Des Bosses', in *Philosophical Papers and Letters*, ed. Leroy E. Loemker (Dordrecht: Reidel, 1969), pp. 596–617. The purpose of the shorter *thèse secondaire*, required for the *doctorat d'état*, was to expound a historical aspect of the *thèse principale*. Until the beginning of the twentieth century, the *thèse secondaire* had to be produced in Latin. For a useful summary of the modern history of the structure of degrees in French higher education, including the dif-

had edited Leibniz's *Monadology*,[8] but Blondel states that he selected his theme as early as 1880, on graduating from lycée and entering Dijon University, where Henry Joly was delivering a course on Leibniz. The correspondence between Leibniz and Des Bosses commences as a discussion about the nature of eucharistic consecration, and in the course of their exchanges the theory of the *vinculum*, or bond, is developed to explain the nature of eucharistic substance. Moreover, as Leibniz's concept of the *vinculum* evolves into that of the *vinculum substantiale*, it begins to acquire a new function as a component of his monadology intended to account for the existence and preservation of all substances in the world. Leibniz did not develop these insights systematically in any of his works between 1706, when the correspondence began, and his death in 1716 which ended it. This was quite possibly because he did not feel entirely happy with it.[9] Blondel, in contrast, argues in a paper for Teilhard that the *vinculum substantiale* is linked intimately with the Incarnation, which he proclaims to be the 'touchstone of a true cosmology, a metaphysics complete within itself':

> The question raised by Leibniz and Des Bosses concerning transubstantiation during the Eucharist leads us to conceive of Christ, without detriment to the constituent monads, as the bond which makes substantiation possible, the vivifying agent for all creation: *vinculum perfectionis*.[10]

Blondel considered the *vinculum substantiale* concept to be of profound metaphysical importance, and regarded Leibniz's failure to appraise its implications fully to be the principal shortcoming of his philosophy:

> Malgré tant d'efforts pour faire de son *vinculum* un sur-être, un vivifiant, un *uniens quid*, Leibniz n'a guère enfanté qu'un mort-né, moins encore, un mot neuter, une sorte d'agrafe, quelque chose d'extrinsèque et de dépendant à la fois; alors qu'il lui eût fallu *une transcendance immanente* à tout ce qu'elle attire, anime et associe du dedans, une sorte d'ébauche de bonté et de perfection. En cela, il retombe encore sous le joug de conceptions qu'il avait cependant voulu et cru dépasser, mais toujours en demeurant à mi-chemin de la libération.[11]

---

ferences between the *doctorat d'université* and the prestigious *doctorat d'état*, see 'Philosophy and the French education system', in Gary Gutting, *French Philosophy in the Twentieth Century* (Cambridge University Press, 2001), pp. 391–93.

[8] G.W. Leibniz, *La Monadologie*, ed. Émile Boutroux (Paris: C. Delagrave, 1881).

[9] E.J. Aiton, *Leibniz: A Biography* (Bristol: Adam Hilger, 1985), pp. 330–32. For the scholastic origins of the concept, see A. Boehm, *Le* vinculum substantiale *chez Leibniz: ses origines historiques*, Études de philosophie médiévale 26 (Paris: Vrin, 1938).

[10] Paper of 5 December 1919, *TBC*, p. 23.

[11] Maurice Blondel, *Une énigme historique: le* vinculum substantiale *d'après Leibniz et l'ébauche d'un réalisme supérieur* (Paris: Beauchesne, 1930), pp. 130–31, emphasis

Blondel argues that neither correspondent recognized the full significance of the doctrine:

> Ni Des Bosses, ni Leibniz lui-même n'ont accordé à la perspective entr'ouverte par le *vinculum* l'importance qu'elle pourrait et qu'elle devrait prendre s'il fallait réorganiser toute la philosophie première en fonction de cette doctrine qui cependant n'est rien si elle rien est l'aboutissement et le couronnement.[12]

The action of the *vinculum substantiale* extends far beyond the Eucharist: «C'est donc la nature entière et toute la métaphysique qui est mise en question par la théorie du *vinculum*.» Blondel argues that this theory responds successfully to Augustine's challenge of providing the necessary conditions for the '"solidification" of the creature', a solidity which, Augustine insists, must be derived from divine truth: 'et stabo atque solidabor in te, in forma mea, veritate tua'.[13] In the specific case of the human self, the *vinculum* is the entity which holds together body and soul in union. Thus John Smith, the Cambridge Platonist, asserts:

> That which determines the Soul to this Body more then that, must be some subtile vinculum that knits and unites it to it in a more Physical way, which therefore Proclus sometimes calls πνευματιχὸν ὄχημα τῆς ψυχῆς, a spiritual kind of vehicle, whereby corporeal impressions are transferr'd to the Mind, and the dictates and decrees of that are carried back again into the Body to act and move it.[14]

---

added: 'Despite so much effort to make with his bond a superior being, a vivifier, a single explanation, Leibniz brought forth scarcely more than a stillborn, even less, a neutral expression, a sort of peg, something simultaneously extrinsic and dependent; whereas he needed to produce a transcendence immanent to all that it causes, animates and binds together from inside, a sort of form of goodness and perfection. In so doing, he falls again under the conceptual yoke that he has wished and believed himself to have surpassed, yet still remains halfway to liberation.'

[12] Blondel, *Une énigme historique,* p. 82. 'Neither Des Bosses nor Leibniz himself gave to the perspective half-opened by the *vinculum* the importance that it could and should assume if it is necessary to reorganize all first philosophy as a function of this doctrine, which is nothing if not its goal and coronation.'

[13] Paper of 19 December 1919, *TBC*, p. 38; cf. Augustine, *Confessions*, XI.xxx (2 vols.; London: Heinemann, 1912), p. 280: 'Then shall I find stability and solidity in you, in your truth which imparts form to me.' Wayne Hankey, *Cent ans de néoplatonisme en France: une brève histoire philosophique*, Collection Zêtêsis (Paris: Vrin, 2004), pp. 154–72, presents the immanentism and Augustinianism of Blondel's *L'Action* as preparing ground for twentieth century French Neoplatonism. Neoplatonic themes are most obvious in Blondel's shorter Latin thesis on Leibniz, not least because it is rooted in a concern to understand the materiality of the world that is absent from *L'Action*, but the content of the shorter thesis did not become nearly so widely known.

[14] John Smith, Discourse 4: 'Of the Immortality of the Soul', IX, in *Select Discourses* (Cambridge: John Hayes, 1673), pp. 109–110.

Fundamental in Teilhard's theology to maintaining the bond between body and soul is the dwelling of the human soul *in Christo*. Indeed the whole of the created order exists *in Christo,* or *in Christo Iesu*, by virtue of its dependence on the human soul for its formation and reformation.[15] Ferdinand Prat, quoting Adolf Deissmann, states that this phrase 'characterizes the relation of the Christian to Jesus Christ as a kind of local presence in the spiritual (mystical) [pneumatischen] Christ'.[16] This notion of the human soul dwelling *in Christo* is a reversal of the Augustinian rhetoric of the human soul as a private inner space of memory and thought, an '*other* in the self' within which Christ dwells and which is metaphysically opposed to the external world.[17] Teilhard believes, in contrast with Augustine, that the opposite relation exists between Christ and creation: the whole created order dwells in Christ. The notion that Christ's presence in the world could be understood as contained within individual human souls appears a strange one indeed when compared with the cosmic christology of Paul and many of the early Church fathers, who believe that Christ is the head of the entire created order.

Teilhard identifies a similarity between the *vinculum* which binds together the human soul and its body, and the links which 'control, in the world, the affinities of the elements in the building up of "natural" wholes'.[18] This organic imagery is more than an analogy. The *vinculum substantiale* is not just a bond between the soul and its body, but subsists spiritually beyond the self. Indeed, the *vinculum* is able to dwell within the self only because it exists beyond the self. It is therefore a bond of *substance* in the sense that it posits the *physical activity* of God in the cosmos, whilst God remains in essence transcendent. Teilhard describes this dimension of the *vinculum substantiale* as follows:

> Little by little, stage by stage, everything is finally linked to the supreme centre *in quo omnia constant*. The streams which flow from this centre operate not only within the higher reaches of the world where human activities take place in a distinctively supernatural and meritorious form. To save and establish these sublime energies, the power of the Word Incarnate

---

[15] e.g. *DM*, p. 107; cf. Rom 3.24.

[16] Ferdinand Prat, *The Theology of Saint Paul*, II (2 vols.; London: Burns, Oates & Washbourne, 1945), p. 392; cf. G. Adolf Deissmann, *Die neutestamentliche Formel „in Christo Jesu"* (Marburg: Elwert, 1892), p. 97. These sources show that the phrase 'In Christo Jesu' occurs most frequently in Ephesians, Phillippians and Colossians.

[17] See Phillip Cary, *Augustine's Invention of the Inner Self: The Legacy of a Christian Platonist* (Oxford University Press, 2000), pp. 141–43.

[18] *DM*, p. 15.

penetrates matter itself; it goes down into the deepest depths of the lower forces.[19]

The power here described 'in which everything consists' is similar to the *'Spermatick Reason* or *Form of the World'* which Ralph Cudworth derives from early Stoicism: 'That which makes all things thus to conspire every where, and agree together into one Harmony.'[20] Teilhard, by focusing in this way on the action of the *vinculum substantiale* on matter, moves closer to Leibnizian cosmology even than Blondel. Of the few philosophers who have considered Leibniz's theory, Blondel complains, most have treated the bond as a *vinculum* but not as a *vinculum substantiale*, as an abstract bond but not as a bond of *substance*.[21] Blondel perpetuates this tendency in his philosophy of action, however, being concerned with the unity of will and intention in the cosmos rather than with materiality. Brandon Look observes of the theory's original development, by contrast:

> The *vinculum substantiale* becomes less metaphorical; it becomes one distinct and important way in which Leibniz attempts to explain the relation between the dominant monad and its subordinate monads. In fact, one might say that this transition explains the move from Leibniz's conception of this entity as a *vinculum* (analogy) to *vinculum substantiale* (a substance-like thing superadded to a group of monads and combining them in a genuine unity).[22]

Leibniz is frequently portrayed as offering no more in his philosophy than a theory of pre-established harmony of material and spiritual principles governed by a dominant monad and then criticised for failing to develop a more convincing metaphysics. In fact, a proper understanding of his theory of substance is crucial in grasping the nature of his break with materialist philosophy. Descartes identified matter with extension, and considered matter to be, along with thought, a substance in itself. Leibniz, by contrast, considers extension to be a phenomenal manifestation of a deeper substantial unity, beginning his late *Principles of Nature and Grace* (1714) by defining substance suggestively as 'a being which is capable of action'.[23] Unformed matter cannot, therefore, be classified as substance.

[19] *DM*, p. 19.

[20] Cudworth, *True Intellectual System*, I, III.xxviii; xxxvii, §23, pp. 133, 167.

[21] See in general Blondel, *Une énigme historique*.

[22] Brandon Look, *Leibniz and the* vinculum substantiale, Studia Leibnitiana 30 (Stuttgart: F. Steiner, 1999), p. 64.

[23] G.W. Leibniz, 'Principles of Nature and Grace, Based on Reason', §1, in *Philosophical Texts*, eds. R.S. Woolhouse and Richard Franks (Oxford University Press, 1998),

This definition does no more than pose the crucial wider question: How is a substance constituted? In the case of simple, indivisible substances like life, soul or spirit, no unifying principle is needed. Composite substances such as bodies require, however, some type of principle to unite the collection of simple substances of which they consist. Composite substance cannot, Teilhard argues, ever be a real or metaphysical unity per se, remaining in isolation no more than an aggregation or phenomenal unity. The question of what makes a substance a substance is crucial, because as Leibniz states above, a thing can only be capable of acting on other substances, and itself able to be acted on by them, if it possesses the real or metaphysical unity of substantiality. Teilhard therefore believes that 'there must lie a supreme centre of convergence and consistence, in which everything is knit together and holds together',[24] and proceeds to construct his metaphysics of substance around this keystone:

> In *natura rerum*, in nature, there is no completed substance, no substance, accordingly, existing in isolation; but every substance is held up by a series of Substances-of-Substance that support one another, step by step, up to the Supreme Centre at which everything converges.[25]

In this cosmology, the 'substantial one and the created multiple fuse without confusion'.[26] The function of the centre of consistence is to preserve individual material substances and individual bodies: it is not true, for instance, that Teilhard uses the concept of the body simply as a metaphor to suggest that the whole world is conscious.[27]

Blondel describes a gradation of being similar to this 'series of Substances-of-Substance' consisting of five stages. The first is extended impenetrable matter, and Teilhard also regards matter as basic and extensionless. The second stage is *conatus*, which is the force animating matter. Affinities are apparent here with Teilhard's theory of spirit, which he later conceives as a life force that motivates the evolutionary process. The third and middle stage in Blondel's progression is the union of primary matter and *conatus* in the monad, which is the fundamental

---

p. 258; cf. Richard A. Watson, *The Downfall of Cartesianism, 1673–1712: A Study of Epistemological Issues in Late 17th Century Cartesianism* (Hague: Nijhoff, 1966), pp. 133–36.

[24] 'Science and Christ' (1921), *SC*, p. 34.

[25] 'My Universe' (1924), *SC*, pp. 52–53.

[26] *DM*, p. 84.

[27] As proposed in Anne Hunt Overzee, *The Body Divine: The Symbol of the Body in the Works of Teilhard de Chardin and Ramanuja* (Cambridge University Press, 1992).

and indivisible unit of substance. The concept of the monad does not, however, provide a complete solution to the metaphysical problems posed by the union of matter and spirit, because once the monad is posited, an explanation of how one monad interacts with another monad is needed. A fourth stage, the semi-mental aggregation of matter and monads, is therefore required, and this leads to a fifth and final stage which posits a grand, dominant or unifying monad which gives consistency to the whole.[28]

Brandon Look identifies a concept related to the *vinculum substantiale* of fundamental importance to the current discussion: a *suppositum*, which is an 'individual substance that arises from the metaphysical union of its constituents'.[29] In the *Summa theologiae*, Aquinas defines a *suppositum* as an individual substance constituted by the combination of matter and form, which is something greater than the sum of its parts: 'If nothing were present in a thing beyond its specific constituents, then there would be no need to distinguish the nature from a supposit in that nature… Yet in fact we find in some subsisting things something that is not part of their specific make-up.'[30] The difference between a substance and a *suppositum* is that whereas the nature of an individual substance belongs essentially to its form, that of a *suppositum* exists in the *combination* of matter and form. Suarez, in his *Disputationes metaphysicae*, considers, for instance, the *suppositum* to be the 'complete individual substance composed of a certain mind and a certain body', mentioning nothing else apart from these two entities.[31] In the specific case of a human being, it is in the *suppositum* that personality inheres, whereas the *vinculum substantiale* forms the deeper unity of body and soul. Significant implications follow for understanding human existence. Look states:

> In claiming therefore that the 'metaphysical union' makes a *suppositum* or a person, Leibniz is making the rather important claim that the 'metaphysical union' between mind and body brings it about that the mind and body act together as if they were an individual substance. In other words, when we have the mind and body together, each acting according to its own laws, the *suppositum* that arises from the two makes it possible for us to treat the

[28] The concept of the monad evidently originates in Hellenic philosophy, as Leibniz recognises in the opening paragraph of his 'Principles of Nature and Grace'. See Leibniz, *Philosophical Texts*, p. 259. An excellent discussion of the Plotinian motifs he employs is Georges Rodier, «Sur une des origines de la philosophie de Leibniz», *RMM* 10 (1902), pp. 552–64.

[29] Look, *Leibniz*, p. 89.

[30] *ST*, IIIa, q. 2, a. 2.

[31] Look, *Leibniz*, p. 61.

actions of the mind and body as if they belonged to one individual substance — a person.[32]

The crucial difference between a *suppositum* and the *vinculum substantiale*, however, is that whereas the *suppositum* is an individual substance *arising from* the metaphysical union of composite substance, the *vinculum substantiale* is an individual substance *able to exist independently* of composite substance.[33] A *suppositum* acts on other substances and *supposita*. The *vinculum substantiale*, by contrast, is a unique and ubiquitous entity unlimited to any particular union or set of unions who provides the ground for them all, and whom Teilhard identifies with Christ.

The fullness of God in Christ

Teilhard contrasts, in many places in his theology, a 'juridical' method with one concerned to develop a 'physical' understanding of reality. These two types of theology might be described, using current terminology, as 'forensic' and 'embodied'. Teilhard sees the distinction between the types as fundamental to both historical and contemporary debates, and as lying at the root of particular doctrinal differences.[34] He traces a juridical, or forensic, theological method to the Latin Fathers, who 'assume the appearance of a legal trial between God and his creatures',[35] and suggests that the fundamental distinction between juridical and physical theologies rests on their understanding of the πλέρωμα (pleroma), or fullness of God. The forensic concept of the fullness of God is one of plenitude: a whole or a totality in which every element or part has its place and function.[36] The interpretation of the πλέρωμα far predates the New Testament: Aristotle and Plato, for instance, both use the term to describe a political society in which every class of person has his or her place within a diverse whole.[37] Teilhard believes these forensic uses of πλέρωμα to be deficient because they fail to describe any physical dynamic within the cosmos that actually causes the ordering. He complains: 'The City of God is too often

---

[32] Look, *Leibniz*, p. 61.

[33] Look, *Leibniz*, p. 89.

[34] e.g. 'Pantheism and Christianity' (1923), *CE*, p. 67.

[35] 'Christology and Evolution' (1933), *CE*, p. 89; e.g Augustine, *De civitate Dei*, XX (7 vols.; Harvard University Press, 1957–72), VI, pp. 249–453.

[36] Prat, *Theology of Saint Paul*, II, p. 295, n. 1.

[37] See Aristotle, *Politics*, 1284a5, *Works* XXI (23 vols.; Harvard University Press, 1926–91), pp. 240–41; Plato, *Republic*, 371e, *Works* V (12 vols.; Harvard University Press, 1914–30), pp. 156–57.

described in conventional and purely moral terms. God and the world governed by God are seen to be a vast and juridical association, conceived of as a family or government.'[38] Teilhard is particularly critical of readings of the vineyard parables which envision a deist *ex machina* God removed from the world, complaining: 'Christ is not something added to the world as an extra, he is not an embellishment, a king as we now crown kings, the owner of a great estate.'[39] The Christian God is portrayed too often as a 'great landowner administering his estates, the world'.[40] Images such as this exert a pervasive influence on theological imagination because they contribute to so many theological categories like reparation, atonement, justification and salvation. Highly organized systematic theology has been produced using these concepts, but it has often failed to relate doctrine explicitly to material life, whether of an individual body or the whole cosmos. Teilhard, by contrast, wishes to consider in detail the implications of doctrine on physical life. He does not, therefore, reject forensic theology altogether, but wishes to 'transpose into terms of physical reality the juridical expressions in which the Church has clothed her faith'.[41]

A realist interpretation of the πλέρωμα, although consigned to comparative obscurity by preachers and theologians, is not only essential to this exercise but is also, Teilhard believes, particularly appropriate to contemporary religious needs.[42] It is closely allied with Teilhard's high valuation of embodiment,[43] which is founded on his appreciation that Christ not only assumed bodily form in a kenotic movement,[44] but lived in intimate relation with the material world, and in so doing blessed it:

> Christ immerses himself in the waters of Jordan, symbol of the energies of the earth. He sanctifies them. And as he emerges, says S. Gregory of Nyssa, he elevates the whole world with the water which runs off his body.[45]

The Baptism of Christ in the Jordan is not only a Jewish ritual which Christ fulfils, but the baptism and sanctification of the whole cosmos by Christ, who is himself the bond of substance:

---

[38] *HP*, p. 211.

[39] 'Science and Christ', p. 34; cf. Mt 20.1–16, 25.14–30.

[40] 'Sketch of a Personalistic Universe' (1936), *HE*, pp. 91, cf. 110. See e.g. John Chrysostom, 'Homily 68', *NPNF*, series I, X, pp. 409–414.

[41] 'How I Believe' (1934), *CE*, p. 128.

[42] 'The Awaited Word' (1940), *TF*, p. 97.

[43] On this theme, see Jean Furness, 'Teilhard de Chardin and Julian of Norwich: A Rapprochement', *Mystics Quarterly* 12 (1986), pp. 67–70.

[44] Retreat note of 24 July 1922, *NR*, p. 98.

[45] *DM*, p. 70; cf. Gregory of Nyssa, 'On the Baptism of Christ: A Sermon for the Day of the Lights', in *NPNF*, series II, V, pp. 518–24.

There must lie a supreme centre of convergence and consistence, in which everything is knit together and holds together. We should be overcome with joy ... to note how admirably Jesus Christ, in virtue of his most fundamental moral teaching and his most certain attributes, fills this empty place which has been distinguished by the expectation of all Nature.[46]

Christ is the 'principle of universal consistence' and 'clothed in the earth' as the 'bond that runs through all things'.[47] He is the 'only true Substance of things'.[48] The entire cosmos participates in his fullness, and is complete only when so doing. Christ's body is the 'active centre, the living link, the organizing soul', or in the words of the letter to the Ephesians, the 'fullness of him who fills all in all'.[49] The πλέρωμα can now be understood in suggestively Byzantine terms as the 'mysterious synthesis of the uncreated and the created'. It is crucial to understand this spiritual synthesis in physical ways which fully recognize the place of the *created* component in the union. God gathers together 'not merely a diffuse multiplicity of souls, but the solid, organic, reality of a universe, taken from top to bottom in the complete extent and unity of its energies'.[50]

Teilhard's depiction of the πλέρωμα is inspired by the Pauline tradition of reflection on the cosmic role of Christ, developed by Paul in order to take full account of the implications for humanity and the cosmos of the fact that the whole fullness of God dwells bodily in Christ.[51] The implications of cosmic christology are not confined, however, to the mutual relations subsisting between the persons of the Godhead. Rather, the Son is 'He in whom everything is reunited, and in whom all things are consummated — through whom the whole created edifice receives its consistency — Christ dead and risen *qui replet omnia, in quo omnia constant*.'[52] Particularly striking is a gloss by Teilhard that combines at least four scriptural passages, which praises Christ as

[46] 'Science and Christ', p. 34.

[47] 'Pantheism and Christianity', pp. 71, 75.

[48] Letter of 13 June 1917 to Berthe Teilhard de Chardin, quoted in Robert Faricy, *All Things in Christ: Teilhard de Chardin's Spirituality* (London: Fount, 1981), p. 16.

[49] Eph 1.23, cf. 3.19, 4.13. See M. Bogdasavich, 'The Idea of Pleroma in the Epistles to the Colossians and Ephesians', *The Downside Review* 83 (1965), pp. 118–30; P. Benoît, «Corps, tête et plérôme», *Exégèse et théologie* 2 (1961), pp. 135–53.

[50] 'The Awaited Word', p. 97. Teilhard had met some members of the Russian Orthodox emigré community of postwar Paris, including Nicholas Berdayev and Vladimir Lossky. (Claude Cuénot, *Teilhard de Chardin: A Biographical Study* (London: Burns & Oates, 1965), p. 261.) There is no evidence, however, that Teilhard's concept of *énergie* was derived from Orthodox sources, not least because Teilhard developed it during the 1930s whilst living in China.

[51] See Col 1.19, 2.9.

[52] *DM*, p. 84.

the Alpha and the Omega, the principle and the end, the foundation stone
and the keystone, the Plenitude and the Plenifier. He is the one who con-
summates all things and gives them their consistence. It is towards him and
through him, the inner life and light of the world, that the universal convergence of all created spirit is effected in sweat and tears. He is the single
centre, precious and consistent, who glitters at the summit that is to crown
the world, at the opposite pole from those dim and eternally shrinking
regions into which our science ventures when it descends the road of matter and the past.[53]

Teilhard's formation in New Testament scholarship at Ore Place, Hastings, inspires him to develop the πλέρωμα concept in this way. His
reading of scripture is original in two senses of the word: creative, but
also a return to an early form of christological expression. During Teilhard's four years' residence at the Jesuit theology scholasticate, important new approaches to Pauline studies were being devised in French
catholic biblical scholarship, and Teilhard lived in community with three
figures of decisive importance in this movement: his tutors Ferdinand
Prat and Albert Durand, and fellow student Joseph Huby.

Prat's christology is best expressed in his two-volume, thousand-page
study *The Theology of Saint Paul*, first published in 1921. Prat affirms of
Christ:

> All things are *in* him because, being the perfect image of God, he com-
> prises the ideal and the model of all things possible, and is thus the exem-
> plary cause of all contingent beings. All things are *by* him, as the efficient
> cause, God, in his outward operations, acting by the Son in the Holy Spirit
> in accordance with the order and harmony of his inmost life. All things are
> *for* him by a double right, both because the creation is his work and
> because God, embracing at a glance the whole multitude of his counsels,
> connected with his Son, in advance and by a special bond of finality, the
> world of nature and the world of grace.[54]

Cyril Martindale, a fellow student of Teilhard's, describes in a letter to
Charles Raven the formative influence of Prat's study of Paul on Teilhard's theology.[55] This enduring inspiration is combined with an earlier
Johannine influence to which Teilhard was subject by his second-year
teacher Albert Durand.[56] The tendency in contemporary New Testament

---

[53] 'Science and Christ', pp. 34–35; cf. Rv 22.13, Col 1.17, Jn 8.12, Rom 8.22.

[54] Prat, *Theology of Saint Paul*, II, p. 146.

[55] Quoted in Charles Raven, *Teilhard de Chardin: Scientist and Seer* (London:
Collins, 1962), p. 46.

[56] *LH*, p. 70, n. 1. Richard W. Kropf, *Teilhard, Scripture and Revelation: A Study of
Teilhard de Chardin's Reinterpretation of Pauline Themes* (Rutherford, NJ: Fairleigh
Dickinson University Press, 1980), pp. 208–215, shows that most of Teilhard's early

circles was to highlight the correspondence between Paul and John rather than the disjunction, with the captivity epistles being taken as forming for this purpose the core of the Pauline corpus.[57] This hermeneutic accounts for the distinctly Johannine mystical and philosophical character of the Pauline christology being developed. Prat's interests were pursued by his pupil Joseph Huby, who was a contemporary of Teilhard's for three year at Hastings, being one year his senior.[58] Henri de Lubac identifies the influence of his theology on Joseph Huby's study *Saint Paul: Les Épîtres de la captivité*, published in the *Verbum salutis* series in 1935.[59] The twelfth edition of this classic study appeared in 1947, and in it Huby states of Christ:

> In him all was created as in the supreme centre of unity, harmony, and cohesion, which gives the world its meaning and its value, and so its reality; or, to put it another way, as in the 'foyer' (*the meeting-point* — Lightfoot) at which all the threads, all the generating forces of the Universe, are woven together and co-ordinated... He is the dominating centre, the keystone of the Universe: 'In him all subsist.'[60]

Huby here interpolates a reference to J.B. Lightfoot's commentary on Colossians: 'All the laws and purposes which guide the creation and government of the Universe reside in Him, the Eternal Word, as their meeting-point.'[61] In the words of Prat once again, the πλέρωμα of God

appeals to scripture are to John. Alfred Durand, «Le Christ 'Premier Né'» 1 (1910), pp. 56–66; «Le Discours de la Cène» 1 (1910), pp. 97–131, 513–39; 2 (1911), pp. 321–49, 521–45; and «La Réponse de Jésus aux noces de Cana» (1912), pp. 157–59, were all published in *RSR* whilst Durand and Teilhard were resident at Ore Place, Hastings as tutor and student.

[57] Kropf, *Teilhard, Scripture and Revelation*, p. 209.

[58] Huby had been censured in Wlodimir Ledochowski, Letter to Provincials of 15 July 1920, 'Doctrina de actu fidei a P. Petro Rousselot p.m. proposita prohibetinur', *Acta Romana Societatis Iesu* 3 (1919–23), pp. 229–33; discussed in Avery Dulles, 'Principal Theses of the Position of Pierre Rousselot', in Pierre Rousselot, *The Eyes of Faith. Answer to Two Attacks* (New York: Fordham University Press, 1990), p. 113. The four works of Huby's cited were: «Miracle et lumière de la grâce», *RSR* 9 (1918), pp. 36–77; «Le Témoignage des convertis», *Études* 155 (1918), pp. 385–400, 558–72, 706–715; «Foi et contemplation d'après saint Thomas», *RSR* 10 (1919), pp. 137–61; *La Conversion* (Paris: Beauchesne, 1919). Teilhard's closeness to Huby is indicated in an unpublished letter to Huby of 13 July 1925 in which Teilhard discusses the proceedings being taken against himself in Rome for his views on original sin. For biography of Huby, see René d'Ouince, «Le Père Joseph Huby», *Études* 259 (1948), pp. 71–80; Henri de Lubac, «Joseph Huby», *RSR* 35 (1948), pp. 321–23.

[59] *LI*, p. 69, n. 3.

[60] Joseph Huby, *Saint Paul: les épîtres de la captivité* (Paris: Beauchesne, 1935), p. 40; trans. in Henri de Lubac, *The Faith of Teilhard de Chardin* (London: Burns & Oates, 1967), p. 34.

[61] J.B. Lightfoot, *St Paul's Epistles to the Colossians and Philemon* (London: Macmillan, 5th edn, 1886), p. 148.

in Christ can no longer be understood as a passing moment of the Word, 'who condescends to plant his tent (ἐσκήνωσεν) for a moment in our midst', as in the Johannine tradition. The πλέρωμα becomes more and more the 'immovable, permanent, and definitive residence (κατοικεῖ) of divinity'[62] in a Pauline cosmos of material substance, human action and human passion. Teilhard affirms of the πλέρωμα of God in Christ that

> we serve to complete it, even by the humblest work of our hands. This is ultimately the value and meaning of our acts. By virtue of the interrelation between matter, soul and Christ, we bring part of the being which he desires back to God in whatever we do. With each one of our works, we labour, separately, but no less really, to build the Pleroma; that is, we bring to Christ a little fulfilment. Every one of our works, by its more or less remote or direct effect upon the spiritual world, helps us to perfect Christ in his mystical totality.[63]

These works are produced by the bond of action, which engenders the bond of substance that gives the world consistency by ordering matter according to a spiritual principle. Teilhard's theological work, his research as a paleontologist, and his practical war service as a stretcher-bearer, are among his own active and passive contributions to this operation.

The concept of πλέρωμα has received divergent theological interpretations, due particularly to its association with the *élément universel* of Stoic philosophy.[64] In this pantheist cosmology, the created order does not participate in divinity; rather, God is coextensive with creation. Stoicism was the most widely accepted philosophical system during the lifetime of Paul of Tarsus, and it is therefore unsurprising that he adapts certain of its concepts for his own use.[65] Jean Maalouf refers uncritically

---

[62] Prat, *Theology of Saint Paul*, I, p. 296.

[63] *DM*, p. 20. Philip Sherrard, in an excellent though critical discussion 'Christian Vision and Modern Science: I. Teilhard de Chardin', in *Human Image, World Image: The Death and Resurrection of Sacred Cosmology* (Ipswich: Golgonooza, 1992), pp. 122–23, objects strongly to this notion that humanity can in any way make Christ present in the world, arguing that it implies a theology in which Christ is saved by humankind. In fact, although Teilhard believes that Christ works through humankind in order to save the world, it by no means follows that humankind, and indeed the whole of the created order, ceases to be dependent on Christ throughout this co-operation. What is more significant about Sherrard's essay, however, is that he demonstrates from an Orthodox perspective just how Western Teilhard's christology is.

[64] See R.A. Markus, 'Pleroma and Fulfilment: The Significance of History in St Irenaeus' Opposition to Gnosticism', *Vigiliae Christianae* 8 (1954), pp. 193–224.

[65] James M. Starr, *Sharers in Divine Nature: 2 Peter 1.4 in its Hellenistic Context* (Stockholm: Almqvist & Wiksell, 2000), p. 165.

to «le Stoicïsme de Teilhard de Chardin»,[66] but it is far from clear that Teilhard adopts a fully Stoic position, even though his long friendship with Léontine Zanta, who produced a study of the reception of Stoicism, enabled him to gain detailed knowledge of the Stoic tradition and its diversity.[67] A more discriminating approach is required to relate Teilhard's cosmology to the Pauline tradition and the particular Stoic elements which it assimilates. For instance, the conception of human unity developed by the later Stoic philosopher Marcus Aurelius in his *Meditations* is grounded in the notion of the *equality* of human beings which results from their forming a single community united by the capacity of each member for rational conduct.[68] This idea exerts a formative influence on the Christian notion of the community of souls regarded as equal in the sight of God.

Teilhard's doctrine of cosmic unity also rests on a belief in human equality, but with that equality conceived in a context of *plurality*. The human soul's capacity to cultivate virtue is due, he suggests, to its vision of its unique place in the cosmos as a member of a network of cosmic relations with other incommensurable beings, and not to a Stoic acceptance of fate, suppression of passion, and submission to a *jus naturae*.[69] In *The Divine Milieu*, Teilhard defends himself against the charge of Stoic pantheism in the following terms:

> At first sight, perhaps, the depths of the divine which St. Paul shows us may seem to resemble the fascinating domains unfolded before our eyes by monistic philosophies or religions. In fact they are very different, far more reassuring to our minds, far more comforting to our hearts. Pantheism seduces us by its vistas of perfect universal union. But ultimately, if it were true, it would give us only fusion and unconsciousness; for, at the end of the evolution it claims to reveal, the elements of the world vanish in the God they create or by which they are absorbed. Our God, on the contrary,

---

[66] Jean Maalouf, «L'Évolutionnisme et le Stoïcisme de Teilhard de Chardin», in *Le Mystère du mal dans l'oeuvre de Teilhard de Chardin* (Paris: Cerf, 1986), pp. 116–38. See also R. Godfrey Tanner, 'Neo-Stoicism in Teilhard de Chardin', in *The Desire to be Human: A Global Reconnaissance of Human Perspectives in an Age of Transformation Written in Honour of Pierre Teilhard de Chardin*, eds. Leo Zonneveld and Robert Muller (Wassenaar: Miranda, 1983), pp. 124–37.

[67] See *LLZ*; Léontine Zanta, *La Renaissance du stoïcisme au XVIe siècle* (Paris: Champion, 1914).

[68] Pierre Hadot, *The Inner Citadel: The Meditations of Marcus Aurelius* (Harvard University Press, 1998) describes this notion with clarity.

[69] Michel Spanneut, «Le Stoïcisme dans l'histoire de la patience chrétienne», *Mélanges de science religieuse* 39 (1982), pp. 128–30, argues that Teilhard reconciles καρτερία, the Stoic concept of patience, with ὑπομονή, the Christian one.

pushes to its furthest possible limit the differentiation among the creatures he concentrates within himself.[70]

Teilhard perhaps has in mind here the strictures of Blondel on immanentist cosmology: 'The more one represents Christ as an innate presence in souls and in the world itself, the more vital it is to lay sharp stress on the absolute transcendence of the divine Gift, on the inescapably supernatural character of the plan towards deification, and thus on the moral transformation and the spiritual expansion which are demanded by and achieved through grace.'[71] Christ is πρὸ πάντων: *before* all things.[72] If the cosmos is truly dependent on divinity, then it follows that divinity must subsist *beyond* the cosmos. Any other understanding of divinity's relation to created being would entail either the dependence of divinity on the cosmos, or its separation from the cosmos.

Teilhard's theory of πλέρωμα also needs to be distinguished from some Gnostic variants. Ferdinand Prat identifies a Gnostic sense of πλέρωμα as referring to the 'whole combination of divine emanations, the sum-total of the divine Being diffused throughout the universe'.[73] Irenaeus records a use of Cerenthius, according to whom the dwelling place of Christ was eternally in the πλέρωμα but only temporarily in Jesus, with Christ entering Jesus at his baptism and departing after teaching humankind the truth of the invisible Father.[74] This conception of the πλέρωμα is clearly incompatible with the Chalcedonian orthodoxy concerning the two natures of Christ, which Teilhard is determined to defend: the historical incarnation of Christ excludes any emanationist sense of his plenitude. Teilhard is as keen as Tertullian to affirm Christ's full humanity,[75] and is therefore staunchly opposed to the Gnostic denigration of embodiment characteristic of its christology, as well as to its exaltation of esoteric forms of knowledge above classic expressions of faith. Teilhard's use of the concept of πλέρωμα is similar to that of Paul of Tarsus, who in his speech at the Areopagus in praise of God in whom 'we live and move and have our being' 'seizes upon it in order to correct the abuse of it'.[76] Teilhard preserves some of the Gnostic insights which

---

[70] *DM*, p. 116.

[71] Paper of 5 December 1919, *TBC*, pp. 26–27.

[72] Col 1.17.

[73] Prat, *Theology of Saint Paul*, I, p. 296.

[74] Irenaeus of Lyons, *Against Heresies*, III, 11; I, 26, *ANF* I, pp. 415, 351–52.

[75] See especially Tertullian, *Adversus Marcionem*, III, vii–xi (2 vols.; Oxford: Clarendon, 1972), I, pp. 186–205.

[76] Prat, *Theology of Saint Paul*, I, p. 296; cf. Acts 17.22–31; see David L. Balch, 'The Areopagus Speech: An Appeal to the Stoic Historian Posidonius against Later Stoics and

entered mainstream Christian theology, such as beliefs in the illumination of the created order by God, and in the possibility of knowledge of
that order by divine revelation.[77] His theology is, at the same time,
unashamedly catholic and non-sectarian, situating faith in a cosmos in
which the revelation of the πλέρωμα of God in Christ is offered to the
whole of humankind.

Christ human and divine

Christianity, Teilhard believes, is essentially the religion of the Incarnation. It 'maintains the value and rights of the flesh, which the Word
assumed, and which he is going to raise to life again'.[78] Teilhard would
have agreed, for this reason, with the observation of William Temple that
Christianity is the most materialistic of the great religions. In its affirmation that the Word was made flesh is 'implicit a whole theory of the relation between spirit and matter'.[79] Teilhard's reflections on materiality
motivate his theological concern to understand the embodiment which
follows from this most fundamental tenet of the Christian faith: that the
Word became flesh in Jesus Christ. Teilhard states: 'Christ, *through his
Incarnation*, is interior to the world, rooted in the world even in the heart
of the tiniest atom.'[80] Teilhard wishes to recover and amplify this insight
of the Christian faith, which 'has always based a large part of its tenets
on the tangible values of the World of Matter'.[81] He states:

> In its dogmas and sacraments, the whole economy of the Church teaches us
> respect for matter and insists on its value. Christ wished to assume, and had
> to assume, a real flesh. He sanctifies human flesh by a specific contact. He
> makes ready, physically, its Resurrection. In the Christian concept, then,
> matter retains its cosmic role as the basis, lower in order but primordial and

the Epicureans', in *Greeks, Romans and Christians*, eds. Everett Ferguson and Wayne
Meeks (Minneapolis, Minn.: Fortress, 1990), pp. 52–79.

[77] For the positive contributions of Gnosticism to emerging Christian orthodoxy, see
Roelof van den Broek, *Studies in Gnosticism and Alexandrian Christianity* (Leiden: Brill,
1996); Alastair Logan, *Gnostic Truth and Christian Heresy: A Study in the History of
Gnosticism* (Edinburgh: T&T Clark, 1996); Simone Pétrement, *A Separate God: The
Christian Origins of Gnosticism* (London: Darton, Longman & Todd, 1991).

[78] 'Social Heredity and Progress' (1938), *FM*, p. 33; 'Introduction to the Christian
Life' (1944), *CE*, p. 169.

[79] William Temple, *Readings in St John's Gospel* (London: Macmillan, 1945), p. xx;
cf. Jn 1.14.

[80] 'Science and Christ' (1921), *SC*, p. 36.

[81] 'The Heart of the Problem' (1949), *FM*, p. 267.

essential, of union; and, by assimilation to the Body of Christ, some part of
matter is destined to pass into the foundations and walls of the heavenly
Jerusalem.[82]

Matter, by virtue of the Incarnation, is transformed, spiritualized and
directed towards the final end of the world: union with Christ and the
spiritual vision of God. Christ is the 'true bond that holds the World
together.'[83] These material works of sanctification and unification are
present most visibly in the Eucharist and the other sacraments, but are
not confined to them. The *vinculum substantiale* is, in fact, a 'close bond
linking all the movements of this world in the single work of the Incarnation'.[84] It is an unceasing operation by which Christ enters into the
world ever more fully and brings the world closer to himself, and is
completed only in the final consummation of the world by Christ. The
coming of Christ as Logos into the human world is not completed in the
birth of Jesus in Palestine. Incarnation is not confined to a discrete event
at a particular point in historical time, but is an ongoing movement
which creates the historical reality which it enters. It is exemplified by
the entry of Jesus Christ into the human world to assume human form,
but its final purpose is the redemption of the whole world:

> The Incarnation is a making new, a restoration, of all the universe's forces
> and powers; Christ is the Instrument, the Centre, the End, of the whole of
> animate and material creation; through him, everything is created, sancti-
> fied, and vivified.[85]

The Incarnation is co-extensive with the spatiality of the world, as well
as with its duration, being the 'visible aspect' of God's creative act.[86]
The divine nature of Jesus Christ, his eternal birth in the Godhead, and
his work of redemption and salvation transform material existence
through all its levels of being. In order that the world be redeemed, it is
necessary for Christ to 'enter into contact with every one of the zones of
the created, from the lowest and most earthly to the zone that is closest
to heaven'.[87] Not to recognize this cosmic character of the work of
Incarnation is to fail to understand the role of Incarnation in the redemption of the created order. Redemption is not a purely spiritual process

---

[82] 'Cosmic Life' (1916), *WW*, p. 64.
[83] 'The Mystical Milieu' (1917), *WW*, p. 142.
[84] *DM*, p. 25.
[85] 'Cosmic Life', p. 58.
[86] 'My Universe' (1924), *SC*, p. 64.
[87] 'Pantheism and Christianity' (1923), *CE*, p. 71.

nor a solely legal one, but a movement into the world that acts on and transforms material substance.

Teilhard possesses a strong sense that the birth of Jesus occurred 'when the time had fully come',[88] and that it therefore needs to be considered, along with the whole of Jesus's life, as part of a redemptive process rather than as an end in itself. It comprises the decisive moment of the eternal birth of Christ from the Father in which history is formed. With allusions to prehistory and the epochs of human religion that followed it, Teilhard states of Christ's birth, in terms which anticipate Karl Rahner's theory of anonymous or implicit Christianity: 'It called for all the fearsome, anonymous toil of primitive humans, for the long drawn-out beauty of Egypt, for Israel's anxious expectation, the slowly distilled fragrance of eastern mysticism, and the endlessly refined wisdom of the Greeks — it called for all these before the flower could bloom on the stock of Jesse and of humankind.'[89]

Teilhard identifies his theology of the cosmic action of Christ on the world with Scotist incarnationalism, which in opposing both the demonstrative mediation of Aquinas and the immediacy theories of earlier Franciscans suggests that the gap between nature and God, who is the necessarily existing first efficient cause of nature, is real and cannot therefore be bridged by any purely natural means but only by the action of Christ. Both Teilhard and Scotus argue for the 'necessity of *some* form of Incarnation' to perform the functions of gathering and uniting the created order.[90] Incarnation is not contingent on the sin of Adam: this would imply divine foreknowledge of Adam's sin, and would entail a greater good (Incarnation) being occasioned by a lesser one (redemption). Christ's Incarnation is a consequence of the reciprocal relation and mutual dependence between God and the material world. Teilhard affirms: 'The world would have no internal coherence were Christ not at hand to give it a centre and to consummate it. Christ, on the other hand, would not be divine if his spirit could not be recognized as underlying

---

[88] Gal 4.3.

[89] 'My Universe', p. 61; cf. Is 11.1; cf. Karl Rahner, 'Christianity and Non-Christian Religions', *TI* V, pp. 115–34.

[90] 'Outline of a Dialectic of Spirit' (1946), *AE*, p. 150. The association is developed in the third interview in Gabriel M. Allegra, *My Conversations with Teilhard de Chardin on the Primacy of Christ, Peking, 1942–1945* (Chicago: Franciscan Herald Press, 1970), pp. 83–107. Gerald O'Collins, 'The Incarnation: The Critical Issues', in *The Incarnation: An Interdisciplinary Symposium on the Incarnation of the Son of God*, eds. Stephen T. Davies, Daniel Kendall and Gerald O'Collins (Oxford University Press, 2002), pp. 16–17, identifies this perspective in Irenaeus, Scotus, Teilhard and Karl Rahner.

the processes which are even now recreating the soul of the earth.'[91] A further comparison can be made with the Scotist christology of Gerald Manley Hopkins: whilst the individualized form (*haeceitas*) of Christ's nature remains transcendent, his attributes are immanent in the world and may be apprehended by human intellect in an analogy between finite and infinite.[92] Since the gap between nature and infinity — Scotus even avoids the term *transcendentalia*, so concerned is he not to objectify divinity — is infinite, this analogy provides the only means of understanding Christ by means of natural faculties. The Incarnation cannot, above all, be established by natural theology: in fact, it is Incarnation which makes natural theology possible. Teilhard states: 'God cannot appear as prime mover (ahead) without first becoming incarnate and without redeeming — in other words *without our seeing that he becomes Christified.*'[93]

Teilhard's theology and philosophy undoubtedly presuppose, despite their frequently speculative character, this *analogia entis* according to which nature exists *in Christo*. Teilhard's christology is, furthermore, fundamental to his understanding of the means by which the material world may be drawn from multiplicity into unity. Only by virtue of Christ's coexisting natures, human and divine, may the spiritual transformation of matter be effected. Christ requires 'both a concrete history and the attributes of divinity'.[94] Teilhard states: 'If Christ was to conquer human life, to dominate it with his own life, he had to do more than stand in juxtaposition to it: he had to assimilate it, in other words to test it, savour it, subdue it in the depths of his own self.'[95] This christology can be seen as a defence of the full humanity of Christ, but is equally part of Teilhard's proclamation of Christ's divinity, manifested in human history but residing fully in the eternally begotten Son, who is the telos of the cosmos.[96] Teilhard states:

> The essential message of Christ … is not to be sought in the Sermon on the Mount, nor even in the drama of the Cross; it lies wholly in the proclamation of a 'divine fatherhood' or, to translate, in the affirmation that God, a

---

[91] 'The Sense of Humanity' (1929), *TF*, p. 38.

[92] See Hywel Thomas, 'Gerard Manley Hopkins and John Duns Scotus', *Religious Studies* 24 (1988), pp. 337–64; Christopher Mooney, *Teilhard de Chardin and the Mystery of Christ* (London: Collins, 1966), pp. 121–22.

[93] 'From Cosmos to Cosmogenesis' (1951), *AE*, p. 263.

[94] 'The Sense of Humanity' (1929), *TF*, p. 37.

[95] 'My Universe', p. 62.

[96] 'Suggestions for a New Theology' (1945), *CE*, pp. 176–77.

personal being, presents Himself to humanity as the goal of a personal *union*.[97]

Teilhard wishes, in his incarnational theology, to deny the dichotomy sometimes presumed to exist between the historical Jesus and the Christ of faith. Indeed, only by allowing the person of Christ to bear, in Chalcedonian terms, 'two natures, without confusion, without change, without division, and without separation', can the unified character of Christ's person be understood: 'It is from his concrete germ, the Man of Nazareth, that Christ-Omega (both theoretically and historically) derives his whole consistence, as a hard experiential fact.'[98] This internal substantial consistency of humanity and divinity in the person of Christ is the corollary of the fact that Christ was born into the created order in order to effect a redemptive union between its material and spiritual principles.

Teilhard denies any dichotomy between the Antiochene historical Jesus and the Alexandrian Christ of faith. Vladimir Lossky describes these contrasting emphases succinctly: the former tending to affirm the 'person of Christ as revealed in his humanity', and the second the 'eternal glory of Christ which he shares with the Father and the Holy Spirit'.[99] Teilhard greatly admires the Christ of faith tradition and regards it as the more ancient of the two, praising the era when 'Christianity made its definitive entry into human thought by boldly identifying the Christ of the gospel with the Alexandrian logos'.[100] Nevertheless, the dichotomy between Antioch and Alexandria is not absolute, with Teilhard's theology of the *person* of Christ being enriched by both traditions:

> The mystical Christ, the universal Christ of S. Paul, has neither meaning nor value in our eyes except as an expansion of the Christ who was born of Mary and who died on the cross. The former essentially draws his fundamental quality of undeniability and concreteness from the latter. However far we may be drawn into the divine spaces opened up to us by Christian mysticism, we never depart from the Jesus of the Gospels. On the contrary, we feel a growing need to enfold ourselves ever more firmly within his human truth. We are not, therefore, modernist in the condemned sense of the word.[101]

The Son is first glimpsed as a historical figure and as the bond of material substance, but fully reveals himself as acting on the world and pre-

[97] 'Human Energy' (1937), *HE*, p. 156.
[98] 'Suggestions for a New Theology', p. 181.
[99] Vladimir Lossky, *The Vision of God* (Crestwood, NY: St Vladimir's, 1983), p. 100.
[100] 'Suggestions for a New Theology', pp. 180–81.

sent in it as its bond and telos. All existing substances are preserved by the 'Word incarnate, our Lord Jesus Christ', who is the 'concrete link which binds all these universal entities together'.[102] This work is made possible by the dual natures of the Word, both human and divine. Teilhard often refers to the human nature of Christ as his *physical* nature. The essential role of this nature in the process of cosmic redemption is also affirmed by Maximus the Confessor, who identifies the universal redemptive principle with a particular person in a *concrete universal*.[103] Teilhard is able thus to develop a dynamic christology whose implications are consistently pursued, believing in Christ as equally the eternal Son born of the Father and the historical son born of Mary. Indeed, it is within this tension in the person of Christ that the temporality and duration of the world reside, held in suspension between future consummation and current reality. This is illustrated in Henry Parry Liddon's discussion of Jesus's statement in Mark 13.32 concerning the coming of Christ: 'About that day or hour no one knows, neither the angels in heaven, *nor the Son*, but only the Father.'[104] The distinction between the humanity and divinity of Christ is most sharply manifested when the eschatological question is posed, in the Son's lack of knowledge of the will of the Father. Liddon identifies this as the single point in the Gospels at which the knowledge of Jesus appears to be limited. He observes of the contrasts which the passage highlights between the human and divine qualities of Christ that 'while they enhance our sense of our Lord's love and condescension' they 'do not destroy our apprehension of the Personal Unity of the Incarnate Christ'. Teilhard would add that they strengthen human perception of that unity, because only through the humanity of Christ will divinity be manifested.

Teilhard distinguishes his christology from that promoted by the group of thinkers and tendencies conveniently labelled 'modernist' by their detractors. The 1907 encyclical of St Pius X, *Pascendi dominici gregis*, defined 'modernism' in terms of a collection of specific theological tendencies: a concern with the phenomenal and with religious expe-

---

[101] *DM*, pp. 78–79.

[102] *DM*, p. 83.

[103] See especially 'The Humanity of Christ and the Faithful' (1920), *CE*, pp. 15–20; David de Pomerai, 'Maximus the Confessor: A Precursor to Teilhard?', *The Teilhard Review* 28, 2 (1993), pp. 16–18; David S. Yeago, 'Jesus of Nazareth and Cosmic Redemption: The Relevance of St Maximus the Confessor', *MT* 12 (1996), p. 177.

[104] Henry Parry Liddon, *The Divinity of Our Lord and Saviour Jesus Christ: Eight Lectures Preached Before the University of Oxford in the Year 1866 on the Foundation of John Bampton* (London: Longmans, 1903), pp. 472–73, emphasis added.

rience; the denial that dogma revealed by the Church is axiomatic; the subordination of religious faith to the natural sciences; a symbolic rather than literal understanding of sacramental efficacy; historical and textual criticism of Scripture; and pantheism.[105] The encyclical describes the 'modernists' as 'inflated like bladders with the spirit of vanity' and 'modernism' itself as the 'synthesis of all heresies'.[106] Few if any individual theologians identified as modernist had espoused all the positions identified in the encyclical, and their synthesis therefore existed more in rhetoric than in reality. Some of the defining features indeed appeared to exclude others: for instance, proponents of religious experience would be unlikely to subordinate faith to the natural sciences. Nevertheless, most of the characteristics associated with modernism were prominent in christological debates or pertinent to them. The encyclical *Pascendi* proclaims that modernists, 'not sparing even the person of the Divine Redeemer, whom, with sacrilegious daring, they reduce to a simple, mere man', had called into question the divine nature of Christ.[107] The implicit reference of this charge is to the christology of Alfred Loisy in his *L'Évangile et l'Église*.[108] The object of Loisy's work had been to refute the argument of Adolf von Harnack in *Das Wesen des Christentums* that the essence of Christianity was the *teaching* of Christ of the fatherhood of God and the solidarity of the human community.[109] Loisy affirmed the divinity of the eternally-born Son, but called into question the divine nature of the historical person of Christ, thereby precipitating huge controversy within Catholic biblical scholarship.

Teilhard also appears to have in his sights the popular christology of figures like Ernst Rénan, who depicted Palestine as a second Eden, a bucolic idyll far removed from the harsh realities of material life.[110] Jesus

---

[105] *Pascendi*, §§6–13, 16–17, 19–21, 29–34, 39, in *PE* III, pp. 71–97. Teilhard swore the anti-modernist oath, made obligatory for all seminarians and clergy by *Pascendi*, on 24 November 1907.

[106] *Pascendi*, §§17, 39.

[107] *Pascendi*, §2.

[108] Alfred Loisy, *L'Évangile et l'Église* (Paris: A. Picard et fils, 1902); trans. *The Gospel and the Church* (London: Isbister, 1903). Donald MacKinnon, 'Teilhard de Chardin: A Comment on his Context and Significance', *The Modern Churchman* 5 (1962), pp. 195–99, explains this context with clarity.

[109] Adolf von Harnack, *Das Wesen des Christentums* (Leipzig: Hinrichs, 1900); trans. *What Is Christianity?* (London: Benn, 5th edn, 1958).

[110] Ernst Rénan, *The Life of Jesus* (London: Kegan Paul, 1893). Albert Schweitzer, *The Quest of the Historical Jesus: A Critical Study of its Progress from Reimarus to Wrede* (London: Black, 2nd edn, 1911), p. 182, comments that Rénan's figures 'might have been taken over in a body from the shop-window of an ecclesistical art emporium in the Place S. Sulpice'. A valuable survey of the French historical Jesus tradition is pro-

Christ, Teilhard protests, is 'not simply the dream figure of literature but its concrete realization in the Christian consciousness'.[111] Whilst affirming that Christians 'breathe the air [Christ] breathed, and something of him is circulating within us', Teilhard believes, as Blondel had reminded him, that a poetic description of Christ 'must go hand in hand with a vocation for the supernatural, with grace offered and received'.[112] Teilhard continues: 'One cannot remain true to Catholicism and be content with a mediocre explanation, a limited outlook which represents Christ as an accident of history, isolating Him in the Cosmos as if He were an episode without proper time and place.'[113] Teilhard therefore insists on the necessity of both the material and the cosmic dimensions of christology.

Teilhard presents this cosmic dimension as providing a response to the challenges of modern critical thought that does not compromise theology in the way which modernist tendencies did. He wishes to articulate Christ's universal power over creation in more than the extrinsic and juridical terms to which he found that power to be so often reduced.[114] Teilhard is inspired in this task by the 1925 encyclical *Quas primas*, proclaiming the feast of Christ the King.[115] This encyclical connects Christ's spiritual reign in hearts and wills with the enthroning of the Sacred Heart by families in their homes and with efforts to combat republican anticlericalism. Promulgated in the sixteenth millennial year of the Council of Nicaea, the encyclical's naming of Christ as King is justified as a consequence of the everlasting kingdom of Christ referred to in the Nicene Creed produced in the Church's confrontation with Arianism. Teilhard depicts Christ's kingship in characteristically material terms. On realizing that the world comprises a single whole

> we begin to see more distinctly rising over our interior world the great sun of Christ the King, of Christ *amictus mundo*, of the Universal Christ. Little by little, stage by stage, everything is finally linked to the supreme centre *in quo omnia constant*.[116]

---

vided in Élian Cuvillier, «La Question du Jésus historique dans l'exégèse francophone: aperçu historique et évaluation critique», in *Jésus de Nazareth: nouvelles approches d'une énigme*, eds. Daniel Marguerat, Enrico Norelli and Jean-Michel Poffet (Geneva: Labor et Fides, 1998), pp. 59–88.

[111] 'The Salvation of Humankind' (1936), *SC*, p. 149.
[112] Letter of 5 December 1919, *TBC*, p. 21.
[113] Paper of 5 December 1919, *TBC*, p. 23.
[114] 'Super-Humanity, Super-Christ, Super-Charity' (1943), *SC*, pp. 165–66.
[115] 'Quas primas', *PE* III, pp. 271–79.
[116] *DM*, p. 19.

Quas primas recognizes Christ as being the 'crowning glory' of the world, and the encyclical's teaching, Teilhard states, makes a 'gesture which marks a decisive stage in the development of dogma ... towards a more universalist and more realist appreciation of the Incarnation'.[117] Teilhard himself employs the image of Christ as King to show how Christ sustains all material things by unifying and governing them. This christology is a natural consequence, he believes, of any serious appraisal of the power of Christ's resurrection in its full extent:

> We are too often inclined to regard the Resurrection as an isolated event in time, with an apologetical significance, as some small individual triumph over the tomb won in turn by Christ. It is something quite other and much greater than that. It is a tremendous cosmic event. It marks Christ's effective assumption of his function as the universal centre.[118]

This cosmic christology appears synonymous with the doctrine of the kingship of Christ contained in *Quas primas*, but is in fact a significant development of it. Teilhard rereads the encyclical on the final day of his 1939 retreat, and demurs that it depicts Christ as possessing an *inferior* primacy to that granted him in the letter to the Colossians, in which Christ is the 'image of the invisible God, the firstborn of all creation', creator and sustainer of all things, whether heavenly and earthly, and the source of their consistency. Teilhard notes: «Relu l'Encyclique du Christ-Roi: Déception... Combien statique! juridique! inférieure à la thèse des Colossiens.»[119] Christ's primacy is too often reduced, Teilhard complains, to purely moral or legal terms,[120] which fail by themselves to communicate its organic character:

> Between Christ the King and the Universal Christ, there is perhaps no more than a slight difference of emphasis, but it is nevertheless all-important. It is the whole difference between an external power, which can only be juridical and static, and an internal domination which, inchoate in matter and culminating in grace, operates upon us by and through all the organic linkages of the progressing world.[121]

James Lyons argues that the term 'universal Christ', first employed by Teilhard in 1918, is virtually synonymous with 'cosmic Christ' but conveys a stronger sense of the *personality* of the second member of the

---

[117] 'The Road of the West' (1932), *TF*, pp. 59, 98.

[118] 'My Universe', pp. 63–64.

[119] Retreat note of 19–27 October 1940, *NR*, p. 167; cf. notes of 18–26 October 1941, 16–24 October 1942, *NR*, pp. 198–99, 214; cf. Col 1.15–20.

[120] 'The New Spirit, 1942', *FM*, p. 94.

[121] 'The Awaited Word' (1940), *TF*, p. 99.

Godhead.[122] The concept of universality thus contains a clearer affirmation of the particularity of Christ and the possibility of humanity entering into a relation with Christ. Teilhard explores, occasionally, a christology which posits the cosmic quality of Christ as a third *nature* distinct from humanity and divinity, declaring for instance: 'Christ possesses "universal" or "cosmic" attributes in addition to his strictly human and divine attributes.'[123] This statement is true if understood to mean that Christ in his two natures bears a cosmic *role*. Christ does not, however, need to possess a third cosmic *nature* in order for his work to have cosmic effects. Between the mid-1920s and mid-1940s, the concept «Christ cosmique» is absent from Teilhard's essays,[124] which suggests that the idea of a third cosmic nature is not itself essential for understanding the cosmic function of Christ, with the human and divine natures alone being sufficient. Lyons explores the possibility of Christ possessing a third nature with interest and approval, asserting that it can be inferred from scripture no more controversially than the Chalcedonian orthodoxy of the two natures of Christ. There is considerable truth in the assessment of Christopher Mooney, however, that Teilhard's third-nature concept is 'more easily open to a total and dangerous misinterpretation', 'untenable in the light of revelation', and 'superfluous to his own system'.[125] The notion of a cosmic nature of Christ seems to offer more hostages to theological fortune than it releases, not least because it undermines the dynamic dualism which Teilhard convincingly establishes between Christ's human and divine natures.

There is a notable rapprochement here with the theological project of Karl Barth, despite several points of disagreement[126]: the whole created order is preserved in being by Christ, seen in the light of Christ, and consummated by Christ. In the *Church Dogmatics*, Barth even refers to an apparently distinct cosmic dimension to Christ's work, asking: 'Does He really exist only as the One He alone is with God, and then as the One

---

[122] James Lyons, *The Cosmic Christ in Origen and Teilhard de Chardin: A Comparative Study* (Oxford University Press, 1982), pp. 39–40, 188; cf. 'The Priest' (1918), *WW*, p. 210.

[123] e.g. 'Some Reflections on the Conversion of the World' (1936), *SC*, p. 122; cf. 'A Sequel to the Problem of Human Origins' (1953), *CE*, p. 236; *J*, 1 September 1944, cahier XIII.

[124] Lyons, 'The instances of "Christ cosmique" in Teilhard's writings', in *Cosmic Christ*, pp. 220–21.

[125] See Lyons, *Cosmic Christ*, pp. 183–98; Mooney, *Teilhard de Chardin and the Mystery of Christ*, p. 178.

[126] For which, see Mary C. Carrington, 'Teilhard de Chardin and Karl Barth', *The Teilhard Review* 17, 2 (1982), pp. 17–24.

He is with and in His community? Does He not already exist and act and achieve and work also as the *Pantocrator*, as the κεφαλὴ ὑπὲρ πάντα, as the One who alone has first and final power in the cosmos?'[127] Although Teilhard could have agreed with Barth about the foundational place of christology in theology, he describes the effects of Christ's action on the world in very different ways. The divine glory, in Barth's dialectical theology, makes possible the manifestation of the 'infinite difference between God and man'.[128] Teilhard, by contrast, expresses the vision of God in more cataphatic, or affirmative, terms as *revealing* something of the action of Christ on the universe.

When considering the relation of christology to history, Teilhard makes a decisive break with the essentially ahistorical and parabolic presentation of scripture characteristic of the Ignatian *Exercises*. Consciously emulating the Franciscan tradition of Bonaventure's *Tree of Life*, the *Exercises* comprise meditations on the historical life of Jesus. Their origins are to be found in the renewed theological interest in the concrete, the historical and the human that characterized the twelfth century renaissance.[129] The *Exercises* are not, however, grounded in a christology of history, and neither do they posit any such christology. Teilhard, by contrast, explicitly identifies in his cosmic christology the effects of the humanity of Christ on world history, and in his theories of action and passion, its implications for human praxis. During a retreat, he even writes that, so far as christology is concerned, there is «rien de commun entre mon attitude et celle de Saint Ignace. À des époques semblables, il cherche à convertir par une sorte 'd'intégrisme', tandis que je penche vers 'l'intégralisme'.»[130] In this comment, Teilhard means to contrast a dogmatic theological method based solely on doctrine and scripture with one which takes explicit account of other sources of human knowledge in formulating theological propositions. He believes that the principal spiritual challenges in his own era are to be found not in a withdrawal from worldly living, such as that of the anchorites driven into the desert in search of purity away from a society increasingly hospitable to religion, but in renewed engagement with a

---

[127] Karl Barth, *Church Dogmatics*, IV/III, 72, 1 (10 vols; Edinburgh: T&T Clark, 1936–77), p. 756, quoted in Lyons, *Cosmic Christ*, p. 57.

[128] Karl Barth, *God in Action* (Edinburgh: T&T Clark, 1936), p. 12.

[129] Ewert H. Cousins, 'Franciscan Roots of Ignatian Meditation', in *Ignatian Spirituality in a Secular Age*, ed. George P. Schner (Waterloo, Ont.: Wilfrid Laurier University Press, 1984), pp. 51–63, provides a useful summary of this genesis.

[130] Retreat note of 19–27 October 1940, *NR*, p. 158.

world whose telos is realized by the co-operative work of Christ and humankind.[131]

Teilhard might be considered, in comparison with many current theologians, to place excessive reliance on christology to account for the consistence of the universe, at the expense of developed doctrines of the Trinity and the Holy Spirit. In a single but significant reflection, he explains part of the reason for this apparent omission:

> If the concept of the Trinity is properly understood, it can only *strengthen* our idea of divine oneness, by giving it the *structure* ... which is the mark of all real living unity, in our experience. If God were not 'triune' (if, that is, he contained no inner self-distinction) we could not conceive the possibility of his subsisting in himself, independently, and without the reaction of some surrounding world; again, if he were not triune we could not conceive the possibility of his creating (and in consequence being incarnate) without totally immersing himself in the world he brings into being.[132]

The significance of the Trinity for Teilhard is as a perichoretic, or reciprocal and interpenetrating, relation internal to the Godhead that preserves the real distinction between God and the created order and is mediated by the Holy Spirit. Teilhard's theology does not anticipate the opportunities explored much more recently by immanentist Trinitarianism which looks for traces or analogies of the Trinity in the world. In fact, Teilhard judged in 1919 that contemporary research into the Trinity seemed dead to most people.[133] So far as christology is concerned, he believes the Trinitarian context to have been superseded by a new need to understand the 'links between Christ and the universe: how they stand in relation to one another, and how they influence one another'. The desire to account for Christ's action on the universe is, however, clearly a primary motivation behind the original development of Western Trinitarian theology, and Teilhard could have chosen to renew this tradition rather than to eschew it. He does not, however, associate different functions with each of the members of the Godhead, such as redemption with

---

[131] Juan Luis Segundo, *The Christ of the Ignatian Exercises* (Maryknoll, NY: Orbis, 1987), especially chapter 7: 'The tensions of a christology', pp. 104–114, and 'A christology encounters history', pp. 115–24. Segundo argues that the christology of Ignatius constitutes the first step in a historical movement from a static 'test' christology towards a dynamic 'project' christology closer to that of the early Fathers. In contrast with many other interpreters, Segundo uses evidence from correspondence and personal biography to argue that Ignatius himself achieves this transition, moving significantly beyond the mysticism of withdrawal from the world that characterizes the early phase of his religious life at Manresa.

[132] 'Introduction to the Christian Life' (1944), *CE*, p. 157–58.

[133] *J*, 5 January 1919, cahier VI.

the Son and sanctification with the Spirit, and argues for the *continuity* of the creation, redemption and consummation of the world in a single movement. It is this conviction that the work of God is one unceasing act, combined with a profound appreciation of the physicality of this act, that leads Teilhard to assign most of the responsibility for the creation, preservation and redemption of the world to Christ rather than to the Holy Spirit.

Eucharistic transformation

Christianity, being the religion of the Incarnation, in which divinity and humanity are fused, is equally the religion of the Eucharist, which in exemplifying this fusion 'belongs to an order of its own among the sacraments'.[134] The initial cosmic role of the Eucharist is to reveal to humanity the extent to which the universe is preserved and sanctified in Christ, of whom it is the visible exemplar. The indwelling of Christ in the substance of the world is analogous to the presence of Christ in the elements of bread and wine following their eucharistic transformation. This analogy should come as little surprise, given that the origins of Blondel's *vinculum substantiale* theory are to be found in Leibniz's discussion about the nature of eucharistic substance. Wolfhart Pannenberg, while regarding Teilhard's theology as immanentist apparently on the basis of *The Human Phenomenon*, acknowledges equally Teilhard's view that 'in the sacraments of the new covenant, and above all in the eucharistic bread and wine, all creation is taken up into the sacramental action of thanksgiving to God'.[135] The doctrine of the *vinculum substantiale* affirms that material substance, being constituted and preserved in Christ, exists in a sanctified state. Christ himself suffuses material substance and sustains it. The eucharistic act is therefore more than one of thanksgiving. It is constituted by the same essential act as that which gives consistency to non-eucharistic substance, and is its type or exemplar. In the Eucharist is made explicit the fact that the human person and all other substances in the world are also given internal consistency by Christ. Inaugurated by Christ and celebrated in remembrance of Christ, as he commanded, the Eucharist is a single, unceasing action in which

---

[134] 'Introduction to the Christian Life', p. 165.
[135] Wolfhart Pannenberg, *Systematic Theology*, II (2 vols.; Edinburgh: T&T Clark, 1994), pp. 34, 75, 113, 121. The quotation is from p. 138.

humanity exists in Christ in a state of *'permanent eucharistic union'*.[136]
Teilhard states: 'All the communions of our life are, in fact, only successive instants or episodes in one single communion.'[137]

Teilhard's eucharistic theology emerges from his cosmic christology,
in which it is *Christ who assimilates the world* rather than the world
which subsumes Christ. In the Eucharist, which is the principal mode of
the indwelling of Christ within the cosmos and of Christ's animation of
the cosmos, on which all other modes of indwelling and animation
depend, Christ draws the cosmos to himself. Teilhard gains this insight,
which is of fundamental importance to his entire eucharistic theology,
from Gregory of Nyssa:

> The bread of the Eucharist is stronger than our flesh; that is why it is the
> bread that assimilates us, and not we the bread, when we receive it.[138]

It is too easy, from a doctrinal standpoint, to regard the eucharistic
species as a portion of bread passed between the ministers who conse-
crate and distribute it and the other persons who receive it.[139] This theology contains the unfortunate critical flaw of denying the decisive transformative action of the Eucharist on the world. Gregory, inspired by the
image of a little yeast raising an entire batch of dough, inverts the visible
power relations between the human body and the eucharistic body in the
following description: 'That body to which immortality has been given it
by God, when it is in ours, translates and transmutes the whole into
itself... The immortal Body, by being within that which receives it,
changes the whole to its own nature... The mere framework of our body
possesses nothing belonging to itself that is cognizable by us, to hold it
together, but remains in existence owing to a force that is introduced into
it.'[140] Humanity is received 'into the mystical extensions' of divine substance'.[141] Teilhard describes his growing awareness of this fact in a
vision immediately after receiving and consuming the Host, stating that
'though the Bread I had just eaten had become flesh of my flesh, nevertheless *it remained outside of me*'.[142] A revealing analogous point about

---

[136] 'The Humanity of Christ and the Faithful' (1920), *CE*, p. 16.

[137] 'Introduction to the Christian Life', p. 166.

[138] 'My Universe' (1924), *SC*, p. 76.

[139] Teilhard writes in a period when it was still standard practice to receive communion in one kind only, i.e. the Host but not the chalice.

[140] Gregory of Nyssa, *The Great Catechism*, §37, *NPNF*, series II, V, pp. 504–506; cf.
I Cor 5.6.

[141] 'The Humanity of Christ and the Faithful', p. 16.

[142] 'Christ in the World of Matter' (1916), *HU*, pp. 52–53.

God's embracing of human nature is made succinctly by Paul Helm: 'In the Incarnation God the Son does not become something that he was not, but assumes humanity into Godhead.'[143] This illustrates just how intimately Teilhard's eucharistic theology is related to and continuous with his cosmology. The role of Christ is fundamental in both, and by virtue of this eucharistic cosmology, humanity exists *in Christo*.

Christian practice often fails to recognize this cosmic setting of the Eucharist, however: there exists a critical danger of 'over-refined piety' which has 'lost contact with the real'.[144] Teilhard's eucharistic theology addresses this problem and thus predates, and in part inspires, the similar argument of Henri de Lubac's 1944 study *Corpus mysticum*: with the rise of late medieval piety, sacramental theology 'shrinks' the space that the eucharist is considered to transform. The eucharistic action was formerly conceived as filling and transforming the created order in eschatological expectation of its consummation. This understanding of the scope of eucharistic action is progressively reduced, however, until the Eucharist comes to be regarded in far more restricted terms as the consecration of a host which occupies a small and specific volume of space.[145] There nevertheless exists a crucial difference between Teilhard's and De Lubac's developing critiques: whereas De Lubac argues for a return to a theology of humanity within the Church as *corpus verum* gathered into unity in Christ, Teilhard places greater emphasis on eucharistic consecration transforming the substance of the whole created order beyond the ecclesial body.[146] Teilhard believes that every particular Eucharist is an instance of what Hans Urs von Balthasar describes as a *cosmic liturgy*,[147] providing his own description of this act in the following striking passage:

> When the priest says the words *Hoc est Corpus meum*, his words fall directly onto the bread and directly transform it into the individual reality of Christ. But the great sacramental operation does not cease at that local and momentary event... Throughout the life of each one of us and the life

[143] Paul Helm, 'Eternal Creation: The Doctrine of the Two Standpoints', in *Doctrine of Creation: Essays in Dogmatics, History and Philosophy*, ed. Colin Gunton (Edinburgh: T&T Clark, 1997), p. 46.

[144] 'The Sense of Humanity' (1929), *TF*, p. 38.

[145] Henri de Lubac, *Corpus mysticum*, trans. Gemma Simmonds (London: SCM, 2005).

[146] Paul McPartlan, *The Eucharist Makes the Church: Henri de Lubac and John Zizioulas in Dialogue* (Edinburgh: T&T Clark, 1996), p. 59.

[147] Hans Urs von Balthasar, *Cosmic Liturgy: The Universe According to Maximus the Confessor* (San Francisco: Ignatius, 2003).

of the Church, and the history of the world — there is only one Mass and
only one Communion... The continuity of a unique act is split up and
fixed, in space and time, for our experience. In fact, from the beginning of
the messianic preparation, up until the Parousia, passing through the historic manifestation of Jesus and the phases of growth of his Church, a single event has been developing in the world: the Incarnation, realized, in
each individual, through the Eucharist.[148]

Teilhard considers the implications of the Eucharist to be as great as
those of the Incarnation. He envisions one communion continuing from
the beginning of creation until its consummation, which takes place in a
cosmic setting and transforms that setting. Individual acts of communion
do not replace, but are instances of, this single, unbroken communion, in
which their full meaning and significance inheres. Teilhard, as well as
regarding the Eucharist as an uninterrupted, everlasting corporate act,
envisions a continuity between the particular material elements used in
its celebration and the matter of the world as a whole:

> In a secondary and generalized sense, but in a true sense, the sacramental
> Species are formed by the totality of the world, and the duration of the cre-
> ation is the time needed for its consecration.[149]

In the Eucharist, the bread offered at the altar by humankind is consecrated and returned as a gift. In this act, a portion of the material world
is offered, substantiated and returned, representing all matter in the cosmos.

Teilhard describes his profound awareness of this cosmic significance
of the Eucharist in an early short story in the style of R.H. Benson.
Although the subject of the narrative is described as a friend, it is clear
that the 'friend' is actually Teilhard himself. He perceives, whilst kneel-
ing before the Blessed Sacrament, that 'through the mysterious expansion of the host the whole world had become incandescent, had itself
become like a single giant host'.[150] The continuity of host and world is

---

[148] *DM*, pp. 85–86. Thomas Merton states of Teilhard and *The Divine Milieu*: 'He is
above all a priest, and the deepest concern of his book is the concern of a priest, a minis-
ter of Christ, one sent by Christ, with a mission to "love the world" as Christ has loved
it, and therefore to seek and to find in it all the good which is hidden there and which
Christ died on the Cross to recover. Only in these priestly and eucharistic perspectives
can we really understand the great work of Teilhard de Chardin and his profound sympathy for everything human and for every legitimate aspiration of modern man, even though
that man may sometimes be a misguided and errant thinker, a heretic, an atheist.' ('The
Universe as Epiphany', in *Love and Living*, eds. Naomi Burton Stone and Patrick Hart
(London: Sheldon, 1979), pp. 183–84.)

[149] *DM*, p. 88.

[150] 'The Monstrance', in 'Christ in the World of Matter', p. 48.

made possible by the 'real, and physical, extensions of the Eucharistic Presence'. The priest's words over the Host therefore possess a twofold reference:

> When the phrase 'Hoc est Corpus meum' is pronounced, 'hoc' means 'primario' the bread; but 'secundario', in a second phase occurring in nature, the matter of the sacrament is the world, throughout which there spreads, so to complete itself, the superhuman presence of the universal Christ. The world is the final, and the real, Host into which Christ gradually descends, until his time is fulfilled.
>
> The priestly act extends beyond the transubstantiated Host to the cosmos itself, which, century after century, is gradually being transformed by the Incarnation, itself never complete. From age to age, there is but one single mass in the world: the true Host, the total Host, is the universe which is continually being more intimately penetrated and vivified by Christ.[151]

In the Eucharist there occurs, Teilhard states, a 'transubstantiation' of the host and a transformation of the cosmos itself. Whether or not the change taking place in the cosmos can accurately be described as transubstantiation in the Thomist sense of the word requires careful consideration, however. Teilhard's eucharistic theology shares many features with the one which prevailed prior to what Andrew Louth describes as the 'collapse of the notion of sacred space'.[152] Transubstantiation, by contrast, is developed in response to the emerging new cosmology of *non*-sacred space that replaced this in an attempt to provide an account of the problematic and unique nature of consecrated eucharistic substance that was the legacy of the end of this cosmology.

The doctrine of transubstantiation states, strictly, the belief that in the Eucharist the substances of bread and wine are replaced by those of the body and blood of Christ, whilst the accidents of bread and wine, including their appearance and taste, remain unchanged.[153] This doctrine is dependent on an adaptation of conventional Aristotelian physics, according to which the accidents of a substance are caused by and inhere in its matter, and if a substance changes, then its accidents must change as well.[154] According to Aristotle, it is impossible for substance to be trans-

---

[151] 'My Universe', p. 65; 'Pantheism and Christianity' (1923), *CE*, pp. 73–74.

[152] Andrew Louth, 'The Body in Western Catholic Christianity', in *Religion and the Body*, ed. Sarah Coakley (Cambridge University Press, 1997), p. 124.

[153] *ST*, IIIa, q. 75, aa. 5–6.

[154] Aristotle, *Metaphysics*, 1027a12–15, *Works* XVII, pp. 302–303. For Aristotle's belief that substance develops, or becomes, over time, see J.W. Felt, 'Whitehead's Misconception of "Substance" in Aristotle', *Process Studies* 14 (1985), pp. 224–36. This interpretation suggests that Aristotle possesses a more dynamic concept of substance than do Descartes or Locke that is closer to Teilhard's own.

formed while the accidents associated with it remain unchanged, because an accident is something which belongs, or does not belong, to a thing (res).[155] Aquinas believes, however, that in the special case of the Eucharist, substance may change whilst accidents persist. The discontinuity which the doctrine of transubstantiation thus posits when one substance is replaced by another is absent in Teilhard's theology, however. In the transformation of substance that Teilhard describes, the original matter of the substance persists. This doctrine cannot, therefore, strictly be described as transubstantiation, even though Teilhard employs this term in places. Neither can the transformation be described as consubstantiation, in which Christ becomes present *in conjunction with* a persisting substance.[156] This is because no other bond of substance exists, in fact, apart from Christ.

In Teilhard's account of the eucharistic transformation of matter, it is the *strength* and *appearance* of the bond of substance that change. He provides an additional twist to standard eucharistic theology in his theory of perception: *vision* transforms human experience of the empirical world so that the world is seen to be preserved in Christ. The world surrounding the person of faith assumes a numinous or sacramental quality. It is therefore possible to speak of a transformation of the accidents of a substance, which is the principal point that the classic Thomist doctrine of transubstantiation denies. There is some similarity here with the doctrine's Cartesian formulation: in the human experience of substances, God intervenes in the perception of sensible qualities, which in the case of the Eucharist provides purely superficial, or surface, contact with the host, which is all to which humanity has access.[157] It would never be possible, for this reason, to establish experimentally whether or not transubstantiation in Aquinas's sense of the term had in fact occurred. Teilhard maintains, nevertheless, that vision of the substance itself is possible. This is because both eucharistic transformation, and humanity's perception of that transformation, are diffused in space. Teilhard states:

[155] Aristotle, *Topica*, 102b3–26, *Works* II, pp. 284–87.

[156] For the distinction between transubstantiation and consubstantiation, see David Burr, 'Scotus and Transubstantiation', *Mediaeval Studies* 34 (1972), pp. 336–60.

[157] See especially René Descartes, 'Fourth Set of Replies', in *Meditations on First Philosophy, The Philosophical Works of Descrates*, II (3 vols.; Cambridge University Press, 1984), pp. 173–77; Richard A. Watson, 'Transubstantiation among the Cartesians', in *Problems of Cartesianism*, eds. Thomas Lennon et al. (Kingston, Ont.: McGill-Queen's University Press, 1982), pp. 127–48.

> When Christ, carrying further the process of his Incarnation, comes down
> into the bread in order to dwell there in its place, his action is not confined
> to the particle of matter that his Presence is at hand, for a moment, to ethe-
> realize. The transubstantiation is encircled by a halo of divinization — real,
> even though less intense — that extends to the whole universe.[158]

There are good reasons to desist from describing this transformation as
transubstantiation. Although Teilhard frequently describes it as such, in
a retreat note written shortly before his death he accepts that «dans
l'Eucharistie la grande affaire n'est plus la 'Transsubstantiation' au
vieux sens du mot (la substitution de 2 Matières) ... [but] Pléromisation»[159]: in other words, the bringing of the fullness of Christ into the
world. The 'halo of divinization' associated with this vision of the fullness of Christ in the world suggests a continuity between substance and
accident rather than an absolute distinction between them. Vision shows
humanity how the substance of the world is sustained by the action of
Christ and progressively unified through his work of Incarnation, which
is exemplified and continued in unceasing eucharistic transformation.

---

[158] 'The Priest' (1918), *WW*, p. 207.
[159] Retreat notes of 27 September – 8 October 1953, *NR*, p. 338. 'In the Eucharist, the
principal point in question is no longer "transubstantiation" in the old sense of the word
(the substitution of one matter for another) [but] "Pléromisation".'

5. VISION

Teilhard is a profoundly visual thinker. At the opening of *The Human Phenomenon*, he affirms the pre-eminent place which vision occupies in human knowledge:

> One could say that the whole of life lies in seeing — if not ultimately, at least essentially. To be more is to be united — and this sums up and is the very conclusion of the work to follow. But unity grows, and we will affirm this again, only if it is supported by an increase of consciousness, of vision. That is probably why the history of the living world can be reduced to the elaboration of ever more perfect eyes at the heart of a cosmos where it is always possible to discern more. Are not the perfection of an animal and the supremacy of the thinking being measured by the penetration and power of synthesis of their glance?[1]

Teilhard employs visual metaphors frequently to suggest this awakening of spiritual awareness. One of his favourite images is the opening of the eyes.[2] He describes the potential which humanity possesses to see the truth, and describes the dazzling of the eyes by revelation.[3] Sensory images are in general important because of their suitability to describe the spiritual experience of the individual person in psychological terms. They are therefore especially prominent in *The Divine Milieu*, whose purpose Teilhard describes as being to 'offer a simple description of a psychological evolution', and in 'The Heart of Matter', in which he provides an account of a 'personal psychological experience: nothing more, but also nothing less'.[4] Vision becomes the principal organ of the imagination, and the means by which humanity gives attention to the sensible reality of the world by perceiving the place of each element within the space and time of the whole.[5]

What, then, is the object to which vision is directed? The person of faith is called to see the world in Christ, who preserves its substance and sustains human action and passion. Christ becomes the medium through

---

[1] *HP*, p. 3.
[2] e.g. 'Cosmic Life' (1916), p. 53; 'The Christic' (1955), p. 85.
[3] Letter of 28 February 1954, *LT*, p. 350; 'The Christic', p. 94.
[4] *DM*, p. xxxi; letter of 18 August 1950, *LTF*, p. 214.
[5] Michel Mansuy, «Pierre Teilhard de Chardin», in *Études sur l'imagination de la vie* (Paris: José Corti, 1970), pp. 175–209.

whom the world is seen,[6] but is also himself seen. Vision, the act of seeing, is crucial to this disclosure. Teilhard states: 'If we had to give a more exact name to the mystical Milieu we would say that it is a Flesh — for it has all the properties the flesh has of palpable domination and limitless embrace.'[7] Teilhard uses the term 'milieu' to describe the active mediation which takes place between the substance perceived and the subject of the perception. The milieu is created by the action of Christ on the world, in which Christ reveals his sustaining presence within it, and by the attention of the subject, which transforms her vision. In practice, the divine milieu can be discovered in a diversity of ways. Teilhard states:

> Whether I am actively impelled towards development by the sensibly perceptible aspirations of my nature, or painfully mastered by material contacts, or visited by the graces of prayer, in each case I am equally moving in the mystical Milieu. First and foremost, I am *in Christo Jesu*; it is only afterwards that I am acting, or suffering, or contemplating.[8]

Teilhard, in employing visual metaphors to describe divine action on the world and presence in it, is clearly inspired by Ignatius Loyola, whose retreat he followed annually for eight days.[9] In the 'Contemplation for Achieving Love', which Teilhard particularly admired,[10] Ignatius urges the retreatant:

> See God living in His creatures: in matter, giving it existence; in plants, giving them life; in animals, giving them consciousness; in men, giving them intelligence.[11]

This is a vision of God active in the world, preserving it and animating it. Significantly, the original subtitle of *The Divine Milieu*, Teilhard's principal theological work, was not *Essai de vie intérieure*, but *Essai de vision intérieure*.[12] Despite making this change to the subtitle, Teilhard

---

[6] 'The Humanity of Christ and the Faithful' (1920), *CE*, pp. 19–20.

[7] 'My Universe' (1924), *SC*, p. 75.

[8] 'My Universe', p. 75.

[9] For comparison of the two figures, see the excellent discussion of Émile Rideau, 'Teilhard's spirituality and the *Spiritual Exercises* of St Ignatius', in *Teilhard de Chardin: A Guide to his Thought* (London: Collins, 1967), pp. 211–220; and Rogelio Garcia-Mateo, „Spiritualität der Welt: Teilhard de Chardin (1881–1955) und ignatianische Spiritualität", in *Gottes Nähe: religiöse Erfahrung in Mystik und Offenbarung: Festschrift zum 65. Geburtstag von Josef Sudbrack SJ*, ed. Paul Imhof (Würzburg: Echter, 1990), pp. 367–81.

[10] Retreat note of 19–27 October 1940, *NR*, p. 169.

[11] Ignatius Loyola, *The Spiritual Exercises* (Wheathampstead: Clarke, 1987), §§230–37.

[12] Haiyan Wang, *Le Phénomène Teilhard: l'aventure du livre 'Le Milieu divin'* (Saint-Étienne: Aubin, 1999), p. 36.

still expresses the original intention of his study in the Preface, in which he identifies its subject to be 'interior vision'.[13] In 'The Heart of Matter' he refers similarly to 'inner vision'.[14] Teilhard has a very specific type of experience in mind here. Interior vision is not the internal spiritual illumination of the individual soul expounded in Augustine's *De trinitate*, in which images of the Trinity found in the sensory world are presented as being, at best, poor analogies for the inner illumination of the soul by God. Augustine proposes in this work an overtly introspective form of illumination: 'Let us put aside all consideration of things we know outwardly through the senses of the body, and concentrate our attention on what we have stated that all minds know for certain about themselves', in other words, their possession of memory, understanding and will.[15] Teilhard recovers, by contrast, a literal sense of vision as that which is given to the human soul by God through objects in the world that are external to the soul.

Light, fire, illumination

In *The Divine Milieu*, Teilhard describes the appearance of the material world by means of striking light metaphors. He writes of its *éclat* (brilliance), *brille* (shine) and *incandescence*. It is *éblouissant* (dazzling), *lumineuse*, *limpide*, and like a *rayon* (ray of light). In an earlier work, he sees the universe 'bathed in light'.[16] Fire and conflagration imagery also capture Teilhard's imagination: humanity lives, he affirms, 'steeped' in the 'burning layers' of the divine and in its 'living light'. Elsewhere, he refers simply to the 'universe ablaze'.[17] Teilhard employs, in addition to these images of the illumination of the substance of the world, similar language to describe the specific case of the union of the individual soul with God. He writes of the dissolution of the 'tension engendered by the encounter between human beings and God' as being 'like a huge fire', and of the 'spirit drawn to God' as being 'like the jet of flame that effortlessly pierces the hardest metal'.[18] He prays: 'Lord, lock me up in the

---

[13] *DM*, p. xxx.

[14] 'The Heart of Matter' (1950), *HM*, p. 35, 38.

[15] Augustine, *The Trinity*, X.14 (Brooklyn, NY: New City Press, 1997), p. 296. Augustine considers these three faculties each to be clear and distinct powers, and forms his final mental image of the divine Trinity from them.

[16] 'My Universe', p. 74.

[17] *DM*, pp. 73–74; 'The Mass on the World' (1923), *HM*, pp. 21–29. For the fire metaphor, see Henri de Lubac, *TBC*, pp. 86–87, n.

[18] *DM*, p. 103.

deepest depths of your heart; and then, holding me there, burn me, purify me, set me on fire.'[19] Teilhard's use of similar images to describe both the illumination of the soul and the illumination of substance suggests that he considers these to comprise two aspects of a single enlightenment. He identifies light as a rational forming principle, as does Plotinus, which transforms the ordinary substance (οὐσία) of intelligible matter (νοητή ὕλη) into illuminated substance (πεφωτισμένη οὐσία).[20] In another essay, Teilhard refers to the coherence which the divine milieu 'introduces into the underlying depths of my mind and heart'.[21] He does not have in mind here, however, the purely individual revelation that has been so prominent in the mystical tradition. Teilhard's fire is not confined within the soul, but is a universal conflagration into which the soul is plunged. He states: '*The Fire of heaven* which consumes us, reaches us in (and after) embracing the world.'[22] This indicates that the divine milieu is dependent on the external world for communicating its revelation. Although Teilhard offers psychological descriptions of the human soul in many of his essays, he insists that the soul can be illumined only through the illumination of the world it inhabits. This illumination is possible because God 'truly awaits us in things', with the soul being absolutely dependent 'upon God's presence in them'.[23] It is through the shared world of substance that the individual soul will attain spiritual vision.

In favouring vision above the other sensory operations, Teilhard stands in agreement with a long tradition of reflection on the respective importance of the various senses. Aristotle recognizes vision to be the most highly developed sense.[24] Robert Grosseteste likewise places vision above the other four senses on the grounds that light, the pure element, is both its object and its power.[25] In the Christian mystical tradition, vision becomes associated with an intellectualist and especially a Dionysian mystical theology which allows the possibility of self-transcendence and the union of the soul with God. This contrasts with vol-

---

[19] 'The Mass on the World', p. 32.

[20] Plotinus, *Enneads*, II.4 (12) 5 (7 vols.; Harvard University Press, 1966–88), pp. 112–117.

[21] 'The Christic', p. 100.

[22] Paper of 29 December 1919, *TBC*, p. 49.

[23] *DM*, pp. 4, 31.

[24] Aristotle, *On the Soul*, III.3, *Works* VIII (23 vols.; Harvard University Press, 1926–91), pp. 154–63.

[25] James McEvoy, *The Philosophy of Robert Grosseteste* (Oxford: Clarendon, 1982), pp. 296–97.

untarist traditions, which have tended to favour images derived from touch, taste and smell, because these images suggest a closer motivational relation between the object and its perceiver. It would be wrong to conclude from this evidence, however, that the more private senses have enjoyed no share of the intellectualist inheritance. This is because apophatic mystical imagery employs, as Denys Turner explains, the following principle of inversion: 'The higher a reality is on the scale of excellence the more appropriate it is to use images of lower things to describe it.'[26] In negative theology therefore, in which the soul's inability to have knowledge of God is emphasized, vision is more likely to be used to describe lower, merely philosophical truths than to depict truths revealed to the soul by God.

The difficulty with using perceptual images derived from touch, taste and smell to describe religious experience, however, is the high degree of intimacy that these forms of sensing demand. There are evidently many everyday situations in which sight would be a far more appropriate sense to employ than, for instance, touch or taste. Sight, it is commonly argued, possesses no physical dimension, in contrast with the other senses.[27] Why, therefore, have the more intimate senses achieved such prominence in religious epistemology? In the case of mystical experience, they often seem to have been preferred because their private character is well-suited to a theory of individual, interior illumination. Teilhard himself employs images drawn from the more intimate and exclusive senses in certain places, such as in his description of savouring the 'unique fragrance' of the glory and wonder of Jesus.[28] Nonetheless, with the exception of early descriptions of touching physical matter, his use of images drawn from the more intimate senses tends to be metaphorical, such as in his descriptions of 'tasting' being. He does not employ these types of images to describe any actual sensory religious experience.

Vision is notable among the sensory operations for the wide range of types of experience it is able to encompass, from the highly interiorized

---

[26] Denys Turner, *The Darkness of God: Negativity in Christian Mysticism* (Cambridge University Press, 1995), pp. 47, 200–201.

[27] As discussed in David Braine, 'The Active and Potential Intellects: Aquinas as a Philosopher in his Own Right', in *Mind, Metaphysics, and Value in the Thomistic and Analytical Traditions*, ed. John Haldane (Notre Dame, Ind.: University of Notre Dame Press, 2002), p. 29.

[28] smell: 'The Priest' (1918), *WW*, p. 211; taste: 'The Mass on the World', p. 30; *DM*, pp. 24 [le goût], 40; hearing: 'The Priest', p. 206; touch: 'Christ in the World of Matter' (1916), *HU*, p. 53; 'The Mass on the World', p. 26; *DM*, pp. 43, 44, 53; 'The Heart of Matter', p. 56.

and intimate to the very public and general. An instance of the use of vision to describe inner revelation is provided by George Herbert's poem 'Love bade me welcome', in which 'quick-eyed love, observing me grow slack' draws the subject from an awareness of her unworthiness to look upon the maker of her eyes and 'taste his meat'.[29] The dialogue form of the poem, and the tasting metaphor, identify it as a description of the revelation of one (divine) person to another (human) person set in no particular material or social context. Vision can, however, describe shared experience equally well as individual experience, and is unique among the senses in possessing this capacity. Neither touch, nor taste, nor smell, nor even hearing, provides the same potential breadth of sensing that seeing may attain. Sight is a qualitatively different sense, being more comprehensive than any other. Visual imagery challenges, therefore, the excessively interiorized conceptions of spiritual illumination that both the historic spiritual tradition and contemporary interest in it have tended to favour. In particular, it enables accounts of religious experience to move beyond the predominant Neoplatonic notion of the soul as the *speculum* of the divine.[30] The world itself now becomes the *speculum*. Teilhard declares:

> To the Christian's sensitized vision, it is true, the Creator and, more precisely, the Redeemer (as we shall see) have steeped themselves in all things and penetrated all things to such a degree that, as S. Angela of Foligno said, 'the world is full of God'.[31]

Elsewhere, Teilhard encapsulates Angela's statement more simply: 'God is everywhere.'[32] Not only the soul, but the world itself, reflects divine glory: 'Everything, in every element and event of the universe, is bathed in light and warmth, everything becomes animate and a fit object for love and worship.'[33]

Much of the mystical tradition of interior illumination is not entirely solitary, having been fostered in the communal setting of the Greek philosophical schools and later Christian monasticism.[34] Such mystical enterprises as these were nonetheless conceived in quite different terms

[29] *George Herbert*, ed. Louis L. Martz (Oxford University Press, 1994), p. 167.
[30] For the Neoplatonic interpretation, see Douglas Hedley, *Coleridge, Philosophy and Religion: 'Aids to Reflection' and the Mirror of the Spirit* (Cambridge University Press, 2000), pp. 109–116.
[31] *DM*, p. 78.
[32] 'Cosmic Life', p. 60
[33] 'My Fundamental Vision' (1948), *TF*, p. 204.
[34] Kevin Corrigan, 'So-Called Solitary Mysticism in Plotinus, Proclus, Gregory of Nyssa and Pseudo-Dionysius', *Journal of Religion* 76 (1996), pp. 28–42.

from Teilhard's. Although the community might have provided common worship, care and other practical assistance to support contemplation, the illumination which contemplation might bring was still conceived as an interior movement occurring within the soul. This communitarianism is expressed in Augustinian ecclesiology, in which love of neighbour is a *consequence* of love of God and love of self: in Augustine's opinion, it follows from the believer's love of God that he will ensure that his neighbour also loves God, because the believer is commanded to love his neighbour as himself.[35] In Teilhard's theology, however, the whole created order constitutes the milieu in which God is seen, thus transforming spiritual practices founded on principles of introversion into disciplines which affirm the goodness of the created order and its existence in Christ. Teilhard, in formulating his theory of vision, criticizes the 'forbidden distortions' of the *illuminati*, or Alumbrados, according to whom the divine will could be communicated immediately and infallibly to the soul following spiritual abandonment (*dexados*).[36] Ignatius Loyola was himself accused of holding this view, which was condemned in the Spanish Inquisition. Teilhard's doctrine of vision is intended to prevent just these kinds of excesses by establishing the shared, public context of the spiritual ascent of the soul. By applying the spiritual senses to the world, the subject is called to test them, in the words of Hugo Rahner, 'against the tangible, the visible, and even ... the reasonable'.[37]

Vision: the end of life

Teilhard believes that the vision of God, given in and through the divine milieu, is the end for which all human life is destined. Vision unifies the partial perspectives of reality gained in the praxis of active and passive existence, which are

> transfigured and clarified for us in the rays of creative union... The whole mass of the universe is gradually bathed in light... A mystical ambience

---

[35] Augustine, *De civitate Dei*, XIX.14 (7 vols.; Harvard University Press, 1957–72), VI, pp. 184–85.

[36] *DM*, p. 78. Hugo Rahner, *Ignatius the Theologian* (London: Chapman, 1968), pp. 156–63, presents a clear contrast between the spiritual doctrines of Ignatius and the Alumbrados. For background, see Alastair Hamilton, *Heresy and Mysticism in 16th-Century Spain: The Alumbrados* (Cambridge: James Clarke, 1992).

[37] Rahner, *Ignatius*, pp. 226–27.

[milieu mystique] appears in which everything floats [tout baigne] and everything converges.[38]

Vision reveals to humanity this 'mystical ambience', which has the property of a 'unifying Centre'.[39] It cannot be understood as a vaguely numinous quality emanating from material objects. Teilhard continues:

> In this most rich and living ambience [milieu], the attributes, seemingly the most contradictory, of attachment and detachment, of action and contemplation, of the one and the multiple, are reconciled without difficulty in conformity with the designs of creative union: everything becomes one by becoming self.[40]

Vision thus reveals a milieu in which apparent dichotomies are harmonized whilst their particularity is preserved. Teilhard, in regarding vision as thus providing the shared telos for individual human life, imparts new significance to an ancient spiritual tradition. Irenaeus of Lyons states that the 'life of the human is the vision of God'.[41] Thomas Aquinas asserts that the correct goal for human life is the direct vision of God.[42] Gottfried Leibniz avers: 'God is the only immediate object of our perceptions which exist outside us, and he alone is our light... We can say that God alone is our immediate external object, and that we see all things through him.'[43] Teilhard himself affirms that 'each one of the elect is called upon to see God face to face.'[44] All four believe that the soul, by means of vision, may gain heightened perception and deeper understanding of the material world. The unifying perspective which vision provides is reminiscent of Ignatius's view of the world *de arriba*, or in Pierre Hadot's expression, the 'view from above'.[45] Vision provides a single true perspective which transcends an infinity of partial

---

[38] 'My Universe' (1924), *SC*, pp. 73–74.

[39] 'Creative Union' (1917), *WW*, p. 175.

[40] 'My Universe', p. 74.

[41] Irenaeus, *Against Heresies*, IV, 20.7, *ANF* I, p. 490. May A. Donovan, 'Alive to the Glory of God', *TS* 49 (1988), pp. 283–97, provides an excellent exposition of this thought.

[42] *ST*, IaIIae, q. 3, a. 8.

[43] G.W. Leibniz, *Discourse on Metaphysics*, §28, in *Philosophical Texts*, eds. R.S. Woolhouse and Richard Francks (Oxford University Press, 1998), p. 80.

[44] *DM*, p. 106. The 'elect' can here be understood to mean any soul with vision.

[45] Pierre Hadot, 'The view from above', in *Philosophy as a Way of Life: Spiritual Exercises from Socrates to Foucault* (Oxford: Blackwell, 1995), pp. 238–50. Teilhard draws a distinction between the 'God of the Above' and 'God of the Ahead'. (e.g. 'The Heart of Matter', pp. 44–46, 97–99.) He wishes in his theology to effect a 'change of direction to the transverse', i.e. from a concept of the God of the Above to one that unifies the Above with the Ahead. ('The Heart of Matter', p. 46.)

perspectives, providing a 'viewpoint from which everything is bathed in light.'[46] In so doing, it makes possible human participation in divine omniscience, fulfilling what Hannah Arendt describes as the 'Archimedean wish for a point outside the earth from which to unhinge the world'. Arendt considers this wish to have been granted from *within* the world by technological intervention in natural processes.[47] Teilhard does not accept, in contrast, that such a point can be attained by purely technical means. Vision provides Teilhard's 'Archimedean point', or as he describes it, a «point d'appui»,[48] because it allows the soul to see the world in its totality and simplicity.

A more precise understanding of the relation which vision establishes between humanity and God can be gained by situating Teilhard's discussion of vision in the context of debates about the nature of mystical experience in classic spiritual writers. Teilhard's devotion was definitively formed, from childhood onwards, by traditional catholic piety, with key figures including Thomas à Kempis, Francis of Assisi, Angela of Foligno, Bonaventure, Vincent de Paul, John of the Cross, and of course Ignatius Loyola.[49] These and other devotional writers remained a continuous presence in his life. Teilhard states that he even considered giving up his geological work during his studies at the Maison Saint-Louis, the Jesuit philosophy scholasticate in Jersey where he spent three years, in order to devote his attention exclusively to prayer, but that one of his tutors managed to deter him from this course of action.[50] A question that arises on reading much of the devotional literature which inspired Teilhard, and which was keenly discussed in early twentieth-century French mystical theology, concerns whether or not the perception of God by humanity is possible in current human life. Teilhard's own opinion about this will be illuminated by a brief consideration of two prominent figures who represent opposing positions in this debate: Auguste Poulain, a Jesuit priest, and Canon Auguste

---

[46] 'The Stuff of the Universe' (1953), *AE*, p. 376.

[47] Hannah Arendt, *The Human Condition* (University of Chicago Press, 1989), p. 262; 'The Conquest of Space and the Stature of Man', in *Between Past and Future: Eight Exercises in Political Thought* (London: Penguin, 1993), p. 279.

[48] 'Spiritual Power of Matter' (1919), *HU*, p. 66; cf. retreat note of 16–24 October 1942, *NR*, p. 222.

[49] 'The Heart of Matter', pp. 45–46; 'Cosmic Life' (1916), *WW*, p. 52; 'The Mystical Milieu' (1917), *WW*, p. 148; 'Cosmic Life', p. 60; letter of 17 December 1919, *MM*, p. 307; *DM*, p. 54, n. 52.

[50] 'The Heart of Matter', p. 46.

[51] Auguste Poulain, *Des grâces d'oraison: traité de théologie mystique* (Paris: V. Retaux, 1901; 10th edn, 1922); Auguste Saudreau, *Les Faits extraordinaires de la vie*

Saudreau.[51] Poulain, to whom Teilhard refers in a letter to Auguste Valensin, affirms:

> From the point of view of the object of vision, *we might say* that these divine things are perceived in the *media* of very sublime *species*, representing the object in a very eminent manner; but it would *perhaps be better* ... to admit that the light of the higher order thus communicated to the mind, is a *certain participation of the light of glory*; consequently, it disposes the intellect so that God Himself may unite Himself to it, *after the manner of an intelligible species*, but in a diminished degree.[52]

In preferring an account of mystical perception based on intelligible species rather than merely sublime ones, Poulain is allowing the possibility that some souls are more inclined to spiritual vision (i.e. vision of intelligible species) than others, according to their state of grace: the perception of sublime species would require the use of common perceptual and intellectual methods. He makes clear that souls inclined to spiritual vision have it revealed to them by a divine illuminative act. Thomas Aquinas also states that some souls see the divine essence more perfectly than others, as they possess greater or lesser shares of the light of glory.[53]

Auguste Saudreau, to whom Teilhard refers in a retreat note and in the same letter to Valensin,[54] maintained, by contrast, a consistently apophatic doctrine of God, concluding his study of the mystical tradition by stating of God in the following unequivocal terms:

> Whatever we can think of him cannot by any possibility come anywhere near the reality. He resembles nothing of which we have cognizance. He infinitely surpasses all that we can represent to ourselves.[55]

In Saudreau's opinion, it follows from this divine otherness or strangeness that no perception of God by humanity is possible in this life, and that God's presence can only be known indirectly. In Poulain's terms, the light of glory is unable to effect any real transformation of human perception. This view seems difficult to defend without undermining either the power or the indeterminacy of divine revelation, however, and

---

spirituelle: état angélique, extase, révélations, visions, possessions (Paris: Vic et Amat, 1908; 2nd edn, 1921).

[52] Auguste Poulain, *The Graces of Interior Prayer: A Treatise on Mystical Theology* (London: Kegan Paul, Trench, Trubner & Co., 6th edn, 1910), p. 569; cf. letter of 21 December 1919, *LI*, pp. 36–37.

[53] *ST*, Ia, q. 12, a. 6.

[54] Retreat note of 23 March 1919, *NR*, p. 76.

[55] Auguste Saudreau, *The Life of Union with God, and the Means of Attaining it, according to the Great Masters of Spirituality* (London: Burns, Oates & Washbourne, 3rd edn, 1927), pp. 324–25.

places apparent limits on what divine action can or cannot achieve in its transformation of humanity. The contentious nature of the debate about the vision of God is illustrated in the second edition of Monseigneur Albert Farges's study *Les Phénomènes mystiques*.[56] Farges defends Poulain from charges brought by Saudreau that Poulain 'invents' the doctrine of intermediate contemplation — that which occurs *'after the manner of an intelligible species'* — by identifying its use by Aquinas.[57] Farges draws the Thomistic distinction between the sensible life in *act*, for which the vision of God is impossible, and the sensible life in *power*, 'in which latter, through the complete silence of the senses, [the vision of God] becomes possible'. This silencing of the senses is, moreover, possible in earthly life.[58] Farges argues against Poulain, however, that although the vision of God perceives *effects* of divine action, rather than divine action itself, it by no means follows that this vision is indirect or 'intermediate', rather than a direct vision. Humanity, Farges argues, is able to see God through the 'divine touch' or 'species' which the logos impresses on the intellect,[59] and this allows 'direct intuition of the act of God'. The analogy of seeing through a *veil* provides a better understanding of this perception than the more mediatory image of reflection in a mirror:

> If, however, these species can in no way act the part of a mirror or of intermediate images, in the sensation of the divine, they may, nevertheless, be compared to transparent veils which diminish the brightness of the divine light and obscure its direct vision.[60]

Farges thus affirms that souls, through the passive effects of God, 'see him in himself and not in an image apart from him', even though the brightness of this vision is dimmed and obscured.[61] In defending Poulain against Saudreau, Farges therefore develops a more cataphatic conception of vision than Poulain himself.

---

[56] Albert Farges, *Les Phénomènes mystiques distingués de leurs contrefaçons humaines et diaboliques* (2 vols.; Saint Dizier: A. Brulliard, 2nd edn, 1925); trans. *Mystical Phenomena, compared with their Human and Diabolical Counterfeits: A Treatise on Mystical Theology in Agreement with the Principles of St Teresa set forth by the Carmelite Congress of 1923 at Madrid* (London: Burns, Oates & Washbourne, 1926).

[57] Cf. Aquinas, *Truth*, q. 18, a. 1 (3 vols.; Indianapolis: Hackett, 1994), II, pp. 338–46; cf. Farges, *Mystical Phenomena*, pp. 266–68.

[58] Cf. *ST*, IIaIIae, q. 174, a. 1; q. 180, a. 5; Farges, *Mystical Phenomena*, p. 273.

[59] Cf. *ST*, Ia, q. 105, a. 3.

[60] Farges, *Mystical Phenomena*, p. 77.

[61] Farges, *Mystical Phenomena*, pp. 276–77.

In at least one place, Teilhard describes the distinctive character of the beatific vision in terms with which Saudreau could have agreed, remarking when learning of the death of his mentor Auguste Valensin that 'now, he sees'.[62] Lying behind this response is a classic theology of the beatific vision as possible only following bodily death. Nonetheless, Teilhard's theory of the divine milieu enables him to defend the possibility of the vision of God during current earthly life. He states that God, 'with the help of the great layers of creation ... will become ... universally tangible and active'.[63] This is the vision of effects described by Farges: direct, but intuited and obscured. In thus maintaining the possibility that some kind of spiritual vision may be gained in this life, Teilhard affirms in principle the view of Thomas Aquinas, who states that some created minds are able to see the essence of God, but remain unable to comprehend it.[64] This vision is, according to Aquinas and the Thomist tradition, due neither to the bodily eyes, nor to the natural powers of created minds.[65] Teilhard accepts, thus far, the Thomist view. He and Aquinas understand the *object* of vision in different ways, however, and this has consequences for Teilhard's understanding of the means by which the object acts on the subject. The Angelic Doctor employs the metaphor of air receiving the form of fire to describe how vision may occur as a result of natural change in the soul: just as air may receive the form of fire, so 'when any created intellect sees the essence of God, the essence of God itself becomes the intelligible form of the intellect'.[66] Teilhard suggests, by contrast, that the created intellect does not, on its transformation, become a different substance. His purpose in using fire imagery is to describe the transformation of the substance which the individual soul *perceives*, rather than the transformation of the substance of the individual soul. The essence of God becomes, as already dis-

---

[62] Letter of 5 January 1954, *LT*, p. 348.

[63] *DM*, p. 3.

[64] *ST*, Ia, q. 12, a. 1. A similar extended discussion occurs in the *Summa contra gentiles*, III/I, aa. 46–63 (5 vols.; Notre Dame, Ind.: University of Notre Dame Press 1975), pp. 154–209. For both theologians, the possibility of spiritual as well as physical sight follows from the fact that humans are composed of spirit as well as body. Archimandrite Elevferiy, 'On Spiritual Sight', *Journal of the Moscow Patriarchate* 1981, 4, pp. 34–35, expresses this idea succinctly.

[65] *ST*, Ia, q. 12, aa. 3–4.

[66] *ST*, Ia, q. 12, a. 6; cf. P. Reeve, 'Exploring a Metaphor Theologically: Thomas Aquinas on the Beatific Vision', in *Studies in Thomistic Theology*, ed. Paul Lockey (Houston: University of St Thomas, 1995), p. 288. For the context of this discussion, see Henri F. Dondaine, «L'Objet et le 'médium' de la vision béatifique au XIIIe siècle», *RTAM* 19 (1952), pp. 60–130.

cussed, the intelligible form of a new spiritual substance which super-venes on material substance.

The effect of this transformation of substance on intellect now requires consideration. Aquinas believes that the *lumen gloriae* illu-mines the intellect, establishing it in a kind of deiformity and enabling it perceive God more perfectly. In other words, the light of glory does not establish a new intellectual medium in the mind in which God is seen, but *enhances* the intellectual *power* by which God is seen.[67] A defla-tionary interpretation of this distinction between medium and power would regard it as similar to the contrast drawn by Aquinas between his own abstractionist theology of the vision of God and the intellectual intuitionism of Augustine or the universal agent intellect theory of Avi-cenna.[68] According to Aquinas's interpretation, the light of glory would represent the *agent* intellect, which gives to the perceiver the conceptual framework needed to provide the 'power to make things actually intelli-gible, by abstraction of the species from material conditions'.[69] Teilhard, whilst considering vision to be a mediated process, interprets the light of glory literally, however. The light of glory implies a medium *in* which God is seen, and *through* which material substance appears in a new, spiritual light. In allowing a form of perception requiring no conceptual meditation, Teilhard here seems to be siding with Augustine against Aquinas, portraying the mind as an essentially passive recipient of God's revelation in visual form. Teilhard remains convinced that in the case of religious experience, the mind is a purely passive recipient of data.

To digress briefly, Teilhard does retain a theory of active intellect to explain *non*-mystical perception, emphasizing continually the universal character of concepts which structure experience, and affirming that the human soul is 'besieged and penetrated by the flow of cosmic influences which have to be ordered and assimilated'.[70] Teilhard develops these particular insights in a distinctive way, arguing for instance that 'con-scious beings are in truth only different local manifestations of a mass which contains them all'.[71] This view is distinctly Avicennan, and pro-

[67] Reeve, 'Exploring a Metaphor', p. 294.

[68] A lucid exposition of these distinctions is given in Wayne Hankey, '*Participatio divini luminis*, Aquinas's Doctrine of the Agent Intellect: Our Capacity for Contempla-tion', *Dionysius* 22 (2004), pp. 149–78.

[69] *ST*, Ia, q. 79, a. 3.

[70] *DM*, p. 17.

[71] 'The Phenomenon of Spirituality' (1937), *HE*, p. 95.

vides foundations for Teilhard's concept of the 'Noosphere' (νοῦς-σφαῖρα), by which he means an expanding realm of shared communication and rationality possessing a real existence distinct from its individuation in human minds. This does not form part of his theory of spiritual vision, however.

Returning to the nature of *mystical* perception, Teilhard presents the dilemma which confronts the theologian when considering whether or not the soul 'can be *tangibly* aware' of Christ:

> *If we say that we can* — that (from the very nature of our emotional make-up) we can sensibly experience the desire to make our way to Christ as the single concrete centre of the present universe — then we are leaning towards the errors that have been condemned in the 'apologetics of immanence'.
>
> *If we say that we cannot* — that the world is moving towards some term (real *or* apparent) other than Christ — then we make faith psychologically impossible, since no authority outside ourselves could have the right or the power to turn our hearts away from an end that makes a more direct emotional appeal to us than Jehovah.[72]

Some useful comparisons and contrasts can be made here with William Alston's reformed mystical epistemology. Both Teilhard and Alston complain that more attention is usually given to arguments for the impossibility of the perception of God than for its necessity, which both accept as axiomatic. Teilhard states:

> Everything that I have written, here and elsewhere, *presupposes* the perception of, or is designed to bring out, this active light which, emanating from Christ, penetrates into us.[73]

Teilhard writes that 'God is as pervasive and tangible as the atmosphere in which we are bathed', and 'tends, by the logic of his creative effort, to make himself sought and perceived by us'.[74] Alston likewise considers some kind of perceptual relation of the believer to God to be fundamental to faith:

> Without God and me being aware of each other in a way that, on my side, is properly called 'perception', there could be no intimate relationship of love, devotion, and dialogue that, according to Christianity, constitutes our highest good.[75]

---

[72] 'Forma Christi' (1918), *WW*, p. 254.

[73] 'Forma Christi', p. 253, emphasis added.

[74] *DM*, pp. 2, 93.

[75] William Alston, *Perceiving God: The Epistemology of Religious Experience* (Ithaca, NY: Cornell University Press, 1995), p. 12; cf. Austin Farrer, *Finite and Infinite: A Philosophical Essay* (Westminster: Dacre, 1943), p. 27, which argues from a standpoint

Both Teilhard and Alston are critical of the affective religious epistemology of William James, on the grounds that it does not describe a
specifically *spiritual* mode of sensing.[76] The two therefore develop and
defend, in response, different varieties of specifically spiritual perception. Alston grounds his account of the vision of God in the similarities
between human perception of ordinary empirical objects and of God,
presenting both as being equally direct and unproblematic. He describes
this as a 'theory of appearing', and as 'direct' and even 'naïve realism',
which implies a willingness to accept phenomena at face value.[77] Teilhard bases his account, by contrast, on the equally *complex* nature of
empirical and spiritual perception: God sustains ordinary material substances in being, and souls may perceive the divine action in the divine
milieu by which this happens. A second point on which Teilhard and
Alston differ is the reliability of sensory perception as a basis for truth
claims. A corollary of Alston's 'direct realism' might appear to be the
assumption that God, being the object of direct spiritual perception,
exists. In fact, Alston wishes simply to analyse claims about the perception of God, and remains agnostic about existence claims and about
whether or not genuine perception of God is actually taking place on any
particular occasion. Throughout his study, Alston therefore refers
implicitly to the 'putative' perception of God.[78] Teilhard, by contrast,
conceives of spiritual perception as grounded in divine revelation, and
conceives it as an inalienable datum of faith.

The divine milieu

Teilhard complains about the 'inexorable and cruel' view of nature
promoted by Hyppolite Taine, who under the inspiration of Comtean
positivism had conceived the milieu which sustains life in profoundly
materialistic terms antagonistic to Christian religion.[79] Auguste Comte,
in laying the foundations of modern sociology, had attached special
importance to the milieu (environment) as the place in which the mind is

---

of 'rational' (i.e. natural) theology for the comparability of finite and infinite and the
necessity, for knowledge, of *apprehension* and not mere inference.

[76] 'The Soul of the World' (1918), *WW*, p. 189; Alston, *Perceiving God*, p. 16.
[77] See also William Alston, *The Reliability of Sense Perception* (Ithaca, NY: Cornell
University Press, 1993).
[78] Alston, *Perceiving God*, pp. 9–11.
[79] Letter of 5–6 August 1915, *MM*, p. 62; *J*, 12 March 1921, cahier VIII.

situated, understanding the milieu to provide all the necessary outside circumstances needed by the mind for its functioning, whilst also recognising the corresponding influence of the mind on its milieu.[80] Taine, in his *Histoire de la littérature anglaise*, first published in 1863, advances his broadly Comtean theory that milieu is the fundamental and inescapable determinism of human life.[81] 'Milieu' describes, along with the German *Umwelt*, Spanish *medio*, Italian *ambiente* and English 'environment' spawned by translations of Taine's ubiquitous work, the 'concept of an aggregate of influences or conditions which shape or determine the being, development, life, or behaviour of a person or thing'.[82] Darwin's use of the idea of the 'fittest' in his theory of the natural selection of species is closely allied with the positivist conception of milieu, suggesting a set of external conditions to which some beings are better fitted than others.[83]

Teilhard's attitude to the positivism of Taine, Comte and Darwin is ambivalent. He praises Comte for his contribution to the development of a material and organic analysis of human society that gradually superseded a legal one.[84] Teilhard adopts however, in opposition to the positivist tradition, the Irenaean motif of the 'two hands of God' to describe how the milieu acts on the soul. Irenaeus uses the image of the two hands to signify a gentle and gradual modelling which surrounds, protects and nurtures its object.[85] Teilhard refers similarly to

> God's creative action, whose Hand has never ceased, from the beginning of time, to mould the human clay that is destined to constitute the Body of his Son.[86]

In *The Divine Milieu*, Teilhard depicts God's

---

[80] Auguste Comte, *System of Positive Polity*, II (4 vols.; New York: Burt Franklin, 1969), pp. 235–39.

[81] Hyppolite Taine, *History of English Literature* (London: Chatto & Windus, 1908), pp. xxvi–xxix.

[82] Leo Spitzer, 'Milieu and *ambiance*: An Essay in Historical Semantics', *Philosophy and Phenomenological Research* 3 (1942), p. 2. For the earlier tradition, see Paul Seligman, 'Soul and Cosmos in Presocratic Philosophy', *Dionysius* 2 (1978), pp. 5–17.

[83] Charles Darwin, *On the Origin of Species by Means of Natural Selection, or the Preservation of Favoured Races in the Struggle for Life* (Harvard University Press, 1964).

[84] 'The Mysticism of Science' (1939), *HE*, p. 172; 'The Formation of the Noosphere' (1947), *FM*, p. 155.

[85] See Réal Tremblay, *La Manifestation et la vision de Dieu selon saint Irénée de Lyon* (Münster: Aschendorff, 1978), p. 20; Jean Mambrino, «Les Deux mains de Dieu dans l'oeuvre de saint Irénée», *NRT* 79 (1957), pp. 355–58. In some places, Irenaeus identifies the two hands with Christ and the Holy Spirit.

[86] 'Cosmic Life' (1916), *WW*, p. 61.

two marvellous hands — the one which holds us so firmly that it is
merged, in us, with the sources of life, and the other whose embrace is so
wide that, at its slightest pressure, all the springs of the universe respond
harmoniously together.[87]

Teilhard describes creation as being 'upheld [*soutenue*] by God', and
refers to the divine operation 'moulding' humankind (*nous pétrit*). His
concept of milieu is, therefore, much closer to the Aristotelian περιέχον, suggesting 'that which surrounds or encompasses', than to the
harsh 'environment' of the emerging positivist tradition. Leo Spitzer
characterizes the classical use of the concept of milieu as opposed to the
'modern brand of fatal determinism envisaged as a menacing force'.[88]
Use of περιέχον in Presocratic philosophy to refer to air, space, sky,
atmosphere or climate also suggests a gradual moulding of humanity by
universal principles. These elements do not constitute a set of conditions
external to humanity that determine its behaviour, but suggest a reciprocal relation between soul and cosmos. Teilhard depicts this relation
using the metaphor of breathing, describing the 'great breath of the universe', the 'breeze that fills and swells [the] soul' of the seeker after
truth and reality, and the breath which uproots and carries the seeker
away.[89] Hippocrates also draws an analogy with the air which
humankind breathes in describing the action of climate on the human
constitution. Through assimilation, transformation and expiration, the
soul and its περιέχον exist in a relation of mutual dependence.[90] In both
cases, the περιέχον provides the setting and complement for human
life.

   Teilhard possesses a clear understanding of the problems associated
with the ordinary empirical perception of material substance. In order to
develop a theory in response to these, he employs Leibniz's concept of
the bond of substance, who is Christ, to portray how monads combine to
form substances, which is discussed in detail elsewhere. Teilhard's theory of substance thus provides the foundation for his theory of spiritual
perception: both substance, and spiritual perception of that substance,
require divine presence and activity. In empirical perception, the preservation of substance by divinity is posited in theory, with no experiential

---

[87] *DM*, pp. 78–79, cf. p. 97.
[88] Spitzer, 'Milieu and *ambience*', p. 11.
[89] *DM*, pp. 4, 30; 'Cosmic Life', p. 16; 'The Spiritual Power of Matter' (1919), *HU*,
p. 62.
[90] See *The Atomists Leucippus and Democritus: Fragments*, ed. C.C.W. Taylor (University of Toronto Press, 1999). For a critical evaluation, see David Konstan, 'Democritus the Physicist', *Apeiron* 33 (2000), pp. 138–41.

knowledge of the bond of substance available for corroboration. In spiritual perception, by contrast, the divine bond reveals Himself in the medium of the milieu. Teilhard states:

> The perception of the divine omnipresence is essentially a seeing, a taste, that is, a kind of intuition bearing upon certain superior qualities in things. It cannot, therefore, be attained directly by any process of reasoning, nor by any human artifice. It is a gift [un don], like life itself, of which it is undoubtedly the supreme experiential perfection.[91]

So far as the concept of divinity is concerned, this 'intimate presence' and 'universal Presence'[92] privilege omnipresence over other attributes like omnipotence or eternity. Teilhard does not wish to deny these other classic attributes: the attribute with experiential connotations is simply the most pertinent to his theological purposes. In identifying omnipresence so closely with the divine milieu, Teilhard nonetheless modifies the traditional understanding of the spatial character of the milieu. He accepts that the περιέχον is 'that which surrounds or encompasses', but regards it equally as a concentrated point:

> The divine milieu, no matter how large it is, is in reality a centre. It therefore has the properties of a centre, that is, above all, the absolute and final power to unite (and consequently to complete) all beings within itself [au sein de lui-même].[93]

This conception of divine omnipresence suggests the opposite of the 'fallacious ubiquity which matter seems to derive from its extreme dissociation'.[94] The divine milieu constitutes, by contrast, a dynamic reality in which all opposition between universal and personal being is annihilated by divine action.[95] In the divine milieu, the presence of Christ is complete at every particular point, rather than diffused through the cosmos.

Experience of the world is the fundamental means by which the soul is illuminated. In the divine milieu, experience is transposed from its ordinary abstractive mode towards a *simplicity* of vision comparable with the *unmittelbare Gotteserfahrung* with which Karl Rahner, in his later theology, associates Ignatius Loyola: 'an ultimate, immediate encounter of the individual with God'.[96] Teilhard's affinity with the tran-

---

[91] *DM*, p. 93.
[92] 'The Christic' (1955), *HM*, pp. 82, 90.
[93] *DM*, p. 76.
[94] *DM*, p. 75.
[95] 'The Christic', p. 101.
[96] Karl Rahner, 'Ignatius of Loyola Speaks to a Modern Jesuit', in *Ignatius of Loyola*, ed. Paul Imhof (London: Collins, 1979), pp. 11–38; 'The Immediate Experience of God

scendental Thomism of Joseph Maréchal is pertinent in considering this point. Maréchal exerted a formative early influence on Teilhard's theory of vision, challenging the agnosticism of Kantian critical philosophy regarding our knowledge of the thing-in-itself.[97] Teilhard and Maréchal had probably first met at Louvain in 1910,[98] and Maréchal offered comments on several of Teilhard's key essays which dealt with Christian philosophical themes.[99] Maréchal questions Kant's view that whereas space, time and causality are transcendental conditions of the active structuring of our experience, the existence of God is a postulate of pure practical reason and therefore less fundamental to cognition, arguing that God's existence can also be deduced transcendentally according to the same method as space, time and causality.[100] What is of especial interest, however, is the active role which Maréchal assigns to the 'object' of perception in structuring the 'subject's' experience of it, which suggests some form of divine agency causing the object to appear in one particular way rather than another.[101] This metaphysics provides the basis for Maréchal's theology of mystical experience, in which objects act on their perceivers rather than providing raw passive data to be structured by active human intellect.

Teilhard also believes that sensory vision rather than abstract intellect provides the 'principal source of our ideas'.[102] Although thus in broad agreement with Maréchal about the relation between the object and sub-

in the Spiritual Exercises of Saint Ignatius of Loyola', in *Karl Rahner in Dialogue*, ed. Harvey D. Egan (New York: Crossroad, 1986), pp. 174–81.

[97] See the Preface to the second (1787) edition of the *Critique of Pure Reason*, xxiv-xxxvii (Cambridge University Press, 1997), pp. 114–120.

[98] Letter of 29 September 1910, *LH*, p. 114.

[99] See letter of Maréchal to Teilhard, 3 July 1934, *LI*, pp. 285–92; letters of 10 January 1920, 29 September 1928, *LI*, pp. 47–48, 181–82; 24 June 1934, *LLZ*, p. 111. These included a selection on evolution and philosophy (probably 'Note on the Essence of Transformism' (1920), *HM*, pp. 107–114; 'On the Notion of Creative Transformation' (1920), *CE*, pp. 21–24; 'Note on the Universal Christ' (1920), *SC*, pp. 14–20; 'The Human Phenomenon' (1930), *VP*, pp. 161–74; 'Christology and Evolution' (1933), *CE*, pp. 76–95). Maréchal's early series of articles was «À propos du sentiment de présence chez les profanes et les mystiques», *Revue des questions scientifiques* 14 (1908), pp. 527–65; 15 (1909), pp. 219–49, 376–426. These served as groundwork for his later study *Études sur la psychologie des mystiques* (Bruges: Beyaert, 1924; 2 vols.; Paris: Desclée, 2nd edn, 1937–38); trans. *Studies in the Psychology of the Mystics* (London, Burns, Oates & Washbourne, 1927). For the later relations of Teilhard and Maréchal, see Robert Speaight, *Teilhard de Chardin: A Biography* (London: Collins, 1967), pp. 154, 203.

[100] Anthony M. Matteo, *Quest for the Absolute: The Philosophical Vision of Joseph Maréchal* (De Kalb: Northern Illinois University Press, 1992), p. 74.

[101] David Brown, *Continental Philosophy and Modern Theology: An Engagement* (Oxford: Blackwell, 1987), pp. 8–9.

[102] 'The Formation of the Noosphere' (1947), *FM*, pp. 167–68.

ject of experience, Teilhard wishes to conceive the activity of the object in an even more radical way, expressing concern that Maréchal's philosophy had become too far estranged from his theology and mysticism.[103] By accepting the Kantian epistemological framework and positing God as a transcendental condition of the active structuring of all experience by intellect, Maréchal appeared not to distinguish, in the experiential realm, the specifically revelatory character of spiritual perception from ordinary forms of perception. This can be seen as part of a larger weakness of transcendental Thomism, which although seeking to combine the insights of Kantian and Thomist philosophy, fails to provide a convincingly doctrine of special revelation with its origin *beyond* human consciousness.

Teilhard provides a radical response to this deficiency, even questioning whether or not intellect is fully individuated, as Kant had so uncompromisingly maintained it was in the figure of the autonomous rational being legislating for humanity. For the ordinary perception of material objects, some form of individuated intellect would be required to form sense data into ideas. Debate about the nature of this individuation originates in controversies surrounding the interpretation of Aristotle's *De anima*. Aquinas maintains that agent intellect, concerned with sense experience, is individuated in particular souls rather than in the cosmos, along with receptive intellect and imagination. In order to perceive objects, the mind needs to remain distinct from the cosmos, with some of its cogitative and memorative powers participating in universal reason in order to command perception by means of certain universal concepts.[104] This was a controversial view to defend in the mid-thirteenth century, and was one of Aquinas's principal contentions with Avicenna (Ibn Sina), who allowed that active intellect resided in the universe as a single intellect. Avicenna believed visual perception to consist in the reception of a sensible form similar to the object being seen but distinct from it, by means of a transparent, diaphanous «milieu intermédi-

[103] Letter to Auguste Valensin, 10 January 1920, *LI*, pp. 47–48.

[104] *ST*, Ia, q. 78, a. 5; Aristotle, *On the Soul*, III.4, *Works* VIII, pp. 164–65.

[105] Gérard Verbeke, «Science de l'âme et perception sensible», in *Avicenna Latinus. Liber de anima seu sextus de naturalibus*, I (2 vols.; Leuven: Peeters; Leiden: Brill, 1968–72), pp. 83–90. This notion sharply contradicted the competing theories of vision, which portrayed light as corpuscular and as emitted in rays from an active *subject*. Democritus supplies similar images for the action of active intellect on individuated minds, believing that the εἴδωλα (ideas) invade humankind from the air, which contains atoms of νοῦς and ψυχή, and that the gods are living εἴδωλα. (See Hippocrates, *Airs, eaux, lieux*, I (Paris: Belles Lettres, 1996), pp. 186–88.)

aire».[105] Teilhard also employs this image of diaphany to suggest that, in vision, the soul receives both the data *and the form* of its experience from God. He writes of a 'Diaphany of the Divine', a 'Christic diaphany' and a 'blaze that is at once Diaphany and Fire'. In another place, he refers to the milieu as the 'golden glow'.[106] What the soul perceives is not a static object but a subject who reveals Himself, and in so doing transgresses the normal boundaries of human experience.

Teilhard agrees with Avicenna that the milieu is transparent, stating that what is essential to its nature 'is not exactly the appearance, but the transparence, of God in the universe'. Teilhard refers to a 'universal transparency aglow with fire' and to a divine fire playing in created beings 'as though in the purest crystal'. He asks:

> Is it not in the heavenly Jerusalem that the elements of the new earth will be so transparent, reflecting so brilliantly, that nothing, seemingly, will subsist but the rays, materialized in us, of God's glory?[107]

The translucence of the divine milieu, Teilhard suggests, prefigures the perfection of the beatific vision. This imagery is inspired by Ignatius Loyola's doctrine of *transparencia*, which refers to the property of visible objects to allow human understanding to penetrate beneath them and thus gain a deeper appreciation of their spiritual significance.[108] This relation of perception and understanding has some similarities with the one prevailing in the divine milieu. Nevertheless, Teilhard relies less on the imagination and emotions than does Ignatius, conceiving of the perception of divine omnipresence as a gift (*un don*)[109] bestowed on the soul by God. Vision, understood in this way, provides a perspective unattainable by solely human effort. Its object is an enduring substance, like that of empirical seeing. In common with the Hegelian *aufheben* and Blondelian negative dialectic, vision surpasses yet retains what has gone before it, constituting a kind of 'metaphysics to the second power'.[110] Vision perceives a 'modification of the deep being of things [l'être profond des choses]'. It does not, however, modify the apparent order of things, just as eucharistic consecration does not modify the appearance

---

[106] 'The Christic', p. 100; *DM*, p. 93; 'The Heart of Matter' (1950), *HM*, pp. 55, 16, 48, 58; letter of 10 October 1948, *LTF*, p. 190.

[107] 'My Universe' (1924), *SC*, p. 75; cf. Rv 21.23.

[108] Rahner, *Ignatius the Theologian*, pp. 3–4.

[109] *DM*, p. 93.

[110] For the final phrase, used as a description of the final chapter of Blondel's *L'Action*, see John J. McNeill, *The Blondelian Synthesis: A Study of the Influence of German Philosophical Sources on the Formation of Blondel's Method and Thought* (Brill: Leiden, 1966), pp. 285–89.

of the elements that are consecrated.[111] Teilhard states of substances in the divine milieu:

> They bathe interiorly in light, but, in this incandescence, they retain — this is not strong enough, they exalt — all that is most specific in their attributes.[112]

Teilhard is so insistent about this retention of specificity and appearance by transfigured substances that he describes mysticism which fails to accept it as 'counterfeit', reflecting in an earlier essay:

> Although all the phenomena of the lower world appear to remain the same (the material determinisms, the vicissitudes of chance, the law of work, the restless activity of humankind, the footfalls of death), the person who *dares* to believe reaches a sphere of created reality in which things, while retaining their habitual texture, seem to be made out of a different substance. Everything remains the same so far as phenomena are concerned, but at the same time everything becomes luminous, animated, instinct with love.[113]

Because Teilhard believes that Christ constitutes the bond of substance, he objects strongly to any mystical theology which regards the substantiality of the world as unimportant, illusory, or dissolved by vision. For this reason, Teilhard's own theology should only be described as 'mystical' with caution. Vision announces the *completion* of substance rather than its annihilation: the divine milieu reveals the true ontological significance of material objects in the world by manifesting their spiritual substance and telos.

Spiritual sense and revelation

Spiritual seeing in the divine milieu requires attention. Teilhard states: 'It is essential to see — to see things as they are and to see them really and intensely.'[114] This mode of seeing contrasts with what Hugo Rahner describes as the 'sluggish or even morbidly inadequate way our untrained senses react, when it comes to seeing, hearing and touching the persons and events bound up with the salvation of our souls'.[115] Teil-

---

[111] *DM*, p. 92.

[112] *DM*, p. 79.

[113] 'Operative Faith' (1918), *WW*, p. 246.

[114] *DM*, p. 16.

[115] Rahner, *Ignatius*, pp. 184-85. John W. Newman, *Disciplines of Attention: Buddhist Insight Meditation, the Ignatian Spiritual Exercises and Classical Psychoanalysis* (New York: Peter Lang, 1996), offers a comparative perspective.

hard describes the transition from the empirical mode of seeing into the spiritual one as a 'transformation ... in the very perception of being'.[116] He refers to finding in the Godhead a 'personal and loving Infinite', the names of whose attributes hold such a sweetness 'that to repeat them seemed a bliss to which there would be no end; it was like the single note produced by the Angel's viol, of which St Francis never wearied'.[117] This allusion provides an important insight into the nature of spiritual sensing. Francis of Assisi, according to one of his companions, when meditating on the joy and glory of heaven 'besought of God to grant him some little foretaste of their bliss. Now while this thought was in his mind, suddenly an angel appeared to him in surpassing glory, having a viol in his left hand and a bow in his right. As St Francis stood in amazement at the sight, the angel drew the bow once across the strings of the viol, when the soul of St Francis was instantly so ravished by the sweetness of the melody, that *all his bodily senses were suspended*, and he believed, as he afterwards told his companions, that if the strain had been continued, the intolerable sweetness would have drawn his soul from his body.'[118] It is the suspension of the bodily senses that makes possible Francis's spiritual perception of the angel. This is an interruption of sight, but also its restoration, and analogous to the healings of physical blindness prolific in the New Testament of Paul, Bartimaeus, and many unnamed figures.[119] It suggests the gift of an entirely new power of 'second sight'[120]: *seeing salvation.*

Teilhard is drawing, in his theory of spiritual sensing, on the concept of the 'eyes of faith' which had recently been revived in the work of Pierre Rousselot, and was promoted following his death by Joseph Huby. The latter makes a distinction which Teilhard would have accepted, opposing «l'idée d'une crédibilité purement naturelle ou d'une foi scientifique de la révélation, d'où l'homme passerait à la foi surnaturelle par l'intermédiaire d'un acte de volonté» in favour of «une nouvelle faculté intellectuelle, — διάνοια — de nouveau yeux, un nouveau don d'interprétation du réel».[121] A key question in this discussion is the

---

[116] *DM*, p. 91.

[117] 'Cosmic Life' (1916), p. 52.

[118] Brother Ugolino, 'Of the sacred and holy stigmata of St Francis and certain considerations thereon', in *The Little Flowers of St Francis of Assisi* (London: Burns, Oates & Washbourne, 1917), p. 193, emphasis added.

[119] Retreat note of 21–29 October 1944, *NR*, p. 250.

[120] 'On Looking at a Cyclotron' (1953), *AE*, p. 350.

[121] Joseph Huby, «Miracle et lumière de la grâce», *RSR* 9 (1918), p. 72, which opposes the 'idea of a purely natural credibility or a scientific faith of revelation, from

relation of this new facultly of seeing to ordinary empirical sight. Aquinas states that Paul, when in rapture, saw the essence of God and was *withdrawn from* the senses.[122] Significantly however, Aquinas identifies the senses exclusively with sense data (*phantasmata*)[123] and does not, therefore, exclude the possibility that sensory operation per se can form part of the vision of God. Instead, Aquinas rules out the possibility that empirical sensing can possess a role in this vision. Moreover, he does not regard separation of the intellect from the body as necessary for Paul's vision of God, noting that the apostle himself did not state clearly whether or not such separation in fact occurred. Teilhard retains a similar agnosticism to Paul's and Aquinas's about the exact means by which the eyes of faith supervene on ordinary seeing. He nevertheless describes lucidly the continuity between the two forms of sight:

> We hardly know in what proportions and under what guise our natural faculties will pass over into the final act of the divine vision. But it can hardly be doubted that, with God's help, it is here below that we give ourselves the eyes and the heart which a final transfiguration will make the organs of a power of adoration, and of a capacity for beatification, particular to each one of us.[124]

Fundamental to any spiritual awakening is the 'role of the created thing [l'objet sensibilisateur] in the sharpening of sensibility'.[125] It is in present life 'here below' that the eyes of faith are awakened. Teilhard believes that the spiritual ascent of the soul needs to make use of the senses because, in the soul's imperfect material state, they are the only possible means which the soul possesses of beginning the ascent.[126] Teilhard states, referring to the perception of ordinary material substance:

> The Real incessantly reawakens us to an impassioned awareness of a wider expansion and an all-embracing unity. It is in the arousing of this restless yearning that the hallowed function of sense-perception finds its consummation.
>
> We imagine that in our sense-perceptions external reality humbly presents itself to us in order to serve us, to help in the building up of our

---

where humanity would pass to supernatural faith by means of an act of will' in favour of a 'new intellectual faculty, new eyes, a new gift of interpreting reality'; cf. Pierre Rousselot, «Les Yeux de la foi», *RSR* 1 (1910), pp. 241–59, 444–75; trans. in *The Eyes of Faith. Answer to Two Attacks* (New York: Fordham University Press, 1990).

[122] *ST*, IIaIIae, q. 175, a. 1.

[123] Brian Davies, *The Thought of Thomas Aquinas* (Oxford: Clarendon, 1992), p. 125.

[124] *DM*, p. 18.

[125] 'The Mystical Milieu' (1917), *WW*, p. 148.

[126] For a similar view, see Richard Southern, *Robert Grosseteste: The Growth of an English Mind in Medieval Europe* (Oxford: Clarendon, 1988), pp. 164–67.

integrity. But this is merely the surface of the mystery of knowledge; the deeper truth is that when the world reveals itself to us it draws us into itself: it causes us to flow outwards into something belonging to it, everywhere present in it, and more perfect than it.[127]

There is a profound humility in the crucial role which Teilhard assigns to sense perception. It is our humblest faculty, but when illumined can bring humanity to its final end: the vision of God. This illumination is a 'second phase in our perceptions' and provides the natural starting point of any spiritual ascent.[128]

Ignatius Loyola describes the movement of the soul by divine impulse that occurs in the Pauline rapture as *sentire* or 'knowledge of the heart'. Hugo Rahner states of this type of knowledge: 'It has nothing to do with any emotional, let alone sensual, impressions; it is a completely intellectual mode of cognition, though it is certainly higher than discursive reasoning and must be ranked among the "spiritual senses".' Knowledge of the heart restores to humanity a spiritualized sensibility which it had formerly lost through being burdened with its earthly senses.[129] Teilhard would concur with interpreters of the *Spiritual Exercises* who have considered the Second Time of election, dependent on knowledge of the heart, to be more excellent than the Third, which is characterized by discursive reason. He nevertheless wishes to establish the end of 'knowledge of the heart' to be the *illumination of intellect*, rather than discernment of the will of God as did Ignatius. Whereas *sentire* seeks knowledge of divine will through the introspective discernment of emotions in the self, *intellectus* gains knowledge of divine truth through seeing God's creative action in the external world. This is why Teilhard does not often discuss the will: the object of *intellectus* lies beyond the soul, and once seen, is able itself to move the soul without the additional volitional principle which Ignatius needs to employ to unify the different tendencies of the soul internally in order to direct them to action externally.

Teilhard's theory of spiritual sensation is illuminated by his distinction between *le sens* (the sense) of the omnipresence of God, and *le sentiment* (the feeling) of the omnipresence of God.[130] The principal differ-

[127] 'The Mystical Milieu', p. 118.

[128] For affinities with modern phenomenology, see Robert E. Doud, 'Wholeness as Phenomenon in Teilhard de Chardin and Merleau-Ponty', *Philosophy Today*, 24 (1980), p. 95.

[129] Rahner, *Ignatius*, pp. 147, 206.

[130] *DM*, p. 92. On related distinctions in Ignatius, see H. Pinard de la Boullaye, «*Sentir, sentimiento, sentido* dans le style de S. Ignace», *Archivum Historicum SI* 25 (1956), pp. 416–30.

ence between these two modes of experience is that *le sens* suggests a qualitatively deeper type of sensing than *le sentiment*. The latter could comprise little more than an ill-defined stream of empirical or intuited experience. Teilhard critically describes the religious epistemologies of William James and R.H. Benson as '"pantheist" (cosmic) mysticism'[131] because, he believes, both fail to establish this crucial distinction between sense and mere feeling. Teilhard affirms that the task of catholic theology should be, in contrast, to '*explicitly Christianize* the compulsion that leads us to divinize the world'. *Le sentiment* is, by implication, insufficient for this task, being unable to reveal any distinctively *religious* truth. *Le sens*, however, is the faculty that 'prolongs, surcreates and supernaturalizes [prolonge, surcrée, surnaturalise]' the '"natural" taste for being' and the 'sense of universal being'.[132] Teilhard describes the acquisition of this faculty and its action as follows:

> The perception of the divine omnipresence is essentially a seeing, a taste, that is, a kind of intuition bearing upon certain superior qualities in things. It cannot, therefore, be attained directly by any process of reasoning, not by any human artifice. It is a gift [un don], like life itself, of which it is undoubtedly the supreme experiential perfection.[133]

The qualitatively different character of spiritual sensing is suggested by a variety of its features: the union of the soul with the Godhead; the finding of a personal and loving Infinite; the heightened consciousness of vision; and the feeling produced by revelation.[134] All these are different ways of describing the unity of the soul with God that spiritual sensing perceives.

Teilhard describes the transition of the soul from empirical to spiritual sensation in Augustinian terms as a 'rising beyond aesthetic dilettantism and the materialism of the lower layers [des couches inférieures] of life'.[135] This is not a turning away from a former life of sinful eroticism: Teilhard does not believe that the soul needs to be converted from a previous fallen condition into a new state of grace. The soul's conversion is, by contrast, *sensory*, with grace causing a 'special sensitizing of the eyes'.[136] Teilhard prays:

[131] 'The Soul of the World' (1918), *WW*, p. 189.
[132] *DM*, p. 92, n. 101.
[133] *DM*, p. 93.
[134] 'Cosmic Life' (1916), *WW*, pp. 47, 52; 'Christ in the World of Matter' (1919), *HU*, p. 53; 'The Mass on the World' (1919), *HU*, p. 26.
[135] 'The Mystical Milieu', p. 119.
[136] 'Introduction to the Christian Life' (1944), *CE*, p. 161.

Lord, it is you who, through the imperceptible goadings of sense-beauty,
penetrated my heart in order to make its life flow out into yourself. You
came down into me by means of a tiny speck of created reality; and then,
suddenly, you unfurled your immensity before my eyes and displayed
yourself to me as Universal Being. Lord, in this first image, so close at
hand and so concrete, let me savour you at length, in all that quickens and
all that fills to overflowing, in all that penetrates and all that envelops — in
sweetness of scent, in light, and love, and space.[137]

Augustine's own best expression of the distinction between spiritual and
empirical sensing is given in book X of the *Confessions*.[138] This description is especially noteworthy for its use of empirical images to describe
spiritual sensing. Addressing the Lord, Augustine asks:

But when I love you, what do I love? It is not physical beauty nor temporal glory nor the brightness of light dear to earthly eyes, not the sweet
melodies of all kinds of songs, not the gentle odour of flowers and oint-
ments and perfumes, nor manna or honey, nor limbs welcoming the
embraces of the flesh; it is not these I love when I love my God. Yet there
is a light I love, and a food, and a kind of embrace when I love my God —
a light, voice, odour, food, embrace of my inner man, where my soul is
floodlit by light which space cannot contain, where there is sound that time
cannot seize, where there is a perfume which no breeze disperses, where
there is a taste for food no amount of eating can lessen, and where there is
a bond of union [haeret] that no satiety can part. That is what I love when
I love my God.[139]

The seeing, hearing, smelling, tasting and touching of Augustine's early
life of sensory estrangement from God are transformed into spiritual
forms of seeing, hearing, smelling, touching and tasting. Teilhard
describes these spiritual senses as 'mystical faculties', a 'complemen-
tary' or 'sixth' sense, and an 'informed eye'.[140] He is particularly insistent on the continuing correspondence in the divine milieu between spiritual and empirical seeing as part of a theology of the 'coincidence of
God and the world'.[141] He states: 'We have only had to go a little
beyond the frontier [la zone] of sensible appearances to see the divine
welling up and shining through.'[142] This correspondence of spiritual
with empirical seeing is similar to the one expounded by Maximus the

[137] 'The Mystical Milieu', p. 120.
[138] For Augustine's place in this tradition, see M. Huftier, «Les Yeux de la foi chez saint Augustin», *Mélanges de science religieuse* 25 (1968), pp. 57–66, 105–12.
[139] Augustine, *Confessions*, X.6 (8) (Oxford University Press, 1998), pp. 86–88, trans. Henry Chadwick.
[140] *DM*, p. 94; 'The Heart of Matter' (1950), 'The Christic' (1955), *HM*, pp. 31, 96.
[141] 'The Heart of Matter', p. 52.
[142] *DM*, p. 73.

Confessor and Hans Urs von Balthasar, who argue that the spiritual senses provide one half of a cosmological vision of transcendent and immanent λόγοι (principles) posited on the correspondence of the visible with the invisible.[143] This continuity provides an illuminating insight into the usually unacknowledged affinity of Teilhard's spiritual cosmology with that of the Orthodox tradition. Philip Sherrard states, for instance: 'The Christocentric attitude adopted by Teilhard, and inherited from western scholasticism, tends to diminish the role of the Spirit in creation, as it further tends to ignore the distinction between the divine Essence and the divine energies through which God penetrates and acts in all things. It is these energies, luminous radiations of the divine rooted in the heart of everything, that animate and transform the world — or would transform it did not man project on to it that opacity which is his as the consequence of the fall.'[144] Whilst Teilhard does not, indeed, conceive of the divine milieu in specifically pneumatological terms, his theory of vision, and especially the language he uses to describe that vision, provides at least some of the perspective which Sherrard finds lacking.

Teilhard believes that the gift of spiritual sensing can be acquired by spiritual discipline, instruction and habituation. He describes the aim of *The Divine Milieu* as being to present a 'practical attitude — or, more exactly perhaps, a way of teaching how to see'.[145] Progress in seeing requires the sharpening of perception (*apprendre le regard*), literally a commitment to *learning how to see*,[146] and the training of vision (*se sensibiliser, fixer l'attention*).[147] The importance which Teilhard attaches to the nurturing of the spiritual senses as part of an ongoing spiritual disci-

---

[143] Nicholas Madden, 'Αἴσθησις νοερά (Diadochus-Maximus)', *SP* 23 (Leuven: Peeters, 1989), pp. 53–60; Hans Urs von Balthasar, *The Glory of the Lord: A Theological Aesthetics*, I (7 vols.; Edinburgh: T&T Clark, 1982–91), pp. 275–84; Karl Rahner, 'Bonaventure', *TI* II, pp. 260–362. For the cosmological as distinct from the theological context of Maximus, see Lars Thunberg, *Man and the Cosmos: The Vision of St Maximus the Confessor* (Crestwood, NY: St Vladimir's, 1985), pp. 137–38; Joost van Rossum, 'The *logoi* of Creation and the Divine "Energies" in Maximus the Confessor and Gregory Palamas', *SP* 27 (Leuven: Peeters, 1993), pp. 213–17. For recent discussion of opposing conceptions of spiritual sensing, see Stephen Fields, 'Balthasar and Rahner on the Spiritual Senses', *TS* 57 (1996), pp. 224–41; and generally, Sarah Coakley, '"Not with the eye only": The Resurrection, epistemology and gender', in *Powers and Submissions: Philosophy, Spirituality and Gender* (Oxford: Blackwell, 2002), pp. 130–52.

[144] Philip Sherrard, 'Christian Vision and Modern Science: I. Teilhard de Chardin', in *Human Image, World Image: The Death and Resurrection of Sacred Cosmology* (Ipswich: Golgonooza, 1992), p. 126.

[145] *DM*, p. 3.

[146] 'Hominization' (1923), *VP*, p. 61.

[147] 'The Mystical Milieu', p. 121; 'The Human Phenomenon' (1928), *SC*, p. 88.

pline places him in the tradition of *exercices spirituels* adumbrated by Pierre Hadot. These are neither «pratiques de soi», as Foucault critically designates them, nor the *reveries* of Descartes and Rousseau. In *exercice spirituel*, intellectual illumination 'deepens and transforms habitual perception, forcing us to become aware of the very fact that we are *perceiving the world*, and that the world *is* that which we perceive'.[148] Vision leads, therefore, not to disengagement from action and passion, but to a renewed commitment to praxis. Teilhard states: 'Lost though he is in a dream, the mystic is still a supreme *realist*.'[149] His use of the image of Jacob, who wrestles with the angel until daybreak, to portray spiritual formation indeed suggests that the acquisition of spiritual sight is like awakening *from* a dream.[150]

The form of intellect employed in the training of the visual faculty is not the *ratio* of contemporary Thomism but the *intellectus* which Pierre Rousselot had argued that Aquinas actually depended on. The created soul sees the underlying consistency of the cosmos by first grasping one simple truth, and from this obtains knowledge of many things.[151] Teilhard describes the cosmos as illumined by intelligence, but this is in the context of a distinction between concepts and *thought*.[152] His description of a 'double perception, intellectual and emotional'[153] suggests that thought, or reason, informs the emotions and is informed by them rather than performing purely discursive functions. One image for this mutuality of intellect and emotion is found in the *Phaedrus*, to which Teilhard alludes in many places, in which the ascent of the chariot of the soul to contemplate the divine principle is made possible by the combination of the *eros* represented by the black horse with the rational negotiation which occurs between the white horse and the charioteer. Indeed each horse, in its effort to see the forms, provides what the other lacks: it is the *eros* of the black horse which impels the chariot to the vision, and

[148] Hadot, 'The sage and the world', in *Philosophy as a Way of Life*, p. 253. Hadot himself resists a Christian interpretation of *exercices spirituels*, despite his view that the classical philosophical schools provided foundations for Christian monasticism. For a critique of his resistance to the possibility of Christian *exercices*, see Wayne Hankey, 'Philosophy as a Way of Life for Christians?', *Laval théologique et philosophique* 59 (2003), pp. 193–224.

[149] 'The Mystical Milieu', p. 139.

[150] *DM*, p. 73; cf. 'Christology and Evolution' (1933), *CE*, p. 93; 'The Mysticism of Science' (1939), *HE*, p. 181; cf. Gen 32.24–31.

[151] Pierre Rousselot, *Intelligence: Sense of Being, Faculty of God* (Milwaukee, Wis.: Marquette University Press, 1999), p. 52.

[152] 'The Heart of Matter', pp. 60, 35.

[153] 'The Christic', p. 82.

the white horse who teaches it rational dialogue and self-control so that the chariot is not destroyed by passion.[154]

Teilhard puts forward a similar argument for the potential goodness of all elements of the soul and the created order, including both emotion and reason. He affirms: 'Nothing here below is profane to those who know how to see. On the contrary, everything is sacred to those who can distinguish this portion of chosen being which is subject to Christ's drawing power [l'attraction du Christ] in the process of consummation.'[155] In perceiving this leaven, the human soul gains an intimation of the heavenly, final end at which action and passion are directed. Spiritual sensing can never be used, therefore, to justify the idolatry of particular material objects: the soul is entirely dependent on the universal within the particular, and not on the particular for its own sake. As Patrick Sherry notes, beauty *anticipates* the final transfiguration of the material world.[156] It therefore possesses an eschatological function, revealing the final end of the created order in the present. Teilhard affirms of the person of vision that

> it is God and God alone whom they pursue through the reality of created things. For them, interest lies truly in things, but in absolute dependence upon God's presence in them. The light of heaven becomes perceptible and attainable to them in the crystalline transparency of beings. But they want only this light, and if the light is extinguished, because the object is out of place, or has outlived its function, or has moved itself, then even the most precious substance is only ashes in their sight.[157]

This transparent milieu is a gift to humanity given by divine action on the world and on the vision which perceives that world. It exists between God and humanity and makes possible the human response to divine grace, having a 'precise concentrated particularity', a 'concrete transcendence' and a nearness yet elusiveness, and is unifying in its universality.[158] The milieu possesses a 'fontal property',[159] revealing the spiritual aspect of everyday objects and encounters that forms their essence. Vision enables the human soul to perceive this milieu, and the possibility of vision is itself due to God's action of self-revelation in Christ in the milieu.

---

[154] G.R.F. Ferrari, *Listening to the Cicadas: A Study of Plato's 'Phaedrus'* (Cambridge University Press, 1987), pp. 190–203; cf. 'Pantheism and Christianity' (1923), *CE*, pp. 57–58.

[155] *DM*, p. 24.

[156] Patrick Sherry, *Spirit and Beauty: An Introduction to Theological Aesthetics* (Oxford: Clarendon, 1992), pp. 156–75.

[157] *DM*, pp. 30–31.

[158] *DM*, p. 74.

[159] *HP*, p. 188.

6. VIRTUE

Action, passion and vision broaden ethical horizons. The moral principles associated with them are grounded in a form of virtue established
by the dependence of the moral subject on God. Virtue is, in this sense,
infused into the human soul by God. Because human moral acts thus
introduce into the material world a non-material principle, their consequences need to be considered metaphysically. Teilhard asserts: 'The
world is ultimately constructed by moral forces; and reciprocally, the
function of morality is to construct the world.'[1] This metaphysics of
morals becomes a single, enfolding cosmology which describes both the
world and the life of the soul within it. In a brief but important essay,
Teilhard states:

> Moral science and metaphysics must inevitably be seen as, structurally, the
> two aspects (the intellectual and the practical) of one and the same system.
> A metaphysics is necessarily backed by a moral science, and vice versa.
> Every metaphysics entails its own moral science, and every moral science
> implies its own metaphysics.[2]

Metaphysical questions are not, therefore, to be separated from the
moral life, but actually determine the forms which the moral life takes.
The inextricable link between the two is described by Joseph Grau as the
'organic tie between morality and "metaphysic", in the sense of a basic
Weltanschauung, or understanding of the world'.[3] These dual elements
of cosmology stand, moreover, in a relation of mutual dependence to
each other. Although a moral system is grounded in a metaphysic, this
metaphysic ultimately retains the status of a hypothesis, because it might
need to be reformulated following the moral experience of action and
passion. Teilhard argues that the 'test of a metaphysics is the moral system which is derived from it', and presents a choice between two different possible moral systems.[4] He employs the Bergsonian distinction

---

[1] 'The Phenomenon of Spirituality' (1937), *HE*, p. 105.

[2] 'Moral Science without a Metaphysical Foundation?' (1945), *TF*, p. 131.

[3] Joseph Grau, *Morality and the Human Future in the Thought of Teilhard de
Chardin: A Critical Study* (Rutherford, NJ: Fairleigh Dickinson University Press, 1976),
p. 365. See also Denis Mermod, *La Morale chez Teilhard de Chardin* (Paris: Éditions
universitaires, 1967), which establishes conditions for morality by analysing basic features of the constitution of the world.

[4] 'Moral Science without a Metaphysical Foundation?', p. 133.

between moralities of balance, established to limit the negative consequences of human autonomy, and moralities of movement, intended to
amplify their positive consequences.[5] When reflecting on the historical
development of moral theory, he imagines an 'original position' thus:

> Morality arose largely as an empirical defence of the individual and soci-
> ety. Ever since intelligent beings began to be in contact, and consequently
> in friction, they have felt the need to guard themselves against each other's
> encroachments. And once an arrangement was in practice discovered
> which more or less guaranteed to each one his due, this system itself felt
> the need to guarantee itself against the changes which would call its
> accepted solutions into question and disturb the established social order.
> Morality has until now been principally understood as a fixed system of
> rights and duties intended to establish a static equilibrium between individ-
> uals, and at pains to maintain it by a limitation of energies, that is to say of
> force.[6]

The consequentialism espoused by John Stuart Mill provides the prime
modern instance of a morality of balance, developed to regulate actions
in burgeoning and increasingly concentrated urban societies in which the
'influences are constantly on the increase, which tend to generate in each
individual a feeling of unity with all the rest'.[7]

Teilhard believes, however, that moralities of balance need to be
revised in light of more recent developments in science, society and politics, because these shifts have fundamentally altered the nature of
human life and understanding of the cosmos. Moralities of movement
forbid some acts which moralities of balance allow, and moralities of
movement likewise permit and even make obligatory many acts which
moralities of balance forbid. In particular, moralities of movement are
less likely to accommodate faults of omission than moralities of balance.
The principle of movement calls humanity to perceive, moreover, new
consequences of action, new duties to follow, and new virtues to nurture.
Teilhard states: 'The morality of the individual was principally ordained
to prevent humans from doing harm. In future it will forbid them a neutral and "inoffensive" existence, and compel them strenuously to free
their autonomy and personality to the uttermost.'[8] Teilhard argues that,

---

[5] *J*, 15 February 1945, cahier XIII; Madeleine Barthélemy-Madaule, *Bergson et Teilhard de Chardin* (Paris: Seuil, 1963), pp. 517–37; cf. Henri Bergson, *Les Deux sources
de la morale et de la religion* (Paris: Alcan, 1932); trans. *The Two Sources of Morality
and Religion* (Notre Dame, Ind.: University of Notre Dame Press, 1977).

[6] 'The Phenomenon of Spirituality', p. 106.

[7] John Stuart Mill, *Utilitarianism*, in *On Liberty and Other Essays* (Oxford University
Press, 1998), p. 166.

[8] 'The Phenomenon of Spirituality', p. 107.

in the modern world, the task of moral theory and the metaphysics of morals has fundamentally altered:

> Now the problem confronting morality is no longer how to preserve and protect individuals, but how to guide them so effectively in the direction of their anticipated fulfilments that the 'quantity of personality' still diffuse in humanity may be released in fullness and security. The moralist was up to now a jurist, or a tightrope walker. They become the technician and engineer of the spiritual energies of the world. The highest morality is henceforth that which will best develop the phenomenon of nature to its upper limits. No longer to protect but to develop, by awakening and convergence, the individual riches of the earth.[9]

Teilhard embraces not only a morality of movement, but the expanded horizons which the Bergsonian metaphysics of morals envisages for 'open morality' as well. He equates, like Bergson, a morality of balance with 'closed' morality, and a morality of movement with 'open' morality.[10] 'Closed' morality is characterized by specific purposes and ends, whereas in 'open' morality, the 'soul opens out, broadens and raises to pure spirituality a morality enclosed and materialized in ready-made rules'. Whilst agreeing with Bergson about the essentially open character of moralities of movement, Teilhard disagrees with him about the indeterminacy of this openness, however. Moralities of movement are not 'open' in the fullest Bergsonian sense of possessing no telos. Teilhard conceives movement, in opposition to Bergson, as directed towards a goal given to humanity and the cosmos by an external power.

The operative virtues: purity, faith, fidelity

A new vision of the world, and new insights into the effects of action and passion in the world, bring about its regeneration by means of the renewal of individual human natures through the virtues of purity, faith and fidelity. Teilhard, using a term employed by Aquinas, describes these three virtues as 'operative virtues', in other words, virtues which belong to the soul rather than to the body. This is because they are powers in reference to act, which relates to soul, rather than in reference to being, which relates to matter.[11] They are the 'three most active and unconfined [illimitées] virtues of all'. Discussion of purity, faith and

---

[9] 'The Phenomenon of Spirituality', p. 106.
[10] Bergson, *Two Sources of Morality and Religion*, pp. 45–52.
[11] *ST*, IaIIae, q. 55, a. 2; *DM*, p. 95.

fidelity close to the end of *The Divine Milieu* might seem misplaced, especially in the case of purity, which is the first virtue considered. The study commences, after all, with a critique of the view that purity of heart provides an adequate account of the motivation to action. Purity of heart is unable to satisfy the longing for spiritual peace or joy, or to confer on the self the hope of bodily resurrection. Purity of heart may reveal a unique milieu in the domain of action,[12] but cannot reveal a divine milieu. Purity has, however, already been identified as a characteristic of both action and passion. It establishes intention, in the domain of action, as a power which unifies the bifurcated human soul. In the domain of passion, it purges the soul of all its material attachments, being a principle of dispersal imposed on the soul externally. In passion, the soul attains purity, moreover, by traversing a 'night' in which it is laid bare and rendered completely subservient to the will of God.

Teilhard states that these active and passive conceptions of purity may be reconciled in the category of operative purity, which is the 'rectitude and the impulse introduced into our lives by the love of God sought in and above everything'.[13] This purity is embodied to the highest degree in Mary the mother of Jesus:

> When the time had come when God resolved to realize his Incarnation before our eyes, he had first of all to raise up in the world a virtue capable of drawing him as far as ourselves. He needed a mother who would engender him in the human sphere. What did he do? He created the Virgin Mary, that is, he called forth on earth a purity so great that, within this transparency, he would concentrate himself to the point of appearing as a child.[14]

Mary is the person by whom and in whom the perfect visible form of the Incarnation is realised. She stands, by virtue of her purity, at the head of the entire created order of nature as 'the eternal feminine'. In an early essay with this title, Teilhard identifies similarities between the status of Mary in the created order and that of the Church in the created order. The 'eternal feminine' questions the reader in the following erotic terms: 'Without the lure of my purity, think you, would God ever have come down, as flesh, to dwell in his creation? Only love has the power to move being.' She continues:

> Lying between God and the earth, as a zone of mutual attraction, I draw them both together in a passionate union — until the meeting takes place in

---

[12] *DM*, p. 12.
[13] *DM*, p. 95.
[14] *DM*, pp. 96–97.

me, in which the generation and plenitude of Christ are consummated throughout the centuries. I am the Church, the bride of Christ. I am Mary the Virgin, mother of all humankind.[15]

The head of the human created order is therefore characterized not as masculine but as feminine. Mary makes possible the unification of transcendent and immanent reality in her Son, whose majesty she shares.[16] In the Incarnation, she brings Christ to birth at a particular point in the material order. The Church as the bride of Christ is similarly the sign that the whole of the material order will be united in Christ, and the principal source of that unification, thereby making possible the historical consummation of the whole.[17]

Faith is present, like purity, in both action and passion. It is affirmed, in the domain of action, in every particular intentional act. In the domain of passion, faith makes possible the resignation of the human soul to diminishment, beyond which lies the transfiguration of passion in Christ. Teilhard reconciles these two particular aspects of faith, and in so doing presents an alternative to the conception of faith that regards it in institutional terms as 'intellectual adherence to Christian dogma'. He defines faith, in contrast, as

> belief in God charged with all the trust in his beneficent strength that the knowledge of the divine being arouses in us ... the practical conviction that the universe, between the hands of the Creator, still continues to be the clay in which he shapes the innumerable possibilities according to his will.[18]

Belief and trust in God bring the human person, through action and passion, to an awareness that God, subsisting apart from the natural order, acts on human intellect and the material substance of the world on which human life depends. The vision of the divine milieu draws the soul, moreover, towards a more profound awareness of the underlying consistency of the cosmos in Christ in the 'revelation of a possible vitalization of the forces of nature in God'.[19]

---

[15] 'The Eternal Feminine' (1918), *WW*, p. 200.

[16] See Henri de Lubac, *The Eternal Feminine: A Study on the Poem by Teilhard de Chardin* (New York: Harper & Row, 1971), pp. 128–29. René Querido, *The Golden Age of Chartres: The Teachings of a Mystery School and the Eternal Feminine* (Edinburgh: Floris, 1987), relates the eternal feminine to the Platonic triad of creation, birth and rebirth.

[17] David Grumett, 'Church, World and Christ in Teilhard de Chardin', *Ecclesiology* 1 (2004), pp. 87–103; Mathias Trennert-Helwig, 'The Church as Axis of Convergence in Teilhard's Theology and Life', *Zygon* 30 (1995), pp. 73–89.

[18] *DM*, p. 97.

[19] *DM*, p. 98.

Teilhard reflects in an earlier essay on the nature of operative faith, describing it as a view of the world from above, or in Ignatius Loyola's phrase, a view *de arriba*:

> If we are to appreciate the harmony of events, they must be looked at 'in descending order'; we must, that is, start from the results which they are set in motion to produce. Looked at from this angle (that is, starting from God, who gathers us to himself) their undisciplined multitude falls into order: but, what is more, we can see how it is bound together in a final purpose (proportionate to our faith) which gives their fluidity a coherence higher than that of the Past.[20]

There is no reference to revelation in this essay, in contrast with the presentation of faith in *The Divine Milieu*: the virtue of operative faith is teleological, but not yet infused. In the final stages of war, Teilhard is apparently concerned to develop a more practical and providential conception of faith. The most distinctive feature of operative faith is not, however, its positing of a providential order to the world, but the fact that it makes possible assent to the existence of the transcendent principle which guarantees its unity. Inherent in operative faith is an acceptance that the source of the organic unity of the cosmos, both its actual consummation and personal recognition of that consummation, must lie beyond the cosmos. Operative faith establishes a dynamic relation between events in the world and their transcendent ordering principle. Teilhard states:

> All the natural links of the world remain intact under the transforming action of 'operative faith'; but a principle, an interior finality, we might almost say an additional soul, is superimposed upon them.[21]

This 'sur-animation' or 'super-animation' can be perceived in different ways. Sometimes it occurs via the 'integration of unimportant or unfavourable events ... within a higher providence', as described in the wartime essay 'Operative Faith'. At other times, however, sur-animation 'expresses itself in miraculous effects — when the transfiguration of causes permits them access to the zone of their "obediential potency"'.[22] Although God normally orders events in the world by means of their secondary causes, divine action on the world also occurs directly in the case of miracles, by means of primary causes. Thomas Aquinas insists that even though a miraculous event contravenes the usual order of the

---

[20] 'Operative Faith' (1918), *WW*, p. 240.
[21] *DM*, p. 98.
[22] *DM*, p. 98.

universe, it cannot be contrary to its nature, because events in the universe are *always* effects of God's will, whether directly or indirectly.[23] This shows how a miracle can reveal the underlying order and consistency of the world: it transcends only the *apparent* causal relationships existing within it. A miracle is literally an event that provokes astonishment,[24] which is a subjective response based on fallible human expectations about the likely succession of events in the world predicted by inductive reasoning.

Use of the *potentia obedientalis* concept to describe this miraculous form of divine action on the world is illuminating, because it suggests that humanity is preconstituted to assent in faith to divine revelation, even though it does not in fact always makes this kind of explicit assent. Karl Rahner, in his 1941 study *Hörer des Wortes*, uses the notion of the *potentia obedientalis* to describe the capacity of humanity to stand open and hear God, which is, in Rahner's view, humanity's defining essence. It suggests, in Rahner's words, an 'original, interior, first and last act' of 'open readiness' to divine revelation which prepares humanity for revelation and is therefore its necessary precondition.[25] Teilhard conceives of faith in similar terms as the explicit assent of humanity to the transcendent principle which providentially orders the world it inhabits.

Faith in the providential action of God consecrates the world, but fidelity communicates with the world, presenting to humanity the possibility of becoming the agent of its providential ordering.[26] If purity concerns the preparation of the inner self for illumination by God, and faith concerns the preparation of the world for illumination by God, then fidelity provides the bond between the two. Incomplete and conflicting formulations of the virtue of fidelity are overcome, as with the cases of purity and faith. Fidelity is regarded abstractly in the domain of action as the affirmation of a cause or a principle. In the domain of passion, it is understood passively as growth. Teilhard's final conception of operative fidelity transcends both these partial understandings. By means of fidelity, humanity situates and maintains itself 'in the hands of God so exactly as to become one with them in their action':

[23] *ST*, Ia, q. 105, a. 6.
[24] Aquinas, *On the Power of God*, q. 6, a. 2 (2 vols.: London: Burns, Oates & Washbourne, 1932–34), II, pp. 162–67.
[25] Karl Rahner, *Hearers of the Word* (London: Sheed & Ward, 1969), p. 173.
[26] *DM*, p. 100.

> Through fidelity … we find ourselves at every moment situated at the exact
> point at which the whole bundle of inward and outward forces of the world
> converge providentially upon us, that is, at the point where the divine
> milieu can, at a given moment, be made real for us.[27]

Inward formation and outward achievement thus comprise a unity in which the absolute reveals itself. The point of unity is, however, always moving away from the subject and withdrawing into the future.[28] Indeed, the final purpose of the task to which fidelity calls humanity will be revealed only in the future. Fidelity continually contradicts human understanding of its nature and of the means by which human knowledge of God will be attained, requiring the abandonment of 'all conceptions of static adherence'. Richard Hardy, in an essay on St John of the Cross, describes fidelity as 'thrust outward toward the future and always yearning for completion'.[29] The New Testament pastoral letter II Thessalonians expresses the eschatological dimension of fidelity just as vividly. The title of Jesus as κύριος forms, in the letter, part of a future-oriented apocalyptic in which present life and activity are portrayed as intimations of a future consummation. The Thessalonians are therefore the firstfruits of salvation, and the good news by which they are called concerns their *future* destiny.[30] Operative fidelity does not, however, remove the material and formal powers of human agency in achieving this destiny. In fact, operative fidelity strengthens and directs those powers. This is because its perspective is one of *generation*: although efficiency and finality are prior in the excellence of their being, matter and form are prior in the process of becoming.[31]

The nature of the three operative virtues of purity, faith and fidelity collectively requires further consideration. Intellectual virtues are perfections of reason, and moral virtues are perfections of appetite. The theological virtues, in contrast, are, in Thomas Aquinas's words, 'superhu-

[27] *DM*, p. 101.

[28] *DM*, p. 102; see also Walter Brueggemann, 'Imagination as a Mode of Fidelity', in *Understanding the Word: Essays in Honor of Bernhard W. Anderson*, eds. James T. Butler et al. (Sheffield: JSOT Press, 1985), pp. 13–36.

[29] Richard P. Hardy, 'Fidelity to God in the Mystical Experience of Fray Juan de la Cruz', *Église et théologie* 11 (1980), p. 73. See also the remainder of this issue 'Expressions of Fidelity', pp. 1–153.

[30] II Thes 2.13–14; see Edgar Krentz, 'Through a Lens: Theology and Fidelity in 2 Thessalonians', in *Pauline Theology*, ed. Jouette Bassler, I (4 vols.; Minneapolis, Minn.: Fortress, 1991–97), pp. 52–62.

[31] Aquinas, *On the Principles of Nature*, §4, in *Selected Writings*, ed. Timothy McDermott (Oxford University Press, 1998), pp. 75–76.

man virtues' whose object is God himself.[32] Teilhard's triad of operative
virtues performs a similar role in his theology to the virtues which
Aquinas describes as theological. The triad is, however, differently composed from that of the theological virtues, which traditionally comprises
faith, hope and love.[33] Consideration of how the two groups of virtues
may be reconciled will provide a better understanding of Teilhard's own
choice of operative virtues. The common element of both triads is *faith*,
which Aquinas places first in the order of generation and last in the order
of perfection. Faith is prior to hope in the order of generation, and both
are prior to love, because it is by means of faith that the intellect appre-
hends the objects of hope and love.[34] In the order of perfection, by contrast, faith and hope rank below love, because they imply estrangement
from their object, whereas love implies its possession.[35] For this reason,
neither faith nor hope remains in glory, whereas love abides.[36]

Teilhard, in contrast with Aquinas, locates faith as the middle operative virtue, after purity but before fidelity. This matches neither the order
of generation nor the order of perfection that Aquinas delineates. Comparison of Teilhard's operative virtues of purity and fidelity with
Aquinas's theological virtues of love and hope explains the reason for
this apparent incongruity. Firstly, Teilhard's concept of *purity* is analogous to Aquinas's concept of *love*. This association of purity with love
is apparent in Aquinas's own argument for the priority of love among
the theological virtues. Love is the only one of the theological virtues
that does not imply distance from God, and this applies equally to Teilhard's operative virtue of purity. Whereas faith compensates a weak
intellect, and fidelity anticipates future perfection, purity is the 'rectitude
and the impulse introduced into our lives by the love of God sought in
and above everything'.[37] It grants to the soul's experience of God an
'ever greater continuity, intensity, and reality'. So far as the third pair of
virtues, *fidelity* and *hope*, is concerned, both cause the soul to tend
towards God as its unfailing source of assistance in attaining the final
good. This entails recognition of God as 'eternal discovery and eternal
growth', and of the ascent of the soul to God as one involving movement

---

[32] *ST*, IaIIae, q. 58, a. 3, r. 3; q. 58, a. 2.
[33] *ST*, IaIIae, q. 62, a. 3; cf. I Cor 13. 'Theological' and 'operative' virtue can be
regarded as synonymous for the purposes of this discussion.
[34] *ST*, IaIIae, q. 62, a. 4.
[35] *ST*, IaIIae, q. 66, a. 6.
[36] *ST*, IaIIae, q. 67, aa. 5–6.
[37] *DM*, p. 95.

and becoming.[38] Human life always remains open to new revelation, by which purity and faith will be renewed. Faith is therefore always mediating between purity, which makes faith possible, and hope, in which faith recognizes its incompleteness.

Teilhard's ordering of purity before faith remains nonetheless open to question. Aquinas asserts that the heart is purified as an *effect* of faith, rather than as its condition.[39] Faith, in other words, precedes purity, and not the reverse, in Aquinas's theology. Teilhard observes, by contrast, that it is 'in faith that purity finds the fulfilment of its fertility'.[40] This is because, in Teilhard's theory of virtue, purity motivates practical action as well as possessing a specifically theological character in the Thomistic sense:

> The purity of beings is measured by the degree of the attraction that draws them towards the divine centre, or, what comes to the same thing, by their proximity to the centre. Christian experience teaches us that it is preserved by recollection, mental prayer, purity of conscience, purity of intention, and the sacraments.[41]

These forms of religious devotion are dependent on the orientation of the soul to God, and are expressions of that orientation. Teilhard therefore preserves the association of purity of heart with the receiving of the grace of God in traditional material forms, and with the freedom from material determination which these can bring.[42] Humanity must 'jealously guard and nourish all the forces of union, of desire, and of prayer that grace offers' because of this freedom which religious devotions inaugurate.[43] Teilhard expresses unease with the contrasting view that faith must precede purity of heart, on the grounds that in his own church, faith is likely to be equated with assent to specific ecclesial teaching rather than as the attraction of the soul to God. He asks rhetorically:

> Is it not a fact, and this I guarantee, that if the love of God were ever to be extinguished in the souls of the faithful, the enormous edifice of rites, hierarchy, and doctrines the Church represents would instantly fall back into the dust from which it came?[44]

[38] *DM*, p. 102; *ST*, IIaIIae, q. 17, a. 6, ad 3.

[39] *ST*, IIaIIae, q. 7, a. 2.

[40] *DM*, p. 97.

[41] *DM*, p. 96.

[42] For discussion of this association, see Gertrude Gillette, 'Purity of Heart in St. Augustine', in *Purity of Heart in Early Ascetic and Monastic Literature: Essays in Honor of Juana Raasch OSB.*, eds. Harriet Luckman and Linda Kulzer (Collegeville, Minn.: Liturgical, 1999), pp. 175–96.

[43] *DM*, p. 96.

[44] *HP*, p. 212.

Authority, tradition, scripture or reason might, of course, form part of the context in which many particular acts of faith in fact occur. Religious commitment itself is nonetheless not motivated by any of these visible elements of religious practice. It is purity of heart in action and passion which orients the soul to God and prepares the soul for faith.

The excellence of virtue

In *The Divine Milieu*, the operative virtues of purity, faith and fidelity are depicted in detail following consideration of the nature of action and passion and their place in the created order. A similar pattern can be identified in the *Summa theologiae*, where the theological virtues, as Aquinas terms them, are not examined until the *Secunda secundae*, after consideration of God, cosmology, the human condition and the different levels of the created order.[45] The operative (or theological) virtues are considered, in both cases, after an examination of the context in which they are engendered. Teilhard and Aquinas both adopt this order of exposition for methodological reasons: each wishes first to situate humanity in a cosmological order before describing how humanity receives revelation. Teilhard has an additional motivation to situate the virtues in this cosmological context: vision reveals God, in his theology, by means of the created order rather than directly in the soul.

Attempts to live a virtuous life conceived in abstract are, Teilhard believes, misguided. His point about virtue is similar to Aristotle's one about goodness: it is pursued through particular activities rather than directly in and for itself. Goodness is not a 'general term corresponding to a single idea'.[46] Attempts to ground ethical theory in notions of 'goodness' established a priori in rules are likely to produce deficient theories which fail to take account of all the elements that are intrinsic to human flourishing and to the complex interrelations of those elements with one other. A large amount of moral theory which defines prohibitions and imperatives has been constructed using this type of model, with the Ten Commandments being the most obvious example, given by God on Mount Sinai to Moses as a representative of humanity. Teilhard's virtue-led approach to ethics has more in common with the Commandments of

[45] See Anna Williams, 'Mystical Theology Redux: The Pattern of Aquinas's *Summa theologiae*', *MT* 12 (1997), pp. 53–74.

[46] Aristotle, *Nicomachean Ethics*, I.vi, *Works* XIX (23 vols.; Harvard University Press, 1926–91), pp. 22–23.

the Seven of Classical Greece, however. These were maxims offering practical guidance for the cultivation of civic and moral excellence, and provide the clearest example from history of a widely-disseminated virtue ethic.[47] Engraved on a stone pillar erected in front of the temple of Apollo at Delphi in the early sixth century BCE, the 137 aphorisms were transcribed by generations of Greek philosophers and transmitted throughout the Greek world and beyond following the conquests of Alexander the Great. Their pithy counsels include 'love friendship', 'long for wisdom', 'control the eye' and 'praise hope'. The positive yet realistic view of human nature which codes of virtue ethics such as these embrace stands in stark contrast to moral systems founded on a negative Hobbesian view of human nature and the attempt to prevent the descent of humanity into anarchy by the definition and enforcement of strict objective moral rules.

Teilhard challenges, in affirming the crucial importance of action and passion for the nurturing of the virtues, the Nietzschean critique of religious practice on its own ground.[48] In *The Anti-Christ*, the Lutheran clergyman's son inveighs against what he regards as the depressive and enervating morality of pity intrinsic to Christian practice and its devaluation of nature and natural values.[49] Teilhard shares this criticism of religious practice, but does not consider such practice to be intrinsic to religion. It is revealing that Teilhard and Nietzsche are united by a profound dislike of the thought of Martin Luther, which is motivated by similar theological concerns. Nietzsche considers Luther's theology to be opposed to a Renaissance revaluation of Christian values achieved by the enthronement of the noble classical virtues, whilst Teilhard perceives it to undermine human self-confidence and the rational method of conquering the world.[50] Luther asserts, for instance, that humanity can possess neither free choice nor any goodness apart from the Spirit.[51] Hostility to Luther is bound up, in Teilhard's case, with the French wartime deployment of catholic imagery to bolster national identity. Teilhard's

[47] See Plato, *Protagoras*, 343a–b, *Works* IV (12 vols.; Harvard University Press, 1914–30), pp. 196–97; *Hipparchus* 228d–229a, *Works* XII, pp. 290–91; Nicolas Oikonomides, 'Records of the "Commandments of the Seven Wise Men" in the 3rd Century BC: The Revered Greek Reading-Book of the Hellenistic World', *Classical Bulletin* 63, 3 (1987), pp. 67–76.

[48] e.g. 'The Moment of Choice' (1939), p. 17.

[49] Friedrich Nietzsche, *The Anti-Christ*, §§7, 38, in *Twilight of the Idols/The Anti-Christ* (London: Penguin, 1990), pp. 130–31, 161–62.

[50] Nietzsche, *The Anti-Christ*, §61, pp. 296–97; 'Operative Faith' (1918), *WW*, p. 244.

[51] Martin Luther, *The Bondage of the Will*, *Works* 33 (55 vols.; Saint Louis, Mo.: Concordia, 1955–76), p. 293.

assessment of Luther illustrates his commitment to defending the continuity of grace with nature as a component of his theory of virtue, even
if its substance is not entirely fair. Teilhard wishes to place greater
emphasis on the capacity of humanity to grow into faith in God through
the free decisions which humanity is capable of making. These are due
not to the action of the Spirit but to the innate potential of humanity for
goodness by virtue of the affirmation of Christ inherent in its action and
passion.

The *potentia* for virtue exists in the human nature even though the
operative virtues are themselves the gifts of God. This partly human origin of theological virtue is affirmed in the description in the 1591 *Directory* to the *Spiritual Exercises*, published more than thirty years after
Ignatius Loyola's death, of the spiritual director as a *midwife*. The comparison suggests that spiritual intensification, whilst assisted by revelation or instruction, consists essentially in the formation of that which is
already present in the human soul. The midwife analogy was excluded
from the later official *Directory* of 1599 on the grounds that it undermined the revelatory character of virtue, and obviously the role of institutional religion in the dissemination of that revelation as well.[52] The
conception of virtue and reason as born within the soul rather than given
to it by an external source possesses an ancient lineage, however.
Socrates is described as the 'son of a good hefty midwife' and as himself assuming the role of a midwife in his questioning and speeches,
eliciting knowledge from within his interlocutors rather than imparting it
to them from an external source. Moreover, only because the midwife
has herself experienced giving birth is she able to assist others.[53] It is
equally clear in the example of the slave-boy mathematician instructed
by Socrates that enlightenment is brought to birth from within the person, rather than being received as an external gift.

Teilhard's theology of virtue constitutes a significant departure from
naturalistic theories of virtue, which are normally grounded in the relation between the virtuous person and the society in which they live. It
challenges, in particular, the prevailing conception of virtue promoted by
'virtue ethicists'. The essence of Aristotle's concept of virtue (ἀρετή) is
typically considered by these theorists, somewhat tautologically, to consist in the pursuit, within a community, of moral excellence as defined
by a particular set of virtues. For practical guidance in difficult cases, the

---

[52] Hugo Rahner, *Ignatius the Theologian* (London: Chapman, 1968), p. 140.
[53] Plato, *Theaetetus*, 148e–151d, *Works* II, pp. 28–39; *Meno*, 82b–85b, *Works* IV,
pp. 304–319; *Phaedrus*, 254b, 246d–248b, *Works* I, pp. 494–97, 472–79.

student of virtue is referred to the example of men whose wisdom has been recognized by their community. Wisdom might, however, call the student beyond the expectations and counsels of the community to a new openness to spiritual inspiration.[54] The official *Directory* to the *Exercises*, published more than forty years after the death of Ignatius, indeed notes the opinion of Aristotle towards the end of the *Eudemian Ethics* that movement by 'the divine in us' (τὸ ἐν ἡμῖν θεῖον) is *superior* to that resulting from knowledge (ἐπιστήμη) or intelligence (νοῦς). Aristotle calls this inspiration (ἐνθουσιασμός): 'A principle of a kind that is better than mind and deliberation.'[55] The theological virtues can in this way be infused into the human soul by God, being 'virtues of men as made partakers in divine grace', and should therefore 'properly be called not human but superhuman or divine virtues'.[56]

The student of virtue might fulfil civic obligations to the community, never infringe the rights of others, and never fail to fulfil legal obligations to political and civil society, but does not need to strive to cultivate personal virtue to the highest possible degree in order to meet these requirements. Nevertheless, without striving (*conatus*) for the best and noblest spiritual character, virtue in the fullest sense remains, at best, only dimly present. Virtue requires, moreover, not only human striving but divine participation in the moral attributes of humanity. This fact is not sufficiently recognized by communitarian virtue ethicists. A guiding aim of these moralists is to liberate ethical discourse from reliance on a single hegemonic account of moral truth. Alasdair MacIntyre, one of their principal representatives, defines the virtues characteristically as 'those dispositions which will not only sustain practices and enable us to achieve the goods internal to practices, but which will also sustain us in the relevant kind of quest for the good'.[57] MacIntyre, in other words, sees virtues not as derived from the good, but as means towards obtaining the good. Another difficulty with communitarian theories of virtue is

---

[54] See Daniel Dombrowski, *The Philosophy of Vegetarianism* (Amherst: University of Massachusetts Press, 1984), pp. 121–26.

[55] *The Spiritual Exercises with the Directorium in Exercitia*, XXVII, 1, ed. W.H. Longridge (London: Scott, 1922), p. 324. Aquinas refers to the *De bona fortuna*, i.e. Aristotle, *Eudemian Ethics*, 1248a24–38, *Works* XX, pp. 466–67, in *ST*, IaIIae, q. 68, a. 1.

[56] *ST*, IaIIae, q. 58, a. 3, ad 3; q. 61, a. 1, ad 2. Anna Williams, 'Argument to Bliss: The Epistemology of the *Summa theologiae*', *MT* 20 (2004), pp. 505–526, argues convincingly that Aquinas's illuminationist epistemology and conception of infused virtue allow the distinction between virtue and gift to be elided, so that all virtues are at once both practical and theological.

[57] Alasdair MacIntyre, *After Virtue: A Study in Moral Theory* (London: Duckworth, 2nd edn, 2000), p. 219.

that the moral theories associated with them frequently conceal absolutist and exclusivist elements. This is because they provide no foundation for moral truth except the self-constituted authority of the community itself.[58] This would be the case even if the moral community were a single global one: the point is not the size of the community, but the ultimate origin of its moral authority. Teilhard argues that virtue calls the soul to transform its shadowy view of goodness as residing within a particular human community into a cosmic and transcendent vision of God, who is the fount of virtue itself. A virtue ethic should not, therefore, be used as part of a postmodern deconstruction of metaphysics, but must ultimately be employed in order to affirm the transcendence of the source of moral truth. Indeed, this kind of transforming virtue is essential if a healthy body politic is to be preserved, because it enables the illumination of contingent material life by eternal truth. As Blondel reminds Teilhard, mystics are the 'great realists among humankind'.[59]

The communion of the human soul with God, in which operative virtue consists, must generate political imperatives for the world. God subsists beyond the world, and is set against the world as currently constituted. Humanity, once abstracted from this relation of communion, is 'continually... dissipated in restless, undisciplined, activity'.[60] In operative virtue, by contrast, contemplation becomes the motive for action, which is a creative moment and a new beginning in which something eternal is brought into being for the first time. Plotinus affirms this generative principle in his statement that producers undertake productive action because they 'want to see their object [of contemplation] themselves and also because they want others to be aware of it and contemplate it, when their project is realised in practice as well as possible'.[61] He describes this as a 'weakening' of contemplation, but also simply as its 'consequence' (παρακολούθημα). Teilhard's understanding of the relation between contemplation and action is closer to Plotinus's second, positive interpretation of the relation: Teilhard refers to the fusion of activity and contemplation as 'mystical activity' and 'reflective action'.[62] These models apply not only to artisanal work but to other forms of

---

[58] John Haldane, 'MacIntyre's Thomist Revival: What Next?', in *After MacIntyre: Critical Perspectives on the Work of Alasdair MacIntyre*, eds. John Horton and Susan Mendus (Cambridge: Polity, 1994), pp. 91–107.

[59] Paper of 5 December 1919, *TBC*, p. 24.

[60] 'Christianity in the World' (1933), *SC*, p. 101.

[61] Plotinus, *Enneads*, III.8 (30) 4 (7 vols.; London: Heinemann, 1966–68), pp. 370–73.

[62] 'My Universe' (1924), *SC*, p. 75; 'Human Energy' (1937), *HE*, p. 141.

praxis as well. Human endeavour, in its supernatural aspect, 'expresses itself and culminates in a sort of participation in the divine life, whereby each individual will find, by conscious union with a Supreme Being, the consummation of their own personality'.[63] The particular operative virtues are, in other words, sustained by divine action on the whole material world, and make possible contemplative activity.

The desire to promote a mystical theology grounded in material life explains why Teilhard prefaces *The Divine Milieu*, his principal study of spirituality, with such a modest statement of aims:

> The following pages do not pretend to offer a complete treatise on asceti-cal theology — they only offer a simple description of a psychological evo-lution observed over a specified period. A possible series of interior per-spectives gradually revealed to the mind in the course of a humble yet 'illuminative' ascent — that is all we have tried to note down here.[64]

Teilhard expresses concern elsewhere about the 'extravagances of peni-tentialism', which he attributes to an essentially Jansenist conception of human nature as depraved, on which is constructed a 'practical system, in which an absolute sanctifying quality is implicitly accorded to suffer-ing and sacrifice' in order that this depraved nature might be redeemed.[65] Teilhard, in his efforts to discourage devotional excesses, stands in a long lineage of spiritual guides and legislators. The final chapter of the *Rule of Saint Benedict*, for instance, sounds a note of strik-ingly similar restraint:

> This Rule has been written in order that, by practising it in monasteries, we may show that we have attained some degree of virtue and the rudiments of monastic observance... Whoever, therefore, thou are that hastenest to thy heavenly country, fulfil first of all by the help of Christ this *little Rule for beginners*. And then at length, under God's protection, shalt thou attain aforesaid loftier heights of wisdom and virtue.[66]

Benedict wishes to devise a rule in which ascetic observance may assist rather than impede the life of service, in contrast with the destructive extravagance of various radical sects that he identifies.[67] Teilhard's objective is similarly to encourage practical action in the world.

---

[63] 'Social Heredity and Progress' (1938), *FM*, p. 34.

[64] *DM*, p. xxxi.

[65] 'The Evolution of Chastity' (1934), *TF*, p. 64.

[66] *The Rule of Saint Benedict*, §73 (London: Sheed & Ward, 1989), emphasis added.

[67] *Rule of Saint Benedict*, §1. Giles Constable, 'Moderation and Restraint in Ascetic Practices in the Middle Ages', in *From Athens to Chartres: Neoplatonism and Medieval Thought*, ed. Haijo Jan Westra (Leiden: Brill, 1992), pp. 315–27, describes the tradition of which Benedict's *Rule* is a part.

Whilst action and passion impel the soul to contemplate God, contemplation motivates the soul's return to action and passion.[68] Mystics are not therefore 'otherwordly' in the sense of desisting from practical living. In fact, nothing distinguishes them outwardly from other people, as shown by Kierkegaard's extraordinary yet anonymous knight of faith. Mystics are nevertheless '*adjutores Dei, patients* in respect to God, *agents* in respect to humankind'.[69] Plotinus also recognizes the movement of the soul from contemplation into action to be a positive and constructive movement for the contemplator and her community, stating:

> The soul must let go of all outward things ... and even ignoring itself, come to be in contemplation of that One, and having been in its company and had, so to put it, sufficient converse with it, *come and announce, if it could, to another that transcendent union.*[70]

This image of the return of the soul back to the material world following its contemplation of ultimate principles persists in both sacred teaching and political theology. It is especially clear in Aquinas's discussion of the respective merits of 'contemplative' and 'active' religious orders, in which he states: 'For even as it is better to enlighten than merely to shine, so is it better to give to others the fruits of one's contemplation than merely to contemplate.'[71] Hannah Arendt argues, moreover, that the political realm needs to be preserved from without, and that choices with political and social implications must be made not solely in accordance with public opinion and the imperatives of production and consumption, but with reference to truth and to values transcending the material world.[72] Teilhard is equally convinced that contemplation can and should motivate determined political action:

> People who are passionately enamoured of the divine milieu will never surrender any essential part of themselves, never let themselves become less a person... In the bliss of feeling themselves conquered by God, they instinctively stiffen their will against evil, and fight, through failures, to make their destiny [sa chance] triumph.[73]

---

[68] For this contrapuntal motif, see Henri de Lubac, 'Ascent and Descent in the Work of Teilhard de Chardin', *TBC*, pp. 143–68.

[69] Bergson, *Two Sources of Morality and Religion*, p. 232. For an Ignatian perspective, see Dominique Bertrand, *La Politique de saint Ignace de Loyola: l'analyse sociale* (Paris: Cerf, 1985).

[70] Plotinus, *Enneads*, VI.9 (9) 7, pp. 328–29, emphasis added.

[71] *ST*, IIaIIae, q. 188, a. 6.

[72] See Hannah Arendt, *Love and saint Augustine* (University of Chicago Press, 1996). This work was first published in 1929, and is discussed in David Grumett, 'Arendt, Augustine and Evil', *HJ* 41 (2000), pp. 154–69.

[73] 'The Mystical Milieu' (1917), *WW*, p. 133.

The new light in which the virtuous person sees the world illumines other persons, social relations, economic and political structures, and the whole created order, transforming human perceptions and priorities as the spiritual telos of the world becomes more clearly revealed. Teilhard describes the contrasting possibility of *un*contemplative activity in the following terms:

> If humans fails to recognize the true nature, the true object of their love, the confusion is vast and irremediable. Bent on assuaging a passion intended for the All on an object too small to satisfy it, they will strive to compensate a fundamental imbalance by materialism or an ever-increasing multiplicity of experiments.[74]

A fundamental contingency abides in material human life, which depends for its right ordering on God, who as Augustine realized is the absolute source of order. When *cupiditas* — love that misguidedly seeks possession of human goods — replaces *caritas* — love of God, but *not* possession of God, which is impossible — the human soul is launched on a fruitless quest for transient goods. The real object of the soul's desire cannot, due to its very nature, be possessed fully in this life. The person of contemplation therefore needs to accept that their commitments, projects and associations are unstable, forming a shifting network and continually dependent for their preservation on divine power.

Divinization: the unification of the created order in God

Teilhard is preoccupied with the imagery of the wings of the soul, undoubtedly derived from Plato's *Phaedrus*, with which he was familiar.[75] Teilhard associates wings with noble passion, the power of flight and the hope in life beyond the walls of the 'prison in which the soul suffocates'.[76] The sprouting of the wings can be a result of ascetical practice,[77] and the monastic virtues of poverty, chastity and obedience represent, in particular, the 'beginnings of a flight beyond the normal

---

[74] 'The Spirit of the Earth' (1931), *HE*, p. 34.

[75] 'Pantheism and Christianity' (1923), *CE*, p. 58. De Lubac, *Eternal Feminine*, p. 32, refers to the importance of Plato's *Symposium* in forming Teilhard's concept of love. This might well be true, although most of Teilhard's explicit Platonic allusions are to the *Phaedrus*.

[76] 'The Great Monad' (1918), p. 190; 'The Evolution of Chastity', p. 77, n. 7; 'Two Principles and a Corollary' (1948), p. 156; 'Christology and Evolution' (1933), *CE*, p. 79.

[77] 'The Sense of Humanity' (1929), *TF*, p. 20.

spheres of earthly, procreative and conquering humanity'.[78] Just as the mind of Plato's philosopher grows wings and gazes aloft like a bird to contemplate true beauty, ἄσκησις allows the ascent of the mind to attain a vision of God. In this state

> the mystic is no longer much concerned with docility of will, or greater natural enrichment, or purity of soul, *in themselves*. They are completely absorbed for the moment in the idea of forming one with the universal Godhead.[79]

The narrative of the translation of Elijah, in which the prophet is borne away to heaven by a 'chariot of fire and horses of fire', provides another metaphor for the spiritual ascent.[80] Teilhard is especially drawn to this passage because it suggests a continuity between material and heavenly life that Plato would wish ultimately to deny: Elijah does not die, but is assumed bodily into heaven. This suggests that physical discipline needs to be situated within an overarching ἄσκησις whose final aim is not material but spiritual, and which does not seek to escape embodiment, but yearns to receive a spiritual body. Asceticism of the purely materialist variety amounts to a 'false mysticism' which destroys embodied humanity. True self-denial, by contrast, 'completes the human being by "loss in something greater than oneself"'.[81]

The spiritual ascent of the soul culminates in θέωσις, or divinization, in which the soul is granted a share in divine life.[82] Teilhard suggests in *The Divine Milieu* that it is more specifically human actions and human passions which are divinized, because it is by means of these that God becomes present to the soul. His use of the concept of divinization should not be controversial, because it is fundamental to both the patristic and Byzantine mystical traditions of the vision of God and participation in the divine life.[83] As II Peter proclaims of God, drawing on the θεοί ἐστε tradition in a text frequently deployed in anti-Arian polemic:

---

[78] *DM*, p. 58; cf. Plato, *Phaedrus*, 249c, *Works* I, pp. 480–81.

[79] 'The Mystical Milieu', p. 135.

[80] 'The Spiritual Power of Matter', (1919), pp. 57–71; cf. II Kgs 2. The same passage is used in Simon Patrick, 'A Sermon Preached at the Funeral of Mr John Smith late fellow of *Queens* Colledge in *Cambridge*', in John Smith, *Select Discourses* (Cambridge: John Hayes, 1763; New York: Garland, 1978), pp. 471–88.

[81] *HP*, p. 187, n.

[82] e.g. Ursula King, *Christ in all Things: Exploring Spirituality with Teilhard de Chardin* (London: SCM Press, 1997), p. 67.

[83] See Gabriel M. Allegra, *My Conversations with Teilhard de Chardin on the Primacy of Christ, Peking, 1942–1945* (Chicago: Franciscan Herald Press, 1970), pp. 41–42; Yakiv Krekhovetsky, 'The Concept of Divinization', *The Teilhard Review* 13 (1978), pp. 112–118.

> His divine power (θείας δυνάμεως) has given us everything needed for life and godliness (ζωὴν καὶ εὐσέβειαν), through the knowledge of him who called us by his own glory and goodness (ἰδίᾳ δόξῃ καὶ ἀρετῇ). Thus he has given us, through these things, his precious and very great promises, so that through them you may escape from the corruption that is in the world because of lust, and may become participants in the divine nature (θείας κοινωνοὶ φύσεως).'[84]

Humanity possesses a pre-eminent place in the cosmos, combining body and intellect in productive ability and mediating material and spiritual principles. Teilhard refers for these reasons to the «rouyauté de l'homme», and to the human person as the «roi de la création».[85] Aquinas similarly considers that humanity 'in a certain sense contains all things': reason which likens it to the angels, sensitive powers which it shares with animals, natural forces also possessed by plants, and the physical embodiment characteristic of matter.[86] Humans can, moreover, by means of grace, merit glory to such a degree that they become equal to the angels in each particular grade, although not to the extent of acquiring an angelic nature.[87] Human beings are created, in the words of the Psalmist, a 'little lower than the אֱלֹהִים' (God, divine beings, or angels), whom the Lord has crowned with glory and honour.[88] Blondel writes in equally poetic terms of the spiritual assimilation of created nature to God that is accomplished in humankind:

> L'homme, destiné à être *sacerdos naturae*, élève en lui à la dignité de la raison, les puissances brutes qui concourent à sa vie ... devenu ainsi le lien universel, il prépare la transubstantiation universelle, par la médiation même de ce corps qui doit devenir un «corps spirituel».[89]

---

[84] II Pt 1.3–4; cf. Jn 10.34, Ps 82.6. For this tradition, see James Starr, *Sharers in Divine Nature: 2 Peter 1.4 in its Hellenistic Context* (Stockholm: Almqvist & Wiksell, 2000); Alan L. Kolp, 'Partakers of the Divine Nature: The Use of 2 Peter 1.4 by Athanasius', *SP* 17, 3 (Elmsford, NY: Pergamon, 1982), pp. 1018–1023.

[85] «Homme» (1912), §§513, 511.

[86] *ST*, Ia, q. 96, a. 2. See Stefan Schneider, „Personale Anthropozentrik: die Personologie im kosmogenetischen Entwurf Teilhard de Chardins und der Personalismus bei Cusanus", in *Menschenbild des Nikolaus von Kues und der christliche Humanismus*, eds. Martín Bodewig, Josef Schmitz and Reinhold Weier, Mitteilungen und Forschungsbeiträge der Cusanus-Gesellschaft 13 (Mainz: Grünewald, 1978), pp. 392–94.

[87] *ST*, Ia, q. 108, a. 8; Ps 8.5.

[88] Ps 8.5.

[89] Letter to Albert Bazaillas, quoted in Xavier Tilliette, «Problèmes de philosophie eucharistique», *Gregorianum* 65 (1984), pp. 622–23: 'The human person, appointed a priest of nature, elevates in himself to the level of reason the primitive powers which make up his life ... becoming also the universal bond, he anticipates a universal transubstantiation by the mediation of his body, which must become a "spiritual body".'

The divinization of faithful humanity by God must, of course, be carefully distinguished from the hubristic attempts of individual human persons, or of collective humanity, to attain divine status by merely human
means. It is in this context that passages of Teilhard's which appear
humanistic to the point of excluding any divine role in human attainment
need to be considered. The following statement, for instance, might
appear to place Teilhard closer to Bergson or even Nietzsche than to any
Church Father:

> The essential law of cosmic development is not the egalitarian fusion of all
> beings, but the segregation that allows a chosen elite to emerge, to mature
> and to stand out alone. And, in this case, the coveted fruit that things work
> to produce, in which all is summed up and fulfilled, in which all finds joy
> and pride, is humankind.[90]

The spiritual dynamic to which Teilhard is here referring is only naturalistic and humanistic, however, to the extent that it is theological and
mystical: the segregation is of humanity from the remainder of the created order, and not of a portion of the human species from the rest of
humankind. Created in the image of Christ, humanity gathers together
the two worlds of matter and spirit in a work analogous to the hypostatic union of the divine and human natures in Christ.[91]

Teilhard believes that the divinization of the individual occurs prior to
collective divinization, and gives several reasons in support of this order
of succession. The first reason is methodological and broadly Aristotelian: it is axiomatic, Teilhard states, that the 'study of particular
cases must precede an attempt at generalization'.[92] His second reason for
considering the divinization of the individual before that of the wider
community is that his theology of salvation entails a movement from
individual existence into a form of existence dependent on solidarity
with the wider human community in which individual existence is nevertheless not annihilated. Teilhard affirms that notwithstanding human
solidarity, each person forms a 'natural unit charged with their own
responsibilities and their own incommunicable possibilities within that
consummation':

> Each individual, though enveloped within the same universe as all other
> individuals, presents an independent centre of perspective and activity for
> that universe (so that there are as many partial universes as there are indi-

[90] 'Cosmic Life' (1916), *WW*, p. 35.
[91] See the discussion of D.S. Wallace-Hadrill, *The Greek Patristic View of Nature*
(Manchester University Press, 1968), pp. 75–79, 119–120.
[92] *DM*, p. 104.

viduals), so in the domain of heavenly realities, however deeply impreg-
nated we may be by the same creative and redemptive force, each one of us
constitutes a particular centre of divinization (so that there are as many partial divine milieus as there are Christian souls).[93]

A contrast between this image of a plurality of individual centres of perspective and that of Bergson's secular 'man of genius' helps to illustrate
the nature of Teilhard's concept of divinization. Bergson's divinized
man is, in each individual case, 'like the creation of a new species, composed of one single individual ... a result which could not have been
obtained at one stroke by humanity as a whole'.[94] The *grand homme*
ethic of the Panthéon that Bergson describes exalts the one over the
many, whereas Teilhard believes that owing to the intrinsic plurality of
human existence, the hope of the soul for unity with God, of which
divinization provides an intimation, will only be realized collectively.
Divinization is ultimately a collective exaltation in two senses. Firstly,
every soul is offered a share in divine life:

> It is not only in the thought of philosophers or the contemplation of mys-
> tics — but in the general consciousness of humankind — that the aware-
> ness of some divine presence underlying evolution demands to be clearly
> recognised as an ultimate and constant support for action.[95]

This does not mean simply that every individual soul will be saved,
however: there is a clear difference between God raising up each soul
one by one, and God consummating the 'collective development of the
world "as a whole"'.[96] In the unification of individual souls with each
other, a common soul is being formed: this is the second sense in which
divinization is collective. It is this common soul, rather than individual
human souls, which will ultimately be unified *in Deo*:

> The ultimate centre of each one of us is not to be found at the term of an
> isolated, divergent, trajectory: rather, it coincides with (though it is not lost
> in) the point of confluence of a human multitude, freely gathered in ten-
> sion, in reflection and in one common mind, upon itself.[97]

This gathering of souls occurs prior to the final collective exaltation of
humanity, and the immanent unification of humanity therefore precedes
its unification with God. Teilhard employs, as Mark Wynn has sug-

---

[93] *DM*, p. 104.
[94] Bergson, *Two Sources of Morality and Religion*, p. 95.
[95] 'Action and Activation' (1945), *SC*, p. 180.
[96] 'The Concept of Christian Perfection' (1942), *TF*, p. 103.
[97] *MPN*, p. 115; cf. 'The Humanity of Christ and the Faithful' (1920), *CE*, p. 16.

gested, the Thomist motif of created nature being transformed into a likeness of God, but believes that it is the world as a whole that will present a likeness to God, rather than individual elements within the world.[98] The collective nature of divinization as both universal and acting on a unified material entity necessarily establishes it as the anticipation of a future event. The most for which humanity can hope in its current continuing state of plurality is a foretaste of this state. The final separation of the collective soul from material things that its divinization brings about cannot be expected until the world has attained a 'stage of development so advanced that its "soul" can be detached without losing any of its completeness, as something wholly formed'.[99]

These references to the formation of a world soul challenge the pronounced trend in Christian mysticism that has associated the soul's illumination with a retreat from collective existence into inner subjectivity. Teilhard accepts that souls need to adhere to the Delphic command Γνῶθι σεαυτόν, 'Know thyself!', but only as preparation for *collective* divinization, stating: 'The total divine milieu is formed by the confluence of our individual divine milieus.'[100] The φυγὴ μόνου προς μόνον, the 'flight from the alone to the alone'[101] with which Porphyry concludes his arrangement of the *Enneads*, is rightly conceived as an ascent from the dispersal and multiplicity inherent in ordinary material living to unimpeded, undistracted union with the One. This union does not necessitate a withdrawal from contact with other souls, however. As the school context of classical Greek philosophical mysticism and the monastic setting of much Christian theology and mysticism show, the individual can participate in divine life only as a member of a community.[102] The divinized soul must likewise exist as part of the community of all human souls if it is to share in divine life.

The collective divinization of human souls is made possible in love, which thus becomes a momentous eschatological sign.[103] Love builds a

[98] Mark Wynn, *God and Goodness: A Natural Theological Perspective* (London: Routledge, 1999), p. 176.

[99] 'The Grand Option' (1939), *FM*, p. 50; cf. 'The Basis and Foundations of the Idea of Evolution' (1926), *VP*, p. 141; *DM*, p. 92.

[100] *DM*, p. 106.

[101] Plotinus, *Enneads*, VI.9 (9) 11.50, vol. VII, pp. 344–45.

[102] See A.H. Armstrong, 'Spiritual or intelligible matter in Plotinus and St Augustine', in *Plotinian and Christian Studies* (London: Variorum, 1979), VII, p. 282.

[103] See Mathias Trennert-Helwig, *Die Urkraft des Kosmos: Dimensionen der Liebe im Werk Pierre Teilhards de Chardin* (Freiburg: Herder, 1993), pp. 158–92; Ursula King, 'Love: A Higher Form of Energy in the Work of Teilhard de Chardin and Sorokin', *Zygon* 39 (2004), pp. 77–102, especially pp. 85–89.

community of souls that waits in anticipation of the transformation of the whole by God: 'The only subject ultimately capable of mystical transfiguration is the whole group of humanity forming a single body and a single soul in charity.'[104] *Caritas* forms therefore the 'beginning and the end of all spiritual relationships'. Teilhard states:

> Christian charity ... is nothing else than the more or less conscious cohesion of souls engendered by their common convergence *in Christo Iesu*. It is impossible to love Christ without loving others (as these others move towards Christ); and it is impossible to love others (in a spirit of broad human communion) without moving nearer to Christ. From now on, automatically, by a kind of living determinism, the individual divine milieus, as they establish themselves, tend to fuse with one another; and in this association they find a boundless increase of their ardour.[105]

Every human relationship presupposes, Teilhard believes, the same kind of telos in which Aelred of Rievaulx grounds friendship: Christ is the principle and goal of friendship, inspiring the love in which it consists.[106] Teilhard describes love of neighbour as a 'tension of communion' in which love of Christ and love of neighbour implicate each other: 'My heart cannot reach your person except at the depths of all that is most individually and concretely personal in every "other" — it is to "others" themselves, and not to some vague entity around them, that my charity is addressed.' The dignity of *caritas* lies in the fact that its object is already possessed, whereas faith and hope both imply a distance from their object.[107] Cultured despisers of religion who argue that its sole function is to provide compensation for things *not* possessed on earth, might be justified in holding this view where faith and hope are concerned. In love, by contrast, religion becomes an eschatological sign of God's will that the whole of humanity be saved, and is being saved.

This love is at once naturally human and divine. Teilhard insists that desire is a 'primordial impulse' and a specifically human capacity.[108] The aim of the spiritual life is not the purgation of this desire, but its *purification*.[109] Souls possess a natural desire for God by virtue of their place in the created order, and it is this desire which properly determines

---

[104] *DM*, p. 108.

[105] *DM*, p. 144.

[106] Aelred of Rievaulx, *Spiritual Friendship*, I.8; II.20 (Scranton, Penn.: University of Scranton Press, 1994), pp. 31, 46.

[107] *ST*, IaIIae, q. 66, a. 6.

[108] 'The Evolution of Chastity' (1934), *TF*, p. 68.

[109] *DM*, p. 106.

all their other loves. Henri de Lubac explains the *désir naturel* of the soul for God in the following terms:

> Reflection enables me to discover in myself, beneath the appearance of servitude, a natural consent that mediates between pure necessity and freedom in the strict sense, an original assent springing from being itself, which the entire role of my free will is to ratify, whatever the cost … In a word, my entire moral life depends on the fact that the Being that gives me being is not a tyrant, that there is something in me that responds to his call, even more, that this call comes from that deep region which is more mine even than myself. In other words, everything depends on my being able to see, or at least to glimpse obscurely, the pure Love that lies behind the figure of the absolute Master.[110]

This possibility of response to the gift of love suggests an essential continuity between nature and grace that grace, in Teilhard's view, neither establishes nor abolishes. Nature is potentially good, and not irredeemably sinful. It points to what Pierre Rousselot describes in his *thèse secondaire* as a physical conception of love, according to which 'every being of creation, in each of its appetitions, desires God more profoundly than the particular object at which it is directed'.[111] This means that the specific objects which are loved provide the primary means by which God is pursued, and does not suggest that the particular objects of love are unimportant. Rousselot defines love using the kind of language that Teilhard would later employ: 'A natural appetite for self-perfection, as a tendency to actualization, and consequently unification.'[112] The more that God possesses the lover, the more the lover *regains* herself. This contrasts with the ecstatic conception of love, which implies a dual-

---

[110] Henri de Lubac, 'A Meditation on the Principle of the Moral Life', *Communio (US)* 26, 2 (1999), p. 423; originally in *Revue apologétique* 65 (1937), pp. 257–66. The doctrine of the *désir naturel* finds its scholastic origins in Scotus's theory of the *appetitus naturalis* for supernatural beatitude, for grace and for glory. See Allan B. Wolter, 'Duns Scotus on the natural desire for the supernatural', in *The Philosophical Theology of John Duns Scotus* (London: Cornell University Press, 1990), pp. 125–47.

[111] Pierre Rousselot, *Pour l'histoire du problème de l'amour au Moyen-Âge*, Extrait des Beiträge zur Geschichte der Philosophie des Mittelalters 6 (Münster: Aschendorffsche, 1908); trans. *The Problem of Love in the Middle Ages: A Historical Contribution* (Milwaukee, Wis.: Marquette University Press, 2001), p. 94. This study has been given surprisingly little attention in theological discussions about love, despite providing a distinction that is in many respects more meaningful than the one proposed by Anders Nygren, *Agape and Eros* (New York: Harper & Row, 1969), between dispassionate self-giving and erotic love. For instance, Henri de Lavalette's essay on Rousselot, «Le Théoricien de l'amour», *RSR* 53 (1965), pp. 462–94, and even John M. McDermott, *Love and Understanding: The Relation of Will and Intellect in Pierre Rousselot's Christological Vision* (Rome: Università Gregoriana, 1983), only discuss the work in passing.

[112] Rousselot, *Problem of Love*, p. 112.

ity between humankind and God that wounds and conquers humanity, and in some theologies, God as well. Ecstasy is violent and irrational, and epitomized in the holy madness of the prophetess of Delphi and the priestesses of Dodona.[113] Many spiritual writers have championed this form of love, but Teilhard believes it to be founded on the mistaken disjunction of the natural and supernatural orders.[114] In fact, the more that the human soul strives to nurture the operative virtues of purity, faith and fidelity, the more it will be impelled to action and passion in the world, thereby contributing to the work of unifying the spiritual and material orders.

Teilhard's three published wedding addresses provide the best discussions in his work of the reciprocal relation between humanity's love for other persons and its love for God. Teilhard conceives of relationships consistently, in this trio of homilies, as establishing a union which enables a common spiritual ideal to be sought. He tells Odette Bacot and Jean Teilhard d'Eyry in 1928 that the 'flame of organic development ... constantly building itself up' is what gives consistency to marriage. Illumined by this flame, the 'world is being impelled upon a centre which lies ahead of it'. Teilhard states: 'It is souls and alliances of souls, it is the energies of souls, that alone possess infallibility, and it is they alone that will endure.'[115] At the marriage of M. and Mme Goublaye de Ménorval in 1935, Teilhard affirms: 'True union, as it brings together, so, and precisely so, it differentiates. It is a continual discovery.'[116] This differentiation is between both the partners of the relationship, and between each partner and God, and is essential because it is intrinsic in establishing a dynamic relation between the three in which each part of the relation destabilizes and enriches the other two. Teilhard's clearest statement of the implications of this teaching is given at the wedding of Christine Dresch and Claude-Marie Haardt in 1948:

> The temptation which besets love, you know, and makes it barren, is to rest upon what is possessed — it is a shared selfishness. To find one another, and to be truly made one, you must seek no other road but that of a strong passion for a common ideal... Between the two of you, remember, no unblemished union can ever exist except in some higher centre which brings you together.[117]

[113] Plato, *Phaedrus*, 244a–245b, *Works* I, pp. 464–69.

[114] See Marc Pelchat, «Pierre Teilhard de Chardin et Henri de Lubac: pour une nouvelle synthèse théologique à l'âge scientifique», *Laval théologique et philosophique* 45 (1989), p. 269.

[115] 'Three Wedding Addresses' (1928–48), *HM*, p. 138.

[116] 'Three Wedding Addresses', p. 140.

[117] 'Three Wedding Addresses', p. 151.

In an era in which relationships are too often regarded as private affairs, involving neither God, nor any other absolute or wider community, renewed reflection on the possibility that they are given consistency only from outside is needed. Teilhard describes, in his early work, the principle that sustains relationships as being one of 'creative union':

> The love that is directed towards the mutual spiritualization of the lovers ... that does not seek to bring them together directly so much as to converge together upon the same divine Centre ... is the love ... within which beings gradually build up their unity.[118]

Human attachments are contingent, being founded on a higher ideal which sustains them and draws them into the future. This is a very different reading of relations between persons from the Levinasian one in *Totality and Infinity*, according to which an infinity is created between them within time when the Other breaches the alterity of the ego he is confronting, thus destroying the unity and totality in which the world previously existed.[119] Teilhard believes, in contrast with Levinas, that relationships in the world always need to be seen as manifestations of a unity established in Christ, and that any moment of suspicion, threat or rupture is subordinated to an encompassing movement of convergence and synthesis that is motivated by a *transcendent* absolute fleetingly present in moments of vision, when the eye is 'enlightened'.[120] In a passage reminiscent of the point in the *Phaedrus* when the soul is struck by the face 'as if by a bolt of lightning' (ἀστράπτω) and recollects the real nature of Beauty,[121] Teilhard describes how

> the centre of attraction suddenly withdraws ahead, to infinity, we might say: and, in order to continue to possess one another more fully in spirit, the lovers are obliged to turn away from the body, and so seek one another in God.[122]

The mutual recognition of the lovers is thus directed beyond itself, with love becoming the 'expression and the agent of universal synthesis'.[123]

---

[118] 'Creative Union' (1917), *WW*, p. 171.
[119] Emmanuel Levinas, *Totality and Infinity: An Essay on Exteriority* (Pittsburgh, Penn.: Duquesne University Press, 2001), pp. 35–36, 102–105.
[120] 'Some Reflections on Progress' (1941), *FM*, p. 69.
[121] Plato, *Phaedrus*, 254b, p. 496.
[122] 'The Evolution of Chastity', p. 85.
[123] 'The Rise of the Other' (1942), *AE*, p. 71.

7. CREATIVE EVOLUTION

Teilhard was continually seeking, in his cosmology, a via media between scientific and theological dogmatism, above all by challenging the widely-held belief that the only viable form of evolutionary theory is Darwinian. He offers, in the words of the composer Edmund Rubbra, 'a picture of a purpose, a oneness, that makes nonsense of any fundamental antagonism or real separation between the world-view of science and of Christianity'.[1] Teilhard was born in the period of hubris which had followed Darwin's destruction of the Linnean classification of sentient life, which had led many geologists and paleontologists to presume that they had uncovered a theory of the evolution of species that dispensed with the need for any motivating final cause. Teilhard wrote, during his time teaching geology and paleontology at the Institut Catholique in Paris: 'Too many evolutionists have, in fact, committed this serious mistake of taking their scientific explanation of life for a metaphysical solution of the world... Zoologists have imagined that they have rendered the primal cause useless because they were discovering a little more clearly the general structure of its work.'[2] He is as critical of Christian fundamentalist refutations of evolution as he is of attempts made by evolutionary science to refute the claims of theism, on the grounds that both enterprises depend ultimately on an anachronistic literal reading of scripture. Just as hazardous are certain conflations of evolutionary and moral insights. After the so-called 'Monkey Trial' in Tennessee, which followed the enactment of the Butler Law in early 1925 prohibiting the teaching of evolutionary theory in schools, Teilhard complains that the case displayed a tendency to regard evolutionary theory as immoral because 'in the name of natural selection it first justifies and then teaches a selfish struggle, the precedence of force over right'.[3]

---

[1] Quoted in Ralph Scott Grover, *The Music of Edmund Rubbra* (Aldershot: Scolar, 1992), p. 151.

[2] 'The Transformist Question' (1921), *VP*, pp. 22–23.

[3] 'Basis and Foundations of the Idea of Evolution' (1926), *VP*, p. 136. The defendant, a science teacher named John T. Scopes, was found guilty of infringing the prohibition and fined $100. See Tom McGowen, *The Great Monkey Trial: Science versus Fundamentalism in America* (New York: Franklin Watts, 1990). In early 2005, legal battles were in progress in Cobb County, Georgia; Dover, Pennsylvania; and Beebe, Arkansas between advocates of the teaching of 'evolutionary' and 'intelligent design' theories of creation in schools.

Teilhard questions, in an early article, the presumption that intelligent human life must possess a different origin from biological life in general: «Il serait prématuré de chercher, dans cette supériorité relative des couches humaines les plus anciennes, des traces ou surtout la preuve d'une révélation première; et les évolutionnistes auraient vite fait d'esquiver le coup.»[4] The catholic magisterium, in contrast, responded to the ascendancy of evolutionism by reasserting the truth of theories of creation that posited a fixed order of species. As late as 1950, the encyclical *Humani generis* asserted that evolution had 'not been fully proven even in the domain of natural sciences' and dismissed the belief that evolution is a continuing process as a 'monistic and pantheistic opinion'.[5] Teilhard begins his response to *Humani generis* by suggesting that because science cannot 'magnify the past' with sufficient clarity to distinguish individual beings, the concept of monogenism — meaning the existence of one original human couple from whom all other humans are descended — is purely theological and dogmatic.[6] The truth of monogenism would be impossible to verify using the methods of the natural sciences, regardless of whether or not an original couple had ever in fact existed. Teilhard argues that because scientists are unable to reach any definitive conclusion about the truth of the monogenetic claim, the theologian enjoys a degree of freedom to 'assume what seems to be dogmatically necessary inside the area of determination created by the imperfect nature of our scientific vision of the past'. Theological propositions should nevertheless still be subject to critical scrutiny. Although they cannot be proven false, their truth can be demonstrated to be improbable. Although the scientist cannot dismiss monogenism completely, it is possible to 'judge that this hypothesis is rendered untenable by all we believe we know so far of the biological laws of "speciation" (or "genesis of species")'. There are two good reasons for rejecting monogenism on these grounds. To begin with, a mutation which transforms an animal couple into a human couple is infinitely improbable and wholly unlikely to propagate itself through a species. Even more significantly, the 'sudden appearance of two individuals *fully complete in their specific development* from the first moment' would require those individuals to have been born adult. As Teilhard responds: '*Contra leges naturae.*'

---

[4] «Pour fixer les traits d'un monde qui s'efface: la semaine d'ethnologie religieuse de Louvain», *Le Correspondant*, 10 November 1912, p. 560.

[5] 'Humani generis: Encyclical of Pope Pius XII Concerning Some False Opinions Threatening to Undermine the Foundations of Catholic Doctrine', §5, *PE*, pp. 175–76.

[6] 'Monogenism and Monophyletism', *CE* (1950), pp. 209–211.

Invention and selection

It is easy to forget the novelty which evolutionary theory held in the
public mind and academic research during the 1920s and in even later
decades. This period was still within living memory of the publication of
Charles Darwin's *On the Origin of Species* and the polemics that surrounded the publication of his subsequent work *The Descent of Man*,
which argued that evolutionary theory could explain not only the origin
of animal species, but that of the human species as well.[7] For paleontologists, it was fortuitous that as a result of political upheavals in China,
new opportunities had arisen to test evolutionary hypotheses. The last
imperial Manchu dynasty, founded in 1644, had been deposed by nationalist forces in 1911, and this had ushered in a period of comparative
intellectual freedom and openness to foreign visitors. Paleontology was
to the 1920s what genetics was to the 1990s. Teilhard enthuses: «C'est
encore l'âge d'or pour les recherches géologiques, en Chine.»[8]

The theories of Darwin were famous throughout the Anglo-Saxon
world, but in France the only British evolutionist whose ideas had been
widely disseminated was the social Darwinist Herbert Spencer. In
France, Darwinian theory itself became generally known only during the
controversies which followed the publication of Bergson's *Creative
Evolution* in 1907, and even then was not accepted as fully as in the
Anglo-Saxon world, Russia or Germany.[9] The true context for Teilhard's study of evolution, crucially, is Lamarckian.[10] Jean Baptiste
Pierre Antoine de Monet, Comte de Lamarck, heralded at the base of his
statue in the Jardin des Plantes as «Fondateur de la Doctrine de l'Évolution», was a Napoleonic deist who coined the term 'transformisme' in
his *Philosophie zoologique* to describe the mutation of species over
time.[11] Lamarck argued that all action is governed by a primordial *senti-*

---

[7] Charles Darwin, *On the Origin of Species by Means of Natural Selection, or the
Preservation of Favoured Races in the Struggle for Life* (Harvard University Press, 1964;
first published, 1859); *The Descent of Man and Selection in Relation to Sex* (2 vols.;
London: Pickering, 1989; first published, 1871; 2nd edn, 1874).

[8] Letter to Christophe Gaudefroy, 14 January 1924, *LI*, p. 107, n. 6.

[9] See Paul Lawrence Farber, 'French Evolutionary Ethics during the Third Republic:
Jean de Lanessan', in *Biology and the Foundation of Ethics*, eds. Jane Maienschein and
Michael Ruse (Cambridge University Press, 1999), pp. 84–97.

[10] Recognition of this fact is rare, but see Noel Keith Roberts, *From Piltdown Man to
Point Omega: The Evolutionary Theory of Teilhard de Chardin*, Studies in European
Thought 18 (New York: Peter Lang, 2000), pp. 115–118.

[11] Jean Baptiste Lamarck, *Philosophie zoologique, ou exposition des considérations
relatives à l'histoire naturelle des animaux* (2 vols.; Paris: Dentu, 1809; Brussels: Cul-

ment intérieure situated within an overarching teleology provided by a universal power which orders the universe in accordance with divine will. These beliefs are broadly identifiable as elements of Aristotelian and scholastic natural law theory.[12] If Lamarck preserves them, then Teilhard reappropriates them for theology in order to compensate the deficiencies of Darwinism. In an early encyclopaedia essay, Teilhard rules out a purely Darwinian theory of human evolution as incompatible with essential axioms of church teaching:

> Nous conclurons au rejet nécessaire d'un évolutionnisme qui, soudant l'homme, par toute l'épaisseur de son être, aux formes inférieures de la vie ou à la matière, ne verrait en lui que le produit d'une transformation, — soit du même au même, par remaniement des combinaisons primitives, — soit du moins au plus, par des accroissements (fussent-ils dus à une source divine), que ne terminerait pas un remaniement brusque et profond, un arrachement au courant commun, plaçant l'Humanité dans une région de transcendence et de stabilité.[13]

The contrast between Lamarckian evolutionism and its Anglo-Saxon equivalent is striking. Darwin had believed that humanity's external natural environment determines the course of its evolutionary development, which consists in the 'automatic selection of the more stable (or progressive) groupings among the immense number of combinations fortuitously and incessantly produced in Nature'. This process of automatic selection implies that evolution is governed by a significant random element, and therefore generates outcomes that can be predicted by statistical laws. Lamarck maintained, by contrast, that the internal motivation of beings possesses a decisive role in their evolution, which is 'being conceived and ensued by psychic forces analogous to our human power of invention'.[14]

---

ture et civilisation, 1983); trans. *Zoological Philosophy: An Exposition with Regard to the Natural History of Animals* (London: Macmillan, 1914; University of Chicago Press, 1984).

[12] See Phillip R. Sloan, 'From Natural Law to Evolutionary Ethics in Enlightenment French Natural History', in *Biology and the Foundation of Ethics*, eds. Maienschein and Ruse, pp. 52–83.

[13] «Homme» (1912), §505: 'We conclude by rejecting necessarily an evolutionism which, linking humanity in the fullness of its being to inferior life forms or to matter, regards it only as the product of a transformation — whether from like to like, by the reshaping of primitive compounds — or from lesser to greater, by increases (which were due to a divine source), that will not culminate in an unanticipated and profound reordering, a rending of the vital current, placing humanity in a region of transcendence and stability.'

[14] 'The Human Rebound of Evolution' (1947), *FM*, p. 199. For the distinction, see Jean-Jacques Barloy, *Lamarck contre Darwin: l'évolution des êtres vivants* (Paris: Firmin Didot, 1980).

The positive achievement of the theories of both Lamarck and Darwin was to free natural history from the 'cold, abstract Linnaean categories'. Nevertheless, Teilhard asserts, the theories of both men contain a 'great deal of defective explanation and false philosophy'. In particular, neither theory includes in its explanation a primal divine cause of existence and change.[15] Darwinian theory possesses, however, an additional serious shortcoming: its concept of the 'survival of the fittest'. The idea as popularly understood — 'Nature, red in tooth and claw'[16] — is subject to particularly trenchant criticism by Teilhard, who denounces this interpretation of evolution because it suggests that development consists in a 'pitiless struggle for domination between individual and individual, between group and group'.[17] To be fairer to Darwin, the survival of the fittest should be understood as suggesting, on the basis of observation of the natural world, that the beings which survive will be those which are best fitted to their environment, rather than the most aggressive ones. Teilhard argues, obviously, that evolution cannot be reduced to a 'selfish struggle, the precedence of force over right'.[18] He also criticizes the more irenic reading of the survival of the fittest, however, on the grounds that it presupposes a *tenacious sense of conservation, of survival*' for which random processes alone are unable to account.[19] Neither version of the survival concept provides a convincing explanation of this desire of beings to persist in being. Teilhard states: 'There can be no natural selection, still less reflective invention, if the individual is not inwardly intent upon "super-living", or at least upon survival.'[20] Darwin ignores this factor when considering the development of plant and animal life. His omission is at this stage significant, but not critical. On entering the realm of human evolution, however, it becomes decisive. The desire to persist in being, Teilhard argues, is basic to any conception of human nature. Indeed, humanity does not just assert its will to persist in being, but also possesses the means of furthering this goal. Among the human species, natural selection as the motivating force of evolution is replaced by the power of *invention*. Biological evolutionary theory, in contrast, 'diminishes' and 'dethrones' humanity by failing to account for

---

[15] 'The Transformist Paradox' (1925), 'The Transformist Question', *VP*, pp. 81, 7, 25.

[16] Alfred Lord Tennyson, *In memoriam*, §56, eds. Susan Shatto and Marion Shaw (Oxford: Clarendon, 1982), p. 80.

[17] 'The Moment of Choice' (1939), *AE*, p. 15.

[18] 'Basis and Foundations of the Idea of Evolution', p. 136.

[19] 'The Zest for Living' (1950), *AE*, pp. 233–34.

[20] 'From the Pre-Human to the Ultra-Human' (1950), *FM*, p. 296.

the inventive power inherent in specifically human evolutionary motivation.[21]

The opinion of Jürgen Moltmann that 'evolution always means *selection*' and the survival of the 'most effective and the most adaptable' of beings is therefore not shared by Teilhard. Moltmann bases his critique of Teilhard on this association of evolution with selection, arguing that Teilhard pays no attention to the 'victims' of evolution, and that he assimilates human catastrophes and natural disasters too easily into a theory of 'sacralized' evolution.[22] In fact, the teleological evolutionary cosmology which Teilhard develops is fundamentally at odds with the Darwinian principles of selection, and neither can be reduced to the other. In particular, the theory of passion enables him to conceive of various forms of suffering within an evolving cosmos in a way that eschews the twin dangers of regarding human suffering as providential, or as meaningless. Teilhard argues that the distinction between the external transformation of species by natural selection, and their internal transformation resulting from invention, is the principal one within evolutionary theory.[23] He elucidates this contrast in an important footnote to *The Human Phenomenon*, in the course of which he defends his view that evolution possesses a 'fundamental impetus'. This note should be quoted in its entirety:

> There inevitably will be those who, in one aspect or another of the following explanation, manage to find the thought too Lamarckian (with exaggerated emphasis on the influence of the 'inside' on the organic arrangement of bodies). But the fact should not be overlooked that I have left a fundamental part in the 'morphogenic' action of instinct, as I understand it here, to the (Darwinian) play of external forces and chance. Life proceeds not only by strokes of luck, but strokes of luck that are recognized and grasped, that is, psychically selected (as I have shown above). Understood correctly, Neo-Lamarckian 'antichance' is not merely the negation, but on the contrary, the utilization of Darwinian chance. There is a function of complementarity between the two factors — a 'symbiosis', one might say.
>
> Let me add only that as soon as we allow a place for the fundamental (although seldom observed) distinction between a biology of small and of large complexes (just as we have a physics of the infinitesimal and of the immense), we notice there is reason to separate out two major zones in the

---

[21] 'The End of the Species' (1952), 'From the Pre-Human to the Ultra-Human', *FM*, pp. 298, 293.

[22] Jürgen Moltmann, *The Way of Jesus Christ: Christology in Messianic Dimensions* (London: SCM, 1990), p. 294. The essence of this criticism is repeated in Richard Bauckham, *The Theology of Jürgen Moltmann* (Edinburgh: T&T Clark, 1995), pp. 194–95.

[23] 'The Christian Phenomenon' (1950), *CE*, p. 203.

unity of the organized world and to treat them in different ways: with, on the one hand, (a) the (Lamarckian) zone of very large complexes (above all, the human being), where antichance visibly predominates; and, on the other, (b) the (Darwinian) zone of small complexes (lower living things), where the only way this same antichance can still be perceived beneath the veil of chance is by reason or conjecture, that is, indirectly.[24]

The Lamarckian form of evolution is, as Bergson observes, the 'only one capable of admitting an internal and psychological principle of development'.[25] Teilhard goes so far as to employ 'Lamarckian evolution' as a synonym for 'human evolution', in which 'biological evolution, from being passive, becomes active in the pursuit of its purpose'.[26] Teilhard does not argue, however, that evolution is wholly purposive, because this would amount to a denial of the role in it of growth and the other forms of human passion. Rather, evolution is the outcome of the combination of a selective outer principle and an inventive inner one. Gerald Bostock correctly identifies the presence in *The Human Phenomenon* of an Origenist conception of humankind as a two-fold creation: inner being made in the image of God, and outer being formed from the dust of the earth.[27] Teilhard describes these dual aspects of specifically human evolution as the 'inside' (or 'within') and the 'outside' (or 'without'), and as tendencies rather than wholly separate realms of being. It is in humankind, and not in the external material world, that the power of invention resides.

In the coexistence of the two tendencies, selection dominates invention. Despite its apparent inferiority to selection, however, invention assumes decisive importance. Teilhard states:

> Compared with this immense passive field (the Darwinian) it may seem that the (Lamarckian) ground gained by our inventive efforts amounts to very little. But let us make no mistake about it. However slight the growth may be, however small the seed, it is precisely here that the power of renewal and rebounding of the living world is concentrated.[28]

Bergson embraces Lamarckian evolutionary theory on the grounds that it posits an immanently purposive universe, thus amounting to a form of cosmic existentialism. He does not, however, accept that it possesses an objective teleology given to it from outside. According to the Bergson-

---

[24] *HP*, pp. 97–98, n.

[25] Henri Bergson, *Creative Evolution* (London: Macmillan, 1911), p. 81.

[26] 'The Human Rebound of Evolution', p. 204.

[27] Gerald Bostock, 'Origen's Philosophy of Creation', in *Origeniana Quinta*, ed. Robert J. Daly (Leuven University Press, 1992), pp. 265–66; cf. *HP*, pp. 22–38.

[28] 'The Human Rebound of Evolution', p. 201.

ian theory of creative evolution, unity and objectivity lie in the past, and
no teleology exists to guide the development of life into the future.
Bergson states: 'Harmony is rather behind us than before. It is due to an
identity of impulsion and not to a common aspiration,' and, 'Life does
not proceed by the association and addition of elements, but by dissociation and division.'[29] In Teilhard's cosmology, however, evolution is
defined by teleology. He states:

> Whereas the Kosmos, in Bergson's *Creative Evolution*, is seen as a radia-
> tion that spreads out from a central source, the picture of the universe we
> are introduced to by 'Creative Union' is that of a concentration, a conver-
> gence, a centripetal confluence... Although both [are] evolutionary, each
> theory is the converse of the other.[30]

To develop this cosmology, Teilhard employs the Lamarckian distinction of organisms from each other according to their degree of biological complexity, which provides a means of liberating some beings from
the evolutionary process governed by external material factors:

> The Darwinian era of survival by Natural Selection (the vital thrust
> [poussée vitale]) is thus succeeded by a Lamarckian era of Super-Life
> brought about by calculated invention (the vital impulse [élan vital]). In
> Humanity evolution is interiorized and made purposeful; and at the same
> time, in the degree in which the strivings of human inventiveness need to
> be controlled in their operation and sustained in their energies, it imposes
> upon itself a moral order and 'mysticizes' itself.[31]

Humanity is able to take control of its future because it exists at the 'critical point' at which evolution by instinct is replaced with evolution by
thought.[32] This feature of Teilhard's evolutionary cosmology becomes
prominent in his social analysis, and he recognizes it as opposing the
Bergsonian thesis of creative evolution:

> It has become rather unconsidered fashion, since Bergson, to decry intelli-
> gence as compared with other forms or aspects of cognition. To the extent that
> this is simply a reaction against a static and abstract rationalism, it is wholly
> salutary; but it becomes pernicious if it goes so far as to cause us to overlook
> what is truly exceptional and essential in the phenomenon of Thought.[33]

Teilhard asserts that 'in line with, and gradually replacing, the thrust
from behind or below, we see the appearance of a force of attraction

---

[29] Bergson, *Creative Evolution*, pp. 54, 94.
[30] 'Creative Union' (1917), *WW*, p. 157.
[31] 'The Human Rebound of Evolution', p. 212.
[32] 'Faith in Humanity' (1947), *FM*, p. 185.
[33] 'Turmoil or Genesis?' (1947), *FM*, p. 219; cf. 'The Human Rebound of Evolution',
p 199.

coming from above', which is bound up with the 'revolutionary superiority of Thought over Instinct'.[34] This motivates the reflective praxis of action and passion, by means of which humanity assumes a creative role in determining the course of its future development.

The zest for life

Teilhard hoped for several decades that the Leibnizian monadology of Blondel could be employed to provide an account of evolution consonant with both scientific and theological objectives. He observes of modern cosmology: 'Traditional conceptions of a God exerting intellectual influence on immortal monads distinct from him reappear, no longer sentimental and instinctive but closely linked to contemporary evolutionary ideas (provided that humankind is not excluded from them).'[35] Elsewhere, Teilhard speculates that theologians 'might one day recognize in the God of evolution an exact equivalent of the attributes accorded to the "*Ens a se*" by medieval philosophy'.[36] The basic principles of this cosmology, above all unity and power, remain his fundamental metaphysical concerns, and to this extent a Leibnizian scheme is identifiable in his work during the 1930s and later.[37]

During that period, Teilhard nevertheless becomes more critical of monadic ontology, on the grounds that it suggests too great a degree of individuation of the substances making up the world. The concept of the monad, originating in Neoplatonist philosophy, is identified by Leibniz as referring to 'unity, or that which is one'.[38] Teilhard is of the opinion that this conception of cosmological unity was destroyed at the Renaissance, when the 'Greek *kosmos* burst asunder, spatially and morally at the same time.'[39] A principal thesis of Leibniz's monadology had been

---

[34] 'On the Probable Coming of an "Ultra-Humanity"' (1950), *FM*, pp. 277, 271.

[35] 'The Spirit of the Earth' (1931), *HE*, p. 46.

[36] 'Sketch of a Personalistic Universe' (1936), *HE*, p. 70

[37] Wolfhart Pannenberg, 'Spirit and Energy in the Phenomenology of Teilhard de Chardin', in *Toward a Theology of Nature: Essays on Science and Faith*, ed. Ted Peters (Louisville, Kent.: Westminster/John Knox, 1993), pp. 138–47; and in *Beginning with the End: God, Science and Wolfhart Pannenberg*, eds. Carol Rausch Albright and Joel Haughen (Chicago: Open Court, 1997), pp. 80–89. Pannenberg does not, however, identify the specifically Leibnizian doctrine of substance in Teilhard's earlier work.

[38] G.W. Leibniz, 'Principles of Nature and Grace, based on Reason', §1, in *Philosophical Texts*, eds. R.S. Woolhouse and Richard Francks (Oxford University Press, 1998), p. 259.

[39] 'The Mysticism of Science' (1939), *HE*, p. 168.

that 'monads have no windows, through which anything could come in
or go out', to which Teilhard responds that 'Leibniz and his closed monads have no place in today's world'.[40]

James Lyons identifies the gradual estrangement of Teilhard's monadology from that of Leibniz, whose monads are thus isolated from one
another in a mechanistic cosmos. Intrinsic to an idea of the universe as
composed of Leibnizian monads with 'neither doors nor windows' is a
static and individualized conception of consistence and unity.[41] Teilhard's monads exist, in contrast, in mutual solidarity in an evolving and
convergent whole: each centre is not only a centre for itself, but also a
partial centre of the whole.[42] Metaphysics needs to jettison its ancient
monadic individualism, he argues, because that individualism provides
no feasible basis for modern cosmology. Teilhard even invokes this critique of individualism against modern existentialists, whom he accuses
of emulating Leibniz when speaking of 'closed being'. He protests: 'To
be cosmically shut up, all together, in the universe; to be shut up, as
individual atoms, each on his own, each inside himself: must we accept
that such is the tragedy of humanity's condition?'[43] Teilhard now
regards the monad not as composed of primary matter and *conatus*, but
as a unity established by a specifically spiritual principle: 'A universe
whose primal stuff is matter is irremediably fixed and sterile; whereas a
universe of "spiritual" stuff has all the elasticity it would need to lend
itself both to evolution (life) and to involution (entropy).'[44] A non-static
universe could, in other words, continue to bring new and increasingly
complex forms of life to birth, or could degenerate into disorder and
death. Humanity is not presented with the 'natural order' of a material
cosmos already completed,[45] Teilhard argues, but with a cosmos which
possesses the potential to evolve continually in accordance with a spiritual principle. An observation of Karl Rahner's about the response of the
Curia to this cosmology shows what is at stake: 'In reprimanding Teilhard de Chardin and repressing his endeavours it manifested too little
understanding for an ontology in which created being is conceived in
principle and in the very beginning as being which is in the process of

[40] G.W. Leibniz, 'Monadology', §7, in *Philosophical Texts*, p. 268; 'The Atomism of
Spirit' (1941), *AE*, p. 37; cf. retreat note of 23–30 October 1943, *NR*, p. 239.

[41] 'The Atomism of Spirit', 'Centrology' (1944), *AE*, pp. 49, 104.

[42] James Lyons, *The Cosmic Christ in Origen and Teilhard de Chardin: A Comparative Study* (Oxford University Press, 1982), pp. 205–206; *J*, 24 August 1944, cahier XIII.

[43] 'A Phenomenon of Counter-Evolution' (1949), *AE*, p. 190.

[44] 'The Spirit of the Earth', p. 23.

[45] 'The Evolution of Chastity' (1934), *TF*, p. 80.

becoming within an entire evolution of the cosmos, which is still in the process of evolution.'[46] In these comments, Rahner appears to be referring to *Humani generis*, even though the encyclical's references to Teilhard are, at most, oblique. Rahner amplifies, in any case, the tremendous importance of a synthetic view of the created order for understanding change within it theologically.

In Teilhard's theory of evolution, the dialectic of action and passion grounded in vision which is expressed in *The Divine Milieu* and 'The Mystical Milieu' persists[47] and assumes a directing role:

> Now that humankind's labour interests it not simply as an operation that brings union with the divine act, but as a work (opus) which is a condition for the presence of God among us, it becomes possible for humankind not only to feel the divine milieu but to form it, and to allow the divine milieu to encompass it like a continually stronger light... It is not enough for humanity to lend itself to purely operative action, but to action aimed at achievement... While humanity was passing through the lower circles of its initiation, space, and matter, and energy, were each in turn divinized in its eyes. Now it is the turn of evolution.[48]

The dynamic of human evolution, Teilhard believes, consists in the action and passion of individual persons, and their confluence in collective action and passion. He places great emphasis in his theory of cosmic convergence on the importance of shared practical activity, rather than purely intellectual apprehension. The movement of the universe towards its final unity in Christ, apprehended in the spatial dimension of vision and the divine milieu, is enacted in the temporal one of action and passion. As Teilhard develops his evolutionary cosmology, the essentially spatial ontology of vision becomes situated more explicitly within this temporal ontology. All the principal features of the spatial ontology are preserved, however, and are indeed required to motivate change in the temporal order. This revised ontology is compatible, Teilhard believes, with a 'correct physics and metaphysics of evolution ... on the lines of the "philosophia perennis": primacy of being, act and potency'.[49] Nevertheless, he wishes to revise the anthropology around which the perennial philosophy has been constructed. He states of evolutionary cosmology: 'This view of the "human phenomenon" is completely different from the old anthropocentrism which made humanity the geometric and

[46] Karl Rahner, 'Natural Science and Reasonable Faith', *TI* V, p. 25.
[47] 'Centrology', pp. 111, 113.
[48] 'The Mystical Milieu' (1917), *WW*, p. 137.
[49] 'Some Reflections on the Conversion of the World' (1936), *SC*, p. 122.

static centre of the universe … it transforms the value and guarantees the immortality of the work we effect — or rather of the work that is effected through us.'[50] Teilhard also comes to realize that God should not be conceived as a pole of consistence, but as a prime mover *ahead*: 'The Higher Life, the Union, the long dreamed-of consummation that has hitherto been sought *Above*, in the direction of some kind of transcendency: should we not rather look for it *Ahead*, in the prolongation of the inherent forces of evolution?'[51] God the pole of consistence becomes God 'the Prime Mover, Gatherer and Consolidator, ahead of us, of evolution'.[52] Arthur Peacocke has noted the tendency of 'Teilhardian theologians' to 'extrapolate into the future from the past',[53] but Teilhard's concept of the God *Ahead* is derived principally from the God *Above* rather than from the Bergsonian notion of an original primordial unity possessing quasi-theistic attributes. This concept of the God *Ahead* provides the evolutionary dynamic, as will later be seen, with a source which subsists essentially in the future, even though continuity exists between this source and the previous evolutionary history which it has motivated.

Jean Maalouf, in his examination of «l'évolutionnisme et le stoïcisme de Teilhard de Chardin», interprets Teilhard as arguing that human collaboration in the work of God, and the freedom which is part of this collaboration, depend on humanity perceiving that cosmic nature possesses a destiny that is a divine work, and on its acceptance of this destiny.[54] Maalouf suggests that humanity's recognition of its destiny necessarily requires resignation, but this cannot be inferred from Teilhard's teleology. In fact, Teilhard refutes the view that humankind is a passive object of its destiny in his critique of Schopenhauerian pessimism.[55] In *The Divine Milieu*, he demonstrates convincingly that the fundamental tension engendering praxis is not the internal tension within *pneuma* (human spirit) that Stoicism posits, but an *external* tension between human spirit and God, 'the tension of communion … for directing us

---

[50] 'The Salvation of Humankind', (1936), *SC*, p. 132.

[51] 'The Heart of the Problem', (1949), *FM*, p. 263. The context makes clear that *Above* and *Ahead* are not being presented as mutually exclusive terms. Similar dialectics are identifiable in the discussion of the interrelations of creation, history and eschatology in Jürgen Moltmann, *Science and Wisdom* (London: SCM, 2003).

[52] *MPN*, p. 121.

[53] Arthur Peacocke, *Creation and the World of Science* (Oxford: Clarendon, 1979), pp. 338–39, 349.

[54] Jean Maalouf, «L'Évolutionnisme et le Stoïcisme de Teilhard de Chardin», in *Le Mystère du mal dans l'oeuvre de Teilhard de Chardin* (Paris: Cerf, 1986), pp. 120–21.

[55] 'Reflections on Happiness' (1943), *TF*, p. 110.

towards our human duty' which exhibits a 'wonderful efficacy' for this purpose.[56] The tension between human spirit and God does not merge matter and form in a «souffle», as Maalouf suggests, but depends for its efficacy on the preservation of the real distinction between form and matter. It is this distinction, and not a cosmic fatalism, which gives to the soul its *inventive* role in directing the course of evolution. The 'flow of cosmic influences ... have to be ordered and assimilated' by the soul, which 'cannot escape from this universal contact nor from this unremitting labour'. Humanity, through its 'own activity, must industriously assemble the widely scattered elements'.[57]

To complete the transposition of his spatial ontology of consistence into a temporal ontology of unity in becoming in which human action and passion continue to perform decisive roles, Teilhard derives from the theories of Bergson and Lamarck the concept of *life* as a force sustaining humanity in being which propels it collectively from the past into the future. He later states:

> What we call evolution develops only in virtue of a certain internal preference for survival (or, of you prefer to put it so, for self-survival) which in humanity takes on a markedly psychic appearance, in the form of a *zest for life*.[58]

During the early 1930s, Teilhard could have made Goethe's complaint about classical metaphysics his own: „Mag der Grieche seinen Ton / Zu Gestalten drücken, / An der eignen Hände Sohn / Steigern sein Entzücken; / Aber uns ist wonnereich / In den Euphrat greifen / Und im flüss'gen Element / Hin und wider schweifen."[59] Humanity, if it lacked a zest for life, would 'lose the heart to act'. Teilhard therefore envisions the history of the world to be unfolding 'as a significant act, instinct with the absolute and the divine, in which the spiritualizing activity of beings emerges as a sacred energy.'[60] It is this zest for life, or for living, which provides the motivation for survival that beings exhibit, and which constitutes their 'fundamental energy'.[61] Teilhard, like Bergson and Goethe,

---

[56] *DM*, p. 107.

[57] *DM*, pp. 17–18.

[58] 'Biology Taken to its Limit' (1951), *SC*, p. 212.

[59] 'Let the Greek mould his clay into shapes and take ever-increasing delight in the child of his own hands. But to us it is an exquisite pleasure to plunge our fingers into the Euphrates and to drift to and fro in the liquid element.' From „Lied und Gebilde", in Johann Wolfgang von Goethe, *Selected Verse*, ed. David Luke (London: Penguin, 1982), p. 236.

[60] 'The Road of the West' (1932), *TF*, pp. 47–48.

[61] 'The Christian Phenomenon' (1950), *CE*, p. 204.

asserts that a visible current of life has arisen in creation.[62] He wishes to designate life in such positive terms as these in order to make clear its crucial role in motivating the evolutionary process: life is not an epiphenomenon constructed from matter, as Darwinian theory suggests, but the 'very essence of phenomenon'.[63]

Some philosophers of science are highly sceptical of any alternative to materialistic reductionism, however. Richard Dawkins ridicules Teilhard and other mystics for their 'fondness' for energy, which creates the 'illusion of scientific content where there is no content of any kind'.[64] The problem with the criticisms of Dawkins and his colleagues is that the 'aseptic positivism',[65] untainted by metaphysics but unfeasibly sterile, with which they propose to replace any spiritual account of evolution, fails to provide a satisfactory alternative response to the serious questions which Teilhard poses, above all to those about the reasons why change, complexity and human development in fact occur. Teilhard's aim is not to present a purely scientific analysis of evolution, but to move beyond scientific description to identify underlying principles which elude scientific definition.

Teilhard's theistic cosmology provides a solution to the perennial question of how the evolutionary process is motivated. He affirms:

> From the moment when humankind recognizes that it is in a state of evolution, it can no longer progress ... unless it develops in itself a deep-rooted, passionate zest for its own evolution.[66]

Teilhard realizes that if evolution is to be understood as composed of linear development rather than cyclical change, there must exist some principle or force motivating that development. William Wordsworth's description of 'A motion and a spirit, that impels / All thinking things, all objects of all thought, / And rolls through all things'[67]

---

[62] Bergson, *Creative Evolution*, p. 27.

[63] *MPN*, p. 18; 'Reflections on an Ultra-Human' (1951), *AE*, p. 272.

[64] Richard Dawkins, *Unweaving the Rainbow* (London: Penguin, 1999), p. 185. Dawkins's sole source for his judgement of Teilhard is an old critical notice by Peter Medawar, 'The Phenomenon of Man', *Mind* 70 (1961), pp. 99–106; reprinted in *The Strange Case of the Spotted Mice; and other Classic Essays on Science* (Oxford University Press, 1996), pp. 1–11; and in *Pluto's Republic* (Oxford University Press, 1982), pp. 242–51. The Medawar review is journalism rather than scholarship, and unpleasantly jingoistic in its criticism of Teilhard for being of French nationality.

[65] The phrase is from Bernard Towers, *Concerning Teilhard; and other Writings on Science and Religion* (London: Collins, 1969), p. 45.

[66] 'The Activation of Human Energy' (1953), *AE*, p. 391.

[67] 'Lines Written a Few Miles above Tintern Abbey', 101–103, in *William Wordsworth*, eds. Stephen Gill and Duncan Wu (Oxford University Press, 1994), p. 59.

hints at what Teilhard has in mind. Evolution, when construed as a self-contained system, is unavoidably reduced to a random statistical process.[68] Such explanations of evolution are deficient, however, being unable to account for the essential transcendence of human praxis. Human evolution must ultimately be described and understood in spiritual terms, and the same applies to the whole of the created order insofar as its evolution is bound up with that of humankind. Teilhard contrasts his own cosmology with the commonly accepted materialistic one thus:

> We still persist in regarding the physical as constituting the 'true' phenomenon in the universe, and the psychic as a sort of epiphenomenon. However … if we really wish to unify the real, we should completely reverse the values — that is, we should consider the whole of thermodynamics as an unstable and ephemeral by-effect of the concentration on itself of what we call 'consciousness' or 'spirit'.[69]
>
> Only *purity of heart* (whether or not assisted by grace, as the case may be) and not *pure science* is capable, confronted by the world in movement or by a miraculous fact, of overcoming the essential indeterminacy of appearances and of unmistakably disclosing a creator behind the forces of nature.[70]

The world is given its current and future consistency, these passages suggest, by spirit, action, passion and grace. This cosmology is clearly opposed to scientific reductionist accounts of evolution, but equally to the strict observance Thomist philosophy of the earlier twentieth century, which proposed a purely extrinsic concept of cause to account for order in the world.[71] Thomist philosophers typically argued that nature possessed only potency, and that God was therefore the primary cause of all events in the world. Such a rigorous form of causal extrinsicism denies that the world possesses any intrinsic order due to human agency or any other natural form of agency, such as biological process. Recent debates in Thomist cosmology have, however, provided a more nuanced conception of the relation of immanent being to transcendent being. In particular, they have sought to elucidate the implications of Aquinas's fundamental cosmological principle that an effect in some way illustrates its cause, which excludes any absolute distinction between act and

---

[68] See e.g. Jacques Monod, *Chance and Necessity: An Essay on the National Philosophy of Modern Biology* (London: Collins, 1972).

[69] 'The Activation of Human Energy', p. 393.

[70] 'On the Modes of Divine Action in the Universe' (1920), *CE*, p. 30.

[71] See Helen James John, *The Thomist Spectrum* (New York: Fordham, 1966), pp. 7–13.

potency.[72] As Olivia Blanchette argues in her examination of Aquinas's theory of perfection, universal causes (formal and final) cannot be purely equivocal because, if they were, then God would not act according to his own similitude. Universal causes are, in fact, analogous with particular (i.e. efficient and material) causes, which display something of their universal causes.[73] Expressed more precisely, God communicates as formal cause the principle of material cause, and communicates as final cause the principle of efficient cause. Blanchette states: 'God does not make the action of natural causes unnecessary, but rather, as the principal cause is the cause of an instrument's action, He is the cause of all true activity in the things of nature.'[74] Teilhard's effort to unify Thomist and evolutionary cosmology can be seen as anticipating some recent work in Thomist anthropology,[75] and suggests possibilities for practical application of their results. Teilhard is clearly closer to accounts which affirm some form of continuity between body and soul, and the created and spiritual orders generally,[76] rather than to readings which reduce either one of the poles to the other.

This reconception of Thomist metaphysics is motivated in part by Blondelian voluntarism and the philosophy of action: in one place, the 'zest for life' is even expressed as a 'will to live'.[77] These elements undergo a Bergsonian transmutation once situated cosmologically and temporally. In this new context, the 'apparent discontinuity of physical life is ... due to our attention being fixed on it by a series of separate acts: actually there is only a gentle slope, but in following the broken line of our acts of attention, we think we perceive separate steps'.[78] Bergson's insistence that life is a continuous movement through time, in opposition to Blondel's essentially atemporal ontology, originates in his *thèse secondaire* on book IV of Aristotle's *Physics*, which is a critique

---

[72] See *ST*, Ia, q. 2, a. 2, resp.; *On the Power of God*, q. 3, a. 7 (2 vols.; London: Burns, Oates & Washbourne, 1932–34), I, pp. 123-35.

[73] Olivia Blanchette, *The Perfection of the Universe According to Aquinas: A Teleological Cosmology* (College Park: Pennsylvania State University Press, 1999), pp. 156–57, 172.

[74] Blanchette, *Perfection*, p. 168.

[75] Key contrasts are presented in Robert C. Miner, 'Recent Work on Thomas in North America', in *Contemplating Aquinas: On the Varieties of Interpretation*, ed. Fergus Kerr (London: SCM, 2003), pp. 147–56.

[76] e.g. Thomas Hibbs, *Virtue's Splendor* (New York: Fordham University Press, 2001).

[77] 'The Zest for Living' (1950), *AE*, p. 231; 'My "Phenomenological" View of the World' (1954), *TF*, p. 214.

[78] Bergson, *Creative Evolution*, p. 3.

of Zeno and the Eleatic tradition.[79] Teilhard also refers to these para-
doxes and their attempts to prove the impossibility of motion.[80] The reason that these puzzles might appear insoluble, he suggests, is that they
assume a static cosmos within which the possibility of motion between
discrete, separated places is identified as problematic. If, however, the
Aristotelian principle is accepted that an act-potency relation may exist
between one place and another, or in other words, that place exerts an
influence on a body occupying it, then movement from one place to
another can be accounted for without difficulty as generated by the
inherently relational nature of spatiality. Bergson continues his refutation of Zeno in his seminal work *Creative Evolution*, in the course of
developing his own concept of the motivating principle of life: the *élan
vital*. He refutes the hypothesis that nothingness is an ontological category, arguing that it represents simply the separation of idea from feeling, and past from present, which can be overcome by human effort.[81]
This conflict over the existence of *le néant* marks the fundamental
breach with Bergsonian *Lebensphilosophie* effected by twentieth century
existentialism. Pete Gunter goes so far as to judge of Jean-Paul Sartre's
existentialist manifesto: 'It is not too far-fetched to consider *Being and
Nothingness* as, in significant respects, a protracted response to the
Bergsonian dismissal of "nothingness" as a pseudo-concept.'[82] Teilhard
similarly asserts that 'pure nothingness is an empty concept, a pseudo-
idea'.[83] At one point, he even states: 'Motion is not independent of the
moving body — on the contrary, the moving body is physically engendered by the motion which animates it.'[84] This apparent denial of the priority of matter and spirit over space and time contrasts with Teilhard's
ontology, but can be explained by his concern to give full recognition to
the Aristotelian insight that change is prior to stasis in the order of being.

Teilhard's own understanding of cosmological change is given particular inspiration by Epicurus, whose theory of motion he praises as pro-

---

[79] Henri Bergson, *Quid Aristoteles de loco senserit* (Paris: Alcan, 1889); trans.
«L'Idée de lieu chez Aristote», *Études Bergsoniennes* 2 (Paris: Albin Michel, 1949),
pp. 32–104; cf. Aristotle, *Physics*, IV, *Works* IV, pp. 274–427.

[80] 'The Transformist Paradox' (1925), 'The Natural Units of Humanity' (1939), *VP*,
pp. 83, 198.

[81] Bergson, *Creative Evolution*, pp. 298–99.

[82] Pete A.Y. Gunter, 'Bergson and Sartre: The Rise of French Existentialism', in *The
Crisis in Modernism: Bergson and the Vitalist Controversy*, eds. Frederick Burwick and
Paul Douglass (Cambridge University Press, 1992), p. 234.

[83] 'The Struggle Against the Multitude' (1917), *WW*, p. 95.

[84] 'My Fundamental Vision' (1948), *TF*, p. 193.

viding a principle of conservation and survival that he describes as an 'obliquity of motion', a bias towards movement, or a 'clinamen' (very slight deviation).[85] Epicurus places special emphasis on the spontaneity of motion, and Walter Englert has for this reason suggested that his mechanics constitutes an ancient antecedent to chaos theory.[86] Epicurus is, moreover, a source for the philosophy of history that Teilhard shares with Karl Marx, who praises the Greek atomist for opposing, according to Lucretius, the consensus that the heavenly or celestial bodies are subject to an ordered motion originating in eternal or divine law.[87] Epicurus regards all heavenly bodies as meteors, moving in a multiple and unregulated way. Their motion introduces a principle of indeterminacy into the heavenly realm, and in them are thus resolved the contradictions between essence and existence, form and matter. This intrusion of spontaneity into an ordered cosmos examined in Marx's doctoral thesis provides part of the philosophical justification for his later hope that the proletariat would arise unprompted against their oppressors as a direct result of their material situation, with no distinct theoretical or ideological persuasion needful. Marx states that, as a result of the heavenly bodies, matter has *'ceased to be abstract individuality; it has become concrete individuality, universality'*.[88] Epicurus, by redeeming matter from the closed and ordered system in which it had previously been confined, demonstrates to Teilhard, as to Marx, the possibility of creative action breaking out of a materially-determined historical process to endow it with a new telos.

Teilhard's belief in the creativity of the evolutionary process also develops and corrects the controversial work of the Louvain professor Henry de Dorlodot, well-known for his efforts to demonstrate the compatibility of Darwinism and magisterial teaching.[89] Augustine is a central figure in Dorlodot's work, having distinguished the spiritual ele-

[85] 'The Zest for Living', p. 234.

[86] Walter G. Englert, *Epicurus on the Swerve and Voluntary Action* (Atlanta, Ga.: Scholars, 1987).

[87] Karl Marx, *The Difference Between the Democritean and Epicurean Philosophy of Nature*, in Karl Marx and Frederick Engels, *Collected Works*, I (49 vols.; London: Laurence & Wishart, 1975–2001), pp. 66–73. For a discussion, see Oded Balaban, 'The Hermeneutics of the Young Marx, According to Marx's Approach to the Philosophy of Democritus and Epicurus', *Diogenes* 148 (1989), pp. 28–41.

[88] Marx, *Difference*, p. 71.

[89] Henry de Dorlodot, *Le Darwinisme au point de vue de l'orthodoxie Catholique* (Brussels: Vromant, 1921); trans. *Darwinism and Catholic Thought* (London: Burns, Oates & Washbourne, 1922); cited in 'The Transformist Question' (1921), 'What Should We Think of Transformism?' (1930), *VP*, pp. 25, 154.

ments of the created order from the material ones on the basis of whether their creation is complete or ongoing.[90] Human souls, which form the principal spiritual element of the created order, were completed at the initial moment of creation. Vegetable, animal and human bodies, and other material elements which would come into being the future, were not by contrast created in their future completed state, but as primordial seeds within the natural order. Dorlodot refutes Augustine's account of the Genesis creation myth on the grounds that it proposes a purely natural theory of evolution, and Dorlodot's arguments against the Bishop of Hippo are instructive. Augustine's figurative interpretation of the seven days, which supports his view that creation is an act which occurred in a single instant, is dependent, Dorlodot argues, on faulty exegesis, because the Hebrew יוֹם can only be read literally.[91] The rest taken by God at the end of the creative process, so important to defenders of the view that creation is a completed process, cannot moreover be 'historically affirmed' in the way that Augustine thinks it can. Dorlodot wishes, in offering these criticisms, to defend a conception of evolution as a continuing process in which God intervenes supernaturally in natural life, because he believes that this is the best way of reconciling Darwinian and Christian accounts of creation. Indeed, Dorlodot specifically argues that this conception of 'special intervention' is compatible with Darwinism.[92] His position is, however, problematic. In the case of miracles, it might be feasible to argue that for God to make special interventions into natural processes does not undermine the basic integrity of the natural order and its independence from the spiritual one. In the case of interventions which alter the future course of historical and biological development, however, it seems difficult to maintain that a realm of pure nature remains intact following those interventions, as Dorlodot claims. Moreover, although Dorlodot's attempt to link special intervention and Darwinism captures the element of spontaneity that Darwin perceives in evolution, it suggests a teleology and a supernatural dimension which were the elements of natural theology that Darwin was most determined to destroy.

---

[90] Augustine, *On the Literal Interpretation of Genesis*, 10, 21, 37, Fathers of the Church 84 (Washington, DC: Catholic University of America Press, 1991), pp. 151, 157–58, 173. A useful review of contemporary literature on the concept, and in particular its relation to 'transformism' (evolution), can be found in C. Boyer, «La Théorie augustinienne des raisons séminales», in *Miscellanea Agostiniana. Studi Agostiniani* (2 vols.; Rome: Poliglotta Vaticana, 1930–31), pp. 795–96.

[91] Dorlodot, *Darwinism*, pp. 141–51.

[92] Dorlodot, *Darwinism*, p. 126.

Teilhard, despite expressing approval of the importance which Dorlodot attaches to Christian humanism, and of his appropriation of the
Greek Fathers, presents a more convincing theology of evolution. To
explain how creation might be ongoing through time, rather than accomplished at a single moment, Teilhard employs, like Dorlodot, Augustine's doctrine of *seminal reason*, but crucially does not conceive it in
purely natural terms. Teilhard states:

> For us duration now permeates the essence of beings to their last fibres. It
> penetrates into their very stuff; not that things thereby become (as has
> often been alleged) fluid and inconsistent, but in the sense that today, how-
> ever fixed we suppose their nature to be, they seem to us termless and
> indefinite during its preparation, maturation and completion. Once consid-
> ered 'point-like' their 'natures' now stretch invisibly before our eyes, along
> the whole length of experiential time. They become to some degree
> 'threadlike'. At certain moments, no doubt, beings are more precisely
> 'born'; that is to say they enter definitely into the field of their internal
> consciousness and of our common experience. But this birth, by which we
> conventionally make them begin, is preceded in reality by a gestation with-
> out assignable origin. By something in itself [quelque chose de soi-même]
> (is not this what St Augustine called *ratio seminalis*?) everything is
> extended into some other preliminary reality, prolonged by something else,
> everything is found linked in its individual preparation and development
> (that is to say its own duration) with a general evolution on which cosmic
> duration records itself. Partially, infinitesimally, without losing any of its
> individual value, each element is co-extensive with history, with the reality
> of the whole.[93]

Teilhard uses Augustine's theory to provide a solution to the vexed
problem of how a greater being can proceed from a lesser being.[94] A
genetic universal is required, Teilhard asserts, instead of abstract and
concrete universals, in order to provide an account of creation as an
ongoing process.[95] It is a mistake, he suggests, to regard humanity as
created once-for-all in the image of an eternal, transcendent God or
form. Instead, the roots of humanity's being 'plunge back and down into
the unfathomable past' and a portion of world history is thus reflected in
every person.[96] The current form which humanity assumes is dependent
on the entire created order throughout all time, both its past evolution
and its future telos. Teilhard even cites Aquinas in support of his inter-

---

[93] 'Basis and Foundations of the Idea of Evolution' (1926), *VP*, p. 129.
[94] 'Evolution of the Idea of Evolution' (1950), *VP*, p. 245.
[95] 'What the World is Looking for from the Church' (1952), *CE*, p. 214; 'Science and
Christ' (1921), *SC*, p. 32.
[96] *DM*, p. 17.

pretation of Augustine: 'Was it not St Thomas who, comparing the viewpoint (fixist as we should call it today) of the Latin Fathers like St Gregory, to the evolutionary viewpoint of the Greek Fathers and St Augustine, said of the latter, *'Magis placet'* — it is more pleasing.'[97] Aquinas himself prefers, perhaps surprisingly, the Augustinian interpretation of the generation of species to the more common 'fixist' view. In the following suggestive comment, Aquinas states that his grounds for preferring Augustine's *ratio seminalis* doctrine over the fixism which one might assume him to have preferred is that the seminal reasons explanation is 'more reasonable and better protects Sacred Scripture from the derision of infidels, which Augustine teaches in his literal interpretation on Genesis is especially to be considered, and so scripture must be explained in such a way that the infidel cannot mock, and this opinion is more pleasing to me'.[98]

This understanding of the *ratio seminalis* as explicating changes in the characteristics of species over time has, however, been contested. Bonaventure employs the concept when arguing that 'matter is full of forms because of seminal principles', which contribute to declaring the action of divine power, wisdom and goodness on the universe.[99] This suggests, as Etienne Gilson has argued, that seminal reasons are no more than static forms instantiated in nature:

> Far from being called upon to explain the appearance of something new, as would be the case with creative evolution, they serve to prove that whatever appears to be new is really not so, and that in spite of appearances, it is still true to say that God 'created all things simultaneously'. This is the reason why seminal reasons, instead of leading to a transformist hypothesis, are constantly called upon by Augustine to account for the stability of species. The elements from which the seminal reasons are made have their own nature and efficacy, and this is the reason why a grain of wheat produces wheat rather than beans, or a man begets a man and not an animal of another species. The seminal reasons are principles of stability rather than of change.[100]

---

[97] 'What Should we think of Transformism?', p. 154.

[98] Thomas Aquinas, *II Scriptum super libros Sententiarum*, d. 12, q. 1, a. 2, resp.; trans. in 'The Work of the Six Days of Creation', in *Selected Writings*, ed. Ralph McInerny (London: Penguin, 1999), pp. 91–92.

[99] Bonaventure, *The Soul's Journey Into God*, I.14, in *The Soul's Journey into God. The Tree of Life. The Life of St Francis*, ed. Ewert Cousins (Mahwah, NJ: Paulist, 1978), pp. 64–65.

[100] Etienne Gilson, *The Christian Philosophy of Saint Augustine* (London: Gollancz, 1961), p. 207.

Gilson is possibly presenting in these comments an implicit critique of
Teilhard's evolutionary cosmology. Further attention reveals, however,
that Gilson and Teilhard are not as far apart as they might appear. Teilhard, in the course of his paleontological work, had realized that nature
ultimately preserves neither the single life nor that of the species.[101] In
the words of Alfred Lord Tennyson: 'From scarped cliff and quarried
stone / She cries, "A thousand types are gone: / I care for nothing, all
shall go.'[102] Tennyson here suggests that the extinction of previously
existing plant and animal species serves to disprove the classical notion
of a stable cosmos ordered by forms. Gilson's comments endorse a
broadly Neoplatonic account of the relation of matter to forming principles to which, he supposes, evolutionary accounts are opposed. The
most obvious response to this would be to consider whether or not the
form of every species requires everlasting and simultaneous instantiation in nature. If not, then the evolutionary process could consist in the
instantiation through time of different permutations of the complete set
of possible forms. It would be quite possible for the evolution of
species to be thus guided by forms. The difficulty with this proposition,
however, is that if evolution is a continual process to which every being
is subject, there would need to be a form subsisting for every being.
This would undermine what is commonly regarded to be a primary purpose of theories of forms, namely to establish ideas of species of which
many particular beings are members. Evolution, being an incremental
process, seems to subvert the notion of discrete species clearly distin-
guishable from each other that are instantiated in the created order. The
problem is curiously similar to the 'third man' objections made to the
Platonic theory of forms in the *Parmenides*,[103] except that it is transposed from an idealist ontology into one of generation. If forms exist of
two beings in which both individuals partake, which for the purposes of
the current discussion can be identified with forms of two related
species, then there must also exist a form of the likeness which they
share. There must then exist a pair of forms of the likeness of the
resemblance to both the individual beings, and then another pair of
forms resembling *those* likenesses, and so on ad infinitum. There is,
thankfully, a simpler response. The view that there exists such a neat
correspondence between species and particular beings, on which 'third
man' objections are based, is not easily reconcilable with the conviction

[101] *HP*, p. 74.
[102] Tennyson, *In memoriam*, §55, p. 148.
[103] Plato, *Parmenides*, 132a–133d, *Works* IV, pp. 216–23.

pervading so much of Plato's cosmology that material beings inhabit a shadowy and *de*formed world. This suggests that not only do individual beings exist imperfectly, but that the relations between them and the species of which they are members are also imperfectly realized. In other words, the forms of species serve as paradigms, and *deficient* likeness is to be expected in the course of evolutionary progression as different species decline and emerge. This theory of forms and their instantiation has more in common with the Aristotelian notion of a form as an object of the understanding than with the classic Platonic one of it possessing real existence in a realm of ideas: from the fact that a property can be predicated of a subject, it does not follow that the property is ontologically present, either in whole or in part, in the subject.[104]

The extent to which the *ratio seminalis* theory accurately describes the relation that Teilhard perceives to exist between ideas and cosmology is ultimately a question of emphasis. He argues that, at the current stage of evolutionary progression, 'duration now permeates the essence of beings to their last fibres' such that possible 'substantial changes' between different natures are no longer regarded as fixed in advance.[105] This might appear to exclude the *ratio seminalis* theory: if the substantial changes are instantiations of forms, they are necessarily preordained. Equally, it could be argued that although instantiations are determined by forms, the *particular* form which is in fact instantiated remains undetermined. Another response would be to distinguish between two 'standpoints' from which creation is regarded: the human, from which 'God's creation is continuously unfolding' as '*creatio continua*', and the divine, from which 'what is created is one temporally extended or ordered universe'.[106] By means such as these, the *ratio seminalis* doctrine remains able to contribute to an account of how, in a theological cosmology, an immanent and teleological creative process unfolds itself and is sustained.

---

[104] Aristotle, *The Categories*, II, *Works* I (23 vols.; Harvard University Press, 1926–91), pp. 14–17.

[105] 'Basis and Foundations of the Idea of Evolution', pp. 128–29.

[106] Jürgen Moltmann cites Teilhard approvingly in support of his own doctrine of continuous creation in *God in Creation: An Ecological Doctrine of Creation* (London: SCM, 1985), p. 211. Philosophical implications of the theory of continuous creation are explored in Paul Helm, 'Eternal Creation: The Doctrine of the Two Standpoints', in *Doctrine of Creation: Essays in Dogmatics, History and Philosophy*, ed. Colin Gunton (Edinburgh: T&T Clark, 1997), p. 35.

The transcendence and immanence of Omega

Maurice Wiles suggested that the open future which an evolutionary model of historical and biological development posits for the world requires a modest mode of Christian theological affirmation.[107] In the case of a static world, Wiles implies, the telos is already given and the cosmological context in which statements of faith are made is everlasting. A greater degree of certainty about the truth of theological propositions is therefore possible. The assumption that evolution is necessarily towards an open future is challenged by Teilhard, however, and therefore the question about the character of Christian affirmation suggested by an evolutionary cosmology remains open. In fact, a key aim of Teilhard's oeuvre is to show how a theory of evolution can provide evidence in support of some of the fundamental tenets of Christian theology. The best known component of his own evolutionary cosmology is the 'Omega point', or end point, prefigured by Tennyson's 'One far-off divine event, / To which the whole creation moves'.[108] The Omega point is

> an ultimate and self-subsistent pole of consciousness, so involved in the world as to be able to gather into itself, by union, the cosmic elements that have been brought by technical arrangement to the extreme limit of their centration — and yet, by reason of its supra-evolutive (that is to say, transcendent) nature, enabled to be immune from that fatal regression which is, structurally, a threat to every edifice whose stuff exists in space and time.[109]

The qualities of the Omega point are defined by the ontological priorities of the Neoplatonic hierarchy of being: simplicity, which is privileged above plurality; unity, which is superior to multiplicity; and rest, which is a higher state of being than linear motion. This is no benediction of Darwinian evolutionary science, but a critique of its basic assumption about the nature of development as materialistic, random and antagonistic.

As the previous Neoplatonic comparison suggests, the Omega point is not an unmoved mover. In the epilogue to *The Human Phenomenon*, Teilhard refers to the 'presence at the head of the world of *something*

---

[107] Maurice Wiles, 'The Incarnation and Development', in *The Religion of the Incarnation: Anglican Essays in Commemoration of 'Lux mundi'*, ed. Robert Morgan (Bristol Classical Press, 1989), p. 84.

[108] Tennyson, *In memoriam*, concluding words of epilogue, p. 148.

[109] 'My Fundamental Vision' (1948), *TF*, p. 185.

still higher, in its line, than the Omega Point'.[110] Omega is the point at which the 'unified plural' *meets* the 'active centre of unification'.[111] This encounter of the created order with Omega is possible as part of a metaphysics of *unire*, Teilhard argues, because such a metaphysics allows intermediate stages of participated being. These are not possible, however, in a Thomist *actus essendi* ontology:

> In a metaphysics of *Esse*, pure act, once posited, monopolizes all that is absolute and necessary in being; and, no matter what one does, nothing can then justify the existence of participated being. In a metaphysics of union, on the other hand, we can see that, when once immanent divine unity is complete, a degree of absolute *unification* is still possible.[112]

Final consummation therefore lies not at the Omega point but *beyond* it. Interpreters of Teilhard are justified in advising caution about religious accounts of evolution which extrapolate too smoothly from scientific and cultural factors to a theological cosmology.[113] Teilhard would share their concerns. Interpreters who have failed to appreciate the transcendence of Omega have committed the same general error as Hegel in his immanentist reading of Plotinus in the *Lectures on the History of Philosophy*: the One, as principle of unity, is not Being (*Sein*), as Hegel maintained Plotinus had proposed, but *beyond Being*.[114] Evolution therefore stands in a similar relation to the absolute as do action and passion: all three both require and posit a transcendent divinity.

Teilhard transposes this Neoplatonic hierarchy into a specifically theological conception of the encounter of act and being in Christ, who is eternally begotten in the Godhead yet acts on the world as Omega. At the head of the created order is

> the centre, at once one and complex, in which, bound together by the person of Christ, may be seen *enclosed one within the other* (one might say)

---

[110] *HP*, p. 214, n.

[111] 'Some General Views on the Essence of Christianity' (1939), *CE*, p. 133.

[112] 'Suggestions for a New Theology' (1945), *CE*, p. 178.

[113] Colin Gunton, *The Triune Creator: A Historical and Systematic Study* (Edinburgh University Press, 1998), p. 188. See also John F. Haught, 'True Union Differentiates: A Response to My Critics', *Science and Christian Belief* 17 (2005), pp. 57–70.

[114] Plotinus, *Enneads*, V.1 (10) 10 (7 vols.; Harvard University Press, 1966–88), p. 44; G.W.F. Hegel, *Lectures on the History of Philosophy*, I (3 vols.; Lincoln: University of Nebraska Press, 1995), pp. 413–16. Hegel's reading is discussed in Eugene F. Bales, 'A Heideggerian Interpretation of Negative Theology in Plotinus', *The Thomist* 47 (1983), pp. 197–208. For lucid comparison of Teilhard and Plotinus on this point, see Marietta Grindler, „Die *henosis* als Zentrum Plotinischen Philosophierens", in *Das holistische Evolutionsmodell Pierre Teilhard de Chardins: ein Vergleich mit den Entwicklungsgedanken bei Plotin, Schelling und Bergson* (Aachen: Shaker, 2000), p. 323.

three progressively deeper *centres*: on the outside, the immanent ('natural')
apex of the humano-cosmic cone; further in, at the middle, the immanent
('supernatural') apex of the 'ecclesial' or Christic cone; and finally, at the
innermost heart, the transcendent, triune, and divine centre: The complete
Pleroma coming together under the mediating action of Christ-Omega.[115]

The deity of natural theology exists beyond this triple centre of the created order. This deity is also personal, however, owing to its transcendence, as in the kalām Islamic systematic theology: not only a physical
or biological prime mover, but a 'psychic prime mover, addressing himself to what is most human in us — to our intelligence, that is, to our
heart and to our power of free choice'.[116] Teilhard's great concern to
address and conserve *personality*, both of humanity and of God, within
a monadic ontology in which the many reflect the one, requires him,
nevertheless, to safeguard divine transcendence at all times. If God were
identical with the Omega point, then the unity, simplicity and rest of that
point would exclude the possibility of God possessing a Trinitarian inner
life, which requires internal differentiation and relationality. This is one
reason why the person of Christ is central in Teilhard's cosmology. The
Godhead, by acting on the world through Christ rather than directly,
does not compromise its own transcendence. Teilhard reflects, during
the final days of his life, that following the consummation of the world
at the Omega point, even Christ will return to the Father, meditating on
the verse from I Corinthians: 'When all things are subjected to him, then
the Son himself will be subjected to the one who put all things in subjection under him, so that God may be all in all.'[117] John Macquarrie
accurately states that although Teilhard 'goes some way towards meeting process philosophies', he ultimately defends traditional theism:
'God is conceived as subsisting beyond the world-process, eternally
complete in his unchanging perfection.'[118]

[115] 'Outline of a Dialectic of Spirit' (1946), *AE*, p. 149.

[116] 'Outline of a Dialectic of Spirit', p. 147. On this point, see Henri de Lubac, 'The
contribution of Teilhard to the knowledge of God', in *Theology in History* (San Francisco: Ignatius, 1996), pp. 543–44. De Lubac grants Teilhard more originality in his personalistic cosmological notion of divinity than Teilhard deserves by leaving its Islamic
antecedents unidentified.

[117] 'The Last Page of Pierre Teilhard de Chardin's Dairy' (1955), *HM*, pp. 103–104;
cf. I Cor 15.28.

[118] John Macquarrie, *Twentieth Century Religious Thought: The Frontiers of Philosophy and Theology, 1900–1980* (London: SCM, rev. edn, 1983), p. 273. John F. Haught,
in his 2004 Boyle Lecture 'Darwin, Design and the Promise of Nature', *Science and
Christian Belief* 17 (2005), pp. 5–20, argues that, in Teilhard's view, trust in cosmic
processes and directionality is indispensable to ongoing creation. This is true, and needs
to be seen as founded in the continued action of God on the cosmos. For comparison of

Teilhard's consistent preservation of a real distinction between God and the created order, even at the moment when its *immanent* convergence is complete, renders any claim that his theory of evolution is 'Hegelian' wholly implausible. Teilhard presents a convincing and nuanced theory of divine nature, which in the terms of the Athanasian Creed neither confounds the divine persons nor divides their substance. The fact that there was virtually no interest in Hegelian philosophy in early twentieth century France, where most elements of Teilhard's theology have their genesis, lends support to this assessment. Dumitru Rosca's thesis concerning the influence of Hegel on Hyppolite Taine, published in Paris in 1928, was considered unusual for its time, and is among the first signs of a revival of Hegelian studies there.[119] Rosca's translation of Hegel's *Life of Jesus* was, moreover, the first work of Hegel's to be published in French translation for fifty years.[120] Teilhard refers to «hégélianisme» in generic and pejorative terms, describes Hegel's metaphysics as an 'ideology', and makes critical comments about Hegel's 'deductive *solution* to the world'.[121] He also suggests that the conflicts between master and slave discussed in the *Phenomenology of Spirit* are irresolvable in the context in which they are set: their resolution lies not in a synthesis of elements, but in the unification of elements by a transcendent power.[122] An apposite description of Teilhard's approach to cosmological questions is provided by Marx's statement that, whereas German (i.e. Hegelian) philosophy 'descends from heaven to earth, here it is a matter of ascending from earth to heaven'.[123]

Teilhard's opposition to *hégélianisme* is further confirmed by his understanding of the *potentia obedientalis* of the created order possessing a natural orientation to divine action. It is here that the transcenden-

Teilhard's evolutionary cosmology with Boyle's physicotheology, see Ernan McMullin, 'Introduction', in *Evolution and Creation* (Notre Dame, Ind.: University of Notre Dame Press, 1985), p. 41.

[119] See Nicolas Tertulian, «Un hégélien roumain: D.D. Rosca», *AP* 63 (2000), pp. 95–109; cf. Dumitru D. Rosca, *L'Influence de Hegel sur Taine: théoricien de la connaissance et de l'art* (Paris: Gamber, 1928).

[120] G.W.F. Hegel, *La Vie de Jésus*, trans. Dumitru D. Rosca (Paris: Gamber, 1928); see Michael Kelly, *Hegel in France* (University of Birmingham Press, 1992), p. 7.

[121] 'Pantheism and Christianity' (1923), *CE*, p. 56; *HP*, p. 212; 'My Fundamental Vision', p. 164.

[122] 'The Human Rebound of Evolution' (1947), *FM*, p. 211; cf. G.W.F. Hegel, *Phenomenology of Spirit* (Oxford University Press, 1977), §§178–96, pp. 111–19.

[123] Karl Marx, *German Ideology*, *Works* V, p. 36. For juxtaposition of Teilhard with Hegel and Rothe, see Sigurd Martin Daecke, *Teilhard de Chardin und die evangelische Theologie: die Weltlichkeit Gottes und die Weltlichkeit der Welt* (Göttingen: Vandenhoeck & Ruprecht, 1967), pp. 186–212.

tal method of a figure like Karl Rahner parts company with Hegelian immanentism,[124] and Teilhard sides with transcendentalism. Hegel's theology has, of course, been appropriated for very different purposes: the religious rationalism of A.E. Biedermann and historical theology of F.C. Baur, through to the historical systematic dialectics of Isaak Dorner and the religious ethical statism of Richard Rothe. Hegel's interpretation of the relation between philosophy and religion consequently remains a debated topic. It is nevertheless the case towards the end of the fairly late *Lectures on the Philosophy of Religion*, which form his most extensive exposition of the philosophy-religion relation, that revelation is explicable in philosophical terms: 'Sustained by philosophy, religion receives its justification from thinking consciousness.'[125] In Teilhard's cosmology, this Hegelian relationship is however transformed: consciousness, being a product of evolution, receives its justification from Christ. Hans Küng, profoundly influenced by Hegelian religious historiography, first denies this contrast between Teilhard and Hegel, but later comes to accept it. Küng, in his study *On Being a Christian*, places Teilhard alongside Hegel and other 'Encyclopaedists' — Lessing, Kant, and Marx — as a theorist of the 'technological evolution of humanity', because of his 'idea of evolution to the "omega point"'.[126] Küng provides, in a later work, a more detailed discussion of Teilhard's theology, suggesting that Teilhard in fact *corrects* Hegelian immanentism by emphasizing that any process of coming-to-be depends on the everlasting existence of God. Teilhard's cosmology, Küng suggests, is pan*en*theistic rather than pantheistic.[127] It was due to Teilhard, Küng moreover argues, that 'theologians increasingly began to observe what new opportunities for the old faith were offered in particular by the evolutive understanding of the world'.[128]

So far as German idealism is concerned, Teilhard's dynamic view of evolution has more in common with the positive philosophy of the later Schelling than with the immanentist spiritualism of the Hegelian closed system: the source of the life force must subsist in *opposition* to the cre-

---

[124] *DM*, p. 98; see Winfried Corduan, 'Hegel in Rahner: A Study in Philosophical Hermeneutics', *Harvard Theological Review* 71 (1978), pp. 285–98.

[125] G.W.F. Hegel, *Lectures on the Philosophy of Religion*, III, §268 (3 vols.; Berkeley: University of California Press, 1984–87), p. 346.

[126] Hans Küng, *On Being a Christian* (London: Collins, 1977), p. 39.

[127] Hans Küng, *Does God Exist? An Answer for Today* (London: Collins, 1980), pp. 171–75.

[128] Küng, *Does God Exist?*, p. 347.

ated order, and not as a vital impulse within it.[129] This is particularly clear in Teilhard's refutation of Bergsonian egoism, according to which humanity 'must, by a strong recoil of our personality on itself, gather up [its] past which is slipping away, in order to thrust it, compact and undivided, into a present which it will create by entering.'[130] The highest degree of self-assertion for which Teilhard can hope is, in contrast, the *'desire to desire being'*.[131] This being is transcendent, and certainly not located in the human ego nor a creation of it. Teilhard argues that humanity motivates the evolutionary process only to the extent that it acts as the agent in which the transcendent absolute recapitulates its creative, unifying act in human action. Bergson fails to see this, and Rose Marie Mossé-Bastide convincingly argues that this is due to his misreading of Plotinus. Bergson wrongly interprets the relation between action and contemplation expounded in the crucial *Ennead* III.8 (30), taking the critique of πρᾶξις (practical action) as a shadow of contemplation to be a critique of action per se rather than as the basis for a distinction between πρᾶξις and ποίησις (creative action), which is symbiotic with the soul's contemplation of the One.[132] Mossé-Bastide concludes that the «rapport essentiel» and «intuition centrale» of both Bergson and Plotinus is the doctrine of the λόγος σπερματικός, of the One descending into corporeal multiplicity and exteriorizing its powers in the world.[133] Bergson nevertheless fails to preserve the transcendence of the One into the present or the future, portraying history as the dispersal of the λόγος itself from unity into multiplicity, with no convergence or consummation therefore possible. Teilhard's understanding of history as being generated by the redemptive action of a unified λόγος on material life is more compatible with Plotinian cosmology. It is also closer to the theology of Justin Martyr in the *First Apology*, in which Christ as λόγος σπερματικός remains the 'first-born of God' and the 'Word of whom every race of men were partakers'.[134] Teilhard believes that Christ coincides with the Omega point as preserver and saviour of

---

[129] Andrew Bowie, *Schelling and Modern European Philosophy: An Introduction* (London: Routledge, 1993), pp. 38–39.

[130] Bergson, *Creative Evolution*, pp. 17, 210–11.

[131] *DM*, p. 40.

[132] Plotinus, *Enneads*, III.8 (30) 4, pp. 369–73; Rose-Marie Mossé-Bastide, *Bergson et Plotin* (Paris: Presses universitaires de France, 1959), p. 393; Henri Bergson, *The Two Sources of Morality and Religion* (Notre Dame, Ind.: University of Notre Dame Press, 1977), p. 221.

[133] Mossé-Bastide, *Bergson et Plotin*, pp. 401–402.

[134] Justin Martyr, *First Apology*, ANF I, §46, p. 178.

evolution and shepherd of the Universe,[135] recognizing as early as 1917 that he needed to give sufficient prominence to this latter redemptive element in his theology.[136] Omega is, moreover, the point at which 'Christic faith comes in to take over from and to consummate faith in humanity.'[137] It is the point at which the unsatisfied hopes and uncompleted projects of humanity are gathered up and consummated *in Christo*.

Karl Barth describes Teilhard's work (specifically *The Divine Milieu*) in a letter as one of several successive *Riesenschlangen* (boa-constrictors) that have swallowed-up the Gospel, suggesting that Teilhard, although assigning to Christ a decisive role, seeks to evaluate and understand Christ from the context of evolution, rather than to honour Christ in his own self-revelation.[138] Barth places Teilhard in the same category, in this letter, as Bultmann and Brunner, and referring to his refutation of the latter's natural theology,[139] states: 'If I said No! then as loudly as I could, do I not really have to do so now?' Barth argues that Teilhard turns the deity into little more than a God of evolution in order to deify the evolutionary principle posited by the natural sciences.[140] Teilhard, he argues, is therefore a classic gnostic theologian. Barth fails to recognize, however, that Teilhard regards Christ as completing and redeeming the evolutionary process and therefore as irreducible to that process. David Fergusson provides, in fact, an accurate description of Teilhard's position in his apparently critical observation that Teilhard's view of the parousia, and the transformation of the whole of nature and redemption of evolution that are associated with it, is 'not a realization of immanent natural forces … but a divine transfiguring of the cosmos intimated in the resurrection of Jesus from the dead'.[141]

---

[135] 'Super-Humanity, Super-Christ, Super-Charity' (1943), *SC*, pp. 164–65; 'Introduction to the Christian Life' (1944), *CE*, p. 156; 'Christology and Evolution' (1933), *CE*, p. 90; 'A Note on Progress' (1920), *FM*, p. 23; 'The Struggle Against the Multitude' (1917), *WW*, p. 105. See Arthur Peacocke, *God and the New Biology* (Gloucester, Mass.: Peter Smith, 1994), p. 78.

[136] *J*, 26 December 1917, p. 243.

[137] 'My Fundamental Vision', p. 203.

[138] Letter to Marie-Claire Barth, 17 August 1963, in Karl Barth, *Letters, 1961–1968*, eds. Jürgen Fangmeier, Hinrich Stoevesandt and Geoffrey W. Bromiley (Edinburgh: T&T Clark, 1981), pp. 116–17.

[139] Exchanges from this debate are presented in Karl Barth and Emil Brunner, *Natural Theology* (London: SCM, 1947). For the detailed issues at stake, see John W. Hart, *Karl Barth vs. Emil Brunner: The Formation and Dissolution of a Theological Alliance, 1916–1936* (Oxford: Lang, 2001).

[140] Letter to Georges Casalis, 18 August 1963, in Barth, *Letters*, pp. 119–20.

[141] David Fergusson, *The Cosmos and the Creator: An Introduction to the Theology of Creation* (London: SPCK, 1998), p. 76.

At this point of consummation, metaphysics ceases to be hypothetical and becomes justified by faith: 'The world is seen to be suspended, by its conscious side, from an Omega Point of convergence, and Christ, in virtue of his Incarnation, is recognized as carrying out precisely the functions of Omega.'[142] Francis Elliot states:

> Omega becomes Christ only by an act of faith, that is to say, an act of personal recognition which is only achieved in the encounter of the call of Christ and the submission of the person who hears it. Omega … becomes a person in the authentic sense only by the mystical encounter which occurs when the person who has perceived the presence of the other submits to deliver themselves up totally, that is to say, to believe in him.[143]

The history of the salvation which Christ-Omega accomplishes is at once religious and cosmic, posited by a Christian narrative of the linear progression of time that contradicts the cyclical models that prevailed in pre-Christian philosophy.[144] The conception of historical development characteristic of 'modernity' is, in other words, established by Christian theology and made a reality in the action of Christ. The evolutionary christology which establishes this dynamic, linear model of historical progression is identifiable in some of the Greek Fathers, who transpose the 'evidence of Revelation into a universe of the non-static type'. Teilhard appropriates, more specifically, the cosmology of Irenaeus of Lyons, in which he identifies an 'astonishing anticipation of our modern views of progress'.[145] Bernard Sesboüé states of Teilhard and Irenaeus:

> Tous deux ont le sens du temps qui n'est pas une répétition stérile des cycles naturels, mais qui construit une véritable histoire. Ils ont le sens du temps humain et de la croissance de l'humanité. Pour tous les deux le Christ est l'Alpha et l'Oméga de l'histoire.[146]

---

[142] 'Super-Humanity, Super-Christ, Super-Charity', p. 166.

[143] Francis G. Elliott, 'The Christology of Teilhard de Chardin', in *Evolution, Marxism and Christianity: Studies in the Teilhardian Synthesis* (London: Garnstone, 1967), p. 97.

[144] Ernst Benz, *Evolution and Christian Hope* (London: Doubleday, 1966), pp. 67–68.

[145] 'Catholicism and Science' (1946), *SC*, p. 189; 'The Mysticism of Science' (1939), *HE*, p. 167, n. For contemporary interest in Irenaean cosmology, see Adhémar d'Alès, «La Doctrine de la récapitulation en saint Irénée», *RSR* 6 (1916), pp. 189–211; D.B. Reynders, «Optimisme et théocentrisme chez saint Irénée», *RTAM* 8 (1936), pp. 227–52; Jean Daniélou, «Saint Irénée et les origines de la théologie de l'histoire», *RSR* 34 (1947), pp. 227–31.

[146] Bernard Sesboüé, *Tout récapituler dans le Christ: christologie et sotériologie d'Irénée de Lyons* (Paris: Desclée, 2000), p. 204: 'Both possess a sense of time which is not a sterile repetition of natural cycles, but which constructs a real history. They possess the sense of human time and the growth of humanity. For both, Christ is the Alpha and the Omega of history.' cf. Dai Sil Kim, 'Irenaeus of Lyons and Teilhard de Chardin: A

Irenaeus believes, moreover, that the vision of God constitutes and exalts the life of humanity. He affirms: 'The glory of God is the living human, and the life of the human is the vision of God'.[147] This theology is humanistic, but only because it is theocentric. In Irenaeus's cosmology, theophanies mark various points in salvation history when humanity is granted the ultimate glory of the vision of God.[148] In Teilhard's cosmology, the vision of God in the divine milieu also provides the means by which Christ recapitulates creation and shepherds it towards its final consummation. The vision of God is therefore a 'restorative vision'.[149] The vision of the cosmos spiritually transfigured performs an analogous function for Teilhard to that of *imagination* in the Ignatian spiritual exercises, which creates «une logique de rupture et d'instauration historique».[150] The imagination does not simply receive images of reality passively, but employs spiritual images to construct that reality.[151]

Biological ethics

The apprentice in Goethe's „Der Zauberlehrling" lays hands, Teilhard states, on 'forces of such power that he begins to be afraid of causing some disaster in Nature'.[152] Teilhard employs this poetic imagery as a metaphor for the capability of modern society to manipulate, with technology, processes that previously occurred naturally. Humanity's capacity for intervention in the processes of nature is forever increasing in ways that are difficult to predict with accuracy. For instance, in considering whether the earth could possibly not constitute the centre of the cosmos, 'all that Galileo's judges could distinctly see as menaced was the miracle of Joshua'.[153] In a world becoming adult, by contrast, the

---

Comparative Study of "Recapitulation" and "Omega"', *Journal of Ecumenical Studies* 13 (1976), pp. 69–93. The latter is an excellent discussion under the three headings of restoration, achievement and deification. Kim's interpretation of Teilhard's cosmology as phenomenological rather than christological means, however, that the affinity between the two theologians is understated.

[147] Irenaeus, *Against Heresies*, IV, 20.7, *ANF* I, p. 490.

[148] Irenaeus, *Against Heresies*, IV, 20.6, p. 489.

[149] Letter of 10 January 1927, *LLZ*, p. 74.

[150] Pierre-Antoine Fabre, *Ignace de Loyola: le lieu de l'image* (Paris: Vrin, 1992), p. 319; cf. Madeleine Barthélemy-Madaule, *Bergson et Teilhard de Chardin* (Paris: Seuil, 1963), p. 86.

[151] *J*, 26 July 1947, cahier XV.

[152] 'The Human Rebound of Evolution', p. 202.

[153] 'Fall, Redemption and Geocentrism' (1920), *CE*, p. 37, n. 1; cf. Jo 10.12–14.

accumulation of powers once attributed solely to divinity is becoming commonplace. The sorcerer's apprentice, after his master's symbolic departure, attempts to harness his powers, rejoicing that „nun sollen seine Geister auch nach meinem Willen leben!" In the poem, the usurpation ends in failure, with the apprentice pleading to his returning Master: „Die ich rief, die Geister, werd' ich nun nicht los."[154] Teilhard believes, by contrast, that there is no returning master about to intervene in the universe to rectify the problems caused by humanity's misuse of technology.

Teilhard is suggesting that relevant theological and ethical principles need to be established to enable humanity in the modern world to make sense of its tremendous powers over nature and to use those powers responsibly and constructively. Moral questions surrounding the use of technology to intervene in biological processes have clearly become far more sharply focused since his lifetime, being intimately related to the ever increasing number of technologies actually available or under development. Teilhard's general analysis of these questions is neverthe-less pertinent, and in places prophetic. He describes an ambivalent and shifting balance between human autonomy and biological determinism, in which 'individual humans have become to some extent subordinate to their work'. The fruits of human labour have, like Victor Frankenstein's monster created during a quest for the source of being, become 'autonomous entities, endowed with unbounding and exacting life'. Humanity's production of new technology is 'more and more patently exceeding its powers of absorption and assimilation'.[155] Jürgen Haber-mas describes this progressive estrangement of material production from consciousness as 'dissonance of intention', and argues that what is needed to counteract it is a renewed understanding of the fusion of nature and soul.[156] Teilhard states a similar belief in his frequent affir-mations that the ordering of nature by soul provides the cosmos with its telos. He believes that the direction of technical production by the moral intention of spirit is a real possibility. He depicts humankind 'now stand-ing upon its own feet' and 'entering into a new era of autonomous con-trol and self-orientation'.[157] The best example of the human appropria-

---

[154] 'Spirits called by him, now banished, / My commands shall soon obey'; 'From the spirits that I called, deliver me!' in Goethe, *Selected Verse*, pp. 173–77.

[155] 'The Spirit of the Earth' (1931), *HE*, pp. 36–37; cf. Mary Shelley, *Frankenstein* (London: Penguin, 1994), p. 49.

[156] Jürgen Habermas, *The Future of Human Nature* (Oxford: Polity, 2003), pp. 60–64.

[157] 'My Fundamental Vision', p. 181.

tion of natural forces that occurred during Teilhard's lifetime is nuclear fission. Reflecting on this technological advance, Teilhard states that humankind 'has succeeded in seizing and manipulating the sources commanding the very origins of matter'.[158] This is clearly an ambivalent achievement, however, having the potential to generate energy to preserve human life as well as to construct weapons capable of destroying it.

Teilhard anticipates the equally acute moral problem of genetic manipulation, observing how humankind feels itself to be 'on the verge of acquiring the power of physico-chemical control of the operations of heredity and morphogenesis in the depths of its own being'.[159] He states:

> As a direct result of its socialization, humankind is beginning, with rational design, to take over the biological motive forces which determine its growth — in other words, it is becoming capable of modifying, or even of creating, its own self.[160]

Biological realities no longer provide a fixed context within which humanity makes moral decisions, and are more likely to become products of those decisions which themselves construct the human subject and thus condition his or her subsequent moral choices. The classic order of a shared conception of static human nature generating an ethic which epistemologically grounds a moral framework and motivates adherence to it no longer applies: 'Material determinisms cease to provide the skeleton of the world; they are merely a secondary effect in the cosmos'.[161] In response to this potential inversion of the historic relationship between nature, ethics and choice, Teilhard calls, as has Habermas more recently, for a renewed sense of an 'ethics of the species'[162] grounded in the most fundamental categories of the human experience so far: consciousness, subjectivity, reason, communication, and Teilhard would add, religion. The power inherent in modern technology to condition human nature, and in part to determine it, is not a usurpation of divine power, but a necessary progression in the history of the cosmos in which humanity becomes increasingly active in the creative process

---

[158] 'The Spiritual Repercussions of the Atom Bomb' (1946), *FM*, p. 142; see also 'On Looking at a Cyclotron' (1953), *AE*, pp. 347–57.

[159] 'The Directions and Conditions of the Future' (1948), 'The Human Rebound of Evolution', *FM*, pp. 234, 197.

[160] 'My Fundamental Vision', p. 181.

[161] 'The Spirit of the Earth', 'The Phenomenon of Spirituality' (1937), *HE*, pp. 29, 102.

[162] Habermas, *Future of Human Nature*, p. 71.

which God directs. Modern technology, far from being a Promethean theft from the deity of a power which is rightly its own,[163] makes possible a necessary sharing by humankind in God's creative power. To preserve and promote human co-operation in this divine action is the new task for ethical theory.

Theology and science

At the core of difficulties in identifying and interpreting Teilhard's theology, and appraising its relation to his scientific oeuvre, has been the hermeneutical question of how the different discourses he employs relate to one another. Teilhard describes his life as 'spent simultaneously in the heart of the Gentile world and in that of the Church',[164] and there is no doubt that in immersing himself in both of these worlds, he recognized their complementarity. He affirms: 'There is no domain, and no point, in which science and religion encroach on one another — nor do one another's work.' There exists, by contrast, a reciprocal and dynamic relation between the two discourses, with both being degraded if this mutuality is denied: science by an excessively mechanized view of reality and process, and religion by its increasing estrangement from the contingencies of material life.[165] Resolution of this antagonism requires the definition of appropriate working relationships between the different sources of authority in order that each may retain a rigorous and consistent methodology which respects the methods of the other. Religious propositions cannot, for instance, be derived from the experimental methods of the natural sciences. Teilhard states:

---

[163] 'The Spiritual Repercussions of the Atom Bomb', p. 147.

[164] 'Christology and Evolution' (1933), CE, p. 77.

[165] 'The Death-Barrier and Co-Reflection' (1955), AE, pp. 404–405. Teilhard's achievement in synthesizing the dual perspectives of scientific evolution and Christian eschatology has been recognized in Ian Barbour, 'Five Ways of Reading Teilhard', Soundings 51 (1968), pp. 115–45; and Arthur Peacocke, Science and the Christian Experiment (London: Oxford Unviersity Press, 1971), pp. 195–96. For more recent positive assessments, see Berthold Suchan, „Die Bedeutung Teilhards de Chardin für das Gespräch zwischen Theologie und Naturwissenschaften", in Von der Suche nach Gott, eds. Margot Schmidt and Fernando Domínguez Reboiras (Stuttgart-Bad Cannstatt: Frommann Holzboog, 1998), pp. 719–30; and Gero Franz Thimm, „Naturwissenschaftliche Erkenntnis und Gotteserfahrung nach Teilhard de Chardin", in Wahrheit: Recherchen zwischen Hochscholastik und Postmoderne, eds. Thomas Eggensperger and Ulrich Engel, Walberberger Studien: Philosophische Reihe 9 (Mainz: Matthias Grünewald, 1995), pp. 314–21.

We shall never be enabled scientifically to see God, because there will never be any discontinuity between the divine operation and the physical and physiological laws which are science's sole concern. Since the chains of antecedents are never broken (but simply bent or extended) by divine action, an analytical observation of phenomena is powerless to enable us to attain God, *even as Prime Mover*. We shall never escape scientifically from the circle of natural explanations.[166]

God acts on the world by means of secondary causes, even in many events which appear miraculous. A true miracle, in the sense of a direct intervention by God in the cosmic order that is independent of secondary causes, is of course theoretically possible. Nevertheless, religious believers need to remain aware of the deficiencies inherent in human scientific knowledge of the way in which the world operates. Just because the cause of a particular event cannot be explained, it does not follow that the event in question is miraculous.[167] Hence Teilhard's examination of the episcopal enquiries into healings at Lourdes hinges on the distinction between establishing that certain facts about healings are 'extra-medical', and interpreting those healings as caused by direct divine action.[168] The same point applies to general theological principles. Teilhard states:

I would never dream ... of deducing Christian dogmas solely from an examination of the properties our reason attributes to the structure of the world. Christ, we must add, is the plenitude of the universe, its principle of synthesis. He is therefore something more than all the elements of this world put together; in other words, although the world can justify our expectation of Christ, he cannot *be deduced from it*.[169]

Scientific method, for instance, can neither prove nor disprove the existence of God. This is because God is believed in by *humanity*, which cannot be defined in solely scientific terms. Teilhard affirms: 'Any number of sciences concern themselves with humankind, but humanity, in that which makes one essentially human, still lies outside science.'[170] The data of theology cannot therefore all be reduced to propositional and quantifiable entities.

One element which the natural sciences and theology have in common is their use of reason to draw conclusions from their respective bodies of

---

[166] 'The Modes of Divine Action in the Universe' (1920), *CE*, p. 28.

[167] *ST*, IaIIae, q. 5, a. 6.

[168] «Les Miracles de Lourdes et les enquêtes canoniques», *Études* 118 (1909), pp. 161–83.

[169] 'Science and Christ' (1921), *SC*, pp. 33–34.

[170] 'The Human Phenomenon' (1928), *SC*, p. 86.

knowledge. Understanding gained in this way is a perfection, but equally a remedy for the *im*perfection and limitation intrinsic to fallen human nature.[171] The origins of discursive knowledge must lie beyond the created order, being given to it by some form of divine illumination. Jacques Derrida's understanding of this form of knowledge as a φάρμακον — a medicine, but also a poison — is suggestive of these inherent ambiguities.[172] If the effects of knowledge are to be medicinal rather than corrosive, both its power and its limitations must be comprehended. The nature of discursive knowledge may be understood better by comparing the similarities of Teilhard's approach to evolution and other scientific questions with that of Pierre Rousselot in his essay «Idéalisme et Thomisme». Rousselot preserves a conceptual, scientific order within a larger supernatural order: «L'être des choses créées n'est qu'une participation analogique de l'Être divin».[173] The supernatural order, far from distorting or transforming pure nature, makes possible its existence as a distinct finite order of being that can be described using appropriate discourses. Rousselot describes in Leibnizian mode the relation between the corporeal world and thinking subjects: «L'harmonie entre elles devrait avoir été préétablie, et réside à l'état conscient dans une intelligence supérieure.» So far as human cognition is concerned, «le principe qui explique l'essence matérielle explique aussi la connaissance conceptuelle».[174] This congruity can be justified, John McDermott argues, on the grounds that the 'deficiency in concepts really corresponds to a deficiency in things'.[175] In the cosmos, like is known by like, as Plotinus states, which means that the imperfect is known by the imperfect.[176] Human knowledge is, in other words, imperfect knowledge of an imperfect world. The scientific and discursive processes on which it depends so heavily are valid, within their limited frame of reference, not because

---

[171] Blanchette, *Perfection*, pp. 270–71; see Aquinas, *Truth*, q. 2, a. 2, resp. (3 vols.; Indianapolis: Hackett, 1994), I, pp. 61–62.

[172] Jacques Derrida, 'Plato's pharmacy', in *Dissemination* (London: Athlone, 1981), pp. 61–171.

[173] Pierre Rousselot, «Idéalisme et thomisme», *AP* 42 (1979), p. 105: 'The being of created things is only an analogical participation of divine being.' This article was not approved by the *réviseurs*, and remained unpublished until 1979.

[174] Rousselot, «Idéalisme et thomisme», pp. 118, 125. 'The harmony between them must have been pre-established, and resides in conscious state in a superior intelligence... the principle which explains material essence also accounts for conceptual knowledge.'

[175] John M. McDermott, *Love and Understanding: The Relation of Will and Intellect in Pierre Rousselot's Christological Vision* (Rome: Università Gregoriana, 1983), pp. 133, 230; cf. Aquinas, *On the Power of God*, q. 1, a. 1, r. 10, vol. I, p. 7.

[176] Plotinus, *Enneads*, II.4 (33) 10, pp. 126–29.

they constitute perfect knowledge, but because they signify true reality incompletely.

Teilhard frequently discusses the conflict considered by many theologians and scientists to exist between religious and scientific views of evolution. He makes clear on the one hand that scientific method will demonstrate that certain theological opinions are false. He asserts that 'it is in actual fact impossible for science to accept' the hypothesis that first only one man, and then only one man and one woman, existed on the earth. Moreover, it is 'impossible to include Adam and the earthly paradise (taken literally) in our scientific outlook'.[177] Scientific method should not, on the other hand, be conceived simply as possessing a right of veto over theological propositions. Teilhard suggests that science, in its engagements with theology and criticisms of it, is seeking some transcendent dimension essential to its own enterprise. He affirms that 'science cannot reach the full limits of itself either in its impetus or in its constructions without being tinged with mysticism and charged with faith', and that physics 'must be checked by a critical reference to a deeper form of experience (perception of the Christic influence)'.[178] Just as scientific method cannot refute theology, nor be appropriated uncritically by it, so foundational principles about the nature of the material world cannot be established, nor proven false, by means of either discipline in isolation from the other.

This does not imply, of course, that no valid non-theological discourse can exist about evolutionary science. Teilhard's own scientific works can indeed be read and discussed with no reference to his theology. Much of the interest in his evolutionary cosmology over the past fifty years has been from people with no specific religious or theological commitment who have evacuated it of any theistic content. The essential complementarity of the two disciplines remains, therefore, crucial but problematic: the controversy that has surrounded Teilhard and his theology has been due in part to his failure to anticipate his detractors in providing easy principles for the resolution of the conflicts between science and religion that he identifies. Critical engagement between the two discourses remains, therefore, possible, reasonable and essential, because the boundaries which exist in practice between their respective spheres of knowledge always remain open to question. Dialogues can and should

---

[177] 'Fall, Redemption and Geocentrism', 'Historical Representations of Original Sin' (1922), *CE*, pp. 36, 47.

[178] *HP*, p. 203; 'My Fundamental Vision', p. 192.

be undertaken to reconcile contesting 'truths': it is an insufficient witness to the truth to hold that contradictory propositions contain equal elements of truth by virtue of being no more than opinions, when they are clearly statements about a single material and spiritual reality. Teilhard regards it as a condition of the continued material and spiritual evolution of the world, and a mark of plain intellectual honesty, that both science and theology be open to the possibility of mutual enrichment and correction in their continuing quests to understand the created order and to shape its future.

8. POLITICS AND SOCIETY

Action, passion and vision provide fundamentally practical principles for living. Action and passion transform the material substance and relationships of the world because they are motivated by God and sustained by Christ. Vision reveals to humanity its telos, illumining social relations in a new light in which the spiritual character of the bond sustaining human activities is clearly perceived. Action, passion and vision thus provide, in combination, the context for specific political and social commitments. Above all, they establish a collective spiritual bond between persons and enable them to see each other, and the whole created order, transfigured in divine light.

In the modern world, the scope of human action has expanded radically. The conditions which motivate action might exist locally, but may equally well originate on the opposite side of the globe. Radio, television, and new forms of transport, Teilhard observes, have extended the 'general control (atomic, chemical, biological and psychic) of the actual driving forces behind our organic and mental structure'.[1] Humanity is drawn ever more closely together 'economically, politically and *mentally*', and is 'daily more thoroughly pounded together and intermixed and more closely bound into one'.[2] Teilhard argues that human consciousness is becoming more homogeneous and that the formation of concepts and the development of rational processes which previously occurred within particular communities are now more likely to take place globally, and thereby to contribute to the formation of a single global consciousness. Action, because it is informed by consciousness, becomes ever more concentrated and concerted, and its power, already amplified by the array of tools and processes at its disposal, is thus further augmented. The result of this conjunction of the convergence of consciousness with enhanced technical power is the 'rapidly increasing influence of a more specifically human factor'. There has occurred in the world an extension of the 'radius of individual action'[3] which brings with it consequences for human action, both positive and negative, of potentially greater quantity, intensity and duration than ever before.

---

[1] 'The Evolution of Responsibility' (1950), *AE*, p. 211.
[2] 'The Mechanism of Evolution' (1951), *AE*, p. 306.
[3] 'The Evolution of Responsibility', p. 210.

The corollary of this convergence of consciousness is the transformation of consciousness's reflective awareness of itself. Teilhard expresses
this shift succinctly in numerous places: humankind 'not only *knows*, but
knows that it knows'.[4] This notion of the modification of consciousness
sounds similar to Hegel's, insofar as the moment when consciousness
grasps the nature of its own essence is decisive in human history.[5] Nevertheless, when describing the unfolding of self-consciousness in history,
Hegel appears to have in mind a development connected with the birth of
specifically modern society in which consciousness is liberated from
primitive forms of subjection and domination. Teilhard, in contrast, refers
to two very different developments, and sometimes conflates them. The
first development he describes as a 'breakthrough of reflection'[6] characteristic of humanity per se as distinct from other forms of sentient life.
This advance was a condition for the birth of rational human life, rather
than a particular stage in its subsequent growth. The second development
to which Teilhard refers is the expanding self-consciousness which he
identifies as the result of new communications technologies, similar to the
Hegelian 'moment of understanding' but identified with twentieth century
Western society rather than the early nineteenth century Prussian state.
Teilhard explains this newly-enlarged self-consciousness using the concept of the 'Noosphere' (i.e. νοῦς-σφαῖρα), which refers to that part of
agent intellect which is not the property of individual souls but a common, global possession. The seeds of this second form of self-consciousness, which he believes are peculiar to modern society, are however contained in the first. Teilhard applies, moreover, insights gained from his
study of human pre-history to his analysis of modern world history. The
'breakthrough of reflection' in which this new form of consciousness is
born is constitutive of humanity, but is equally a moment in an ongoing
process of reflective growth or 'spiritualization' characterized by the
enhanced dominance of reflection over automatic reactions and instinct.[7]
The effect of these combined shifts in consciousness is an increased
'sense of responsibility' among humanity for itself and the whole created
order that is experienced forcefully by every individual person.[8]

[4] 'My Fundamental Vision' (1948), 'My "Phenomenological" View of the World'
(1954), *TF*, pp. 171, 213; 'The Human Phenomenon' (1930), 'Hominization and Speciation' (1952), *VP*, pp. 161, 261; 'The Planetization of Humankind' (1945), 'On the Probable Coming of an Ultra-Humanity' (1950), *FM*, pp. 133, 270.
[5] G.W.F. Hegel, *Phenomenology of Spirit*, §89 (Oxford University Press, 1977), p. 57.
[6] 'My Fundamental Vision', p. 174.
[7] 'My Fundamental Vision', p. 183.
[8] 'The Evolution of Responsibility in the World', p. 207; cf. Madeleine Barthélemy-

Each person thus forms, notwithstanding human solidarity, a 'natural unit charged with its own responsibilities and its own incommunicable possibilities within that consummation'.[9] This dialectic between individuated existence and universal telos provides the dynamic of Teilhard's political theology: he always approaches political and social analysis from a metaphysical perspective. The titles and concepts he employs sometimes cause confusion, however, about the nature of the theories he advocates. It might, for instance, be assumed that 'The Struggle Against the Multitude' refers to a Nietzschean (or Maurrassian) assault on popular culture and democracy. In fact, the essay unfolds multiplicity as sin, death and non-being, and proceeds to discuss how the bond of unity which *caritas* and faith in Christ bring may transform these.[10] Teilhard, far from embracing libertarianism and other forms of radical individualism, in fact argues that they threaten to 'bring to matter a fragmentation, dispersion, and consequent return to multiplicity'.[11] The actual political doctrines which he accepts and defends are best identified by an examination of his practical statements and commitments.

Fascism and Marxism

The political figures and doctrines prominent in French catholic circles during the early twentieth century are crucial to understanding Teilhard's social and political theories. The reactionary Action Française movement of Charles Maurras is especially significant. Teilhard, like many other French catholics, expressed sympathy for it during his early life, applauding the party's high public profile and electoral successes[12] and reading some of its publications.[13] Also in common with many fellow catholics, he approved of the 1910 condemnation by the Holy Office

Madaule, *Bergson et Teilhard de Chardin* (Paris: Seuil, 1963), pp. 403–407, and generally, Georges Ordonnaud, *L'Ère nouvelle de la coresponsabilité* (Paris: Pedone, 1991).
    [9] *DM*, p. 104.
    [10] 'The Struggle Against the Multitude' (1917), *WW*, pp. 93–114.
    [11] 'Basis and Foundations of the Idea of Evolution' (1926), *VP*, p. 140.
    [12] Letters of 16 May 1913, 10 May 1914, *LP*, pp. 74, 130.
    [13] Letters of 20 August 1916, 17 November 1918, *MM*, pp. 122, 253. Pierre-Louis Mathieu, *La Pensée politique et économique* (Saint Étienne: Aubin, new edn, 2000), pp. 100–102, provides an excellent assessment of this period of Teilhard's life. Jean-Yves Calvez, «Pierre Teilhard de Chardin (1885–1955)», in *Chrétiens penseurs du social: Maritain, Fessard, Teilhard de Chardin, De Lubac (1920–1940)* (Paris: Cerf, 2002), pp. 107–136, gives a lucid overview of Teilhard's political and social thought, despite the incorrect birth date.

of the pioneering Christian democratic movement Le Sillon, founded by Marc Sangnier in 1894.[14] Church authorities considered this movement to be conspiring with the modernist alliance condemned by the encyclical *Pascendi dominici gregis* of St Pius X promulgated in the same year, and colluding with the virulently secularist Third Republic. Teilhard's right-wing allegiances in this early part of his life were normal for the son of a well-bred, provincial catholic family.

Teilhard was not, however, an active supporter of Action Française. Pierre-Louis Mathieu states that, prior to about 1920, Teilhard rarely expressed his political views. Politics were of little interest to him, Mathieu adds, and he accepted fairly uncritically the views of his family and the church.[15] Suggestions that the precepts of Action Française form part of Teilhard's developing theological cosmology are false, and based typically on the classification of Teilhard as a social evolutionist who affirms the Darwinian view of natural selection as a political principle for human society. This constitutes a serious misapprehension of his theory of evolution, and of the distinctive Lamarckian character of evolutionary discourse in France more widely that has already been discussed. Action Française and other contemporary right-wing movements were usually hostile to evolutionary science, considering its view of historical development to be too closely allied with Marxism, which they vehemently opposed.[16] Maurras's manifesto for the remedying of the ills of the French nation included the restoration of a nationalist monarchy, and he founded his political doctrines on the assumption that human life is comprehensively determined by historical and biological laws. He considered liberal egalitarianism and democracy corrupt on the grounds that the human autonomy and freedom on which they are predicated are phantasms. Maurras was an atheist who wished to preserve the utility of religion as a means of social control without accepting its metaphysical claims.[17] He did not believe in a cosmic *Christus*, as did Teilhard, but in a utilitarian *Chrestus* in the tradition of Suetonius, Kant's *Religion Within the Bounds of Mere Reason* and the Savoyard Vicar of Rousseau's *Émile*. Despite the political and religious claims of Action Française, however, for Teilhard and other catholics to have opposed them would have undermined the coherence of the catholic position as being one of

---

[14] Letter of September 1910, *LH*, p. 110.

[15] Mathieu, *La Pensée politique et économique*, p. 102.

[16] Mathieu, *La Pensée politique et économique*, pp. 103–104.

[17] See Thomas Molnar, «L'État et le problème de la religion chez Maurras» *Études Maurrassiennes* 5, 1 (1986), pp. 283–91.

obedience to the Church. The Curia and the French catholic hierarchy gave tacit support to Action Française as a preferable alternative to the radical republicanism under which the religious orders had been sent into exile and church assets liquidated. Action Française indeed ended up undermining itself precisely by opposing the church: despite its claim to exalt authority in general and that of the papacy in particular, it responded to its condemnation by the Holy Office in 1926 with a series of attacks on its official journal *Osservatore Romano*, and by implication, on Pius XI himself. This was in stark contrast to Le Sillon's submission to its 1910 condemnation, following which it disbanded its organisation and journal and thereby demonstrated its acceptance of the authority of the Church whose mission it had been seeking to promote. For St Pius X to have denounced Le Sillon, a Christian movement which promoted democracy and world peace, whilst tolerating Action Française, an atheist organisation that was nationalistic and reactionary, was in fact the fundamental contradiction, and not Teilhard's response to these events. The Curial policies are explained by the relations existing between Church and state in early twentieth century France, and the close affinities perceived to exist between liberalism and modernism, although are not justified by them.[18]

Teilhard's critique of fascism will shed further light on his attitude towards Action Française. The nationalism inherent in fascist doctrines is, Teilhard argues, 'obsolete', 'dreadfully primitive and narrow' and 'reactionary', because it promotes an ever more outdated form of fragmented political organisation.[19] Teilhard applies similar criticisms to Franco's *Falange* at the opening of the Spanish Civil War.[20] He also refers to the 1938 pastoral letter of the Bishops' Conference at Fulda, suppressed by the Nazi party, which criticized Nazism for seeking to replace Christianity with an immanentist «doctrine et religion de l'en

---

[18] Hugues Petit, *L'Église, le Sillon et l'Action française* (Paris: Nouvelles éditions latines, 1998), examines the condemnations of both Le Sillon and Action Française, reactions to the condemnations, and the contradictions inherent in them.

[19] *MPN*, p. 101; letter of 18 June 1940, *LTF*, p. 145. His writings on this and other social topics are part of the manifesto genre characteristic of the 1930s and later in which Catholic intellectuals contributed to public debates about many pressing political questions with a recognition that they had not received since prior to the Revolution. See Joseph A. Komonchak, 'Returning from Exile: Catholic Theology in the 1930s', in *The Twentieth Century: A Theological Overview*, ed. Gregory Baum (Maryknoll, NY: Orbis, 1999), p. 37.

[20] Letters of 11 and 15 August 1936, cited in Mathieu, *La Pensée politique et économique*, p. 106.

deçà».[21] The principal flaw in fascist ideologies, Teilhard contends, is their refusal to accept that the only future basis for society and politics will be an international one. Despite the fascist rhetoric of harmony with nature and destiny, fascism's illusory national science actually forges false gods by failing to recognize the true direction of the cosmic process, which is towards ever closer unity.[22] It fails to recognize the power of the 'irresistible material bonds that have now permanently introduced civilization to the stage of internationalism'.[23] Teilhard asserts:

> It will not be long before the human mass closes in upon itself and groups all its members in a definitely realized unity. Respect for one and the same law, one and the same orientation, one and the same spirit, are tending to overlay the permanent diversity of individuals and nations.[24]

This vision of political convergence towards a shared truth has far more in common with Leibnizian internationalism[25] than with any Spencerian triumph of the most assertive beings, Darwinian survival of the best-fitted species, or nationalist politics of exclusion. The evolutionary theories of Spencer and Darwin are, apart from anything else, incomplete, because they lack any guiding spiritual principle. Teilhard's evolutionism is, by contrast, grounded in human freedom and self-transcendence. His political ethic is one of unity gained through convergence and inclusion, and not by means of opposition or exclusion. The fascist precept of the superiority of one race over others, its lust for territorial expansion, and its deployment of myth and rhetoric, are fundamentally opposed to Teilhard's metaphysic of the spiritual transformation of the material elements of life in the progress of the world towards an all-comprehending unity.

Teilhard is especially critical of the inclusion and exclusion of persons from political communities on grounds of race. The racist ideal, in appealing to the tendencies of primitive biological nature, is false and

---

[21] *J*, 18 July 1944, cahier XIII. A portion of the pastoral letter is reproduced in *The Persecution of the Catholic Church in the Third Reich: Facts and Documents* (London: Burns Oates, 1940), pp. 30–33. Teilhard alludes to the Nazi denial of the immortality of the soul and of a future life, which the document opposes.

[22] *J*, 23 April and 29 May 1946, cahier XIV. It is unfortunate that cahiers X–XII, which cover some or all of the period from 18 July 1925 to 17 July 1944, have been lost, as they would be likely to shed further light on Teilhard's response to Nazism.

[23] 'The Salvation of Humankind' (1936), *SC*, pp. 140–41.

[24] 'The Great Monad' (1918), *HM*, p. 184.

[25] Mathieu, *La Pensée politique et économique*, p. 245, n. 13.

[26] 'The Moment of Choice' (1939), *AE*, p. 17; *HP*, p. 173.

contrary to the spiritual laws which govern developed human nature.[26] Teilhard complains that Japanese society, as well as Nazi Germany, is operating a politics of racial exclusion, 'centred on blood and common origin much more than on spirit and convergence ahead'.[27] This division of society into 'ethnic units' is a result of the 'mechanism of dispersion' which governs the pre-human form of evolution. The persistence in modern human society of this essentially pre-human form of association is due to 'asphyxiation', which Teilhard defines as the frequently violent attempts of nations and individuals to break out of global society and preserve, in isolation, their own particular identities.[28] He perceives, in opposition to such isolationism, an irreversible movement towards racial inclusion in global politics motivated by the 'compression of Humankind on the closed surface of the planet':

> Economically and psychically the entire mass of Humankind, under the inexorable pressure of events and owing to the prodigious growth and speeding up of the means of communication, has found itself seized in the mould of a communal existence — large sections tightly encased in countless international organisations, the most ambitious the world has ever known.[29]

The links which accentuate national interdependence are causing previously distinct units of humanity to merge and combine.[30] Particular races within the human species are coalescing according to an inescapable dynamic of synthesis, which is contributing materially to the development of an 'international ethic'. This movement reveals the essential complementarity of distinct ethnic groups as part of a global shift towards mutual acceptance and 'joyful unity'.[31] Teilhard identifies the fascist tendencies in the nascent communist republics of wartime Europe, as well as the more obvious instances of fascism in Germany and Italy, as having been subsumed into a single reactionary political tendency in opposition to this convergent internationalism:

> Only five years ago it was still possible to contrast the internationalism of communism and the democracies with the particularism of the axis powers. This distinction would no longer be possible today. Governed by the very

---

[27] 'The Spiritual Contribution of the Far East' (1947), *TF*, p. 140.
[28] 'Reflections on the Compression of Humankind' (1953), *AE*, p. 342.
[29] 'The Directions and Conditions of the Future' (1948), 'The Planetization of Humankind', *FM*, pp. 233, 127.
[30] 'Faith in Peace' (1947), *FM*, p. 150; 'The Reflection of Energy' (1952), *AE*, p. 321.
[31] 'The Natural Units of Humanity' (1939), *VP*, pp. 202, 211–12, 215. See John Morgan, 'Ethnicity and the Future of Man', *The Teilhard Review* 11 (1976), pp. 16–20.

nature of the economic and spiritual environment in which they are developing, racialist nationalisms have rapidly evolved into systems or mystiques so all-embracing as to be without limit, with the result that no difference (except in methods of presentation and realization) distinguishes them any longer from the opposite camp.[32]

Teilhard predicts that, following a period of conflict, the differences between these different 'racialist nationalisms' will be resolved. In 1947, he moreover observes prophetically of capitalist and communist society: 'Two great human blocks alone remain confronting one another. Is it not inevitable that in one way or another these two will eventually coalesce?'[33] Always appreciative of the decisive power of thought and concepts in shaping human relationships and behaviour, Teilhard regarded the conflict between communism and fascism as an ideological battle. It was a 'war of ideals' in which 'two opposed concepts of humankind are confronting one another'.[34] At the same time, he regarded different political ideologies as fragments of a single truth that are 'seeking one another'.[35] The bringing into consciousness, as ideologies, of conflicting personal and political identities, was a decisive stage, he suggested, of their resolution.

Teilhard began to discover left-wing political movements and ideas in the aftermath of the First World War. Pierre-Louis Mathieu describes him as «un homme de droite» until about 1920. Following the end of the war, however, Teilhard was plunged into many new political currents, and progressively discovered the emerging movements and theories of the left and the extreme left.[36] It is striking just how much Teilhard's views evolve during the 1920s, following the shock of service in the Great War and the new vistas which this revealed to him. Mathieu notes that as early as 1924, Teilhard expresses greater fear of «conservateurs» than of the «gens de gauche»: this is notable, given the anticlerical character of French republicanism and the fact that Action Française was not censured until 1926.[37] When the condemnation of Action Française occurred, Teilhard expressed his approval, though was shocked at the brutality of its implementation, and above all at the withholding of the sacraments from sympathizers and the suspension of sup-

---

[32] 'Universalization and Union' (1942), *AE*, p. 81.
[33] 'The Formation of the Noosphere' (1947), *FM*, p. 175.
[34] 'The Moment of Choice', p. 19.
[35] 'The Salvation of Humankind', p. 142.
[36] Mathieu, *La Pensée politique et économique*, p. 102.
[37] Letter of 13 July 1924 to an unnamed recipient, cited in Mathieu, *La Pensée politique et économique*, p. 104.

porters among the clergy.[38] Teilhard states his explicit opposition to Action Française in his unpublished journal more than two years earlier, however, and in the course of so doing makes a strong statement advocating liberal polity on epistemological grounds reminiscent of John Stuart Mill's:

> Je considère comme des adversaires les A.F. et leur clan, parce que sur terrain intellectuel, je vois que le libéralisme est absolument nécessaire, liberalisme, c'est-à-dire non droit égal du vrai et du faux, mais attitude expectante et chercheuse, admettant que rien n'est achevé ni trouvé complètement.[39]

A society in which ideas can be debated and tested is, Teilhard argues, the only type of society that will possess the capacity for continued growth and development. Two months later, he writes critically of «la fausse accusation de A.F. [que] ceux qui croient à l'intuition sont des 'sentimentaux'», and follows this critique of Action Française's rationalism by expressing dissatisfaction with the movement's lack of imagination and inability to conceive of any way of life other than the routine.[40]

Teilhard's social analysis shares with Marx's a profound dissatisfaction with the path that modern industrialization has taken. He decries

> the human personality stifled by the collective monsters which a pitiless necessity of life has compelled us to set up everywhere around us. Great cities, great industries, great economic organization... Heartless and faceless Molochs.[41]

Factory work is 'unmistakable slavery', but Teilhard does not see the creation of a strong state to suppress capitalists as the likely means of transforming economic relations: political state control can itself be bru-

---

[38] Letter of 12 November 1926, cited in Mathieu, *La Pensée politique et économique*, p. 105.

[39] *J*, 23 January 1922, cahier VIII: 'I consider myself to be an adversary of Action Française and its associates, because on intellectual grounds I regard liberalism as absolutely necessary, liberalism, that is to say, not as an equal right to truth and falsehood, but as an expectant and seeking attitude, accepting that nothing is finished nor completely certain.' cf. John Stuart Mill, 'On the Liberty of Thought and Discussion', in *On Liberty and Other Essays* (Oxford University Press, 1998), pp. 20–61.

[40] *J*, 12 March 1922, cahier IX.

[41] 'Sketch of a Personalistic Universe' (1936), *HE*, p. 80; cf. Lv 18.21, II Kgs 23.10, Jer 32.35. William C. French, 'Subject-centred and Creation-centred Paradigms in Recent Catholic Thought', *Journal of Religion* 70 (1990), p. 63, critiques Teilhard's 'sweeping endorsement of technological and industrial development' as characteristic of a subject-centred (i.e. human-centred) paradigm, but Teilhard locates this movement within a creation-centred (i.e. cosmos-centred) approach and is alert to its ambiguities.

tal and atomizing.[42] Indeed, by 1941 it is 'the collective', rather than industrialized, urban society, that Teilhard describes as a 'terrifying Moloch'.[43] In places where workers have grown conscious,[44] the conditions exist for the birth of a new society. The form which this society should take is not communist, however. Teilhard considers communism to have appropriated elements of advanced capitalist social analysis which a Christian political theology is in fact compelled to disavow. This is particularly true of communism's materialist ontology and associated determinism, which comprises its principal defect and provides the underlying reason why communism fails to acknowledge the uniqueness and irreducibility of the human person. Marxism, Teilhard states, is a species of 'materialist ideology', and is as such 'born from a fundamental error of perspective'.[45] In conceiving human history as mere process, communism has reduced it to the 'mechanical development of a soulless collectivity'.[46] By subsuming humankind into classes and construing history as an ongoing conflict between those classes, Marxist and advanced capitalist politics alike have, moreover, denied to individual persons and even to great statesmen any agency in the making of history.

Teilhard, despite his critique of historical materialism, anticipates liberation theologians in seeking to correct the critique of religion put forward by Marx in the Introduction to his projected *Critique of Hegel's 'Philosophy of Right'*. Teilhard states: 'Religion can become an opium. It is too often understood as a simple soothing of our woes. Its true function is to sustain and spur on the progress of life.'[47] He contends that Marx has failed to justify his atheism convincingly. A critique of particular religious institutions or sentiments cannot, after all, be construed as a critique of faith itself. Teilhard asserts: 'Marxist atheism is not absolute, but ... simply rejects an "extrinsical" God, a *deus ex machina* whose existence can only undermine the dignity of the Universe and weaken the springs of human endeavour.'[48] He embraces, in contrast to

---

[42] *MPN*, p. 100.

[43] 'The Atomism of Spirit' (1941), *AE*, p. 47.

[44] *HP*, p. 161.

[45] 'The Place of Technology' (1947), *AE*, pp. 161–62; 'Science and Christ' (1921), *SC*, p. 28. It is this Marxist interpretation of the equality of all peoples that Teilhard appears to be rejecting in his letter of 26 January 1936, *LLZ*, pp. 116–117.

[46] 'The Salvation of Humankind', p. 140.

[47] 'The Spirit of the Earth' (1931), *HE*, p. 44; cf. 'Christology and Evolution' (1933), *CE*, p. 93.

[48] 'The Heart of the Problem' (1949), *FM*, pp. 266–67.

Marx, a concept of religion which gives as prominent a place to the active life as to the passive one.

Teilhard, in common with many liberation theologians, salvages intellectual resources from Marxist social analysis to employ in his political theology. He also suggests that Marxism possesses within itself the potential to be transformed into a Christian movement. Noting its unifying dynamic, Teilhard states that 'neo-humanist Marxism ... seems destined to become Christianized'.[49] Assessments such as these raise inevitable questions about Teilhard's impact on liberation theologies, but the importance of any direct exchange of ideas should not be overstated: similarities are in many cases more likely to be the result of the common paternity of Blondel, whose large impact on liberation movements is usually disregarded. One theologian who does not commit this particular error, however, is Jürgen Moltmann, who acknowledges that liberation theology, far from being founded on secular Marxist ideology, possesses its 'own theological dynamic' which appropriates Blondel's theology of action.[50] So far as Teilhard's impact on liberation theology is concerned, Gustavo Gutiérrez provides a balanced discussion which demonstrates both the usefulness and the limitations of Teilhard's theology for a liberationist agenda. He agrees with Teilhard that humanity has acquired a high degree of control over nature and the evolutionary process.[51] Gutiérrez accepts, moreover, that the 'naïve optimism which denies the role of sin in the historical development of humanity', although associated with Teilhard, is not actually endorsed by him, and goes on to praise Teilhard's dynamic and temporal conception of the Church in opposition to more traditional ecclesiologies based on static spatial imagery.[52] Furthermore, Gutiérrez and other liberation theologians concur with Teilhard's criticisms of anti-progressive theologies and social theories, which are likely to be motivated by the wish of governing classes to preserve the status quo and to prevent structural political change. Gutiérrez, whilst praising these various positive features of Teilhard's theology, nevertheless complains that 'politically, his vision

---

[49] 'Two Converse Forms of Spirit' (1950), *AE*, p. 225; 'The Christian Phenomenon' (1950), *CE*, p. 199.

[50] Jürgen Moltmann, *Experiences in Theology: Ways and Forms of Christian Theology* (London: SCM, 2000), p. 238.

[51] Gustavo Gutiérrez, *A Theology of Liberation: History, Politics and Salvation* (London: SCM, 1974), pp. 21–22, 147; cf. John W. Cooper, 'Teilhard, Marx and the Worldview of Prominent Liberation Theologians', *Calvin Theological Journal* 70 (1990), pp. 48–72.

[52] Gutiérrez, *Theology of Liberation*, pp. 102, 147.

is, on the whole, neutral'.[53] From a liberationist perspective, Gutiérrez argues, Teilhard appears too concerned with problems surrounding the 'faith-science conflict and the application of science to the transformation of the world' which detract from social and political action aimed at the immediate amelioration of material hardships which restrict human flourishing.

Social democracy and globalization

Teilhard's critiques of communism and fascism show, when combined with his cosmology, that during the European political upheavals of the 1930s he advocated some form of social democratic governance. His political theology comprises several elements of a social democratic *Weltbild* of a specifically Christian variety: the value of every individual person, based on their existence under divine grace; the creativity and transcendence of human action; concern for workers and the unemployed; and the future for humanity as being one of international unity. Pierre-Louis Mathieu correctly states that Teilhard's political reflections lead naturally to a specifically Christian definition of democracy which is enriched by its contact with history and appropriates elements of both liberal democracy and social democracy.[54] Teilhard was brought to re-engage with political questions following his return to the France in the aftermath of the Second World War, after twenty years spent mainly in China, and expresses vividly his hope for a democratic future in writings produced during the years he spent in Paris and New York from 1946 until his death in 1955.[55] He considers in these essays ways of renewing democratic politics by formulating new justifications and ideals for it, in order to safeguard society from future totalitarian challenges: fascist and communist dictatorships develop, he observes, in societies in which democracy is poorly-organized and weakly-justified.[56] Teilhard here espouses the democratic politics, internationalism and religious inclusivism advocated by Le Sillon, the pioneering Christian social democratic movement which had disbanded on threat of Curial censure forty years earlier.[57] This body and its leader, Marc Sangnier, had sought to

[53] Gutiérrez, *Theology of Liberation*, p. 101.
[54] Mathieu, *La Pensée politique et économique*, p. 178.
[55] Brought together in the collection *FM*.
[56] *J*, 17 June 1947, cahier XV.
[57] For the distinction between social democracy and the older social catholicism of the

prove to an anticlerical and atheist Third Republic that it was possible to be Christian and Republican at the same time, and that Christian faith, as distinct from mere observance, strengthened the civic responsibility and respect for others which enable democracy to flourish. Many of these social democratic values had also been espoused by the Popular Front, the left-wing political alliance led by Léon Blum which gained power in France in 1936. Teilhard expressed his approval of this regime, although recognized its limited capacity to effect social change due to the circumstances of the time.[58]

Although Teilhard played no direct role in social or political movements, it is possible to trace his connections with left-wing groups through his contacts with activists in Christian social movements. Two colleagues with whom Teilhard shared the draft manuscript of *The Divine Milieu* were leading figures in the Association Catholique de la Jeunesse Française: Père Corbillé, the association's national chaplain from 1911 to 1940, and Benoît Emonet, its chaplain in Marseille from 1903 to 1940.[59] Teilhard indeed expresses the hope that his writing will contribute to a spiritual revival within the movement, whose «froideur» he considers part of a wider ecclesial malaise: «L'ACJF, tout en s'occupant *pro Deo*, de choses humaines, ne participe pas assez aux courants humains, — ne les prolonge pas assez, donc, dans son surnaturel.»[60] The ACJF, along with Action Populaire and the Semaines Sociales, became the champion of many of the principles of the Sillonist movement following its condemnation,[61] and Jesuits continued to occupy key positions in all these organizations.[62] Interest in *The Divine Milieu* among

---

1891 encyclical *Rerum novarum*, see Jean-Claude Delbreil, «Les Formes politiques de la démocratie chrétienne en France au vingtième siècle», in *Catholicism, Politics and Society in Twentieth-Century France*, ed. Kay Chadwick (Liverpool University Press, 2000), pp. 119–21.

[58] Letters of 25 July 1937, 20 November 1938, *LLS*, pp. 99, 121; cf. Julian Jackson, *The Popular Front in France: Defending Democracy, 1934–38* (Cambridge University Press, 1988).

[59] Letters to Auguste Valensin, 11 November 1927, 14 February 1928, *LI*, pp. 166, 169. See Charles Molette, *L'Association catholique de la jeunesse française, 1886–1907: une prise de conscience du laïcat catholique* (Paris: Colin, 1968), p. 442. Teilhard and Emonet had apparently been good friends since well before the First World War, as Teilhard records with great surprise a chance meeting with him during their war service. (*J*, 10 September 1915, p. 21.)

[60] *J*, 17 April 1919, cahier VI.

[61] For the relation of the ACJF with Le Sillon and other smaller movements that continued after 1910, see Jean Boissannat and Christophe Grannec, *L'Aventure du Christianisme social, passé et avenir* (Mayenne: Desclée, 1999), pp. 74–87.

[62] Action Française sympathizers were more numerous among Dominicans, especially

left-wing figures was promoted by a private printing in Lyons by Victor Carlhian, the founder and editor of the journal *Le Van* (1921-39).[63] Etienne Fouilloux describes the instrumental role played by Carlhian, the Lyons industrialist, in the production and distribution of this and other texts produced by Teilhard, Pierre Rousselot and others.[64] Several shorter works of Teilhard's appeared in *Le Van* itself.[65] Carlhian's printing house, «La Source», was in the former premises of the Lyons branch of Le Sillon, which Carlhian had founded after joining the movement whilst a student in Paris, and had previously served as its press.[66] Teilhard's affinity with social catholic values needs also to be situated within the omnipresent Blondelian context. Maurice Blondel had been Sangnier's teacher and had played an active part in the inception of Sangnier's *Sillon* movement by contributing to its political journals, conferences, education and other projects.[67] Blondel presents, under the pseudonym of Testis, or 'witness', a sustained defence of Christian social democratic values in the *Annales de philosophie chrétienne* on both moral and religious grounds.[68] These projects helped to spawn the

strict-observance Thomists, such as Réginald Garrigou-Lagrange, for whom there was often an affinity between theological and political rationalism. See André Laudouze, *Dominicains français et Action française, 1899-1940: Maurras au couvent* (Paris: Éditions ouvrières, 1990). This statement is not intended, however, to deny the breadth of allegiance within the Dominican order.

[63] Henri de Lubac, *The Religion of Teilhard de Chardin* (London: Collins, 1970), p. 21.

[64] Étienne Fouilloux, *Une église en quête de liberté : la pensée française entre modernisme et Vatican II, 1914-1962* (Paris: Desclée, 1998), pp. 162–65, 238.

[65] 'What Should We Think of Transformism?', 'Sinanthropus pekinensis' (1930); 'The Human Phenomenon' (1931); 'The Prehistoric Excavations of Peking' (1934).

[66] For biography, see Régis Ladous, «Victor Carlhian aux sources du personnalisme», in *Cent ans de catholicisme social à Lyons et en Rhône-Alpes: la postérité de Rerum novarum* (Paris: Éditions ouvrières, 1992), pp. 171–79; R. Voog, «Carlhian, Victor», in *Dictionnaire du monde religieux dans la France contemporaine*, VI (9 vols.; Paris: Beauchesne, 1985–96), pp. 95–96.

[67] René Virgoulay, *Blondel et le Modernisme: la philosophie de l'action et les sciences religieuses, 1896–1913* (Paris: Cerf, 1980), pp. 149–79; Peter Bernardi, 'Social Modernism: The Case of the *Semaines Sociales*', in *Catholicism Contending with Modernity: Roman Catholic Modernism and Anti-Modernism in Historical Context*, ed. Darrell Jodock (Cambridge University Press, 1999), pp. 277–307. For Blondel's opposition to Maurras following their early close friendship, see Michael Sutton, *Nationalism, Positivism and Catholicism: The Politics of Charles Maurras and French Catholics, 1890–1914* (Cambridge University Press, 1982), pp. 123–62.

[68] Testis (= Maurice Blondel), «La Semaine sociale de Bordeaux et le monophorisme», *Annales de philosophie chrétienne* 4, 9 (1909), pp. 5–22, 162–84, 245–78; 10 (1910), pp. 372–92, 449–72, 561–92; 11 (1910), pp. 127–62. Peter Bernardi, 'Maurice Blondel and the Renewal of the Nature–Grace Relationship', *Communio (US)* 26 (1999), pp. 806–45, summarizes the articles and is followed by the author's translation of the third, pp. 846–74.

worker-priest movement, for which Teilhard demonstrates considerable support, although he laments its haphazard organization.[69] Much earlier in his life, Teilhard had himself served a workers' community and orphanage at the glass works at Le Bourget in Paris, but had not himself been employed there.[70]

Some of Teilhard's most concrete political reflections concern the changing nature of work and the organization of production processes. When discussing the unemployment precipitated by the Great Depression, he reflects: 'Humanity began to be without occupation (at least potentially) from the first moment when its new-born mind was released from perception and immediate action.'[71] Teilhard's theology of action suggests a connection between the acting person and the results of their action similar to the bond which John Locke envisages between the worker and the product of their labour. By subduing and improving the earth for the benefit of human life, Locke argues, the worker has laid 'something upon it that was his own, his labour', and 'thereby annexed to it something that was his property, which another had no title to, nor could without injury take from him'.[72] In industrial society, Teilhard suggests, this bond has been severed. The most serious practical effect of this separation of the worker from the product of their work has not, however, been the expropriation of workers by capitalists. Teilhard complains, in contrast, of the 'ever-growing onslaughts of the *taedium vitae*' which commenced with the advent and subsequent growth of leisure time. The progressively more detailed division of labour increases, on one hand, the efficiency of the production process so that workers need to spend fewer hours at work. On the other hand, tasks become more specialized, and people have leisure time in which to reflect on their paid work whilst using and consuming resources in more personally enriching ways. Teilhard criticizes the Vichy regime as an example of the privatized, hyper-reflective social morality which industrial society has spawned.[73] Vichy was, he suggests, a society founded on expedience to preserve the personal security of the majority rather than on principles of

---

[69] 'Research, Work and Worship' (1955), *SC*, p. 218.

[70] Various letters of 13 October 1912 – 14 October 1913, *LP*, pp. 36, 42, 47, 54, 67, 75, 111, 113.

[71] 'Christianity in the World' (1933), *SC*, p. 101.

[72] John Locke, 'On property', in *The Second Treatise of Government*, §32, in *Political Writings*, ed. David Wootton (London: Penguin, 1993), p. 277.

[73] Letters to Max and Simone Bégouën, 20 September 1940, and Claude Aragonnès, 20 November 1940, *LT*, pp. 267, 271; Mathieu, *La Pensée politique et économique*, pp. 107–108.

justice and human rights for all. Following the end of the war, he reflects:

> The believers in progress think in terms of a Golden Age, a period of euphoria and abundance: and this, they give us to understand, is all that Evolution has in store for us. It is right that our hearts should fail us at the thought of so 'bourgeois' a paradise.[74]

Teilhard comes close to offering, in places such as this, an Arendtian *Zeitkritik*: the mass of humanity is partly responsible for its own subjugation through its acquiescence in the values of a society founded on the tenets of consumption, which continually demands new products to annihilate. Teilhard complains of the spiritual vacuity of this consuming material power, in contrast with the transforming quality of God's power of *spiritual* consumption: «L'erreur des Molochs est de le faire 'dévorant' matériellement, sans la transformation de ce terme et de l'opération entitative qu'il désigne.»[75] Teilhard even suggests that the leisure and boredom characteristic of consumer society result in an excess of accumulated energy which becomes a motivating force for warfare.[76] He is equally ill-at-ease with the physical landscape of industrial society, protesting that the 'disappearance of solitude and nature in favour of the factory and town is intellectually and physically enervating', and lamenting the 'ugliness, vulgarity and servitude with which the growth of industrialism has undeniably sullied the poetry of primeval pastures'.[77] Maybe there can be detected here a yearning for a return to the Auvergnat life of his childhood prior to the deluge of the Great War, curiously reminiscent of the bucolic idyll of post-capitalist society portrayed by Marx in which citizens would 'hunt in the morning, fish in the afternoon, rear cattle in the evening, criticize after dinner'.[78] Teilhard here professes, in any case, what Simone Weil describes as humanity's enduring 'need for roots'. This suggests that the universality of consciousness, communication, and the Church, which Teilhard experiences so strongly, needs to be grounded in a particular locality.

[74] 'The End of the Species' (1952), *FM*, p. 303.

[75] Retreat note of 28 July 1922, *NR*, pp. 103–104. 'The error of the Molochs is to turn consumption into a material principle, without transforming the term nor the act which it designates.'

[76] 'Life and the Planets' (1945), 'The End of the Species' (1952), 'The Spiritual Repercussions of the Atom Bomb' (1946), *FM*, pp. 121, 303, 146.

[77] 'The Compression of Humankind' (1953), *AE*, p. 341; 'Does Humankind Move Biologically Upon Itself?' (1949), *FM*, p. 250.

[78] Karl Marx, *German Ideology*, in Karl Marx and Frederick Engels, *Collected Works*, 5 (49 vols.; London: Laurence & Wishart, 1975–2001), p. 47.

This discussion has shown how the *nouvelle théologie* of Teilhard and others of his generation develops, from its early origins in Blondel, in a social and political context and possesses social and political implications. The humanist, universalist and inclusivist politics which Teilhard in particular espouses provide a basis for discourse between adherents of different religions, and between religious believers and those of no faith, and thus offer a much-needed alternative to postmodern 'end of dialogue' theses.[79] Being motivated by the action of Christ on the world, converging religious pathways are themselves graced. Teilhard has much to contribute to constructive political theology both in his concrete discussions and in his wider theological cosmology. In an age of religious extremism and global terrorism undertaken in the name of religion, the postmodern celebration of difference, incommensurability and conflict might constitute an accurate diagnosis of the symptoms of religious and social antagonisms, but it is hard to see how it could provide constructive intellectual resources for their amelioration or resolution. Teilhard, by contrast, correctly perceives that in a shrinking and increasingly interdependent world, humanity will one day be compelled to 'unite in some form of human whole organized on the basis of human solidarity'.[80]

Regarding the other

The breadth of vision which Teilhard's theology offers can sometimes be gained at the expense of specificity. What appears as inclusivity might not be realized in sufficient particularity: a generalized love of the world, rather than love for any of its real features. James McClendon, who believes that ethics must form the starting point of any systematic theology, comments that the danger of Teilhard's 'enlarged foci' for ethics is the difficulty of justifying any particular moral standpoint within them.[81] These foci reverse, McClendon adds, the normal order of moral knowledge, which begins with concrete human experience rather than abstract principles. Teilhard's theology also appears at times to sub-

---

[79] e.g. John Milbank, 'The End of Dialogue', in *Christian Uniqueness Reconsidered: The Myth of a Pluralistic Theology of Religions*, ed. Gavin D'Costa (Maryknoll, NY: Orbis, 1990), pp. 174–91.

[80] 'The Human Rebound of Evolution' (1947), *FM*, p. 198.

[81] James W. McClendon, *Systematic Theology*, I (3 vols.; Nashville: Abingdon, 1986–2000), pp. 87–88.

ordinate personal relations to a greater and more purely spiritual good. Teilhard's frequent use of facial imagery as metaphor, rather than literally, suggests that he neglects the significance of relations between persons, certainly if judged by current theological standards. He recalls the *renovabis faciem terrae* tradition of Psalm 104.30, referring to the '*human face of the earth*' and the 'face of [the] world'.[82] He refers to the 'countenance of the world' and 'of nature', and to the 'radiant smile' in every part of nature.[83] He even employs the image of the laughter of the waves, alluding to the ἀνήριθμον γέλασμα of Aeschylus.[84] Teilhard has in mind, in these places, the generic sense of *faciem* as 'form' or 'appearance', rather than the specific revelation of a human person in a human face.

Teilhard's view of the relation between the illumination of nature and the illumination of humanity alters significantly, however. Initially, he regards the whole of nature as infused with spirit, expressing an illness at ease with the human world that is commonly found in nature mystics. He states: 'I felt that I was less a part of society... I obediently yielded to the thirst for being alone, and, to find a less irksome life [pour vivre plus à l'aise], I made my way into the desert.' He goes on to recognize, nevertheless: 'The person who finds their neighbour too heavy a burden must inevitably be weary already of bearing the burden of their own self.'[85] Teilhard seeks to understand, from this point onwards, the role of the universal dimension of vision, on which he continues to reflect, within the particular and the personal. He comes to realize that vision in fact calls its subject to be especially attentive to the other human souls who inhabit the illumined world: 'What is really serious, and even mortal, is turning towards *an* other: it is loving *some one*.'[86] He prays:

> Grant, O God, that the light of your countenance may shine for me in the life of these 'others'. The irresistible light of your eyes shining in the depth of things has already guided me towards all the work I must accomplish, and all the difficulties I must pass through. Grant that I may see you, even and above all, in the souls of my brothers and sisters, at their most personal, and most true, and most distant.[87]

[82] *DM*, pp. 13, 55; 'The Mass on the World' (1923), *HM*, p. 34.
[83] 'Cosmic Life' (1916), *WW*, pp. 27, 32; cf. 'The Christic' (1955), *HM*, pp. 91, 100; 'The Promised Land' (1919), *WW*, p. 278.
[84] 'Cosmic Life', 'The Eternal Feminine' (1918), *WW*, pp. 29, 195; cf. Aeschylus, *Prometheus Bound*, 90 (Cambridge University Press, 1932), p. 54.
[85] 'Cosmic Life', pp. 30–31.
[86] 'The Evolution of Chastity' (1934), *TF*, p. 75.
[87] *DM*, p. 108.

This vision of the divine light shining in the face of another person is made possible by charity, 'that wonderful virtue which makes us see and cherish Christ in every person'.[88]

Teilhard understands this highest of the virtues as a loving openness to the other that is grounded in the transcendent. One example he gives is seeing the eyes of Christ in the glance of a dying soldier.[89] Virtue directed towards others initially requires a respectful distancing from its object that is distinct from the way in which a friend is regarded. Teilhard states honestly, addressing himself to God:

> Just as much as I have derived intense joy in the superhuman delight of dissolving myself and losing myself in the souls for which I was destined by the mysterious affinities of human love, so I have always felt an inborn hostility to, and closed myself to, the common run of those whom you tell me to love. I find no difficulty in integrating into my interior life everything above and beneath me (in the same line as me, as it were) in the universe — whether matter, plants, animals; and then powers, dominions and angels: these I accept without difficulty and delight to feel myself sustained within their hierarchy. But 'others', my God — by which I do not mean 'the poor, the halt, the lame and the sick', but 'others' quite simply as 'others', those who seem to exist independently of me because their universe seems closed to mine, and who seem to shatter the unity and the silence of the world for me — would I be sincere if I did not confess that my instinctive reaction is to rebuff them? and that the mere thought of entering into spiritual communication with them disgusts me?[90]

Teilhard identifies the challenge, but also the necessity, of existing in relationship with the other. He continues:

> You want me to be drawn towards 'others', not by simple personal sympathy, but by what is much higher: the united affinities of a world for itself, and of that world for God.[91]

At this point, as so often, Teilhard fuses metaphysical and theological analysis. His 'other' is both a material substance and a spiritual being capable of initiative and response. His Leibnizian cosmology, in which the individual and indivisible monad is axiomatic and relations between monads are problematic, presents considerable challenges to any theory of how individual persons interact with one another. The priority which Teilhard gives, in the order of generation, to the particular over the collective provides, in isolation, considerable resources for a theology of

---

[88] 'Cosmic Life', p. 51.
[89] 'Christ in the World of Matter' (1916), *HU*, p. 46.
[90] *DM*, p. 108.
[91] *DM*, p. 109.

'mutual suspicion', according to which differing perspectives on life and faith are irreconcilable because the entities possess in themselves no means of overcoming their individuality. This atomized perspective on individuality needs, however, to be seen as a realistic attempt to describe the way in which individuals might enter into dialogue in a world of conflicting perspectives in which each dialogue partner is committed to the integrity of his or her own beliefs. Teilhard's theology, viewed in its wider eschatological context, combines a recognition of the reality of conflict between individuals in the world with an account of how antagonisms will ultimately be transcended. Many proponents of mutual suspicion do not, by contrast, give a convincing account of why antipathy cannot be overcome as part of a movement of convergence in and through dialogue. John Milbank has, for instance, argued that religious convergence implies a capitulation to political and social secularization, relativistic religious pluralism, and their concomitant liberal values.[92] The fundamental problem with the mutual suspicion thesis is that it excludes the possibility that convergence might be motivated by specifically religious factors, such as trust or hospitality.[93] Although Teilhard presents, like Milbank, an individualized model of human personality that is clearly applicable to large sectors of modern society, he situates it, unlike Milbank, within a general telos of convergence in which difference between persons can be mediated. Teilhard proposes a metaphysics of convergence in which trust, hospitality and other concrete acts of reaching out to the other in 'basic human sympathy' can be situated and understood as forming part of a salvation history in which God in Christ is active.[94] Milbank is, by contrast, unwilling to accept the cosmic christology in which this conviction is founded, decrying 'christocentric fixation' despite his wish to defend and extend Christian theological discourse in the face of competing narratives.[95] Teilhard believes that the partial perspectives which foster mutual suspicion can be overcome in a genuinely Christian transcendence of difference grounded in the action of Christ on the world, rather than in a politically or socially determined discourse

[92] Milbank, 'End of Dialogue', pp. 181–82.

[93] For trust, see Patricia Sayre, 'The Dialectics of Trust and Suspicion', *Faith and Philosophy* 10 (1993), pp. 567–84, who argues that the attitude of trust is more fundamental to religious sensibility than that of suspicion. For hospitality, see Michael Barnes, *Theology and the Dialogue of Religions* (Cambridge University Press, 2002), especially pp. 249–52.

[94] 'Faith in Humanity' (1947), 'The Planetization of Humankind' (1945), *FM*, pp. 191, 135.

[95] Milbank, 'End of Dialogue', p. 179.

which evacuates religious claims of any truth or falsity. He maintains, in common with Aristotle, that the material cosmos is ordered towards a final unity, and suggests that action, passion and vision provide the dynamic of unification by means of the spiritual transformation of material substance which impels the cosmos towards its final spiritual unity. Action, passion and vision therefore possess a double reality, being, in a phrase of Blondel's, 'simultaneously the expression of a being's incommunicability and a factor within the Whole'.[96] Their dual identity is due to the uniqueness of individual reflection, in which the human monad becomes personalized and 'lives for itself, as much as and at the same time as for others'.[97] Teilhard believes that humanity makes contact with the universal through that which is most incommunicably personal in it.[98] This is Christ, the bond of substance, who preserves the consistency of particular objects in the cosmos in the unity of the whole, and in whom body and soul are unified to form an enduring single substance.

Hope in a future for the world

In June 1928, Pope Pius XI promulgated the encyclical *Miserentissimus redemptor* on Reparation to the Sacred Heart. Teilhard praises the encyclical's focus on the Heart, but criticizes the interpretation it gives of the doctrine of expiation. The document asserts, for instance, that the duty of expiation is 'laid upon the whole race of men since, as we are taught by the Christian faith, after Adam's miserable fall, infected by hereditary stain, subject to concupiscences and most wretchedly depraved, it would have been thrust down into eternal destruction'.[99] Theologians who teach that humanity possesses any natural virtue prior to the granting of special grace are, the encyclical continues, committing the error of Pelagius. Teilhard describes this argument as a 'typical example of Christian pessimism' in which 'world history is presented as a long series of evils' requiring rectification.[100] One of the charges some-

---

[96] Maurice Blondel, paper of 5 December 1919, *TBC*, pp. 22–23.
[97] 'Super-Humanity, Super-Christ, Super-Charity' (1943), *SC*, p. 160.
[98] 'How I Believe' (1934), *CE*, pp. 97–98.
[99] *Miserentissimus redemptor*, §8, *PE* III, p. 323.
[100] 'The Sense of Humanity', (1929), *TF*, p. 34. Christopher Mooney, *Teilhard de Chardin and the Mystery of Christ* (London: Collins, 1966), p. 135, is critical of Teilhard's negative assessment of reparation, which he considers that Teilhard associates too closely with the juridical theories of atonement and fails to employ in the same constructive way that he does other theological concepts.

times levelled against Teilhard is, in contrast, that his teleology of history amounts to an unequivocal endorsement of actual lived history that ignores individual and structural sin and rebellion against God. Francis Schüssler Fiorenza and John Galvin consider this to be an inevitable outcome of Teilhard's use of a 'coherence theory' to explain the relation of theology and science: 'Theology in continuity with evolutionary theory too easily promotes an optimistic view about historical progress and about the rational and moral perfectibility of humanity. This optimism cannot stand up to the test of human experience.'[101] The view of progress which Teilhard presents is, however, more nuanced than his critics usually acknowledge. He identifies both 'regressive' currents of history and 'progressive, or constructive' ones, and states: 'If you tell me that as time goes on humankind is getting "better" or "worse", I hardly know or care what the words mean.'[102]

Any response to the charges of Panglossian optimism brought against Teilhard needs to be grounded in the eschatological character of the progress he envisions. Humanity is 'awaiting the parousia' in which the 'historic is to be fused in the transcendent'.[103] This eschatological progress provides a clear alternative to a theology of despair, and some theologians will react to it with natural hostility:

> The learned may smile, or be angered, to hear us speak of progress. They may smugly enumerate the scandals of the present day, or argue about original sin, to prove that nothing good can come from the earth. We may disregard these pessimists, who seem never to have questioned history, or reason, or their own hearts. But have they the faintest suspicion, these people, that their scepticism will end logically in making the world unintelligible, and in destroying our capacity to act? Deny that consciousness is better than unconsciousness. Deny, too, that if humans are to act they must know that their effort has some use — and in so doing you will have denied the necessity of progress. But you will at the same time have destroyed, with your theories, our true reasons for living.[104]

Maurice Blondel, after enumerating the qualities inherent in action — being, creation, willing, teleology — and contrasting them with the 'system of co-ordinates' posited by nothingness — pessimism, an evil universe, illusory existence — concludes similarly: 'To posit nothingness is to affirm at a stroke this entire system of co-ordinates... Thus the

---

[101] Francis Schüssler Fiorenza and John P. Galvin, *Systematic Theology*, I (2 vols.; Minneapolis, Minn.: Fortress Press, 1991), p. 229.

[102] *MPN*, p. 32; 'The Stuff of the Universe' (1953), *AE*, p. 380.

[103] *DM*, pp. 113–118; 'Two Principles and a Corollary' (1948), *TF*, p. 153

[104] 'My Universe' (1924), *SC*, p. 81.

will for nothingness is necessarily incoherent and it harbours in itself a struggle wherein it cannot succumb in spite of the lie and the error; for error is not nothing, it is nothingness that is the error.'[105] Teilhard throws the challenge presented by the Blondelian option between everything and nothing back onto the 'sceptic and the dilettante',[106] for whom pessimism is a pose within which impossible contradictions are concealed. Teilhard wishes ultimately, like Blondel, to encompass all positive affirmations of being in one single synthetic action. Pessimism is, by contrast, essentially a self-contradiction, and even equated by Bernard Towers with neurosis.[107] The choice is between truth and despair, life and cynicism, existence and decay, everything and nothing. There exists, in the phrase of Karl Rahner, an essential active self-transcendence grounded in the 'absolute and infinite mystery of God',[108] which humanity can either accept or refuse. This dynamic of self-transcendence propels humanity to the point at which it is confronted with the option to choose between action and nothingness, and defines the absolute character of this choice.

The natural human hope that the future of the world will be consummated in Christ is justified by the discernment of signs of future life and new creation in the world.[109] Teilhard portrays these signs using the image of natality. They emerge as part of a bringing to birth of the successive stages of the work of God in the heart of material life in a movement of 'universal childbirth'.[110] The world is undergoing 'immense travail' and 'growing-pains',[111] with God working to achieve its salvation through the ongoing act of creation.[112] God's action does not operate as an 'intrusive thrusting of His works into the midst of pre-exisitent

---

[105] Maurice Blondel, *Action: Essay on a Critique of Life and a Science of Practice*, §§38-39 (Notre Dame, Ind.: University of Notre Dame Press, 2003), p. 50.

[106] 'The Spirit of the Earth' (1931), *HE*, p. 37.

[107] See the excellent essay of Bernard Towers, 'Optimism and Pessimism in Contemporary Culture', in *Concerning Teilhard, and other Writings on Science and Religion* (London: Collins, 1969), pp. 115–23.

[108] Karl Rahner, 'Christology within an Evolutionary View of the World', *TI* V, pp. 165–66, 190. Rahner states at the opening of his essay that what separates him from Teilhard is not necessarily his conclusions, but his method: Rahner wishes to proceed entirely through theological and philosophical reasoning and does not wish to employ a posteriori insights from the natural sciences.

[109] On this topic, see Michel Rancourt, «La Foi au monde chez Teilhard de Chardin», in *Questions actuelles sur la foi* (Montreal: Fides, 1984), pp. 77–102.

[110] 'The Transformist Paradox' (1925), 'Basis and Foundations of the Idea of Evolution' (1926), *VP*, pp. 102, n. 1, 137.

[111] 'The New Spirit, 1942' (1942), 'Faith in Humanity', *FM*, pp. 90, 187; cf. Rom 8.22.

beings'.[113] Teilhard states that, in fact, 'nothing makes a complete beginning. All things are born from what existed before them.'[114] Hope therefore amounts to prophecy, which does not create future events by changing the course of history, but perceives their causes or signs which already exist. This is why Paul Tillich also affirms a 'right to hope' as part of his theology of culture:

> Where there is genuine hope, then that for which we hope, has already some presence. In some way, the hoped for is at the same time here and not here. It is not yet fulfilled and it may remain unfulfilled. But it is here, in the situation and in ourselves as a power which drives those who hope into the future. There is a beginning here and now. And this beginning drives towards an end. The hope itself, if it is rooted in the reality of something already given, becomes a driving power and makes fulfilment, not certain, but possible.[115]

Hans Schwarz recognizes that this hope does not amount to a 'naïve and blind trust in the future', stating of Teilhard's theology: 'The eschatological goal of salvation is of cosmic dimension. It is a gift provided by God's grace and not the result of human achievement.'[116] Humankind is waiting to attain its future state, just as Christ is 'waiting to reappear until the human collectivity has at last become capable (because fully realized in its natural potentialities) of receiving from him its supernatural consummation'.[117] Humanity is living in the eternal present of action, passion and vision, which bind it to Christ in realizing the future of the world and awaiting its final transfiguration.

[112] 'Human Energy' (1937), *HE*, p. 141.

[113] 'The Transformist Paradox', p. 102, n. 1

[114] 'Basis and Foundations of the Idea of Evolution', p. 130.

[115] 'The Right to Hope: A Sermon', in *Paul Tillich: Theologian of the Boundaries* (London: Collins, 1987), p. 327. W.J.P. Boyd, 'Teilhard de Chardin and Modern Protestant Theology', in *Teilhard Reassessed*, ed. Anthony Hanson (London: Darton, Longman & Todd, 1970), pp. 143–55, identifies affinities between Teilhard and Tillich on the grounds of the fundamental place that both give to christology.

[116] Hans Schwarz, 'Twelfth locus: eschatology', in Carl E. Braaten and Robert W. Jenson (eds.), *Christian Dogmatics*, II (2 vols.; Philadelphia, Penn.: Fortress, 1984), pp. 530, 532.

[117] 'Two Principles and a Corollary', p. 155.

EPILOGUE

Theism and humanism

Teilhard is concerned that the Church has become progressively estranged from what the inaugural words of *Gaudium et spes* describe as the 'joys and hopes and the sorrows and anxieties of people today'.[1] He identifies in his oeuvre reasons for this estrangement, and proposes ways of reducing it. Teilhard considers the origins of the divergence of interests between Church and world to lie in fifteenth century Renaissance humanism, when a significant corpus of science, art and learning began, for the first time in Christian society, to flourish independently of ecclesial patronage.[2] The Church need not have perceived this as a threat, but because it had come to regard the axioms on which its theology was constructed as necessary rather than contingent, it was unable to assimilate many of the new scientific, artistic and intellectual insights offered to it, with the usual response to them being, instead, suspicion and retrenchment. Responsibility for the designation of the fruits of the Renaissance as 'secular' rests, therefore, primarily with the Church. Teilhard describes the resulting clash between Church and the 'secular' world proclaimed by numerous theologians in the following stark terms:

> Think of all the infantile maledictions pronounced by Churchmen against new ideas! Think of all the avenues of enquiry that have at first been forbidden and later found to be rich in results! Think of all the futile subterfuges designed to make people believe that the Church was directing a movement by which it was, in fact, being forcibly dragged along![3]

Teilhard suggests in his later essays that the current stage of historical development is not simply a continuation of the same process, but a qualitatively new phenomenon, which he terms 'neo-humanism'.[4] This is characterized by humanity's emerging awareness of its decisive role in the political and biological development of the world. Whereas

---

[1] *DEC* II, p. 1069.

[2] e.g. 'The Sense of Humanity' (1929), 'Two Principles and a Corollary' (1948), *TF*, pp. 21, 156.

[3] 'Mastery of the World and the Kingdom of God' (1916), *WW*, pp. 86–87.

[4] 'My Fundamental Vision' (1948), *TF*, pp. 192, 202–203; 'The Basis of my Attitude' (1948), *HM*, p. 147.

humankind used, typically, to be controlled by events and its material circumstances, it now increasingly determines these. Humanity is becoming adult, and is as part of this maturation becoming conscious of its global existence. Similarities with the earlier form of humanism may, nonetheless, be identified: above all, the challenges which both have presented to established religious institutions. Theologians need to respond to neo-humanism by developing an 'authentic Christian humanism' which affirms the intrinsic value and goodness of humanity.[5]

Teilhard communicates the Christian message to people living in a world interconnected and dominated by science and technology as never before. The universal is surpassing the local as the principal unit of human affiliation. Some of Teilhard's statements about these developments now sound prophetic. He notes, for instance: 'What we call civilization is weaving its web around us with a terrifying rapidity.'[6] In our own internet age, a 'single gigantic network girdling the earth' which amounts to a new form of consciousness, is being realized in terms more concrete than even Teilhard could have imagined:

> No one can deny that a network (a world network) of economic and psychic affiliations is being woven at ever increasing speed which envelops and constantly penetrates more deeply within each one of us. With every day that passes it becomes a little more impossible for us to act or think otherwise than collectively.[7]

Individual people and communities are being drawn materially, intellectually and spiritually to perceive the intimate connections between the universal and the particular: 'The scope of each human molecule, in terms of movement, information and influence, is becoming rapidly coextensive with the whole surface of the globe.'[8] This is William Blake's vision of a 'world in a grain of sand, / And a heaven in a wild flower', or as Teilhard expresses it, 'nature's masterpiece within itself'.[9] In a global society ever more unified by intellect and language, shared con-

---

[5] Thomas Corbishley, *The Spirituality of Teilhard de Chardin* (London: Fontana, 1971), p. 111.

[6] 'The Grand Option' (1939), *FM*, p. 43.

[7] 'The Formation of the Noosphere' (1947), *FM*, pp. 171, 166.

[8] 'Formation of the Noosphere', p. 170. Christopher F. Mooney, 'Cybernation, Responsibility and Providential Design', *Theological Studies* 51 (1990), pp. 286–309, offers imaginative reflections on the consequences of this expansion of information networks for human responsibility.

[9] 'The Human Phenomenon' (1930), *VP*, p. 173; cf. 'Auguries of Innocence (c. 1804)', in *William Blake*, ed. Michael Mason (Oxford University Press, 1994), p. 173. For the affinity of Teilhard with Blake, see Eileen Sanzo, 'The Convergence of Blake and Teilhard', *The Teilhard Review* 12 (1977), pp. 16–20.

cepts and signs acquire a new potency, and as a result, perspectives on truth converge. This is not to say that a single truth can or should be accepted as the complete and sole truth by the whole of humanity, as claimed by totalitarian political regimes. It suggests, rather, that the remedy for imperfect human knowledge will be found above and beyond any consensus currently imaginable. Truth is not simply the opinion of the majority, nor even the totality, of humanity. Truth nevertheless needs to be believed and lived if action, passion and reflection are to endure. Teilhard expresses concern about the 'extent to which the lie (a relatively minor evil in more restricted groups) is fast becoming an inhibiting major vice in large social organisms'.[10] The belief that truth subsists above and beyond the created order is required if particular truths are to be accepted, and is implied by particular truths whenever they are sincerely affirmed.

Teilhard believes that the ideological, cultural and existential conflicts apparent in the modern world just described are a product not of atheism but of *'unsatisfied theism'*. 'In spite of appearances,' he states, 'our age is more religious than ever.'[11] Teilhard's frequent complaints that religion and theology have come to assume excessively juridical forms, at the expense of more organic conceptions of faith, are motivated by his anxiety that religion and theology have lost contact with the wider true reality existing beyond them. He responds by affirming that theology needs to be governed by a 'principle of *the primacy of the organic over the juridical'*.[12] This typically does not happen. Theologians have, in so

---

[10] 'The Human Rebound of Evolution' (1947), *FM*, p. 203, n. 1. Stephen Jay Gould, 'Piltdown Revisited', in *The Panda's Thumb: More Reflections in Natural History* (London: Penguin, 1983), pp. 92–104; 'Teilhard and Piltdown', in *Hen's Teeth and Horse's Toes* (London: Penguin, 1990), pp. 199–250, have generated great controversy by implicating Teilhard in the Piltdown Man hoax. Gould's arguments have been shown to be unsupportable in several places, including Mary Lukas, 'Teilhard and Piltdown: A Re-Reassessment', in *Humanity's Quest for Unity: A United Nations Teilhard Colloquium*, ed. Leo Zonneveld (Wassenaar: Mirananda, 1985), pp. 61–70. John Haught states of Teilhard's accusers: 'Something much more contentious is occurring here than merely scientific disagreement. What really repels them is Teilhard's suggestion that a metaphysically adequate explanation of any universe in which evolution occurs requires — at some point beyond the limits that science has set for itself — a transcendent force of attraction to explain the *overarching* tendency of matter to evolve toward life, mind, and spirit.' (*God After Darwin: A Theology of Evolution* (Boulder, Col.: Westview, 2000), p. 83.)

[11] 'The Awaited Word' (1940), *TF*, p. 93; cf. 'The Zest for Living' (1950), *AE*, pp. 239–40.

[12] 'Note on the Universal Christ' (1920), *SC*, p. 19. John Haught, *Deeper than Darwin: The Prospect for Religion in the Age of Evolution* (Oxford: Westview, 2004), p. 65, endorses Teilhard's assessment.

many cases, surrendered any ambition to provide a comprehensive description and explanation of the material and spiritual world, focusing instead on church life and salvation history abstracted from human life and world history rather than rooted in them. In fact, if theology is to remain relevant to human life, it is essential that it preserve both its dogmatic *and* human references, or in the words of Blondel, 'to go forward towards a realism which is self-consistent throughout, towards a total reality which puts the metaphysics of Christianity in accord with the mystical theology lived by the saints and even by the faithful following'.[13] This conception of the theological enterprise requires theologians to take cosmology seriously. Teilhard's contribution to this task is a theology in which individual and universal, soul and cosmos are given their harmony and consistency by one single unifying substance, who is Christ. Teilhard's theology is motivated by an experience of the world similar to that of Samuel Taylor Coleridge, who on hearing the music of the spheres asks: 'And what if all of animated nature / Be but organic harps diversely framed, / That tremble into thought, as o'er them sweeps / Plastic and vast, one intellectual breeze, / At once the Soul of each, and God of all?'[14] Teilhard's response to Coleridge's question would be that this harmonious unity in diversity is preserved by a bond which exists within the cosmos, yet also subsists beyond it. Individual, embodied human beings, and other particular substances, do not exist apart from this cosmological bond.

The primary obstacle to providing a theological account of the body has been the understanding of spiritual illumination as the dwelling of Christ *within* the body rather than as the recognition that Christ himself forms and sustains that body. Teilhard recovers a more ancient theology of the body in which it is a 'microcosm reflecting in itself a cosmic story' rather than an 'interpreter of human inwardness'.[15] His determination to develop a coherent theology of the body and its relation with spirit is painfully lacking in mainstream contemporary Christian religion, with the result that nowadays in the West, the kinds of people who would in previous ages have provided institutional churches with spiritual leadership and finance are more likely to be practitioners of yoga or

---

[13] Maurice Blondel, paper of 5 December 1919, *TBC*, p. 23.

[14] 'The Eolian Harp', §§44–48, in *Samuel Taylor Coleridge*, ed. H.J Jackson (Oxford University Press, 1994), p. 28.

[15] Andrew Louth, 'The Body in Western Catholic Christianity', in *Religion and the Body*, ed. Sarah Coakley (Cambridge University Press, 1997), p. 129, provides these categories.

feng shui than of Christianity. Such privatized forms of embodied and spatialized spiritual living, rediscovered in the West on sites evacuated by historic Christianity, present it with immense challenges and opportunities to reaffirm the importance to human flourishing of the *decentring* of the self to give attention to the Word of God present in human bodies and other substances in the wider world, sustaining them, and animating them.[16]

Two particular elements of Teilhard's theology enable him to reappraise the relation between the universal and the particular in this critical and imaginative way. Firstly, his ontology of present human and cosmic fallenness enables a positive assessment of human freedom and diversity as directed towards a future consummation. Teilhard accepts the Aristotelian view that beings may be imperfect in numerous different ways yet perfect in only one: whilst perfection implies unity and a univocal conception of being, imperfection signifies multiplicity, disunion, and a diversity of equally valid perspectives on the truth. No theology can, in other words, possess a monopoly of truth, and new departures and creative reappropriations of past discussions, such as those about the body, are a valid and indeed essential part of the theological enterprise. The second element of Teilhard's theology that accounts for its critical and imaginative qualities is contextual: that it is lived and developed within a community and a spiritual discipline. French Jesuits comprised, during the twentieth century, a remarkable body: exiled by their people, they ministered, fought and died for them in war; suppressed by their Church, they provided many of its foremost theologians. These tensions explain why French Jesuit theology inheres so strongly in its community and the challenges that confronted it. Its creativity and commitment to the search for truth is evinced in letters exchanged and conversations continued across several decades, when many key texts could not be published nor officially discussed. It is these dialogues, grounded in the community life of prayer, worship, work and the freedom of movement characteristic of the Jesuit order, that sustained radical and controversial theological ideals. They contrast sharply with the conservative neo-Thomism of the emerging generation of lay theologians led by Jacques Maritain and Étienne Gilson, whose identity was established in a far less challenging set of circumstances.[17] The community context of Jesuit theology enables the preservation of a sense of excitement and even

---

[16] 'Reflections on Happiness' (1943), *TF*, pp. 118–29.

[17] See Claude Langlois, «La Naissance de l'intellectuel catholique», in *Intellectuels chrétiens et esprit des années 1920*, ed. Pierre Colin (Paris: Cerf, 1997), pp. 220–21.

humour in the face of challenges, based on the belief that something real is at stake in theological arguments, and that those arguments can have great practical consequences. The development of modern French Jesuit theology is, indeed, located in real life events just as much as is German Protestant theology through the twentieth century, and above all in the crisis of religious exile and the perils of foreign missions. This context is a world removed from the academic round of publishing and conferences, as well as from the systematized ministerial diet of 'applied', 'pastoral' or 'practical' theology. Teilhard's theology is freed from secondary considerations by its rootedness in a life given to it — what Blondel calls *le vécu*, which includes worship, action, passion and vision — and thus able to undertake its primary task of reflecting on the Word of God. Teilhard devotes his life's energy to the spiritual quest for truth and holiness in an ethical context of responsibility to others.[18]

A renewed emphasis on the organic and the embodied in theology has the potential to contribute to a renewal of metaphysical concepts by showing that they inevitably contain a theological component. Teilhard considers metaphysics to extend far beyond the analytical boundaries within which it is often confined, posing questions which only theology can ultimately answer. Teilhard's theology is therefore far more than a French Catholic counterpart to *Kulturprotestantismus*: he aims to order and synthesize metaphysics and the other sciences, whose appropriate object is the created order, with the theology which is properly directed towards the source of creation and revelation, in an encounter which renews both disciplines. He avers:

> Metaphysics has over-emphasized an abstract, physically indeterminate idea of being. Science, for its part, used certain exact 'parameters' to define for us the nature and requirements, in other words the physical stuff, of 'participated' being. It is these parameters that must in future be respected by every concept of Creation, Incarnation, Redemption and Salvation — as, indeed, of course by every 'demonstration' of the existence of God.[19]

The scientific 'parameters' to which Teilhard refers are, more precisely, the organic and atomic natures of the universe, and the primordial function in it of the dynamic of unification. These parameters bind theology, however, to a particular metaphysics. Teilhard sometimes commits the

---

[18] Michael D. Barber, 'The Ethical Eloquence of the Silenced: A Levinasian Reading of Teilhard de Chardin's Silencing', in *Trying Times: Essays on Catholic Higher Education in the 20th Century*, eds. William M. Shea with Daniel Van Slyke (Atlanta, Ga.: Scholars, 1999), pp. 153–71, provides an illuminating analysis of the ethical and ecclesial context of Teilhard's theology.

fallacy with which he indicts his critics of proposing that a particular
metaphysic will be valid for all theology for all time, such as the neo-
Aristotelianism of which contemporary Thomists were enamoured. It
certainly seems strange for him not to have accepted more clearly that
the continuing progression of research in the natural sciences might in
the future present new data which will indicate the need for further read-
justments in theology and metaphysics.

Teilhard sometimes exaggerates the degree of reassessment of traditional theological categories that he effects, such as when asserting: 'It is
impossible to think of Christ as "evolver" without at the same time having to rethink the whole of Christology.'[20] Such statements do little to
help his cause in the eyes of less adventurous theologians, and seem to
be at variance with his use of Pauline sources and contemporary scholarly interpretation of them for this theological 'revolution'. Teilhard's
project should more accurately be described as one of *ressourcement*
than of creating a wholly *new* theology. Nevertheless, if by 'Christology'
he is referring to a clearly and objectively defined component of Church
dogmatic teaching, it is possible to understand what he means: simply
that formal magisterial teaching is radically challenged by developments
in the scientific understanding of the world. Indeed, Teilhard refers more
credibly to the 'increasing necessity we are experiencing today of read-
justing the fundamental lines of our Christology to a new universe'.[21]
This language of adjustment gives a more accurate portrayal of his theological method than one of dismantling and reconstruction, despite his
own equivocation on this point. It also suggests that there will be more
opportunities to employ insights from his theology in mainstream theological debates. Donald MacKinnon described Teilhard's work as 'profoundly suggestive for the constructive philosopher and theologian'.[22]

This adjustment of theological concepts challenges the boundaries
within which theological language has previously been conceived. Teilhard's neologisms are well-known, although less essential to his theology than has sometimes been claimed. Critics might charge him with
obscurantism, but this is in no way his intention. Teilhard is seeking to
articulate and communicate a profound spiritual experience which is, as

---

[19] Letter to Emmanuel Mounier, 2 November 1947, cited in *SC*, pp. 222–23.
[20] 'The Stuff of the Universe' (1953), *AE*, p. 382.
[21] 'Christ the Evolver' (1942), *CE*, p. 139.
[22] Donald MacKinnon, 'Teilhard's Achievement', in *Teilhard de Chardin: Pilgrim of the Future*, ed. Neville Braybrooke (London: Darton, Longman & Todd, 1965), p. 60.

such, strictly incommunicable.[23] His aim is, in other words, not to create a 'new theology' or new set of doctrines, but to think through the implications for modern living of the theology and devotion of the Christian tradition.[24] Teilhard employs, like George Herbert, theological terms in what have often been regarded to be non-theological contexts, and thus makes their theological sense 'strange'. He believes, as does Herbert, that theological technicalities are 'technicalities of great contemporary moment', and need to be formulated in terms derived from human experience at any particular time, whatever that experience might be.[25] Being unafraid to employ theological terms in new ways seems to be part of what it means to be a theologian living in a changing world, in which even the ways in which change is experienced are changing. To take an example, the description of Christ as 'evolver' seems to point to a reasonable and required dimension of human experience of the creative and redeeming power of Christ in a world commonly believed to be in a state of linear biological progression, and challenges many scientific notions of that progression as well. It is too easy to cast neologisms as mere histrionics. Jon Sobrino argues that, in christology, the 'creation of new titles is justified and even required' because they 'spell out the significance of Jesus today' in an exercise that is doing no more than 'continuing the logic of the New Testament' of calling Christ by new names. If this were not true, then humankind would be inhabiting a theologically 'complete' world that is simply waiting for its past speculations to be proven true. Humankind cannot however assume that it has yet reached this stage of possessing a complete theological explanation of the world. Until it has, the task of naming will continue. It is essential, nonetheless, to remember that only the figure of Jesus provides the meaning of the titles used to describe him,[26] which all refer ultimately to him and therefore have the potential continually to reveal new aspects of

---

[23] Jacques Maritain, 'Teilhard de Chardin and Teilhardianism', in *The Peasant of the Garonne: An Old Layman Questions Himself about the Present Time* (London: Chapman, 1968), pp. 124–25.

[24] Étienne Gilson, «Trois leçons sur le thomisme et sa situation présente», *Seminarium* 17 (1965), p. 720. In his letter to Henri de Lubac of 13 May 1962, Gilson had however suggested provocatively that Teilhard was the advocate of a new religion to replace Christianity. De Lubac judges (n. 1) that Gilson never read Teilhard seriously, and when he did, suffered from an inherent bias against him. (*Letters of Étienne Gilson to Henri de Lubac* (San Francisco: Ignatius, 1988), pp. 59–66.)

[25] For Herbert, see Rowan Williams, *Anglican Identities* (London: Darton, Longman & Todd, 2004), p. 58.

[26] Jon Sobrino, *Christology at the Crossroads: A Latin American Approach* (London: SCM, 1978), p. 272, n. 12.

divine revelation. At least Teilhard cannot be charged with attempting to rewrite intellectual history in order to suit his own theological agenda. He is refreshingly candid in identifying when he is departing from the views of particular thinkers.

Teilhard's reapplication of historic christological categories is by modern standards, and certainly by postmodern ones, radical. He states:

> Understood in their full sense, creation, incarnation and redemption are not facts which can be *localized* at a given point in time and space; they are true dimensions of the world (not objects of perception, but a condition of all possible perceptions).
> It is nevertheless true that all three can take the form of particular *expressive* facts, such as the historical appearance of the human type (creation), the birth of Christ (incarnation), his death (redemption). These historical facts, however, are only a special heightened expression of a process which is 'cosmic' in dimensions.[27]

Teilhard recovers in his christology, above all else, the awareness present in early Christian theology that the sacrifice of Christ encompasses not only his death on the cross but the whole of his earthly ministry, from Incarnation to Ascension.[28] The relation between theology and history that Teilhard espouses, with its Rahneresque reference to the conditions necessary for all possible perceptions, appears less novel when considered alongside the cosmic speculations of Tertullian, Justin Martyr, Gregory of Nyssa, Irenaeus of Lyons, and other early Church Fathers on whose work he draws. Teilhard's attempts to establish pairs of theological and metaphysical concepts is best understood in this pre-Nicaean context. He identifies, for instance, heaven, catholicity, and the city of souls with, respectively, the future, universality, and personality, and in the course of an account of the rebirth of the universe in Christ ('christogenesis'), equates creation, incarnation and redemption with motive principle, unifying mechanism and ascensional work.[29] Teilhard does not wish to deny the theological content of these pairs. Rather, he believes that their theological meaning will emerge from the dynamic relation between the members of the pair itself. He therefore proposes *coherence* and *fertility* as truth principles.[30] The best theological categories are, in other words, those which relate doctrine to human experi-

---

[27] 'Some General Views on the Essence of Christianity' (1939), *CE*, p. 135.

[28] Dom Gregory Dix, *The Shape of the Liturgy* (London: Continuum, 2nd edn, 2001), pp. 746–48, provides an excellent classic discussion of this point.

[29] 'The Salvation of Humankind' (1936), *SC*, p. 147; 'Introduction to the Christian Life' (1944), *CE*, p. 155.

[30] 'The Natural Units of Humanity' (1939), *VP*, p. 206.

ence, and those which aid reflection and bring inspiration. Teilhard believes that whenever theological language becomes estranged from the categories with which humanity understands the world, theology ceases to have any reference to that world or to its life.

Teilhard shows that theological categories are essential for describing humanity's transformed vision of the world in Christ gained in the divine milieu, and for preparing humanity for practical living in the world. People, objects and projects attain a new significance when regarded contemplatively, in and through divine light. What has previously appeared as void and absence assumes fresh radiance, whilst other habitual attachments appear less important. Empirical sensory process is not essential to this new vision: the vision is in fact a divine gift of which humanity seeks understanding. Vision challenges the understanding of contemplation as drawing the person of faith out of the material world. In fact, contemplation provides an impulsion into ever more active spiritual engagement with the world, in the *in actione contemplativus* tradition of Ignatius's disciple Jerónimo Nadal. Contemplation does not precede nor succeed action, but accompanies it.[31]

Powerful currents in contemporary Christian theology give, at best, insufficient emphasis to the intimate relation between religious faith and action and passion in the world, and at worst actively discourage reflection on this relation. Forms of Barthian and postmodern theology often promote the incommensurability of religious and non-religious discourse, suggesting either that there is no possibility of arbitration between theology and other discourses, or that their engagement will be not through attentive listening but by means of power and rhetoric. Apophatic theology, in accentuating the unknowability and incommunicability of the data of faith, can moreover expedite a withdrawal into the 'interior castle' of the soul that might be accompanied by a reliance on mores and liturgical ritual to define religious identity.[32] Both postmodern and apophatic theology can certainly maintain, in fairly generalized ways, an understanding of contemplation as vision, whether by gaze or by metaphor. Nevertheless, in Teilhard's eschatological christology, once contemplation is understood as vision the completely ordinary

---

[31] See Jérôme Nadal, *Contemplatif dans l'action: écrits spirituels ignatiens (1535–1575)* (Paris: Desclée, 1994), pp. 19–21; cf. Philip Endean, *Karl Rahner and Ignatian Spirituality* (Oxford University Press, 2001), pp. 69, 74.

[32] For discussions of the two approaches, see Merold Westphal, *Overcoming Onto-Theology: Toward a Postmodern Christian Faith* (New York: Fordham University Press, 2001); David Burrell, 'Beyond Onto-Theology: Negative Theology and Faith', *Lonergan Workshop* 15 (1999), pp. 1–11.

human activity of seeing becomes transformed by divine action, so that the whole cosmos is seen in concentrated and transfigured form. Teilhard recognizes the 'considerable traces of fusionism in the appeals directed towards the inexpressible by an Eckhart or even a John of the Cross', but cannot be reconciled to apophatic description, believing that 'God is arrived at not in a negation, but in an extension, of the world'.[33]

This cosmic, eschatological focus is not widely diffused in large sectors of current church or academic theology. Expressing the current situation in Luther's terms, so many practitioners and writers of theology have not yet emerged from the stage of trial into the realm of hope.[34] The psychological categories of weakness and vulnerability have, in their preoccupation with morbidity,[35] attained credal status, displacing the Pauline conceptions of mission and ministry as requiring ambition for Christ, strength to undertake demanding tasks, protection from assault, and geographical mobility.[36] It is deeply ironic that it is from precisely these kinds of psycho-theological perspectives, which are in reality neither psychological nor theological, that Teilhard is likely to face criticism for allegedly conflating different categories of analysis and departing from scriptural and historical Christian theology. The threat he presents to these viewpoints, and to those of atheist writers of popular science such as Peter Medawar determined to refute evolutionary christology, is obvious. By undermining discourses that associate religion with disempowerment, Teilhard threatens to dismantle the control mechanisms of rational professionalism that are dominant both within and outside the visible church, whose most formidable opponents are those with a happy, embodied, hopeful faith grounded in their experience of God in Christ.

Words of a Lutheran contemporary of Teilhard's express in more concrete terms some of the implications of the theology that this study has presented for practical church ministry. The theologian and pastor Dietrich Bonhoeffer, following his arrest by the Gestapo, wrote from Tegel Prison in Berlin:

[33] 'Two Converse Forms of Spirit' (1950), *AE*, p. 225; 'Christianity in the World' (1933), *SC*, p. 106. For Teilhard as a cataphatic theologian, see Ursula King, 'Consumed by Fire from Within: Teilhard de Chardin's Pan-Christic Mysticism in Relation to the Catholic Tradition', *HJ* 40 (1999), p. 459.

[34] Martin Luther, *Lectures on Romans*, *Works* 25 (55 vols.; Saint Louis, Mo.: Concordia, 1955–76), pp. 291–96; cf. Rom 5.3–4.

[35] 'From the Pre–Human to the Ultra–Human' (1950), *FM*, p. 296.

[36] Rom 15.20, II Tm 4.17, Heb 11.34, Eph 6.10-17. References to missionary journeys are too numerous to list.

> The secrets known to a man's valet — that is, to put it crudely, the range of his intimate life, from prayer to his sexual life — have become the hunting-ground of modern pastoral workers. In that way they resemble (though with quite different intentions) the dirtiest gutter journalists... There is a kind of evil satisfaction in knowing that everyone has his failings and weak spots... The more isolated a man's life, the more easily he falls a victim to this attitude.[37]

Teilhard identifies, like Bonhoeffer, a negative and inquisitorial attitude towards humanity as characteristic, sociologically, of the 'bourgeois spirit' of 'those who simply wish to make the world a comfortable dwelling-place',[38] routinized, controlled and predictable. Bonhoeffer suggested that the origins of the set of 'professional' theories and attitudes which fortify this spirit, prevalent both within and beyond the church, are located in a juridical or static mode of *theology*. The Lutheran pastor referred to these theories as the

> secularized offshoots of Christian theology ... who demonstrate to secure, contented, and happy mankind that it is really unhappy and desperate and simply unwilling to admit that it is in a predicament about which it knows nothing, and from which only they can rescue it. Wherever there is health, strength, security, simplicity, they scent luscious fruit to gnaw at or to lay their pernicious eggs in. They set themselves to drive people to inward despair, and then the game is in their hands.[39]

Such attitudes are frequently considered by ministerial and vocational theory as suitable responses to declining participation by large sectors of society in the theology, mission and ministry of the historic churches. In fact, they are symptoms of that decline. The means of ecclesial renewal that Teilhard envisions is the re-engagement by the Church with the fundamental expressions of its faith and life. The essential manifestations of the Church's faith in which Christ acts are everlasting: baptism, prayer, eucharist, action, passion, the vision of God. It is solely in these that Christ is made present to the world, and solely in these that the world is brought closer to consummation by Christ and in Christ. These fundamental expressions of faith could constitute the core of a new 'Christian

---

[37] Dietrich Bonhoeffer, letter to Eberhard Bethge, 8 July 1944, in *Letters and Papers from Prison: The Enlarged Edition*, ed. Eberhard Bethge (London: SCM, 1986), pp. 344–45. For comparisons of Teilhard and Bonhoeffer, see Charles M. Hegarty, 'Bonhoeffer and Teilhard on Worldly Christianity', *Science et esprit* 21 (1969), especially pp. 67–70; Noel Keith Roberts, *From Piltdown Man to Point Omega: The Evolutionary Theory of Teilhard de Chardin*, Studies in European Thought 18 (New York, Lang, 2000), pp. 218–220.

[38] 'The Planetization of Humankind' (1945), *FM*, p. 139.

[39] Bonhoeffer, letter of 8 June 1944, *Letters and Papers*, p. 326.

humanism', which remains open to creative divine revelation whilst preserving and exalting all that is most properly human in humanity.[40] Such
Christian humanism would invigorate the Church by liberating it from
static, hypercritical and ultimately dehumanizing theologies. Teilhard
describes proponents of these latter types of theology as 'juridicists', and
contrasts them with physicalists and mystics.[41] In the first half of the
twentieth century, as at the opening of the twenty-first, it frequently
seems that the visible Church is controlled by juridicists, with the physicalists and mystics either outside it or on the margins. Teilhard opposes
this balance of power, instead embracing Bergson's view that religion is
essentially dynamic and not static, and that mysticism provides its essential impulse. Fideism, whether Catholic or Protestant, blows like a cold
wind over the 'religion of the heart' which he embraces.

Teilhard's theological insights and method have much to offer the
Church and its theology. One commentator, however, sums up Teilhard's current status in the following terms:

> His fame, it would seem, is on a 'back burner'. In a faint odour of sulphur,
> votive candles admittedly flicker about 'Teilhard's thought', while 'Teil-
> hard Associations' are born and endure. But as the echo of his hard-fought
> battle dies down, does the power of his message also wane?... The
> Catholic Church is in great need of the abrasive, energizing breath of a new
> Teilhard. Or, in the interim (why not?) a return to Teilhard? Or, quite sim-
> ply, a welcome for Teilhard?[42]

Max Wildiers believed Teilhard to have set a threefold task for present-
day theology: to proceed with an attitude of openness towards the natural sciences; to transpose Christian dogmas into the structure provided
by a new view of the world; and to reflect seriously on the religious
value of temporal, human endeavour.[43] Wildiers' definition of Teilhard's
middle objective needs to be interpreted as being to establish a mutually-
informing dialogue between dogma and society. These three points then
provide an accurate summary of Teilhard's agenda, which provides a

---

[40] 'Social Heredity and Progress: Notes on the Humanist-Christian Value of Education' (1938), *FM*, p. 34.

[41] e.g. 'My Universe' (1924), *SC*, p. 55.

[42] Jean Lacouture *Jesuits: A Multibiography* (London: Harvill, 1996), p. 441. An
excellent recent collection of practical spiritual resources drawn from and inspired by
Teilhard's work, organized into 15 sessions, is Robert Faricy and Lucy Rooney, *Knowing
Jesus in the World: Praying with Teilhard de Chardin* (London: St Paul's, 1999), with a
commendatory preface by Hans-Peter Kolvenbach, the Jesuit Superior General.

[43] N. Max Wildiers, *An Introduction to Teilhard de Chardin* (London: Fontana,
1968), p. 125.

commendable set of theological priorities for church life and mission. Many of the challenges, dilemmas and conflicts confronting society and Church today, such as nationalism, bioethics and sexuality, would bene-fit from a theology which privileges movement and change over stasis, and from one that is able to conceive of humanity and life in organic terms and to accept and work with the many consequences of organic, embodied existence.

In fact, much current spiritual and theological reflection is abstract and vacuous, lacking meaningful references in the material world. Many assertions are made in popular and quasi-academic writing on spiritual-ity, for instance, about the nature of a person's 'spiritual journey'. Although the language of journeying can provide a welcome poetic anti-dote to models of religion based on practice and their inherent dangers of introversion and stasis, there persists the real hazard of abstracting notions of soul and spirit from a universal metaphysical context and thereby precluding any distinctively theological understanding of them. Theologies of individual spiritual journeying often seem to possess no more in common with classic spirituality, which emphasizes specific marks of holiness like attention and humility, than does the Star Wars imagery of voyaging and landmarks which they deploy. Teilhard's con-ception of spiritual progression is quite different from this current post-modern conception of individual journeying because it grounds individ-ual testimony in participation in a *collective* material and spiritual movement that both precedes individual persons and persists beyond them. Teilhard articulates this movement using the language of action, passion and vision, whose references are transcendent, and has no need of the interconnecting narratives employed by figures like Alastair Mac-intyre to restore some degree of dignity to an essentially narcissistic communitarianism.[44] Whenever Teilhard employs relational spiritual images — such as his conception of the 'other', and in the wedding addresses — they are inalienably located in a public, cosmic context. Much closer to the time of Christ's life on earth, anchorites were driven into the desert not to seek tranquility, but to engage in spiritual combat away from the increasingly institutionalized forms of Christianity. Teil-hard identifies the equivalent spiritual challenge in his own era to lie not in withdrawal from worldly religion, but in renewed engagement with societies in increasingly urgent need of religious renewal. In an era when

---

[44] Alasdair MacIntyre, *After Virtue: A Study in Moral Theory* (London: Duckworth, 2nd edn, 1999), pp. 216–221.

Christian faith and values are questioned as never before, the world becomes the principal theatre of spiritual challenge.

Paying attention to the world by means of attentive seeing is crucial to engagement with it. The gift of vision which makes this engagement possible attests the spiritual dimension of human and organic life. It affirms that human evolution is directed towards Christ, and that it can be consummated neither by biological processes nor by human effort. It is opposed to much current christology that dispenses in Marcionite fashion with any metaphysics of the creation and preservation of the cosmos by Christ, or which conceives of metaphysics in purely analogical terms and supposes that the whole of theology can be summed up in the statement that 'God is love'. Vision informs science and politics with transcendent values, and reminds practitioners of the imperfection of their theory and practice, but equally of their vocation to bring socialized humanity closer to God. Vision provides a new principle for praxis.[45]

Teilhard has left Christian theology with 'issues', not in the all too usual sense of concerns to be expressed in ongoing discussion and criticism, but in the sense of ends, outcomes, openings and options.[46] These are presented to theology as it continues its everlasting quest of imaginative reflection on how the created order is brought into being, sustained and consummated by the revelation of God in Christ. This reflection requires an ongoing dialogue between theology and other discourses in which theology situates and interprets the whole of human experience as recapitulated at any particular point of history in the various fields of human knowledge and their methodologies. Theology, through its participation in this dialogue, reinvigorates itself, manifests itself in new historical forms, and at its best, enriches the discourses with which it interacts. This mutual renewal is instrinsic to Teilhard's vision of the unification and future consummation of embodied humanity and the entire created order in action, passion, vision, virtuous living, evolution and social life, all motivated by the power of the ever greater Christ.

---

[45] Some of these themes are explored in Helmut Riedlinger, „Das göttliche Milieu: der Mystiker Pierre Teilhard de Chardin auf dem Weg der großen Kommunion mit dem immer größeren Christus", in *Gemeinsam Kirche sein: Theorie und Praxis der Communio*, eds. Günter Biemer and Bernhard Casper (Freiburg: Herder, 1992), pp. 207–234.

[46] Christopher F. Mooney, *Teilhard de Chardin and the Mystery of Christ* (London: Collins, 1966), p. 17.

BIBLIOGRAPHY

Works of Pierre Teilhard de Chardin[1]

Essays

1909 «Les Miracles de Lourdes et les enquêtes canoniques», *Études* 118, pp. 161–83.
1912 «Pour fixer les traits d'un monde qui s'efface: la semaine d'ethnologie religieuse de Louvain», *Le Correspondant*, 10 November, pp. 553–60.
«Homme: IV: l'homme devant les enseignements de l'Église et devant la philosophie spiritualiste», *Dictionnaire apologétique de la foi catholique*, II, 4 vols.; Paris: Beauchesne, 4th edn, 1924–28, §§501–514.
1916 * 'Christ in the World of Matter', *HU*, pp. 39–55.
'Cosmic Life', *WW*, pp. 13–71.
'Mastery of the World and the Kingdom of God', pp. 73–91.
1917 'Creative Union', *WW*, pp. 151–76.
* 'The Mystical Milieu', *WW*, pp. 115–49.
* 'Nostalgia for the Front', *HM*, pp. 167–81.
'The Struggle Against the Multitude', *WW*, pp. 93–114.
1918 'The Eternal Feminine', *WW*, pp. 191–202.
'Forma Christi', *WW*, pp. 249–69.
'The Great Monad', *HM*, pp. 182–95.
* 'My Universe', *HM*, pp. 196–208.
'Operative Faith', *WW*, pp. 225–48.
* 'The Priest', *WW*, pp. 203–224.
'The Soul of the World', *WW*, pp. 179–90.
1919 'The Names of Matter', *HM*, pp. 225–39.
'Note on the Presentation of the Gospel in a New Age', *HM*, pp. 209–224.
'The Promised Land', *WW*, pp. 277–88.
'The Spiritual Power of Matter', *HU*, pp. 57–71.
'The Universal Element', *WW*, pp. 289–302.
1920 'Fall, Redemption and Geocentrism', *CE*, pp. 36–44.
'Note on the Essence of Transformism', *HM*, pp. 107–114.
'Note on the Physical Union Between the Humanity of Christ and the Faithful in the Course of their Sanctification', *CE*, pp. 15–20.
'Note on the Modes of Divine Action in the Universe', *CE*, pp. 25–35.
'A Note on Progress', *FM*, pp. 11–24.
'Note on the Universal Christ', *SC*, pp. 14–20.
'On the Notion of Creative Transformation', *CE*, pp. 21–24.

---

[1] Items marked * provide an engaging and representative selection of Teilhard's theology.

1921 'Science and Christ, or Analysis and Synthesis', *SC*, pp. 21–36.
      'How the Transformist Question Presents Itself Today', *VP*, pp. 7–25.
1922 'Note on Some Possible Historical Representations of Original Sin', *CE*,
      pp. 45–55.
1923 'Hominization: Introduction to a Scientific Study of the Human Phenom-
      enon', *VP*, pp. 51–79.
      * 'The Mass on the World', *HM*, pp. 119–34.
      'Pantheism and Christianity', *CE*, pp. 56–75.
1924 * 'My Universe', *SC*, pp. 37–85.
1925 'The Transformist Paradox, or the Latest Criticism of Transformism by
      M. Vialleton', *VP*, pp. 80–102.
1926 'The Basis and Foundations of the Idea of Evolution', *VP*, pp. 116–42.
1927 * *The Divine Milieu*.
1928 'The Human Phenomenon', *SC*, pp. 86–97.
      'At the Wedding of Odette Bacot and Jean Teilhard d'Eyry', *HM*, pp.
      135–38.
1929 'The Sense of Humanity', *TF*, pp. 13–39.
1930 'The Human Phenomenon', *VP*, pp. 161–74.
      'What Should We Think of Transformism?', *VP*, pp. 151–60.
1931 'The Spirit of the Earth', *HE*, pp. 19–47.
1932 * 'The Road of the West', *TF*, pp. 40–59.
1933 'Christianity in the World', *SC*, pp. 98–112.
      'Christology and Evolution', *CE*, pp. 76–95.
      'Modern Unbelief: Its Underlying Cause and Remedy', *SC*, pp. 113–117.
      * 'The Significance and Positive Value of Suffering', *HE*, pp. 48–52.
1934 'The Evolution of Chastity', *TF*, pp. 60–87.
      'How I Believe', *CE*, pp. 96–132.
1935 'At the Wedding of M. and Mme de la Goublaye de Ménorval', *HM*, pp.
      139–42.
1936 'The Salvation of Humankind', *SC*, pp. 128–50.
      'Sketch of a Personalistic Universe', *HE*, pp. 53–92.
      * 'Some Reflections on the Conversion of the World', *SC*, pp. 118–27.
1937 'Human Energy', *HE*, pp. 113–62.
      'The Phenomenon of Spirituality', *HE*, pp. 93–112.
1938 'Social Heredity and Progress: Notes on the Humanist-Christian Value of
      Education', *FM*, pp. 25–36.
1939 'The Grand Option', *FM*, pp. 37–60.
      'The Moment of Choice: A Possible Interpretation of War', *AE*, pp.
      11–20.
      'The Mysticism of Science', *HE*, pp. 163–81.
      'The Natural Units of Humanity: An Attempt to Outline a Racial Biology
      and Morality', *VP*, pp. 192–215.
      'Some General Views on the Essence of Christianity', *CE*, pp. 133–37.
1940 *The Human Phenomenon*.
      'The Awaited Word', *TF*, pp. 92–100.
1941 'The Atomism of Spirit: An Attempt to Understand the Structure of the
      Stuff of the Universe', *AE*, pp. 21–57.
      'Some Reflections on Progress', *FM*, pp. 61–81.

1942 * 'Christ the Evolver', *CE*, pp. 138–50.
'Humanity's Place in Nature', *VP*, pp. 175–82.
'A Note on the Concept of Christian Perfection', *TF*, pp. 101–106.
'The New Spirit, 1942', *FM*, pp. 82–96.
'The Rise of the Other', *AE*, pp. 59–75.
'Universalization and Union: An Attempt at Clarification', *AE*, pp. 77–95.

1943 'Reflections on Happiness', *TF*, pp. 107–129.
'Super-Humanity, Super-Christ, Super-Charity: Some New Dimensions for the Future', *SC*, pp. 151–73.

1944 'Centrology: An Essay in a Dialectic of Union', *AE*, pp. 97–127.
* 'Introduction to the Christian Life', *CE*, pp. 151–72.

1945 'Action and Activation', *SC*, pp. 174–86.
* 'Can Moral Science Dispense with a Metaphysical Foundation?', *TF*, pp. 130–33.
* 'Christianity and Evolution: Suggestions for a New Theology', *CE*, pp. 173–86.
'A Great Event Foreshadowed: The Planetization of Humankind', *FM*, pp. 124–39.
'Life and the Planets: What is Happening at this Moment on Earth?', *FM*, pp. 97–123.

1946 'Catholicism and Science', *SC*, pp. 187–91.
'Outline of a Dialectic of Spirit', *AE*, pp. 141–51.
'Some Reflections on the Spiritual Repercussions of the Atom Bomb', *FM*, pp. 140–48.

1947 'Faith in Humanity', *FM*, pp. 185–92.
'Faith in Peace', *FM*, pp. 149–54.
'The Formation of the Noosphere: A Biological Interpretation of Human History', *FM*, pp. 155–84.
'The Human Rebound of Evolution and its Consequences', *FM*, pp. 196–213.
'The Place of Technology in a General Biology of Humankind', *AE*, pp. 153–63.
* 'Reflections on Original Sin', *CE*, pp. 187–98.
'The Spiritual Contribution of the Far East: Some Personal Reflections', *TF*, pp. 134–47.
'Turmoil or Genesis? The Position of Humanity in Nature and the Significance of Human Socialization', *FM*, pp. 214–26.

1948 'The Basis of my Attitude', *HM*, pp. 147–48.
'The Directions and Conditions of the Future', *FM*, pp. 227–37.
'My Fundamental Vision', *TF*, pp. 163–208.
'Two Principles and a Corollary (or a *Weltanschauung* in Three Stages)', *TF*, pp. 148–61.
'At the Wedding of Christine Dresch and Claude-Marie Haardt', *HM*, pp. 150–51.

1949 'Does Humankind Move Biologically Upon Itself? Galileo's Question Restated', *FM*, pp. 244–59.
'The Heart of the Problem', *FM*, pp. 260–69.

Man's Place in Nature.

'A Phenomenon of Counter-Evolution in Human Biology, or the Existential Fear', *AE*, pp. 181–95.

1950 'The Christian Phenomenon', *CE*, pp. 199–208.

'A Clarification: Reflections on Two Converse Forms of Spirit', *AE*, pp. 215–27.

'Evolution of the Idea of Evolution', *VP*, pp. 245–47.

'The Evolution of Responsibility in the World', *AE*, pp. 206–214.

'From the Pre-Human to the Ultra-Human: The Phases of a Living Planet', *FM*, pp. 289–97.

* 'The Heart of Matter', *HM*, pp. 15–61.

'Monogenism and Monophyletism: An Essential Distinction', *CE*, pp. 209–211.

'On the Probable Coming of an "Ultra-Humanity"', *FM*, pp. 270–80.

* 'The Spiritual Energy of Suffering', *AE*, pp. 245–49.

* 'The Zest for Living', *AE*, pp. 229–43.

1951 'Can Biology, Taken to its Extreme Limit, Enable us to Emerge into the Transcendent?', *SC*, pp. 212–13.

'The Evolution of Responsibility in the World, *AE*, pp. 205–214.

'A Mental Threshold Across our Path: From Cosmos to Cosmogenesis', *AE*, pp. 251–68.

'Note on the Present Reality and Significance of a Human Orthogenesis', *VP*, pp. 248–55.

'Reflections on the Scientific Probability and the Religious Consequences of an Ultra-Human', *AE*, pp. 269–80.

'The Transformation and Continuation in Humankind of the Mechanism of Evolution', *AE*, pp. 297–309.

1952 'The End of the Species', *FM*, pp. 298–305.

'Hominization and Speciation: The Present Discomforts of Anthropology', *VP*, pp. 256–67.

'The Reflection of Energy', *AE*, pp. 319–37.

'What the World is Looking for from the Church of God at the Moment: 'A Generalizing and a Deepening of the Meaning of the Cross', *CE*, pp. 212–220.

1953 'The Activation of Human Energy', *AE*, pp. 385–93.

'The Contingence of the Universe and Humankind's Zest for Survival, or 'How Can One Rethink the Christian Notion of Creation to Conform with the Laws of Energetics?', *CE*, pp. 221–28.

'The God of Evolution', *CE*, pp. 237–43.

'On Looking at a Cyclotron: Reflections on the Folding-Back Upon Itself of Human Energy', *AE*, pp. 347–57.

'Reflections on the Compression of Humankind', *AE*, pp. 339–46.

'A Sequel to the Problem of Human Origins', *CE*, pp. 229–36.

'The Stuff of the Universe', *AE*, pp. 373–83.

1954 'The Singularities of the Human Species', *AM*, pp. 208–270.

'A Summary of my "Phenomenological" View of the World: The Starting-Point and Key of the Whole System', *TF*, pp. 212–215.

1955 * 'The Christic', *HM*, pp. 80–102.

'The Death-Barrier and Co-Reflection, or the Imminent Awakening of Human Consciousness to the Sense of its Irreversibility', *AE*, pp. 395–406.
'Research, Work and Worship', *SC*, pp. 214–220.
'The Last Page of Pierre Teilhard de Chardin's Dairy', *HM*, pp. 103–104.

Correspondence

Letters from Egypt, 1905–1908, New York: Herder & Herder, 1965.
Letters from Hastings, 1908–1912, New York: Herder & Herder, 1968.
Letters from Paris, 1912–1914, New York: Herder & Herder, 1967.
The Making of a Mind: Letters from a Soldier-Priest, 1914–1919, London: Collins, 1965.
* *Pierre Teilhard de Chardin – Maurice Blondel: Correspondence*, New York: Herder & Herder, 1976.
Lettres intimes à Auguste Valensin, Bruno de Solages, Henri de Lubac, André Ravier, 1919–1955, Paris: Aubier Montaigne, 1972.
Letters from a Traveller, 1923–1955, London: Collins, 1962.
Letters to Two Friends, 1926–1952, London: Rapp & Whiting, 1970.
Letters to Léontine Zanta, New York: Harper & Row, 1969.
Letters to Lucile Swan, Washington, DC: Georgetown University Press, 1993.

Journal and retreat notes

Cahiers I–V (26 August 1915 – 4 January 1919): *Journal, 1914–1919*, eds. Nicole and Karl Schmitz-Moormann, Paris: Fayard, 1975.
Cahiers I–VII (26 August 1915 – 25 February 1920): *Tagebücher*, eds. Nicole and Karl Schmitz-Moormann, 3 vols.; Olten/Freiburg: Walter, 1974–77; vol. III includes Cahiers V–VII (14 May 1918 – 25 February 1920).
Notes de retraites, 1919–1954, ed. Gérard-Henry Baudry, Paris: Seuil, 2003.

Unpublished material

Cahiers VI–IX and XIII–XXI (5 January 1919 – 17 July 1925, 18 July 1944 – 7 April 1955), transcribed by Nicole Schmitz-Moormann. Cahiers X–XII have not been recovered.
Notes de lecture, 3 vols.; I & II, 1945; III, n.d. (but not earlier than 1952).
Letter of Teilhard de Chardin to Joseph Huby, 13 July 1925.
These materials are held at the Archives Françaises de la Compagnie de Jésus, 92170 Vanves, France.

Secondary works

Aelred of Rievaulx, *Spiritual Friendship*, Scranton, Penn.: University of Scranton Press, 1994.
Aeschylus, *Prometheus Bound*, Cambridge University Press, 1932.

Aiton, E.J., *Leibniz: A Biography*, Bristol: Adam Hilger, 1985.

Alès, Adhémar d', «La Doctrine de la récapitulation en saint Irénée», *RSR* 6 (1916), pp. 189–211.

Alexander, Ian W., *Bergson: Philosopher of Reflection*, London: Bowes & Bowes, 1957.

Allegra, Gabriel M., *My Conversations with Teilhard de Chardin on the Primacy of Christ, Peking, 1942–1945*, Chicago: Franciscan Herald Press, 1970.

Alston, William, *Perceiving God: The Epistemology of Religious Experience*, Ithaca, NY: Cornell University Press, 1995.

The Reliability of Sense Perception, Ithaca, NY: Cornell University Press, 1993.

Anderson, Gary A., 'The Garments of Skin in Apocryphal Narrative and Biblical Commentary', in *Studies in Ancient Midrash*, ed. James Kugel, Harvard University Center for Jewish Studies, 2001, pp. 101–143.

Anonymous, «L'Oeuvre de la 'Jeune Turquie': Notes de Constantinople», *Études* 118 (1909), pp. 199–235.

Anselm, *Proslogion*, Notre Dame, Ind.: University of Notre Dame Press, 1979.

Aquinas, Thomas, *Summa theologiae*, 60 vols.; London: Blackfriars, 1962–76.

Summa contra gentiles, 5 vols.; Notre Dame, Ind.: University of Notre Dame Press, 1975.

On the Power of God, 2 vols.; London: Burns, Oates & Washbourne, 1932–34.

Truth, 3 vols.; Indianapolis: Hackett, 1994.

Selected Writings, ed. Ralph McInerny, London: Penguin, 1998.

Selected Philosophical Writings, ed. Timothy McDermott, Oxford University Press, 1998.

Arendt, Hannah, *The Human Condition*, University of Chicago Press, 1989.

Between Past and Future: Eight Exercises in Political Thought, London: Penguin, 1993.

Love and Saint Augustine, University of Chicago Press, 1996.

Aristotle, *Works*, 23 vols.; Harvard University Press, 1926–91.

Armagnac, Christian d', «De Blondel à Teilhard de Chardin: nature et intériorité», *AP* 21 (1958), pp. 298–312.

Armstrong, A.H., *Plotinian and Christian Studies*, London: Variorum, 1979.

The Architecture of the Intelligible Universe in the Philosophy of Plotinus: An Analytical and Historical Study, Cambridge University Press, 1940.

Arnou, René, *Le Désir de Dieu dans la philosophie de Plotin*, Paris: Alcan, 1921.

Atkin, Nicholas, 'The Politics of Legality: The Religious Orders in France, 1901–1945', in *Religion, Society and Politics in France Since 1789*, eds. Frank Tallett and Nicholas Atkin, London: Hambledon, 1991, pp. 149–65.

Augustine, *De civitate Dei*, 7 vols.; Harvard University Press, 1957–72.

The Trinity, Brooklyn, NY: New City Press, 1997.

Confessions, 2 vols.; London: Heinemann, 1912.

On the Literal Interpretation of Genesis, Fathers of the Church 84, Washington, DC: Catholic University of America Press, 1991.

Earlier Writings, ed. John Burleigh, London: SCM, 1953.

Bachelet, Xavier-Marie Le, «Baius», in *Dictionnaire de théologie catholique*, II, 15 vols.; Paris: Letouzey et Ané, 1915–50, cols. 38–111.

Bainvel, Jean-Vincent, *Devotion to the Sacred Heart: The Doctrine and its History*, London: Burns, Oates & Washbourne, trans. from 5th edn, 1924.

Balaban, Oded, 'The Hermeneutics of the Young Marx, according to Marx's Approach to the Philosophy of Democritus and Epicurus', *Diogenes* 148 (1989), pp. 28–41.

Balch, David L., 'The Areopagus Speech: An Appeal to the Stoic Historian Posidonius against Later Stoics and the Epicureans', in *Greeks, Romans and Christians: Essays in Honor of Abraham J. Malherbe*, eds. David L. Balch, Everett Ferguson and Wayne Meeks, Minneapolis, Minn.: Fortress, 1990, pp. 52–79.

Bales, Eugene F., 'A Heideggerian Interpretation of Negative Theology in Plotinus', *The Thomist* 47 (1983), pp. 197–208.

Balthasar, Hans Urs von, *The Glory of the Lord: A Theological Aesthetics*, 7 vols.; Edinburgh: T&T Clark, 1982–91.

Heart of the World, San Francisco: Ignatius, 1979.

Cosmic Liturgy: The Universe According to Maximus the Confessor, San Francisco: Ignatius, 2003.

Barber, Michael D., 'The Ethical Eloquence of the Silenced: A Levinasian Reading of Teilhard de Chardin's Silencing', in *Trying Times: Essays on Catholic Higher Education in the 20th Century*, eds. William M. Shea with Daniel Van Slyke, Atlanta, Ga.: Scholars, 1999, pp. 153–71.

Barbour, Ian, 'Five Ways of Reading Teilhard', *Soundings* 51 (1968), pp. 115–45.

Barloy, Jean-Jacques, *Lamarck contre Darwin: l'évolution des êtres vivants*, Paris: Firmin Didot, 1980.

Barnes, Michael, *Theology and the Dialogue of Religions*, Cambridge University Press, 2002.

Barth, J. Robert, *The Sacramental Vision of Gerald Manley Hopkins*, Regina: Campion College, 1989.

Barth, Karl, *Church Dogmatics*, 10 vols.; Edinburgh: T&T Clark, 1936–77.

God in Action, Edinburgh: T&T Clark, 1936.

Letters, 1961-1968, eds. Jürgen Fangmeier, Hinrich Stoevesandt and Geoffrey W. Bromiley, Edinburgh: T&T Clark, 1981.

Barth, Karl, and Emil Brunner, *Natural Theology*, London: SCM, 1947.

Barthélemy-Madaule, Madeleine, *Bergson et Teilhard de Chardin*, Paris: Seuil, 1963.

Bauckham, Richard, *The Theology of Jürgen Moltmann*, Edinburgh: T&T Clark, 1995.

Becco, Anne, «Leibniz et François Mercure van Helmont: bagatelle pour des monades», in *Magia naturalis und die Entstehung der modernen Naturwissenschaften*, eds. Albert Heinekamp and Dieter Mettler, Wiesbaden: Steiner, 1978, pp. 119–42.

Becker, Annette, *War and Faith: The Religious Imagination in France, 1914–1930*, Oxford: Berg, 1998.

Becker, Thomas, *Geist und Materie in den ersten Schriften Pierre Teilhard de Chardins*, Freiburger theologische Studien 134, Freiburg: Herder, 1987.

Benoît, P., «Corps, tête et plérôme», *Exégèse et théologie* 2 (1961), pp. 135–53.

Benz, Ernst, *Evolution and Christian Hope*, London: Doubleday, 1966.

Bergson, Henri, *Oeuvres complètes*, 7 vols.; Paris: Presses universitaires de France, 6th edn, 2001.

Creative Evolution, London: Macmillan, 1911.

Essai sur les données immédiates de la conscience, Paris: Alcan, 1889; trans. *Time and Free Will: An Essay on the Immediate Data of Consciousness*, London: Macmillan, 1910.

Matière et mémoire, Paris: Alcan, 1896; trans. *Matter and Memory*, London: Macmillan, 1911.

Quid Aristoteles de loco senserit, Paris: Alcan, 1889; trans. «L'Idée de lieu chez Aristote», *Études Bergsoniennes* 2, Paris: Albin Michel, 1949, pp. 32–104.

Les Deux sources de la morale et de la religion, Paris: Alcan, 1932; trans. *The Two Sources of Morality and Religion*, Notre Dame, Ind.: University of Notre Dame Press, 1977.

Cours, 4 vols.; Paris: Presses universitaires de France, 1990–2000.

Bernardi, Peter, 'Social Modernism: The Case of the *Semaines Sociales*', in *Catholicism Contending with Modernity: Roman Catholic Modernism and Anti-Modernism in Historical Context*, ed. Darrell Jodock, Cambridge University Press, 1999, pp. 277–307.

'Maurice Blondel and the Renewal of the Nature–Grace Relationship', *Communio (US)* 26 (1999), pp. 806–845.

Bertrand, Dominique, *La Politique de saint Ignace de Loyola: l'analyse sociale*, Paris: Cerf, 1985.

Blake, William, *William Blake*, ed. Michael Mason, Oxford University Press, 1994.

Blanchette, Olivia, *The Perfection of the Universe According to Aquinas: A Teleological Cosmology*, University Park: Pennsylvania State University Press, 1999.

Blondel, Maurice, *Oeuvres complètes*, 10 vols.; Paris: Presses universitaires de France, 1995– .

L'Action: essai d'une critique de la vie et d'une science de la pratique, Paris: Alcan, 1893; trans. *Action: Essay on a Critique of Life and a Science of Practice*, Notre Dame, Ind.: University of Notre Dame Press, 2003.

De vinculo substantiali et de substantia composita apud Leibnitium, Paris: Alcan, 1893; trans. *Le Lien substantiel et la substance composée d'après Leibniz*, Louvain: Nauwelaerts, 1972.

Une énigme historique: le vinculum substantiale *d'après Leibniz et l'ébauche d'un réalisme supérieur*, Paris: Beauchesne, 1930.

«Un interprète de Spinoza: Victor Delbos, 1862–1916», *Chronicum spinozanum* 1 (1921), pp. 290–300.

«L'Évolution du spinozisme et l'accès qu'elle ouvre à la transcendance», *L'Archivio di Filosofia* 11, 4 (1932), pp. 3–12; and in *Dialogues avec les philosophes: Descartes, Spinoza, Malebranche, Pascal, Saint Augustin*, Paris: Aubier Montaigne, 1966, pp. 11–40.

(writing as Bernard Aimant), «Une des sources de la pensée moderne: l'évolution du spinozisme», *Annales de philosophie chrétienne* 64 (1894), pp. 260–75, 324–41.

(writing as Testis), «La Semaine sociale de Bordeaux et le monophorisme», *Annales de philosophie chrétienne* 4, 9 (1909), pp. 5–22, 162–84, 245–78; 10 (1910), pp. 372–92, 449–72, 561–92; 11 (1910), pp. 127–62; trans. of (1909), pp. 245–78 in 'Maurice Blondel and the Renewal of the Nature–Grace Relationship', *Communio (US)* 26 (1999), pp. 846–74.

Boehm, Alfred, *Le vinculum substantiale chez Leibniz: ses origines historiques*, Études de philosophie médiévale 26, Paris: Vrin, 1938.

Bogdasavich, M., 'The Idea of Pleroma in the Epistles to the Colossians and Ephesians', *The Downside Review* 83 (1965), pp. 118–30.

Boissannat, Jean, and Christophe Grannec, *L'Aventure du Christianisme social: passé et avenir*, Mayenne: Desclée, 1999.

Bonaventure, *The Soul's Journey into God. The Tree of Life. The Life of St Francis*, ed. Ewert Cousins, Mahwah, NJ: Paulist, 1978.

Bonhoeffer, Dietrich, *Letters and Papers from Prison: The Enlarged Edition*, ed. Eberhard Bethge, London: SCM, 1986.

Bostock, Gerald, 'Origen's Philosophy of Creation', in *Origeniana Quinta*, ed. Robert J. Daly, Leuven University Press, 1992, pp. 253–69.

Bowie, Andrew, *Schelling and Modern European Philosophy: An Introduction*, London: Routledge, 1993.

Boyd, W.J.P., 'Teilhard de Chardin and Modern Protestant Theology', in *Teilhard Reassessed*, ed. Anthony Hanson, London: Darton, Longman & Todd, 1970, pp. 113–55.

Boyer, C., «La Théorie augustinienne des raisons séminales», in *Miscellanea Agostiniana. Studi Agostiniani*, 2 vols.; Rome: Poliglotta Vaticana, 1930–31, pp. 795–819.

Braaten, Carl E., and Robert W. Jenson (eds.), *Christian Dogmatics*, 2 vols.; Philadelphia, Penn.: Fortress, 1984.

Braine, David, 'The Active and Potential Intellects: Aquinas as a Philosopher in his Own Right', in *Mind, Metaphysics, and Value in the Thomistic and Analytical Traditions*, ed. John Haldane, Notre Dame, Ind.: University of Notre Dame Press, 2002, pp. 18–35.

Bréhier, Émile, *Les Idées philosophiques et religieuses de Philon d'Alexandrie*, Paris: Vrin, 1908; third edn, 1950.

Brock, Stephen L., *Action and Conduct: Thomas Aquinas and the Theory of Action*, Edinburgh: T&T Clark, 1998.

Broek, Roelof van den, *Studies in Gnosticism and Alexandrian Christianity*, Leiden: Brill, 1996.

Brown, David, *Continental Philosophy and Modern Theology: An Engagement*, Oxford: Blackwell, 1987.

Brueggemann, Walter, 'Imagination as a Mode of Fidelity', in *Understanding the Word: Essays in Honor of Bernhard W. Anderson*, eds. James T. Butler et al., Sheffield: JSOT Press, 1985, pp. 13–36.

Bruteau, Beatrice, 'Sri Aurobindo and Teilhard de Chardin on the Problem of Action', *International Philosophical Quarterly* 12 (1972), pp. 193–204.

Buccellati, Giorgio, 'Ascension, Parousia, and the Sacred Heart: Structural Correlations', *Communio (US)* 25 (1998), pp. 69–103.

Burr, David, 'Scotus and Transubstantiation', *Mediaeval Studies* 34 (1972), pp. 336–60.

Burrell, David, 'Beyond Onto-Theology: Negative Theology and Faith', *Lonergan Workshop* 15 (1999), pp. 1–11.

Cabanel, Patrick, «Le Grand exil des congrégations enseignantes au début du XXᵉ siècle», *Revue d'histoire de l'Église de France* 81 (1995), pp. 207–217.

Callahan, Annice, *Karl Rahner's Spirituality of the Pierced Heart: A Reinterpretation of Devotion to the Sacred Heart*, Lanham, Md.: University Press of America, 1985.

Calvez, Jean-Yves, «Pierre Teilhard de Chardin (1885–1955)», in *Chrétiens penseurs du social: Maritain, Fessard, Teilhard de Chardin, De Lubac (1920–1940)*, Paris: Cerf, 2002, pp. 107–136.

Carrington, Mary C., 'Teilhard de Chardin and Karl Barth', *The Teilhard Review* 17, 2 (1982), pp. 17–24.

Cary, Phillip, *Augustine's Invention of the Inner Self: The Legacy of a Christian Platonist*, Oxford University Press, 2000.

Chantraine, Georges, «La Théologie du surnaturel selon Henri de Lubac», *NRT* 119 (1997), pp. 218–35.

Charles, Pierre, *La Prière de toutes les heures*, 2 vols.; Bruges: Beyaert, 1923; trans. *Prayer for all Times*, 1 vol.; London: Fount, 1983.

Charlesworth, Max, *Philosophy and Religion: From Plato to Postmodernism*, Oxford: Oneworld, 2002.

* Clark, Mary T., 'The Divine Milieu in Philosophical Perspective', *The Downside Review* 80 (1962), pp. 12–25.

Clavel, Pierre, «De Newman à Teilhard: une piste de recherche — 1: Ore Place à l'arrivée de Teilhard en 1908», in *Newman et l'histoire*, eds. Claude Lepelley and Paul Veyriras, Presses Universitaires de Lyon, 1992, pp. 245–55.

Climacus, John, *The Ladder of Divine Ascent*, London: Faber & Faber, 1959.

Coakley, Sarah, '"Not with the eye only": The Resurrection, epistemology and gender', in *Powers and Submissions: Philosophy, Spirituality and Gender*, Oxford: Blackwell, 2002, pp. 130–52.

Coleridge, Samuel Taylor, *Samuel Taylor Coleridge*, ed. H.J Jackson, Oxford University Press, 1994.

Colin, Pierre, *L'Audace et le soupçon: la crise moderniste dans le catholicisme français, 1893–1914*, Malakoff: Desclée, 1997.

Colin, Pierre (ed.), *Intellectuels chrétiens et esprit des années 1920*, Paris: Cerf, 1997.

Comte, Auguste, *System of Positive Polity*, 4 vols.; New York: Burt Franklin, 1969.

Constable, Giles, 'Moderation and Restraint in Ascetic Practices in the Middle Ages', in *From Athens to Chartres: Neoplatonism and Medieval Thought*, ed. Haijo Jan Westra, Leiden: Brill, 1992, pp. 315–27.

Cooper, John W., 'Teilhard, Marx and the Worldview of Prominent Liberation Theologians', *Calvin Theological Journal* 70 (1990), pp. 48–72.

* Corbishley, Thomas, *The Spirituality of Teilhard de Chardin*, London: Collins Fontana, 1971.

Corduan, Winfried, 'Hegel in Rahner: A Study in Philosophical Hermeneutics', *Harvard Theological Review* 71 (1978), pp. 285–98.

Corrigan, Kevin, 'So-Called Solitary Mysticism in Plotinus, Proclus, Gregory of Nyssa and Pseudo-Dionysius', *Journal of Religion* 76 (1996), pp. 28–42. 'Plotinus and St Gregory of Nyssa: Can Matter really have a Positive Function?', *SP* 27, Leuven: Peeters, 1993, pp. 14–20.

Coudert, Allison, Richard Popkin and Gordon Weiner (eds.), *Leibniz, Mysticism and Religion*, London: Kluwer, 1998.

Cousins, Ewert H., 'Franciscan Roots of Ignatian Meditation', in *Ignatian Spirituality in a Secular Age*, ed. George P. Schner, Waterloo, Ont.: Wilfrid Laurier University Press, 1984, pp. 51–63.

Coutagne, Marie-Jeanne, «Le Christ et l'énigme du monde: la christologie blondélienne, 1916–1925», in *Le Christ de Maurice Blondel*, ed. René Virgoulay, Paris: Desclée, 2003, pp. 85–114.

Cudworth, Ralph, *The True Intellectual System of the Universe*, Stuttgart: Frommann, 1964.

* Cuénot, Claude, *Teilhard de Chardin: A Biographical Study*, London: Burns & Oates, 1965.

Cuvillier, Élian, «La Question du Jésus historique dans l'exégèse francophone: aperçu historique et évaluation critique», in *Jésus de Nazareth: nouvelles approches d'une énigme*, eds. Daniel Marguerat, Enrico Norelli and Jean-Michel Poffet, Geneva: Labor et Fides, 1998, pp. 59–88.

Dadrian, Vahakn N., *The History of the Armenian Genocide: Ethnic Conflict from the Balkans to Anatolia to the Caucasus*, New York: Bergham, 6th rev. edn, 2004.

Daecke, Sigurd Martin, *Teilhard de Chardin und die evangelische Theologie: die Weltlichkeit Gottes und die Weltlichkeit der Welt*, Göttingen: Vandenhoeck & Ruprecht, 1967.

Daniélou, Jean, «Saint Irénée et les origines de la théologie de l'histoire», *RSR* 34 (1947), pp. 227–31.

Darwin, Charles, *The Descent of Man and Selection in Relation to Sex*, 2 vols.; London: Pickering, 1989; first published, 1871. *On the Origin of Species by Means of Natural Selection, or the Preservation of Favoured Races in the Struggle for Life*, Harvard University Press, 1964; first published, 1859.

Davies, Brian, *The Thought of Thomas Aquinas*, Oxford: Clarendon, 1992.

Dawkins, Richard, *Unweaving the Rainbow*, London: Penguin, 1999.

Dawson, Christopher, *The Mongol Mission: Narratives and Letters of the Franciscan Missionaries in Mongolia and China in the Thirteenth and Fourteenth Centuries*, London: Sheed & Ward, 1955.

Deissmann, G. Adolf, *Die neutestamentliche Formel „in Christo Jesu"*, Marburg: Elwert, 1892.

Delbos, Victor, *Le Problème moral dans la philosophie de Spinoza et dans l'histoire du spinozisme*, Paris: Alcan, 1893. «Maurice Blondel, L'Action», *Revue philosophique de la France et de l'étranger* 38 (1894), pp. 634–41.

Delbreil, Jean-Claude, «Les Formes politiques de la démocratie chrétienne en France au vingtième siècle», in *Catholicism, Politics and Society in Twentieth-Century France*, ed. Kay Chadwick, Liverpool University Press, 2000, pp. 119–41.

Derrida, Jacques, *Dissemination*, London: Athlone, 1981.

Desaymard, Joseph, *H. Bergson à Clermont-Ferrand*, Clermont-Ferrand: Bellet, 1910.

Descartes, René, *Principles of Philosophy*, Dordrecht: Reidel, 1983.
   The Philosophical Works of Descartes, 3 vols.; Cambridge University Press, 1984.

Dix, Dom Gregory, *The Shape of the Liturgy*, London: Continuum, 2nd edn, 2001.

Dombrowski, Daniel, *The Philosophy of Vegetarianism*, Amherst: University of Massachusetts Press, 1984.

Dondaine, Henri F., «L'Objet et le 'médium' de la vision béatifique au XIIIᵉ siècle», *RTAM* 19 (1952), pp. 60–130.

Donovan, May A., 'Alive to the Glory of God', *TS* 49 (1988), pp. 283–97.

Dorlodot, Henry de, *Le Darwinisme au point de vue de l'orthodoxie catholique*, Brussels: Vroment, 1921; trans. *Darwinism and Catholic Thought*, London: Burns, Oates & Washbourne, 1922.

Doud, Robert E., 'Wholeness as Phenomenon in Teilhard de Chardin and Merleau-Ponty', *Philosophy Today* 24 (1980), pp. 90–103.

Downes, David A., *The Ignatian Personality of Gerard Manley Hopkins*, Lanham, Md.: University Press of America, 1990.

Dunne, George H., *Generation of Giants: The First Jesuits in China*, London: Burns & Oates, 1962.

Dupré, Wilhelm, 'Anselm and Teilhard de Chardin: Remarks on the Modification of the Ontological Argument in the Thought of Teilhard de Chardin', *Analecta Anselmiana* 4 (1975), pp. 323–31.

Durand, Alfred, «Le Christ 'Premier Né'», *RSR* 1 (1910), pp. 56–66.
   «Le Discours de la Cène», *RSR* 1 (1910), pp. 97–131, 513–39; 2 (1911), pp. 321–49, 521–45.
   «La Réponse de Jésus aux noces de Cana», *RSR* 3 (1912), pp. 157–59.

Eckhart, Meister, *Sermons and Treatises*, ed. Maurice O'C. Walshe, 3 vols.; Shaftesbury: Element, 1987.
   Selected Writings, ed. Oliver Davies, London: Penguin, 1994.
   Meister Eckhart: Teacher and Preacher, eds. Bernard McGinn with Frank Tobin and Elvira Borgstadt, New York: Paulist, 1986.
   The Essential Sermons, Commentaries, Treatises and Defense, eds. Edmund Colledge and Bernard McGinn, London: SPCK, 1981.

Elevferiy, Archimandrite, 'On Spiritual Sight', *Journal of the Moscow Patriarchate* 1981, 4, pp. 34–35.

Eliot, T.S., *Four Quartets*, London: Faber & Faber, 1959.

Elliott, Francis G., 'The Christology of Teilhard de Chardin', in *Evolution, Marxism and Christianity: Studies in the Teilhardian Synthesis*, eds. Bernard Towers and Anthony Dyson, London: Garnstone, 1967, pp. 86–98.

Endean, Philip, *Karl Rahner and Ignatian Spirituality*, Oxford University Press, 2001.

Englert, Walter G., *Epicurus on the Swerve and Voluntary Action*, Atlanta, Ga.: Scholars, 1987.

Fabre, Pierre-Antoine, *Ignace de Loyola: le lieu de l'image*, Paris: Vrin, 1992.

Farber, Paul Lawrence, 'French Evolutionary Ethics during the Third Republic: Jean de Lanessan', in *Biology and the Foundation of Ethics*, eds. Jane Maienschein and Michael Ruse, Cambridge University Press, 1999, pp. 84–97.

Farges, Albert, *Les Phénomènes mystiques distingués de leurs contrefaçons humaines et diaboliques*, 2 vols.; Saint Dizier: A. Brulliard, 2nd edn, 1925; trans. *Mystical Phenomena, Compared with their Human and Diabolical Counterfeits: A Treatise on Mystical Theology in Agreement with the Principles of St Teresa set forth by the Carmelite Congress of 1923 at Madrid*, London: Burns, Oates & Washbourne, 1926.

* Faricy, Robert, *All Things in Christ: Teilhard de Chardin's Spirituality*, London: Fount, 1981.

 * 'The Heart of Christ in the Spirituality of Teilhard de Chardin', *Gregorianum* 69 (1988), pp. 261–77.

* Faricy, Robert and Lucy Rooney, *Knowing Jesus in the World: Praying with Teilhard de Chardin*, with preface by Hans-Peter Kolvenbach, London: St Paul's, 1999.

Farrer, Austin, *Finite and Infinite: A Philosophical Essay*, Westminster: Dacre, 1943.

Fédou, Michel, «Origène et le langage du coeur», *Christus* 190 (2001), pp. 58–62.

Felt, J.W., 'Whitehead's Misconception of "Substance" in Aristotle', *Process Studies* 14 (1985), pp. 224–36.

Fergusson, David, *The Cosmos and the Creator: An Introduction to the Theology of Creation*, London: SPCK, 1998.

Ferrari, G.R.F., *Listening to the Cicadas: A Study of Plato's 'Phaedrus'*, Cambridge University Press, 1987.

Fields, Stephen, 'Balthasar and Rahner on the Spiritual Senses', *TS* 57 (1996), pp. 224–41.

Fouilloux, Étienne, *Une église en quête de liberté: la pensée française entre modernisme et Vatican II, 1914–1962*, Paris: Desclée, 1998.

Frémont, Christiane, *L'Être et la relation; avec trente-sept lettres de Leibniz au R.P. Des Bosses*, Paris: Vrin, 2nd edn, 1999.

French, William C., 'Subject-Centred and Creation-Centred Paradigms in Recent Catholic Thought', *Journal of Religion* 70 (1990), pp. 48–72.

Furness, Jean, 'Teilhard de Chardin and Julian of Norwich: A Rapprochement', *Mystics Quarterly* 12 (1986), pp. 67–70.

Garcia-Mateo, Rogelio, „Spiritualität der Welt: Teilhard de Chardin (1881–1955) und ignatianische Spiritualität", in *Gottes Nähe: religiöse Erfahrung in Mystik und Offenbarung: Festschrift zum 65. Geburtstag von Josef Sudbrack SJ*, ed. Paul Imhof, Würzburg: Echter, 1990, pp. 367–81.

Gillette, Gertrude, 'Purity of Heart in St. Augustine', in *Purity of Heart in Early Ascetic and Monastic Literature: Essays in Honor of Juana Raasch OSB*, eds. Harriet Luckman and Linda Kulzer, Collegeville, Minn.: Liturgical, 1999, pp. 175–96.

Gilson, Étienne, «Trois leçons sur le thomisme et sa situation présente», *Seminarium* 17 (1965), pp. 682–737; and in *Les Tribulations de Sophie*, Paris: Vrin, 1967, pp. 15–99.

Letters of Étienne Gilson to Henri de Lubac, San Francisco: Ignatius, 1988.

Goethe, Johann Wolfgang von, *Faust: A Tragedy*, New York: Norton, 2nd edn, 2001.

Selected Verse, ed. David Luke, London: Penguin, 1982.

Gould, Stephen Jay, 'Piltdown Revisited', in *The Panda's Thumb: More Reflections in Natural History*, London: Penguin, 1990, pp. 92–104.

'Teilhard and Piltdown', in *Hen's Teeth and Horse's Toes*, London: Penguin, 1990, pp. 199–250.

Grandmaison, Léonce de, Foreword to Pierre Rousselot, *L'Intellectualisme de saint Thomas*, Paris: Beauchesne, 2nd edn, 1924, pp. v–xl.

Grau, Joseph, *Morality and the Human Future in the Thought of Teilhard de Chardin: A Critical Study*, Rutherford, NJ: Fairleigh Dickinson University Press, 1976.

Gray, Donald, *The One and the Many: Teilhard de Chardin's Vision of Unity*, London: Burns & Oates, 1969.

Gregory of Nyssa, *Homilies on Ecclesiastes*, ed. Stuart George Hall, Berlin: De Gruyter, 1993.

Grindler, Marietta, *Das holistische Evolutionsmodell Pierre Teilhard de Chardins: ein Vergleich mit den Entwicklungsgedanken bei Plotin, Schelling und Bergson*, Aachen: Shaker, 2000.

Grogin, Robert, *The Bergsonian Controversy in France, 1900-1914*, University of Calgary Press, 1988.

Grosholz, Emily, 'Plato and Leibniz against the Materialists', *Journal of the History of Ideas* 57 (1996), pp. 255–76.

Grover, Ralph Scott, *The Music of Edmund Rubbra*, Aldershot: Scolar, 1992.

* Grumett, David, 'Church, World and Christ in Teilhard de Chardin', *Ecclesiology* 1 (2004), pp. 87–103.

'Arendt, Augustine and Evil', *HJ* 41 (2000), pp. 154–69.

Gunter, Pete A.Y., 'Bergson and Sartre: The Rise of French Existentialism', in *The Crisis in Modernism: Bergson and the Vitalist Controversy*, eds. Frederick Burwick and Paul Douglass, Cambridge University Press, 1992, pp. 230–44.

Gunton, Colin, *The Triune Creator: A Historical and Systematic Study*, Edinburgh University Press, 1998.

Gustavo Gutiérrez, *A Theology of Liberation: History, Politics and Salvation*, London: SCM, 1974.

Gutting, Gary, *French Philosophy in the Twentieth Century*, Cambridge University Press, 2001.

Habermas, Jürgen, *The Future of Human Nature*, Oxford: Polity, 2003.

Hadot, Pierre, *Philosophy as a Way of Life: Spiritual Exercises from Socrates to Foucault*, Oxford: Blackwell, 1995.

The Inner Citadel: The Meditations of Marcus Aurelius, Harvard University Press, 1998.

Haffner, Paul, *Mystery of Creation*, Leominster: Gracewing, 1995.

Haldane, John, 'MacIntyre's Thomist Revival: What Next?', in *After MacIntyre: Critical Perspectives on the Work of Alasdair MacIntyre*, eds. John Horton and Susan Mendus, Cambridge: Polity, 1994, pp. 91–107.

Hamilton, Alastair, *Heresy and Mysticism in 16th-Century Spain: The Alumbrados*, Cambridge: James Clarke, 1992.

Hamon, Auguste, *Histoire de la dévotion du Sacré-Coeur*, 5 vols.; Paris: Beauchesne, 1939.

Hankey, Wayne, *Cent ans de néoplatonisme en France: une brève histoire philosophique*, Collection Zêtêsis, Paris: Vrin, 2004, pp. 123–268.

'*Participatio divini luminis*, Aquinas's Doctrine of the Agent Intellect: Our Capacity for Contemplation', *Dionysius* 22 (2004), pp. 149–78.

'Philosophy as a Way of Life for Christians?', *Laval théologique et philosophique* 59 (2003), pp. 193–224.

'Aquinas's First Principle: Being or Unity?', *Dionysius* 4 (1980), pp. 133–72.

Hardy, Richard P., 'Fidelity to God in the Mystical Experience of Fray Juan de la Cruz', *Église et théologie* 11 (1980), pp. 57–75.

Harnack, Adolf von, *Das Wesen des Christentums*, Leipzig: Hinrichs, 1900; trans. *What Is Christianity?*, London: Benn, 5th edn, 1958.

Hart, John W., *Karl Barth vs. Emil Brunner: The Formation and Dissolution of a Theological Alliance, 1916-1936*, Oxford: Lang, 2001.

Haught, John, *Deeper than Darwin: The Prospect for Religion in the Age of Evolution*, Oxford: Westview, 2004.

'Darwin, Design and the Promise of Nature', Boyle Lecture 2004, and 'True Union Differentiates: A Response to My Critics', *Science and Christian Belief* 17 (2005), pp. 5–20, 57–70.

Hebblethwaite, Brian, *Evil, Suffering and Religion*, London: SPCK, rev. edn, 2000.

The Ocean of Truth, Cambridge University Press, 1988.

Hedley, Douglas, *Coleridge, Philosophy and Religion: 'Aids to Reflection' and the Mirror of the Spirit*, Cambridge University Press, 2000.

Hegarty, Charles M., 'Bonhoeffer and Teilhard on Worldly Christianity', *Science et esprit* 21 (1969), pp. 35–70.

Hegel, G.W.F., *Phenomenology of Spirit*, Oxford University Press, 1977.

Lectures on the Philosophy of Religion, 3 vols.; Berkeley: University of California Press, 1984–87.

Lectures on the History of Philosophy, 3 vols.; Lincoln: University of Nebraska Press, 1995.

La Vie de Jésus, trans. Dumitru D. Rosca, Paris: Gamber, 1928.

Heidegger, Martin, *Pathmarks*, Cambridge University Press, 1998.

Helm, Paul, 'Eternal Creation: The Doctrine of the Two Standpoints', in *Doctrine of Creation: Essays in Dogmatics, History and Philosophy*, ed. Colin Gunton, Edinburgh: T&T Clark, 1997, pp. 29–46.

Henry, Paul, «Bulletin critique des études plotiniennes (1929–31)», *NRT* 8 (1932), pp. 707–35; 9 (1933), pp. 785–803; 10 (1934), pp. 906–925.

Herbert, George, *George Herbert*, ed. Louis L. Martz, Oxford University Press, 1994.

Hibbs, Thomas, *Virtue's Splendor*, New York: Fordham University Press, 2001.

Hick, John, *Evil and the God of Love*, Basingstoke: Macmillan, 2nd edn, 1977.

Hippocrates, *Airs, eaux, lieux*, Paris: Belles Lettres, 1996.

Hopkins, Gerald Manley, *Gerald Manley Hopkins*, ed. Catherine Phillips, Oxford University Press, 1995.

Huby, Joseph, *Saint Paul: les épîtres de la captivité*, Paris: Beauchesne, 1935.

«Miracle et lumière de la grâce», *RSR* 9 (1918), pp. 36–77.

«Le Témoignage des convertis», *Études* 155 (1918), pp. 385–400, 558–72, 706–715.

«Foi et contemplation d'après saint Thomas», *RSR* 10 (1919), pp. 137–61.

La Conversion, Paris: Beauchesne, 1919.

Huey, F.B., and John H. Walton, *The Genesis Debate*, Nashville: Thomas Nelson, 1986.

Huftier, M., «Les Yeux de la foi chez saint Augustin», *Mélanges de science religieuse* 25 (1968), pp. 57–66, 105–12.

Hunt Overzee, Anne, *The Body Divine: The Symbol of the Body in the Works of Teilhard de Chardin and Ramanuja*, Cambridge University Press, 1992.

Ignatius Loyola, *The Spiritual Exercises*, Wheathampstead: Clarke, 1987.

The Spiritual Exercises with the Directorium in Exercitia, ed. W.H. Longridge, London: Scott, 1922.

Jackson, Julian, *The Popular Front in France: Defending Democracy, 1934–38*, Cambridge University Press, 1988.

John of the Cross, *The Dark Night of the Soul*, London: Rider, 2002.

John of Damascus, *On the Divine Images: The Apologies Against those who Attack the Divine Images*, New York: St Vladimir's, 1980.

John, Helen James, *The Thomist Spectrum*, New York: Fordham, 1966.

Kant, Immanuel, *Critique of Pure Reason*, Cambridge University Press, 1997.

Critique of Practical Reason, Cambridge University Press, 1997.

Groundwork of the Metaphysics of Morals, Cambridge University Press, 1997.

Kelly, Michael, *Hegel in France*, University of Birmingham Press, 1992.

Kim, Dai Sil, 'Irenaeus of Lyons and Teilhard de Chardin: A Comparative Study of "Recapitulation" and "Omega"', *Journal of Ecumenical Studies* 13 (1976), pp. 69–93.

* King, Thomas M., *Teilhard's Mass: Approaches to 'The Mass on the World'*, New York: Paulist, 2005.

King, Ursula, *Christ in all Things: Exploring Spirituality with Teilhard de Chardin*, London: SCM, 1997.

The Spirit of One Earth: Reflections on Teilhard de Chardin and Global Spirituality, New York: Paragon, 1989.

'Consumed by Fire from Within: Teilhard de Chardin's Pan-Christic Mysticism in Relation to the Catholic Tradition', *HJ* 40 (1999), pp. 456–77.

'Love: A Higher Form of Energy in the Work of Teilhard de Chardin and Sorokin', *Zygon* 39 (2004), pp. 77–102

Kolp, Alan L., 'Partakers of the Divine Nature: The Use of 2 Peter 1.4 by Athanasius', *SP* 17, 3, Elmsford, NY: Pergamon, 1982, pp. 1018–1023.

Komonchak, Joseph A., 'Returning from Exile: Catholic Theology in the 1930s', in *The Twentieth Century: A Theological Overview*, ed. Gregory Baum, Maryknoll, NY: Orbis, 1999, pp. 35–48.

Konstan, David, 'Democritus the Physicist', *Apeiron* 33 (2000), pp. 125–44.

Krekhovetsky, Yakiv, 'The Concept of Divinization', *The Teilhard Review* 13 (1978), pp. 112–18.

Krentz, Edgar, 'Through a Lens: Theology and Fidelity in 2 Thessalonians', in *Pauline Theology*, ed. Jouette Bassler, I, 4 vols.; Minneapolis, Minn.: Fortress, 1991–97, pp. 52–62.

* Kropf, Richard W., *Teilhard, Scripture and Revelation: A Study of Teilhard de Chardin's Reinterpretation of Pauline Themes*, Rutherford, NJ: Fairleigh Dickinson, 1980.

Küng, Hans, *On Being a Christian*, London: Collins, 1977.

Does God Exist? An Answer for Today, London: Collins, 1980.

Lacouture, Jean, 'Obedience and Teilhard', in *Jesuits: A Multibiography*, London: Harvill, 1996, pp. 431–41.

Ladous, Régis, «Victor Carlhian aux sources du personnalisme», in *Cent ans de catholicisme social à Lyons et en Rhône-Alpes: la postérité de Rerum novarum*, ed. Jean-Dominique Durand, Paris: Éditions ouvrières, 1992, pp. 171–79.

Lahitton, Joseph, *Le Chemin de croix national pour le temps de la guerre*, Mont de Marsan: Legrand, 1914.

Lamarck, Jean Baptiste, *Philosophie zoologique, ou exposition des considérations relatives à l'histoire naturelle des animaux*, 2 vols.; Paris: Dentu, 1809; Brussels: Culture et civilisation, 1983; trans. *Zoological Philosophy: An Exposition with Regard to the Natural History of Animals*, London: Macmillan, 1914; University of Chicago Press, 1984.

Lane, David H., *The Phenomenon of Teilhard: Prophet for a New Age*, Macon, Ga.: Mercer University Press, 1996.

Langan, Janine, 'Pascal and Teilhard de Chardin: *frères spirituels*', *Communio (US)* 12 (1985), pp. 425–35.

Lapidge, Michael, 'Stoic Cosmology', in *The Stoics*, ed. John M. Rist, Berkeley: University of California Press, 1978, pp. 180–84.

Lapomarda, Vincent, 'France', in *The Jesuits and the Third Reich*, Lewiston, Ma.: Mellen, 1989, pp. 266–301.

Laudouze, André, *Dominicains français et Action française, 1899–1940: Maurras au couvent*, Paris: Éditions ouvrières, 1990.

Lavalette, Henri de, «Le Théoricien de l'amour», *RSR* 53 (1965), pp. 462–94.

Ledochowski, Wlodimir, 'Doctrina de actu fidei a P. Petro Rousselot p.m. proposita prohibetinur', *Acta Romana Societatis Iesu* 3 (1919–23), pp. 229–33.

Leibniz, G.W., *La Monadologie*, ed. Émile Boutroux, Paris: C. Delagrave, 1881.

Philosophical Texts, eds. R.S. Woolhouse and Richard Franks, Oxford University Press, 1998.

'Correspondence with Des Bosses', in *Philosophical Papers and Letters*, ed. Leroy E. Loemker, Dordrecht: Reidel, 1969, pp. 596–617.

The Atomists Leucippus and Democritus: Fragments, ed. C.C.W. Taylor, University of Toronto Press, 1999.

Levinas, Emmanuel, *Totality and Infinity: An Essay on Exteriority*, Pittsburgh, Penn.: Duquesne University Press, 2001.

Liddon, Henry Parry, *The Divinity of Our Lord and Saviour Jesus Christ: Eight Lectures Preached Before the University of Oxford in the Year 1866 on the Foundation of John Bampton*, London: Longmans, 1903.

Lightfoot, John B., *St Paul's Epistles to the Colossians and Philemon*, London: Macmillan, 5th edn, 1886.

Locke, John, *Essay Concerning Human Understanding*, Oxford: Clarendon, 1975.

Political Writings, ed. David Wootton, London: Penguin, 1993

Logan, Alastair, *Gnostic Truth and Christian Heresy: A Study in the History of Gnosticism*, Edinburgh: T&T Clark, 1996.

Loisy, Alfred, *L'Évangile et l'Église*, Paris: A. Picard et fils, 1902; trans. *The Gospel and the Church*, London: Isbister, 1903.

Look, Brandon, *Leibniz and the* vinculum substantiale, Studia Leibnitiana 30, Stuttgart: F. Steiner, 1999.

Lossky, Vladimir, *The Vision of God*, Crestwood, NY: St Vladimir's, 1983.

Lottin, Odon, «Les Premières définitions et classifications des vertus au Moyen-Âge», *Revue des sciences philosophiqes et théologiques* 18 (1929), pp. 369–407.

Louth, Andrew, 'The Body in Western Catholic Christianity', in *Religion and the Body*, ed. Sarah Coakley, Cambridge University Press, 1997, pp. 111–30.

Lubac, Henri de, *Oeuvres complètes*, 50 vols.; Paris: Cerf, 1998–.

The Religion of Teilhard de Chardin, London: Collins, 1970.

* *The Faith of Teilhard de Chardin and Note on the Apologetics of Teilhard de Chardin*, London: Burns & Oates, 1965.

The Eternal Feminine: A Study on the Poem by Teilhard de Chardin, London: Collins, 1971.

'Tradition and innovation in the position of the problem of God in Father Teilhard de Chardin', in *Theology in History*, San Francisco: Ignatius, 1996, pp. 505-540.

'The contribution of Teilhard to the knowledge of God', in *Theology in History*, pp. 541-62.

Histoire et l'esprit: l'intelligence de l'Écriture d'après Origène, Paris: Aubier, 1950.

Surnaturel: études historiques, Paris: Aubier Montagne, 1946; Desclée, 2nd edn, 1991.

Corpus mysticum, trans. Gemma Simmonds, London: SCM, 2005.

At the Service of the Church: Henri de Lubac Reflects on the Circumstances that Occasioned his Writings, San Francisco: Communio, 1993.

'A Meditation on the Principle of the Moral Life', *Communio (US)* 26 (1999), pp. 418–28; originally in *Revue apologétique* 65 (1937), pp. 257–66.

«Joseph Huby», *RSR* 35 (1948), pp. 321–23.

«Deux Augustiniens fourvoyés: Baius et Jansénius», *RSR* 21 (1931), pp. 422–43, 513–40.

Lukas, Mary, 'Teilhard and Piltdown: A Re-Reassessment', in *Humanity's Quest for Unity: A United Nations Teilhard Colloquium*, ed. Leo Zonneveld, Wassenaar: Mirananda, 1985, pp. 61–70.

Lussier, E., 'Universal Conflagration at the Parousia', *Catholic Biblical Quarterly* 12 (1950), pp. 243–47.

Luther, Martin, *Works*, 55 vols.; Saint Louis, Mo.: Concordia, 1955–76.

* Lyons, James, *The Cosmic Christ in Origen and Teilhard de Chardin: A Comparative Study*, Oxford University Press, 1982.

Maalouf, Jean, *Le Mystère du mal dans l'oeuvre de Teilhard de Chardin*, Paris: Cerf, 1986.

McClendon, James W., *Systematic Theology*, 3 vols.; Nashville: Abingdon, 1986–2000.

McDermott, John M., *Love and Understanding: The Relation of Will and Intellect in Pierre Rousselot's Christological Vision*, Rome: Università Gregoriana, 1983.

McEvoy, James, *The Philosophy of Robert Grosseteste*, Oxford: Clarendon, 1982.

McGowen, Tom, *The Great Monkey Trial: Science versus Fundamentalism in America*, New York: Franklin Watts, 1990.

MacIntyre, Alasdair, *After Virtue: A Study in Moral Theory*, London: Duckworth, 2nd edn, 1999.

* MacKinnon, Donald, 'Re-Review: Pierre Teilhard de Chardin's *Le Milieu divin*', *The Modern Churchman* 25 (1983), pp. 49–53.

 * 'Teilhard's Achievement', in *Teilhard de Chardin: Pilgrim of the Future*, ed. Neville Braybrooke, London: Darton, Longman & Todd, 1965, pp. 60–66.

 * 'Teilhard de Chardin: A Comment on his Context and Significance', *The Modern Churchman* 5 (1962), pp. 195–99.

McMullin, Ernan, 'Introduction', in *Evolution and Creation*, Notre Dame, Ind.: University of Notre Dame Press, 1985, pp. 1–56.

McNeill, John J., *The Blondelian Synthesis: A Study of the Influence of German Philosophical Sources on the Formation of Blondel's Method and Thought*, Leiden: Brill, 1966.

Macquarrie, John, *Twentieth Century Religious Thought: The Frontiers of Philosophy and Theology, 1900–1980*, London: SCM, rev. edn, 1983.

McPartlan, Paul, *The Eucharist Makes the Church: Henri de Lubac and John Zizioulas in Dialogue*, Edinburgh: T&T Clark, 1996.

Madden, Nicholas, 'Αἴσθησις νοερά (Diadochus-Maximus)', *SP* 23, Leuven: Peeters, 1989, pp. 53–60.

Mambrino, Jean, «Les Deux mains de Dieu dans l'oeuvre de saint Irénée», *NRT* 79 (1957), pp. 355–70.

Mansuy, Michel, «Pierre Teilhard de Chardin», in *Études sur l'imagination de la vie*, Paris: José Corti, 1970, pp. 175–209.

Maréchal, Joseph, *Études sur la psychologie des mystiques*, Bruges: Beyaert, 1924; 2 vols.; Paris: Desclée, 2nd edn, 1937–38; trans. *Studies in the Psychology of the Mystics*, London: Burns, Oates & Washbourne, 1927.

«À propos du sentiment de présence chez les profanes et les mystiques», *Revue des questions scientifiques* 14 (1908), pp. 527–65; 15 (1909), pp. 219–49, 376–426.

Marion, Jean-Luc, «La Conversion de la volonté selon *L'Action*», *Revue philosophique de la France et de l'étranger* 177 (1987), pp. 33–46.

Maritain, Jacques, *The Peasant of the Garonne: An Old Layman Questions Himself about the Present Time*, London: Chapman, 1968.

Saint Thomas and the Problem of Evil, Milwaukee, Mich.: Marquette University Press, 1942.

Markus, R.A., 'Pleroma and Fulfilment: The Significance of History in St Irenaeus's Opposition to Gnosticism', *Vigiliae Christianae* 8 (1954), pp. 193–224.

Martin, Malachi, *The Jesuits: The Society of Jesus and the Betrayal of the Roman Catholic Church*, London: Simon & Schuster, 1988.

Marty, Élie, *Le Témoignage de Pierre Rousselot SJ, d'après ses écrits et sa correspondance*, Paris: Beauchesne, 1941.

Marx, Karl, and Frederick Engels, *Collected Works*, 49 vols.; London: Laurence & Wishart, 1975–2001.

Massis, Henri, *Le Sacrifice*, Paris: Plon, 1917.

* Mathieu, Pierre-Louis, *La Pensée politique et économique de Teilhard de Chardin*, Saint Étienne: Aubin, new edn, 2000.

Matteo, Anthony M., *Quest for the Absolute: The Philosophical Vision of Joseph Maréchal*, De Kalb: Northern Illinois University Press, 1992.

Maybaum, Ignaz, *The Face of God after Auschwitz*, Amsterdam: Polak & Van Gennep, 1965.

Medawar, Peter, 'The Phenomenon of Man', *Mind* 70 (1961), pp. 99–106; reprinted in *Pluto's Republic*, Oxford University Press, 1982, pp. 242–51; and in *The Strange Case of the Spotted Mice; and other Classic Essays on Science*, Oxford University Press, 1996, pp. 1–11.

Melson, Robert, *Revolution and Genocide: On the Origins of the Armenian Genocide and the Holocaust*, University of Chicago Press, 1992.

Mermod, Denis, *La Morale chez Teilhard de Chardin*, Paris: Éditions universitaires, 1967.

Merton, Thomas, 'The Universe as Epiphany', and 'Teilhard's Gamble', in *Love and Living*, eds. Naomi Burton Stone and Patrick Hart, London: Sheldon, 1979, pp. 171–84, 185–91.

Milbank, John, *The Word Made Strange: Theology, Language, and Culture*, Oxford: Blackwell, 1997.

'The End of Dialogue', in *Christian Uniqueness Reconsidered: The Myth of a Pluralistic Theology of Religions*, ed. Gavin D'Costa, Maryknoll, NY: Orbis, 1990, pp. 174–91.

Mill, John Stuart, *On Liberty and Other Essays*, Oxford University Press, 1998.

Miner, Robert C., 'Recent Work on Thomas in North America', in *Contemplating Aquinas: On the Varieties of Interpretation*, ed. Fergus Kerr, London: SCM, 2003, pp. 137–62.

* Modemann, Christian, *Omegapunkt: christologische Eschatologie bei Teilhard de Chardin und ihre Rezeption durch F. Capra, J. Ratzinger und F. Tipler*, Münster: Lit, 2004.

Molette, Charles, *L'Association catholique de la jeunesse française, 1886–1907: une prise de conscience du laïcat catholique*, Paris: Colin, 1968.

Molnar, Thomas, «L'État et le problème de la religion chez Maurras» *Études Maurrassiennes* 5, 1 (1986), pp. 283–91.

Moltmann, Jürgen, *God in Creation: An Ecological Doctrine of Creation*, London: SCM, 1985.

The Way of Jesus Christ: Christology in Messianic Dimensions, London: SCM, 1990.

Experiences in Theology: Ways and Forms of Christian Theology, London: SCM, 2000.

Science and Wisdom, London: SCM, 2003.

Monod, Jacques, *Chance and Necessity: An Essay on the National Philosophy of Modern Biology*, London: Collins, 1972.

* Mooney, Christopher, *Teilhard de Chardin and the Mystery of Christ*, London: Collins, 1966.

'Cybernation, Responsibility and Providential Design', *TS* 51 (1990), pp. 286–309.

'Blondel and Teilhard de Chardin: An Exchange of Letters', *Thought* 37 (1962), pp. 543–62.

Morgan, John, 'Ethnicity and the Future of Man', *The Teilhard Review* 11 (1976), pp. 16–20.

Mossé-Bastide, Rose-Marie, *Bergson et Plotin*, Paris: Presses universitaires de France, 1959.

Murphy, Francis X., 'Conflagration: The Eschatological Perspective from Origen to John Chrysostom', *SP* 18, 1, Kalamazoo, Mich.: Cistercian, 1985, pp. 179–85.

Nadal, Jérôme, *Contemplatif dans l'action: écrits spirituels ignatiens (1535–1575)*, Paris: Desclée, 1994.

Newman, John W., *Disciplines of Attention: Buddhist Insight Meditation, the Ignatian Spiritual Exercises and Classical Psychoanalysis*, New York: Peter Lang, 1996.

Nichols, Aidan, *Catholic Thought Since the Enlightenment: A Survey*, Leominster: Gracewing, 1998.

Nietzsche, Friedrich, *Twilight of the Idols. The Anti-Christ*, London: Penguin, 1990.

Nygren, Anders, *Agape and Eros*, New York: Harper & Row, 1969.

O'Cleirigh, P.M., 'Prime Matter in Origen's World Picture', *SP* 16, Berlin: Akademie, 1985, pp. 260–63.

O'Collins, Gerald, 'The Incarnation: The Critical Issues', in *The Incarnation: An Interdisciplinary Symposium on the Incarnation of the Son of God*, eds. Stephen T. Davies, Daniel Kendall and Gerald O'Collins, Oxford University Press, 2002, pp. 1–27.

Oikonomides, Nicolas, 'Records of the "Commandments of the Seven Wise Men" in the 3rd Century BC: The Revered Greek Reading-Book of the Hellenistic World', *Classical Bulletin* 63, 3 (1987), pp. 67–76.

Ordonnaud, Georges, *L'Ère nouvelle de la coresponsabilité*, Paris: Pedone, 1991.

Origen, *On First Principles*, New York: Harper, 1966.

Traité des principes, 5 vols.; Paris: Cerf, 1978–84.

Homélies sur la Genèse, eds. Henri de Lubac and Louis Doutreleau, Sources Chrétiennes 7b, Paris: Cerf, 1944; rev. 2nd edn, 2003.

Ouince, René d', *Un prophète en procès: Teilhard de Chardin dans l'Église de son temps; Teilhard de Chardin et l'avenir de la pensée chrétienne*, 2 vols.; Paris: Aubier Montaigne, 1970.

«Le Père Joseph Huby», *Études* 259 (1948), pp. 71–80.

Pannenberg, Wolfhart, *Systematic Theology*, 2 vols.; Edinburgh: T&T Clark, 1994.

'Spirit and Energy in the Phenomenology of Teilhard de Chardin', in *Toward a Theology of Nature: Essays on Science and Faith*, ed. Ted Peters, Louisville, Kent.: Westminster/John Knox, 1993, pp. 138–47; and in *Beginning with the End: God, Science and Wolfhart Pannenberg*, eds. Carol Rausch Albright and Joel Haughen, Chicago: Open Court, 1997, pp. 80–89.

Pascal, Blaise, *Pensées*, London: Penguin, rev. edn, 1995.

Patrick, Simon, 'A Sermon Preached at the Funeral of Mr John Smith late fellow of *Queens* Colledge in *Cambridge*', in John Smith, *Select Discourses*, Cambridge: John Hayes, 1763; New York: Garland, 1978, pp. 471–88.

Peacocke, Arthur, *God and the New Biology*, Gloucester, Mass.: Peter Smith, 1994.

Creation and the World of Science, Oxford: Clarendon, 1979.

Science and the Christian Experiment, London: Oxford University Press, 1971.

Pelchat, Marc, «Pierre Teilhard de Chardin et Henri de Lubac: pour une nouvelle synthèse théologique à l'âge scientifique», *Laval théologique et philosophique* 45 (1989), pp. 255–73.

Petit, Hugues, *L'Église, le Sillon et l'Action française*, Paris: Nouvelles éditions latines, 1998.

Pétrement, Simone, *A Separate God: The Christian Origins of Gnosticism*, London: Darton, Longman & Todd, 1991.

Philo, *Works*, 12 vols.; London: Heinemann, 1929–54.

Pinard de la Boullaye, H., «*Sentir, sentimiento, sentido* dans le style de S. Ignace», *Archivum Historicum SI* 25 (1956), pp. 416–30.

Plato, *Works*, 12 vols.; Harvard University Press, 1914–30.

Plotinus, *Enneads*, 7 vols.; Harvard University Press, 1966–88.

Les Ennéades de Plotin, trans. Marie-Nicolas Bouillet, 3 vols.; Paris: Hachette, 1857–61.

Poggi, Vincenzo, «Saint Jean Climaque et saint Ignace de Loyola», *Proche Orient Chrétien* 32 (1982), pp. 50–85.

Polato, Franco, *Blondel e Teilhard de Chardin (convergenze e divergenze)*, Studi e Ricerche 18, Bologna: Zanichelli, 1966.

Pomerai, David de, 'Maximus the Confessor: A Precursor to Teilhard?', *The Teilhard Review* 28, 2 (1993), pp. 16–18.

Poulain, Auguste, *Des grâces d'oraison: traité de théologie mystique*, Paris: V. Retaux, 1901; 10th edn, 1922; trans. *The Graces of Interior Prayer: A Treatise on Mystical Theology*, London: Kegan Paul, Trench, Trubner & Co., 6th edn, 1910.

Poulat, Émile, *Les Prêtres-ouvriers: naissance et fin*, Paris: Cerf, 2nd edn, 1999.

Prat, Ferdinand, *La Théologie de saint Paul*, 2 vols.; Paris: Beauchesne, 1908–1912; trans. *The Theology of Saint Paul*, 2 vols.; London: Burns, Oates & Washbourne, 1945.

Origène: le théologien et l'exégète, Paris: Bloud, 1907.

Proclus, *The Elements of Theology*, Oxford: Clarendon, 2000.

Quantin, J.L., and Antionina Bevan, 'The Fathers in Seventeenth Century Roman Catholic Theology', in *Reception of the Church Fathers in the West: From the Carolingians to the Maurists*, ed. Irena Backus, II, 2 vols.; Leiden, Brill, 1997, pp. 951–86.

Querido, René, *The Golden Age of Chartres: The Teachings of a Mystery School and the Eternal Feminine*, Edinburgh: Floris, 1987.

Rahner, Hugo, *Ignatius the Theologian*, London: Chapman, 1968.

Rahner, Karl, *Theological Investigations*, 23 vols.; New York: Crossroad, 1974–92.

Hearers of the Word, London: Sheed & Ward, 1969.

'Ignatius of Loyola Speaks to a Modern Jesuit', in *Ignatius of Loyola*, ed. Paul Imhof, London: Collins, 1979, pp. 11–38.

'The Immediate Experience of God in the Spiritual Exercises of Saint Ignatius of Loyola', in *Karl Rahner in Dialogue*, ed. Harvey D. Egan, New York: Crossroad, 1986, pp. 174–81.

Rancourt, Michel, «La Foi au monde chez Teilhard de Chardin», in *Questions actuelles sur la foi*, eds. Thomas R. Potvin and Jean Richard, Montreal: Fides, 1984, pp. 77–102.

* Raven, Charles, *Teilhard de Chardin: Scientist and Seer*, London: Collins, 1962.

Reeve, P., 'Exploring a Metaphor Theologically: Thomas Aquinas on the Beatific Vision', in *Studies in Thomistic Theology*, ed. Paul Lockey, Houston: University of St Thomas, 1995, pp. 283–300.

Rénan, Ernst, *The Life of Jesus*, London: Kegan Paul, 1893.

Reynders, D.B., «Optimisme et théocentrisme chez saint Irénée», *RTAM* 8 (1936), pp. 227–52.

Riches, John, 'Balthasar's Sacramental Spirituality and Hopkins' Poetry of Nature: The Sacrifice Imprinted upon Nature', in *Christ: The Sacramental Word*, eds. David Brown and Ann Loades, London: SPCK, 1996, pp. 168–80.

Rideau, Émile, *Teilhard de Chardin: A Guide to his Thought*, London: Collins, 1967.

Riedlinger, Helmut, „Das göttliche Milieu: der Mystiker Pierre Teilhard de Chardin auf dem Weg der großen Kommunion mit dem immer größeren Christus", in *Gemeinsam Kirche sein: Theorie und Praxis der Communio*, eds. Günter Biemer and Bernhard Casper, Freiburg: Herder, 1992, pp. 207–234.

* Robbins, Lee, 'Being in Darkness: A Jungian Commentary on Teilhard's "Passivities of Diminishment"', *Anima* 11, 1 (1984), pp. 17–23.

Roberts, Noel Keith, *From Piltdown Man to Point Omega: The Evolutionary Theory of Teilhard de Chardin*, Studies in European Thought 18, New York, Peter Lang, 2000.

Rodier, Georges, «Sur une des origines de la philosophie de Leibniz», *RMM* 10 (1902), pp. 552–64.

Rondet, Henri, *Le Péché originel dans la tradition patristique et théologique*, Paris: Fayard, 1967; trans. *Original Sin: The Patristic and Theological Background*, Shannon: Ecclesia, 1972.

Problèmes pour la réflexion chrétienne: Le Péché originel, L'Enfer et autres études, Paris: Spes, 1946.

Le Mystère du péché originel, Le Puy: X. Mappus, 1943.

Rondet, Michel, «La Tradition médiévale», *Christus* 190 (2001), pp. 63–66.

Rosca, Dumitru D., *L'Influence de Hegel sur Taine: théoricien de la connaissance et de l'art*, Paris: Gamber, 1928.

Rossum, Joost van, 'The *logoi* of Creation and the Divine "Energies" in Maximus the Confessor and Gregory Palamas', *SP* 27, Leuven: Peeters, 1993, pp. 213–17.

Rousselot, Pierre, *Intelligence: Sense of Being, Faculty of God*, Milwaukee, Wis.: Marquette University Press, 1999.

Pour l'histoire du problème de l'amour au Moyen-Âge, Extrait des Beiträge zur Geschichte der Philosophie des Mittelalters 6, Münster: Aschendorff, 1908; trans. *The Problem of Love in the Middle Ages: A Historical Contribution*, Milwaukee, Wis.: Marquette University Press, 2001.

«Idéalisme et thomisme», *AP* 42 (1979), pp. 103–26.

«Les Yeux de la foi», *RSR* 1 (1910), pp. 241–59, 444–75; trans. in *The Eyes of Faith. Answer to Two Attacks*, New York: Fordham University Press, 1990.

Russo, Antonio, «Rome et Teilhard», *RSR* 69 (1981), pp. 485–507.

Ruzhitaky, Konstantin, 'The Teaching of the Holy Fathers and other Church Writers on Matter', *Journal of the Moscow Patriarchate*, 1989, 1, pp. 17–18.

Sanzo, Eileen, 'The Convergence of Blake and Teilhard', *The Teilhard Review* 12 (1977), pp. 16–20.

Saudreau, Auguste, *Les Faits extraordinaires de la vie spirituelle: état angélique, extase, révélations, visions, possessions*, Paris: Vic et Amat, 1908; 2nd edn, 1921; trans. *The Life of Union with God, and the Means of Attaining it, According to the Great Masters of Spirituality*, London: Burns, Oates & Washbourne, 3rd edn, 1927.

Sayre, Patricia, 'The Dialectics of Trust and Suspicion', *Faith and Philosophy* 10 (1993), pp. 567–84

Schiwy, Günter, *Teilhard de Chardin: sein Leben und seine Zeit*, 2 vols.; Munich: Kösel, 1981.

Schleiermacher, F.D.E., *On Religion: Speeches to its Cultured Despisers*, Cambridge University Press, 2nd edn, 1997.

Schmutz, Jacob, 'Escaping the Aristotelian Bond: The Critique of Metaphysics in Twentieth-Century French Philosophy', *Dionysius* 17 (1999), pp. 169–200.

Schneider, Stefan, „Personale Anthropozentrik: die Personologie im kosmogenetischen Entwurf Teilhard de Chardins und der Personalismus bei Cusanus", in *Menschenbild des Nikolaus von Kues und der christliche Humanismus*, eds. Martín Bodewig, Josef Schmitz and Reinhold Weier, Mitteilungen und Forschungsbeiträge der Cusanus-Gesellschaft 13, Mainz: Grünewald, 1978, pp. 375–94.

Schüssler Fiorenza, Francis, and John P. Galvin, *Systematic Theology*, 2 vols.; Minneapolis, Minn.: Fortress, 1991.

Schweitzer, Albert, *The Quest of the Historical Jesus: A Critical Study of its Progress from Reimarus to Wrede*, London: Black, 2nd edn, 1911.

Segundo, Juan Luis, *The Christ of the Ignatian Exercises*, Maryknoll, NY: Orbis, 1987.

Seligman, Paul, 'Soul and Cosmos in Presocratic Philosophy', *Dionysius* 2 (1978), pp. 5–17.

Sesboüé, Bernard, *Tout récapituler dans le Christ: christologie et sotériologie d'Irénée de Lyons*, Paris: Desclée, 2000.

«Le Surnaturel chez Henri de Lubac: un conflit autour d'une théologie», *RSR* 80 (1992), pp. 374–408.

Shelley, Mary, *Frankenstein*, London: Penguin, 1994.

* Sherrard, Philip, 'Christian Vision and Modern Science: I. Teilhard de Chardin', in *Human Image, World Image: The Death and Resurrection of Sacred Cosmology*, Ipswich: Golgonooza, 1992, pp. 102–130.

Sherry, Patrick, *Spirit and Beauty: An Introduction to Theological Aesthetics*, Oxford: Clarendon, 1992.

Sloan, Phillip R., 'From Natural Law to Evolutionary Ethics in Enlightenment French Natural History', in *Biology and the Foundation of Ethics*, eds. Jane Maienschein and Michael Ruse, Cambridge University Press, 1999, pp. 52–83.

Smith, John, *Select Discourses*, Cambridge: John Hayes, 1673.

Sobrino, Jon, *Christology at the Crossroads: A Latin American Approach*, London: SCM, 1978.

Solages, Bruno de, *Teilhard de Chardin: témoignage et étude sur le développement de sa pensée*, Toulouse: Privat, 1966.

Soloviev, Vladimir, *War, Progress, and the End of History: Three Conversations, including a Short Story of the Anti-Christ*, Herndon, Va.: Lindisfarne, 1990.

Southern, Richard, *Robert Grosseteste: The Growth of an English Mind in Medieval Europe*, Oxford: Clarendon, 1988.

Spanneut, Michel, «Le Stoïcisme dans l'histoire de la patience chrétienne», *Mélanges de science religieuse* 39 (1982), pp. 101–130.

Speaight, Robert, *Teilhard de Chardin: A Biography*, London: Collins, 1967.

Spinoza, Benedict, *Ethics*, London: Penguin, 1996.

Spitzer, Leo, 'Milieu and *ambiance*: An Essay in Historical Semantics', *Philosophy and Phenomenological Research* 3 (1942), pp. 1–42, 169–218.

Starr, James M., *Sharers in Divine Nature: 2 Peter 1.4 in its Hellenistic Context*, Stockholm: Almqvist & Wiksell, 2000.

Strenski, Ivan, *Contesting Sacrifice: Religion, Nationalism and Social Thought in France*, University of Chicago Press, 2002.

Suchan, Berthold, „Die Bedeutung Teilhards de Chardin für das Gespräch zwischen Theologie und Naturwissenschaften", in *Von der Suche nach Gott*, eds. Margot Schmidt and Fernando Domínguez Reboiras, Stuttgart-Bad Cannstatt: Frommann Holzboog, 1998, pp. 719–30.

Sutherland, D. Dixon, 'A Theological Anthropology of Evil: A Comparison in the Thought of Paul Ricoeur and Teilhard de Chardin', *Neue Zeitschrift für systematische Theologie und Religionsphilosophie* 34 (1992), pp. 85–100.

Sutton, Michael, *Nationalism, Positivism and Catholicism: The Politics of Charles Maurras and French Catholics, 1890-1914*, Cambridge University Press, 1982.

Taine, Hyppolite, *History of English Literature*, London: Chatto & Windus, 1908.

Tanner, R. Godfrey, 'Neo-Stoicism in Teilhard de Chardin', in *The Desire to be Human: A Global Reconnaissance of Human Perspectives in an Age of Transformation Written in Honour of Pierre Teilhard de Chardin*, eds. Leo Zonneveld and Robert Muller, Wassenaar: Miranda, 1983, pp. 124–37.

Teilhard de Chardin, Marguerite-Marie, *L'Énergie spirituelle de la souffrance*, ed. Monique Givelet, Paris: Seuil, 1951.

Françoise Teilhard de Chardin, Petite-Soeur des Pauvres: soeur Marie Albéric du Sacré-Coeur, 1879–1911: lettres et témoignages, Paris: Beauchesne, 1975; Clermont-Ferrand: Bellet, 1914; or alternative edn, *Soeur Marie-Albéric du Sacré-Coeur, petite soeur des pauvres, 1879–1911*, Rennes: Oberthur, 1935.

Temple, William, *Readings in St John's Gospel*, London: Macmillan, 1945.

Tennant, F.R., *The Sources of the Doctrines of the Fall and Original Sin*, Cambridge University Press, 1903.

Tennyson, Alfred Lord, *In memoriam*, eds. Susan Shatto and Marion Shaw, Oxford: Clarendon, 1982.

Tertulian, Nicolas, «Un hégélien roumain: D.D. Rosca», *AP* 63 (2000), pp. 95–109.

Tertullian, *Adversus Marcionem*, 2 vols.; Oxford: Clarendon, 1972.

Théobald, Christoph, «Une manière ignatienne de faire la théologie», *NRT* 119 (1997), pp. 375–96.

Thimm, Gero Franz, „Naturwissenschaftliche Erkenntnis und Gotteserfahrung nach Teilhard de Chardin", in *Wahrheit: Recherchen zwischen Hochscholastik und Postmoderne*, eds. Thomas Eggensperger and Ulrich Engel, Walberberger Studien: Philosophische Reihe 9, Mainz: Matthias Grünewald, 1995, pp. 314–21.

Thomas, Hywel, 'Gerard Manley Hopkins and John Duns Scotus', *Religious Studies* 24 (1988), pp. 337–64.

Thucydides, *History of the Peloponnesian War*, 4 vols.; London: Heinemann, 1919–23.

Thunberg, Lars, *Man and the Cosmos: The Vision of St Maximus the Confessor*, Crestwood, NY: St Vladimir's, 1985.

Tillich, Paul, *Systematic Theology*, 3 vols.; University of Chicago Press, 1951–63.

'The Right to Hope: A Sermon', in *Paul Tillich: Theologian of the Boundaries*, London: Collins, 1987, pp. 324–31.

Tilliette, Xavier, «Problèmes de philosophie eucharistique», *Gregorianum* 64 (1983), pp. 273–305; 65 (1984), pp. 605–634.

Towers, Bernard, *Concerning Teilhard; and other Writings on Science and Religion*, London: Collins, 1969.

Tremblay, Réal, *La Manifestation et la vision de Dieu selon saint Irénée de Lyon*, Münster: Aschendorff, 1978.

Trennert-Helwig, Mathias, *Die Urkraft des Kosmos: Dimensionen der Liebe im Werk Pierre Teilhards de Chardin*, Freiburg: Herder, 1993.

* 'The Church as Axis of Convergence in Teilhard's Theology and Life', *Zygon* 30 (1995), pp. 73–89.

Turner, Denys, *The Darkness of God: Negativity in Christian Mysticism*, Cambridge University Press, 1999.

Ugolino, Brother, *The Little Flowers of St Francis of Assisi*, London: Burns, Oates & Washbourne, 1917.

Vale, Carol Jean, 'Teilhard de Chardin: Ontogenesis vs. Ontology', *TS* 53 (1992), pp. 313–37.

Verbeke, Gérard, «Science de l'âme et perception sensible», in *Avicenna Latinus. Liber de anima seu sextus de naturalibus*, I, 2 vols.; Leuven: Peeters; Leiden: Brill, 1968–72, pp. 83–90.

Virgoulay, René, *Blondel et le modernisme: la philosophie de l'action et les sciences religieuses, 1896–1913*, Paris: Cerf, 1980.

«La Question du mal dans la pensée et l'expérience spirituelle du P. Teilhard de Chardin», *RSR* 56 (1982), pp. 33–51.

Wagner, Jean-Pierre, *Henri de Lubac*, Paris: Cerf, 2001.

Wallace-Hadrill, D.S., *The Greek Patristic View of Nature*, Manchester University Press, 1968.

Wang, Haiyan, *Le Phénomène Teilhard: l'aventure du livre 'Le Milieu divin'*, Saint-Étienne: Aubin, 1999.

Watson, Richard A., 'Transubstantiation among the Cartesians', in *Problems of Cartesianism*, eds. Thomas Lennon et al., Kingston, Ont.: McGill-Queen's University Press, 1982, pp. 127–48.

The Downfall of Cartesianism, 1673–1712: A Study of Epistemological Issues in Late 17th Century Cartesianism, Hague: Nijhoff, 1966.

Westphal, Merold, *Overcoming Onto-Theology: Toward a Postmodern Christian Faith*, New York: Fordham University Press, 2001.

Wildiers, N. Max, *An Introduction to Teilhard de Chardin*, London: Collins Fontana, 1968.

Wiles, Maurice, 'The Incarnation and Development', in *The Religion of the Incarnation: Anglican Essays in Commemoration of 'Lux mundi'*, ed. Robert Morgan, Bristol Classical Press, 1989, pp. 74–84.

Williams, Anna, 'Argument to Bliss: The Epistemology of the *Summa theologiae*', *MT* 20 (2004), pp. 505–526.

'Mystical Theology Redux: The Pattern of Aquinas's *Summa theologiae*', *MT* 12 (1997), pp. 53–74.

Williams, Norman Powell, *The Ideas of the Fall and of Original Sin*, London: Longmans, Green & Co., 1927.

Williams, Rowan, *Anglican Identities*, London: Darton, Longman & Todd, 2004.

Winslow, Donald F., *The Dynamics of Salvation: A Study in Gregory of Nazianzus*, Cambridge, Mass.: Philadelphia Patristic Foundation, 1979.

Wojtyla, Karol, *The Acting Person*, Analecta Husserliana 10, Dordrecht: Reidel, 1979.

Wolter, Allan B., 'Duns Scotus on the natural desire for the supernatural', in *The Philosophical Theology of John Duns Scotus*, London: Cornell University Press, 1990, pp. 125–47.

Wordsworth, William, *William Wordsworth*, eds. Stephen Gill and Duncan Wu, Oxford University Press, 1994.

Wynn, Mark, *God and Goodness: A Natural Theological Perspective*, London: Routledge, 1999.

Yeago, David S., 'Jesus of Nazareth and Cosmic Redemption: The Relevance of St Maximus the Confessor', *MT* 12 (1996), pp. 163–93.

Zaehner, R.C., *Our Savage God*, London: Collins, 1974.

Evolution in Religion: A Study in Sri Aurobindo and Pierre Teilhard de Chardin, Oxford: Clarendon, 1971.

Zanta, Léontine, *La Renaissance du stoïcisme au XVIe siècle*, Paris: Champion, 1914.

Reference works

Ante-Nicene Fathers of the Christian Church, 10 vols.; Grand Rapids, Mich.: Eerdmans, 1993.

Decrees of the Ecumenical Councils, 2 vols.; London: Sheed & Ward, 1990.

Dictionnaire du monde religieux dans la France contemporaine, 9 vols.; Paris: Beauchesne, 1985–96.

Établissements des Jésuites en France depuis quatre siècles, ed. Pierre Delattre, 5 vols.; Enghien: Wetteren, 1939–57.

The Ethiopian Book of Enoch, 2 vols.; Oxford: Clarendon, 1978.

Myths from Mesopotamia, ed. Stephanie Dalley, Oxford University Press, 1991.

New English Hymnal, Norwich: Canterbury Press, 1995.

Nicene and Post-Nicene Fathers of the Christian Church, 28 vols.; Grand Rapids, Mich.: Eerdmans, 1961.

The Papal Encyclicals, 5 vols.; Pierian: Ann Arbor, 1990.

The Persecution of the Catholic Church in the Third Reich: Facts and Documents, London: Burns Oates, 1940.

The Rule of Saint Benedict, London: Sheed & Ward, 1989.

INDEX

PRINTED ON PERMANENT PAPER • IMPRIME SUR PAPIER PERMANENT • GEDRUKT OP DUURZAAM PAPIER - ISO 9706

N.V. PEETERS S.A., WAROTSTRAAT 50, B-3020 HERENT